Praise for the First Edition
A CHOICE Outstanding Academic Title, 2015

"Wayne Wu in *Attention* not only motivates and defends his distinctive account of attention; he also provides a sweeping but rigorous overview of empirical and philosophical work on attention, spanning the last several decades. Indeed, one of the book's most admirable features is the way it handles the interdisciplinary nature of work on the mind. … [A] well-written and engaging book that should prove valuable to anyone interested in attention."

– **Markos Valaris**, *Australasian Journal of Philosophy*

"[A] welcome addition to the philosophical literature on attention. It launches a new and exciting topic of research in attention – selection for action. I hope that philosophers will be enough inspired by Wu's arguments to continue the discussion on the relationship between attention and action."

– **Carolyn Dicey Jennings**, *Notre Dame Philosophical Reviews*

"Attention is a hot topic in cognitive science and philosophy. … [This] book is both a rich philosophical exploration of attention, and, now, with its clear and comprehensive accounts of classic and recent empirical work, the indispensable starting point for anyone with a philosophical interest in attention. Summing up: Essential."

– **William Seager**, CHOICE

"A ground-breaking exploration of what happens when we attend to things, *Attention* provides a thorough and original examination of the nature and functions of attention and its relationship to classical problems in philosophy and psychology. If you read only one book on attention this year, make it this one."

– **Berit Brogaard**, *University of Miami, USA*

"A masterful survey of current work on attention, at once highly informative and readily accessible. It covers all the main current theories and empirical findings about how attention operates, its neural underpinnings, and its ties with agency, perception, cognition, and consciousness, adding much that is novel and challenging. This will be rich and rewarding reading for anybody curious about attention and the mind generally, and a must for anybody in philosophy of mind, philosophy of psychology, and cognitive science."

– **David Rosenthal**, *Graduate Center, City University of New York, USA*

ATTENTION

Wayne Wu's *Attention* was the first book to provide a systematic overview and assessment of different empirical and philosophical works on attention. In this revised and expanded second edition, Wu discusses the following central topics and problems:

- the nature of attention and the structure of the theory of attention.
- explanatory integration of the psychology and neuroscience of attention.
- attention's intimate relation to agency.
- attention and memory.
- the phenomenology of attention and attention as a gate on consciousness.
- introspective attention of consciousness.
- skill in attention.
- the epistemology and ethics of attention.
- attention in thought.

Updated throughout, this edition includes new chapters on working memory, automaticity and skill, and attention and ethics. The breadth of coverage provides materials for advanced students and researchers in psychology, cognitive science, and philosophy. Additional features include chapter summaries, a glossary, and suggestions for further reading, making this also an ideal introduction for those new to attention.

Wayne Wu is Professor in History and Philosophy of Science at the University of Pittsburgh, USA.

"*New Problems of Philosophy* is developing a most impressive line-up of topical volumes aimed at graduate and upper-level undergraduate students in philosophy and at others with interests in cutting edge philosophical work. Series authors are players in their respective fields and notably adept at synthesizing and explaining intricate topics fairly and comprehensively."

- **John Heil**, *Monash University, Australia, and Washington University in St. Louis, USA*

"This is an outstanding collection of volumes. The topics are well chosen and the authors are outstanding. They will be fine texts in a wide range of courses."

- *Stephen Stich, Rutgers University, USA*

New Problems of Philosophy

Series Editor: José Luis Bermúdez

The *New Problems of Philosophy* series provides accessible and engaging surveys of the most important problems in contemporary philosophy. Each book examines either a topic or theme that has emerged on the philosophical landscape in recent years or a longstanding problem refreshed in light of recent work in philosophy and related disciplines. Clearly explaining the nature of the problem at hand and assessing attempts to answer it, books in the series are excellent starting points for undergraduate and graduate students wishing to study a single topic in depth. They will also be essential reading for professional philosophers. Additional features include chapter summaries, further reading and a glossary of technical terms.

Embodied Cognition, Second Edition
Lawrence Shapiro

Self-Deception
Eric Funkhouser

Relativism
Maria Baghramian and Annalisa Coliva

Empathy
Heidi Maibom

Moral Disagreement
Richard Rowland

Perception
Adam Pautz

Thinking and Perceiving
Dustin Stokes

Emotion
Charlie Kurth

Skepticism
Annalisa Coliva and Duncan Pritchard

Self-Control
Marcela Herdova, Stephen Kearns, and Neil Levy

Noncognitivism in Ethics, Second Edition
Mark Schroeder

Attention, Second Edition
Wayne Wu

Explanation and Understanding
Arnon Levy

For more information about this series, please visit: https://www.routledge.com/New-Problems-of-Philosophy/book-series/NPOP

ATTENTION

Second Edition

Wayne Wu

Routledge
Taylor & Francis Group
LONDON AND NEW YORK

Designed cover image: *Detailed view of the fixing points and lugs of a climbing wall*, by geogif. Courtesy of Getty Images.

Second edition published 2025
by Routledge
4 Park Square, Milton Park, Abingdon, Oxon OX14 4RN

and by Routledge
605 Third Avenue, New York, NY 10158

Routledge is an imprint of the Taylor & Francis Group, an informa business

First edition published by Routledge 2014

British Library Cataloguing-in-Publication Data
A catalogue record for this book is available from the British Library

ISBN: 978-1-032-12178-9 (hbk)
ISBN: 978-1-032-12177-2 (pbk)
ISBN: 978-1-003-22345-0 (ebk)

DOI: 10.4324/9781003223450

Typeset in Joanna
by SPi Technologies India Pvt Ltd (Straive)

To my parents, Mabel and Gideon Wu

CONTENTS

PREFACE TO THE SECOND EDITION

This book substantially revises the first edition. It is almost a new book though demonstrably a progeny of the first. Space constraints and new material required excising some previous content. There are now thirteen substantive chapters rather than eight. One past chapter, "Attention and Demonstrative Thought", has been compressed into one section in Chapter 13. Material about attention and representational theories of consciousness has been largely excised. Debates on those topics have become less central relative to other issues discussed in this volume. Readers interested in representationalism will find the first edition a continued resource.

I have substantially revised my discussion of empirical and relevant conceptual material on attention treated in Chapters 1 and 2 of the first edition. These are replaced by Chapters 1 to 5 of the present book along with a new discussion of attention and working memory in Chapter 6. Chapters 1 to 3 provide a theoretical framework for attention of use to philosophers and scientists. This framework is deployed to organize experimental and computational work on spatial attention, discussed in Chapter 4, and on visual search, discussed in Chapter 5. The aim is to review the science by showing how a Common Conception of attention, derived from methodological assumptions, organizes scientific work into a structured explanation of what attention is. Introspection gets a separate chapter, Chapter 8, and three new chapters conclude the book: Chapter 11 on automaticity, habits, and skill in attention; Chapter 12 on ethical and normative issues regarding attention; and Chapter 13 on varieties of thinking as attention.

The many acknowledgements for the first edition carry over to this one since this book would not be possible without the first. For this edition, I thank a number of researchers for their helpful feedback: Brian Anderson, Nic Bommarito, Laura Callahan, Maurizio Corbetta, Florian Cova, Rachel Denison, Tim Donovan, François Kammerer, Anna Giustina, Carolyn Dicey Jennings, Chris Mole, Jessie Munton, Ruth Rosenholtz, Gordon Shulman, Henry Taylor, and Jeremy Wolfe as well the anonymous reviewers for the press. Thanks to Tony Bruce for inviting me to do a new edition and Adam Johnson for keeping things on track.

Let me record one final acknowledgement. A half-century ago, my parents emigrated to the United States. My father went ahead for seminary studies and to prepare things for his young family. My mother, left behind, raised an infant first son (me) for nearly two years on her own before joining her husband in the States. Over the next 18 years, they worked hard to ensure that my brother and I had the opportunities to succeed. I understand now the sacrifices that they made when they opted to run a photo development shop, then a small convenience store, and finally a Greek deli (yes, that's right) instead of doing what they were trained, and hoped, to do. After my brother left for college, my parents finally returned to their heart's work, to minister to the spiritual needs of Chinese people across the world. They were Christian missionaries in Buenos Aires, Vladivostok, Saipan, with occasional forays into China. They faced racism, physical dangers, and the absence of basic necessities, the same challenges facing the migrant Chinese laborers they ministered to. What is plain to me, however, in looking at pictures of them during this time is how happy and fulfilled they were and how many lives they positively touched, people far from their own homes who found a home through my parents' efforts. I am so grateful that Ma and Pa were able for many years to do what they loved and to love others in a way that expressed their deep humanity. This book, indeed this author, would not be possible without the sacrifices they made. It is gratefully and lovingly dedicated to them.

INTRODUCTION

Attention insinuates itself into what we do, perceive, and think. When you listen carefully for the too-infrequent beeping of a battery-drained fire detector in the middle of the night, examine the complex and uncanny texture of an object with your fingers, try to isolate the hint of strawberry in a red wine, or just look frantically for your keys before leaving the house late for a meeting, you deploy attention, sometimes successfully, sometimes not. Attention can involve movement as when you use your fingers to search for something under the couch or shift your eyes as you follow someone moving across a room. It can be furtive as when you pretend to listen to a conversation yet covertly eavesdrop on the person behind you or you look at someone "out of the corner of your eye." Attention is not always voluntary. It is involuntary when a loud noise or awful smell pulls your focus to it. Even in thought, attention plays a central role: the embarrassing event of yesterday that pulls your thoughts to it against your will, distracting you throughout the day; the attempt to remember the name of a person and then, as if by magic, finally recalling it; or just thinking, working through specific reasons to make a decision and thereby following a train of thought. Attention is a fundamental capacity of the mind. It is central to what we do, and it is what this book is about.

DOI: 10.4324/9781003223450-1

The book's goals are to provide a comprehensive overview of the nature of attention understood from philosophical and empirical perspectives and to draw consequences from that multidimensional picture for topics of broader philosophical concern. Some readers have kindly mentioned to me how much they enjoyed, even admired, the first edition of *Attention*. As these readers will see, the book is substantially revised.

In the introduction to the first edition, I noted empirical skepticism regarding attention, but I now feel that I did not adequately confront it. To do better, I extract a functional characterization that William James expressed long ago, one that enables philosophers and scientists to anchor their discussions to the core function of attention in guiding behavior. This function provides a unification principle to bridge empirical work across different modes of analysis. It also allows philosophers to draw on that productive work, captured in nearly *fifty thousand papers* with "attention" in the title, registered in PubMed from 1950 to 2024. Indeed, philosophical reflection on attention, especially in ethics and epistemology, seems to be undergoing a renaissance, and the book reflects this wave of new work.

The book can be divided into four parts:

(1) A conceptual framework for attention

(2) Empirical and philosophical accounts of attention

(3) Consciousness and attention and

(4) Philosophical work drawing on attention.

In the first part (Chapters 1–3), I argue that a shared conception anchors empirical paradigms for probing attention: a subject's mentally selecting a target to deal with, say her visually selecting an object to pick up or put into memory. This links attention both to task performance in experimental settings and to actions in the world, providing the conceptual clarification needed to construct an adequate theory of attention. In the second part (Chapters 4–7), I begin reviewing empirical work on attention focusing on two paradigms: indirect spatial cueing of visual attention (Chapter 4) and visual search (Chapter 5). The goal of these chapters is to cover salient results of cognitive science in a way that merges them in a unified explanation of concrete attentional phenomena. This explanation is inspired by David Marr's approach to explaining what vision is. I demonstrate how much has already been cohesively explained. We know what attention is as deployed in many experimental tasks. I also provide new coverage of the crucial relation between attention and working memory, highlighting cognitive attention as studied in cognitive science (Chapter 6), and conclude with an overview of four philosophical theories in the analytical tradition of what attention is (Chapter 7).

I should note the change in presentation of the empirical material. The first edition separated the psychology of attention from the neuroscience of attention, reviewing each separately. Such overviews can be found in any textbook. Here, I take a different approach. Chapter 1 argues that experimental paradigms probing attention share a Common Conception of attention that underscores its role in guiding behavior. If so, this functional role provides a means of unifying scientific work at all levels of analysis. Accordingly, I show how explanatory unity can be achieved regarding two central experimental paradigms: spatial cueing and visual search. I use the Common Conception to show how experimental and computational results interlock. Readers wanting a review of some of the psychology and neuroscience of attention can focus on Chapters 1, 4, and 5 (with perhaps a dash of Chapter 2, namely Section 2.5). Those interested in attention and working memory can also read Chapter 6.

In the third part (Chapters 8–10), I discuss attention and consciousness. It is important to understand the central role that introspection plays in constructing theories of consciousness, and attention in introspection receives its own chapter in this edition. Chapter 8 characterizes introspective attention used to generate data regarding conscious phenomena, and the following two chapters cover material carried over and updated from the first edition, focusing on attention's effects on conscious experience and whether attention gates consciousness. Finally, the fourth part (Chapters 11–13) discusses philosophical topics, namely the automaticity of attention and skill (Chapter 11), the ethics of attention (Chapter 12), and the role of attention in varieties of thought (Chapter 13). These hardly exhaust the philosophical significance of attention such as its relation to the emotions, attention and aesthetics, and a more concerted discussion of attention and epistemology. Nevertheless, I hope that in these chapters, readers will be able to take the framework for attention from Chapters 1 to 7 and apply them to their own work.

I want to underscore the anchor of my discussion, the Common Conception of attention. This is expressed in James' description of attention as we the folk experience it, what we all know. The conception can be put this way: a subject's attending is the subject mentally selecting a target in order to deal with it, this necessitating withdrawal from other things. Readers can recognize this as being at the core of the earlier banal situations that manifest a subject's attending to things. Folk and empirical psychology intersect at this conception, for the guidance of behavior conception of attention is common in the sciences. It is built into the shared empirical methods of the science of attention. If so, then in accepting the empirical approach to attention, we commit ourselves to a common functional structure exemplified in each experimental paradigm. Because many philosophers of attention are sensitive to empirical work driven by these paradigms, this part of selection for action should be *ground zero* for philosophical reflection. Neutrality regarding this point closes off engagement with empirical work and obscures the inherent unity therein. Assertions of alternative pictures of attention invite the question of why take a different path that avoids, even contradicts, basic (axiomatic) assumptions in empirical methodology? Crucially, if we begin with what is common, unity is present at the get-go.

***

As I noted in the first edition, it is helpful to articulate clear questions regarding attention. Here are seven:

Metaphysical:	What is attention?
Function:	What role does attention play?
Taxonomy:	What kinds of attention are there and how are they related?
Properties:	What are characteristic features of attention?
Mechanism:	How is attention implemented?
Consciousness:	What is the relation between attention and consciousness?
Philosophical:	What is the philosophical significance of attention?

A complete theory of attention answers these questions, and constructing such a theory will require both empirical and philosophical work. The questions do not exhaust what we can ask about attention, and they can be rendered in more specific versions. I note them to frame the discussions to come. That said, I will not keep score. Readers are encouraged to come back to these questions or their preferred versions of them, indeed to articulate others and add them above, tracking the answers found in the book and how those answers link together. As they do so, readers will recognize that attention is one of the best understood of mental phenomena.

It has been gratifying to see a recent resurgence of interest in attention, especially in ethics and epistemology. These were areas only lightly covered in the first edition. Further, the coverage in the first edition was limited in ways that now seem to me unfortunate. Still, glaring omissions remain of which I shall mention a few: the history of theories of attention across all intellectual traditions; the absence of engagement with philosophical discussions of attention outside Western thought, especially the growing interest in Buddhist approaches to attention; silence regarding the link between moods, emotions, and attention; passing over the phenomenological approach such as found in the works of Edmund Husserl, Maurice Merleau-Ponty, and others; lack of discussion of the pathologies and deficits of attention as occur in attention-deficit/hyperactivity disorder, schizophrenia, obsessive-compulsive disorder, depression, and other conditions; skirting the relation between attention and imagery and attention and aesthetic experience; and inadequate coverage of the epistemology of attention. In the end, time and limited expertise imposed salient limits on what I could adequately cover. I highlight these topics here so readers will know of the gaps. The framework presented in this book should provide a foundation to approach any of those topics, and I hope readers will be inspired to pursue them and to engage with the many researchers who are setting a path forward.

1

A THEORETICAL FRAMEWORK FOR ATTENTION

1.1 Introduction

Much of what we know about attention comes from work in cognitive science, and yet empirical theorists have raised questions about whether we understand attention at all. Russell Poldrack noted:

> I don't think we know what "attention" is. It's a concept that's so broad and over-used as to be meaningless. There's [sic.] lots of things people in psychology and neuroscience study that they call "attention" that are clearly different things.
>
> (quoted in Goldhill 2018)

Such skepticism is long-standing. A century earlier, Karl Groos observed:

> To the question, "What is Attention?", there is not only no generally recognized answer but the different attempts at a solution even diverge in the most disturbing manner.
>
> (Groos 1896)

DOI: 10.4324/9781003223450-2

Linked across a century, Poldrak and Groos strikingly voice the same worries: there is no accepted answer to the question "What is attention?" and there are too many answers to it. We do not have an adequate answer to the Metaphysical Question, "What is attention?" Two articles announce that "There is no such thing as attention" (Anderson (2011); see also Anderson (2021)) and "No one knows what attention is" (Hommel et al. 2019). Yet there is a thriving research program on attention with over fifty thousand papers with "attention" in the title since 1950 (PubMed search, September 14, 2024). How can we reconcile such pessimism with such productivity? Is the entire field confused? Fragmented? Empty?

Among experimentalists, such skepticism does not induce much concern perhaps because attention research thrives without an answer to the Metaphysical Question. Science doesn't need metaphysics to make progress. Instead, I offer a different explanation. Progress is made because experimentalists operate with a shared conception of what attention is, one sewn into the fabric of experimental practice: Attention is the subject's selection of a target to perform an (instructed) action. Scientists already agree, implicitly, on a uniform answer to the Metaphysical Question, one implied by the standard attentional paradigms. Our goal is to uncover this *Common Conception* to establish a shared starting point for theorists of attention who take empirical work seriously. Skeptics about attention are answered by showing that, in accepting the standard paradigms, they, like us, are committed to a uniform characterization of attention as a target of empirical understanding. The Common Conception as a core assumption of experimental work on attention unifies that work. That conception captures William James's well-known characterization of the folk psychology of attention, what everyone knows: a subject attending to X is the subject's selecting X to respond to. This chapter reveals the Common Conception as a methodological principle that unifies experimental and theoretical traditions. It is, as James noted, what we all (implicitly at least) know.

Section 1.2 outlines basic conceptual problems in the theory of attention. Section 1.3 introduces a Marrian multilevel explanatory structure that we will draw inspiration from to constitute an explanation of attention. In Section 1.4, we respond to skepticism about attention by identifying a Common Conception, an assumption that scientists are committed to if they are committed to the validity of standard experimental paradigms. Section 1.5 argues against the proliferation of attention into different kinds. Finally, in Section 1.6, we add more detail to what a unified explanation of attention will look like, one that we apply in reviewing two major experimental research traditions in attention research: spatial cueing (Chapter 4) and visual search (Chapter 5).

1.2 Conceptual Problems in the Theory of Attention

This chapter examines attention through conceptual analysis. An all-too-common objection to this approach is that it perseverates about nomenclature, plays with words, or is "just semantics". This common complaint derails substantive discussion. Worse yet, it is based on fundamental confusions. Certainly, in explaining what X is, we set "X"'s semantic value, namely what "X" means. Yet while disputes about what X is uses the word "X", it is a *use-mention* fallacy to conclude that the dispute is about words.

The "just semantics" complaint conflates two distinct claims:

Attention = X
"Attention" means X

The first is a claim about the world *using* the word "attention". The second is a claim about the word "attention" *mentioning* it. Cognitive science is in the first instance concerned with the identity claim, what attention is. It is not directly concerned with language, as in the second claim. The charge that metaphysical investigation of what attention is, the identity claim, is really just legislating the meaning of words commits this use-mention confusion. Our investigation concerns a psychological-biological phenomenon, not language. The analysis that follows clarifies what attention is by connecting it to other aspects of mind and world within a psychological theory about the nature of mental reality. We aim to carve reality at its joints.

That said, the word "attention" is overused in empirical descriptions, reflecting a stylistic reflex to add "attention" or "attentional" in descriptions of any *selective* phenomena. Britt Anderson (2011) proposed a helpful exercise. Take any passage in which "attention" is deployed in explanations or descriptions, cross out the word, and see if anything is lost. Anderson demonstrated such excision on a passage from one of the pioneers of the psychology of attention, Anne Treisman:

> For example, when Treisman (1985) writes "Some discriminations appear to be made automatically ~~without attention~~ and spatially in parallel across the visual field. Other visual operations ~~require focused attention and~~ can be performed only serially." The references to attention can be struck out without losing any understanding of the empirical results, and their inclusion doesn't deepen our theoretical understanding.
>
> (Anderson 2011, 4)

I would add the following: anytime one reads "attentional process" in a journal, replace "attentional" with "selective", and typically no change in meaning will result.

Attention is selective, and one might conclude that attention *is* selection – that is, attention to X is selection of X. Yet not every selective process is attention. Consider the standard account of attention offered in textbooks and scientific review articles (Koester et al., 2021, Chapter 25; Holt et al. 2019, 225; Bear et al., 2020, Chapter 21; Workman and Taylor 2021, 50; Bahmani et al. 2019, 129; Störmer 2019), the *simple identification*:

> attention is the selection of information for further processing.

We can read this as expressing either identity or predication. As predication, the statement claims that attention exhibits the property of informational selectivity. This is true, yet the claim so understood yields an incomplete answer to the Metaphysical Question since there are many forms of informational selectivity not all of which are attention. The required next step is to say what kind of informational selectivity is at issue, a point we shall return to. In contrast, identity answers the Metaphysical Question since it tells us what attention is. On the simple identification, attention is identical to a kind of process, namely processes of selecting information for further processing.

The problem is that the simple identification *overgeneralizes*, finding attention everywhere in information processing systems. Yet selective information processing is present where attention is not. This shows that the account as stated is false. For example, at the human retina, there is selection of information from light of specific wavelengths for further processing. By the simple identification, there is attention on the retina. This is false, and to my knowledge, no one has ever made the latter claim. The optical processing of the photoreceptors is not sufficient for attention even if it exhibits informational selection of specific wavelengths of light. The reader can easily construct further counterexamples as an exercise. The counterexamples enjoin us to narrow the aim of the selective processing that counts as attention, what such processing is *for*.

Implicit endorsement of identity in the simple identification explains an untoward linguistic practice, namely the stylistic reflex of applying the term "attention" to diverse types of selective processing. So, "attention" comes to refer to too many things, as Groos and Poldrack observed. On the simple identification, attention is many things and "attention" means many things. This brings us back to the century-old problem noted earlier.

The (over)emphasis on linguistic failure obscures the logical flaws of the theory of attention. Take the empirical theory of attention as including the totality of reasonable claims widely accepted by scientists and theorists about attention. Now consider the following formal schema.

1. A = X

2. A = Y

3. X ≠ Y

4. Thus: X = Y or, alternatively, *A ≠ A*

The logic is perspicuous, the result, theoretically devastating. Let there be psychological or neural phenomena X and Y such that X ≠ Y (premise 3) and where many scientists S_1 say that attention is X (premise 1) while many S_2 say that attention is Y (premise 2). Note, sometimes, $S_1 = S_2$. Readers are invited to select a random set of papers on attention, look for identity claims endorsed in those papers (i.e., attention is...), and run the argument as an exercise.

To give a concrete example, consider the generic idea of *biased competition* in behavior (cf. the biased competition theory of attention, Chapter 2.5). One situation demanding biased competition is when two visible targets compete for control of behavior such as when you are looking at two containers of desirable ice cream, say rocky road and chocolate chip. Each container competes for the control of your behavior, namely reaching for one of the two to consume. For you to reach for one rather than the other, you and hence your brain have to resolve this competition. We will use the term *bias* to name the disparate factors that resolve this behavioral conflict. For example, a decision to go for chocolate chip today resolves the behavioral competition, and you reach for that flavor.

There are two positions in the empirical literature regarding how attention is related to biases that resolve behavioral competition. The most common, a "spotlight" account of attention, treats attention as a *cause*, identifying it as the bias that resolves neural competition in the brain and, ultimately, behavioral competition needed for the subject to act. After all, if your brain fails to resolve the correlated processing competition between the two visible targets, you will not act. On this view, attention is an internal mechanism that biases processing toward a specific target. Yet Robert Desimone and John Duncan, who presented a biased competition theory of attention, explicitly rejected this spotlight conception. Instead, they identified attention to be the *effect* of, or explained by, the resolution of competition. So, on one view, attention is the bias that causes resolution of competition; on the other, attention is the effect of such resolution. Yet arguably here, cause ≠ effect. Conjoining the two positions into a single theory entails that the cause of biased competition = the effect of biased competition (transitivity of identity from [1] cause = attention and [2] attention = effect). We end up with an inconsistent theory that divides nature in an incoherent way. (For another version of this argument, see below.)

Contradiction is avoided by the proliferation of different types of attention: attention_1, attention_2, and so on. This blocks deriving the contradiction which relies on the tautology *attention = attention*. While logically on point, the move strikes me as questionable. The issue is not with proliferation *per se*. After all, we divide memory into different kinds, so why not attention? Proliferation, however, is not something we should unthinkingly affirm. What justifies this psychological fission? What unifies the resulting proliferation? Since it seems theoretically desirable to avoid a disjunctive conception of a psychological kind where each disjunct has little substantive connection to others, we want a principle that identifies what the species share that unifies them into a coherent kind. For example, isotopes of an element are grouped as an atomic kind because they have the same number of protons, so the same atomic number. In the case of memory, perhaps the principle is something like *an experience dependent change of a psychological representation/capacity*. Arguably, this unifies episodic memory with priming, two seemingly disparate phenomena standardly categorized as mnemonic. The present point is not to take a strong stand on what explains types of memory as belonging to a single kind but to note that something ought to. In this way, proliferation of instances of a psychological kind is coherent.

We already have an intelligible way to proliferate types of attention. Consider the following *logical frame* for claims about attention that we will use throughout the text:

S m-attends to *T*

S, the *subject* variable, takes as values subjects who pay attention, typically persons (you and I); m, the *mode*, takes adverbial modification corresponding to different psychological capacities like vision (visual attention), audition (auditory attention), cognition of various forms (mnemonic attention), and so on; *T*, the target, identifies the item to which attention is directed. From this frame, it is easy to identify species of attention, such as visual or auditory attention to features, mnemonic attention to a past episode or a fact (episodic and semantic recall), top-down attention to a location or bottom-up attention to a loud sound, and so on. This is a familiar partitioning into coherent types of attention we understand. For example, the simple identification gives us the following principle of unification for all these types:

S m-attends to *T* = *S m*-selecting *T* for further processing

So, top-down visual attention to a color and bottom-up cognitive attention to a disturbing past event all share a core, namely each is a type of selection of a target for further processing by the subject. Unfortunately, as we saw, the simple identification is demonstrably false. Let's consider another demonstration of this.

Consider two common claims: (1) attention is a mechanism/process P, and (2) attention is a limited resource R. This distinction is clearly articulated by Daniel Kahneman (1973) in his book, *Attention and Effort*, and different versions of (1) and (2) are common today. (We shall discuss attention as resource further in Chapter 3.4.) We have already seen a version of (1) in the idea of attention as the bias that causes resolution of competition. Here, attention is identified by neuroscientists as the neural mechanism that changes processing, shifting it to a relevant target. The idea that attention is a resource is often left open-ended in that very few have stated precisely what the resource is. Nevertheless, when theorists speak of *more or less* attention, namely that attention can be graded, they are expressing the resource idea. Now, since P uses R, P ≠ R. This allows us to derive a contradiction from any theory that endorses both (1) and (2) since we can derive that P = R, as in the previous example. Proliferation avoids contradiction by saying that process and resource are two kinds of attention.

But what unifies these species as being of the same genus? Consider auditory and visual attention to perceptible features. The simple identification, were it true, allows us to unify these two putative species of attention as being of the same genus, namely psychological processes that select information for further processing. Yet why do attention as resource and attention as process count as species of the same genus, attention? This is not clear. My worry here is that proliferation has become a linguistic, not empirical claim. That is, it is not that R and P are, in fact, species of a single psychological kind, attention. No argument for this is given in the literature. Rather, the field has chosen to call two distinct phenomena "attention". This is a word game, not an evidentially supported inference about the world.

Without principled empirical or theoretical reasons to divide attention into distinct species, the theory of attention comes to be inconsistent; consequently, its representation of psychological reality is incoherent. Groos voiced a complaint about the theory of attention, and 120 years later, Poldrack re-expressed it. We have, by common consent, failed to solve this century-old conceptual-logical problem. Contradiction shows us that we must solve it.

1.3 Marrian Explanation

To make progress, I want to draw inspiration from a theory of scientific explanation provided by David Marr. Marr's goal was to explain vision (seeing). He begins his book, *Vision*, as follows:

> What does it mean, to see? The plain man's answer (and Aristotle's, too) would be, to know what is where by looking. In other words, vision is the *process* of discovering from images what is present in the world, and where it is.
> (Marr 1982, 3)

Marr's opening question, transposed to attention, suggests two of our questions.

Metaphysical: What is attention?
Function: What role does attention play?

Marr begins with the Metaphysical Question regarding vision, "What is vision?" but answers it by considering the Functional Question, "What is the purpose of vision?" To see, Marr notes, is to know what is where by looking, to acquire knowledge of the external world. To specify vision's function is to answer what seeing is. This provides the anchor for his proposal for how to explain vision. Marr reformulates the Aristotelian and common answer in this restatement: "Vision is *therefore*, first and foremost, an information-processing task" (3, my italics). That shift involves a translation of the common sense idea of seeing into a mathematical function. In vision, the function maps a two-dimensional retinal input into a representation of the three-dimensional world. The mathematization of the initial functional description of vision is a key step in the Marrian account. It provides the *computational theory*, the top-level of the explanation.

Beyond the computational theory, there are two further explanatory levels. The level below the computational theory is the *algorithmic level* specifying the algorithms needed to compute the mathematical function of the computational theory, including identifying the representations the algorithm operates over. The algorithm is realized in a physical system described in the implementation or hardware level. Marr is sometimes criticized for invoking only three levels. We leave open how many levels of analysis are needed to explain the target phenomenon, the *explanandum*. (We will suggest a fourth level, the *architectural level*, in Chapter 5.4 and Figure 6.1.) The aim is to build a multilevel *vertical* analysis of psychological capacities such as vision or attention that provides an explanatory structure for those capacities. The relation between each level is perhaps *constitution*, *implementation*, or *realization*. So, in vision, the neural substrate implements an algorithm that realizes the computation of the mathematical function.

Properly filled out, the explanatory structure answers the question "What is X?" where X is a psychological phenomenon. The multiple levels of analysis are "the different levels at which an information-processing device *must* be understood before one can be said to have understood it completely" (24; my italics). Marr's insight is that if we can find the right computational theory, this provides an *organizing principle* for other levels of analysis.

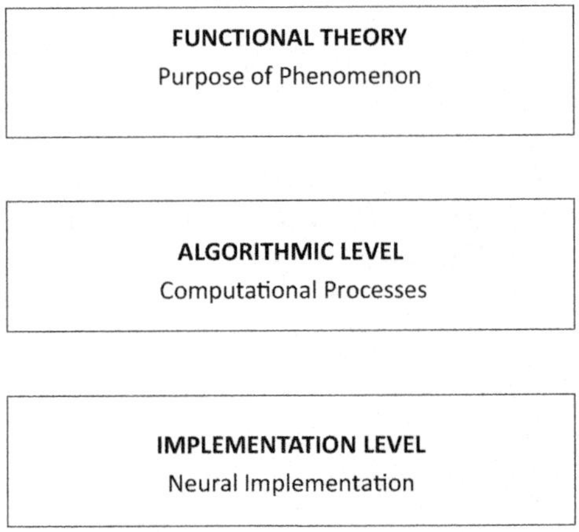

Figure 1.1 The explanatory structure.

We will not take on Marr's specific explanatory program. Instead, it inspires us to suggest a unified, multilevel approach to explaining what attention is. We will give a functional description of attention, specifically what selection of information is *for*. We leave open the possibility that this can be translated into a mathematical function, but it need not be. To mark this divergence, I shall speak of a *functional theory* as opposed to a computational theory. The functional theory provides a description of attention's point which will guide us in finding algorithms and neural substrates that allow the realization of attention's selective function. So, our explanations will be "Marrian" in the sense that a functional description will be the starting point and that other levels of analysis will be vertically organized with the functional theory as unifying principle. This provides a way to explain what attention is.

The functional description of attention, what I shall call the *Common Conception*, was articulated by William James as what we all know. Chapters 4 and 5 will use the explanatory framework to organize empirical work drawing on two of the main experimental paradigms for attention: spatial cueing (Chapter 4) and visual search (Chapter 5).

1.4 Attention as Selection for Behavior (Action)

The science of attention is *methodologically committed* to a specific functional conception of attention entailed by James's well-known characterization (Wu 2024b). Bracketing your own theoretical commitments, read James's description and see if it matches your experience of attention, especially the parts italicized:

> Everyone knows what attention is. *It is the taking possession by the mind*, in clear and vivid form, *of one out of what seem several simultaneously possible objects or trains of thought*. Focalization, concentration, of consciousness are of its essence. *It implies withdrawal from some things in order to deal effectively with others.*
>
> (James 1890, 402, my italics)

The folk conception that James articulates, what we all know, highlights attention deployed as part of doing something intentionally. In doing things, our minds *actively* take possession of a target. This form of attention is what cognitive scientists often refer to as *voluntary*, *endogenous*, or *top-down* attention. In contrast, attention outside of the agent's control would involve the taking possession of our mind by an object, what is often called *automatic*, *exogenous*, or *bottom-up* attention. Note that, as described, both forms of attention are captured in James's description. We begin with the top-down form, extracting the functional core of attention in James's description as follows:

> attention is the subject's mentally selecting a target in order to deal effectively with it.

We will return to automatic attention in Chapter 11, but for now, we focus on the agent's dealing with something as the agent's acting intentionally in response to it. To act involves a selective response to a specific target rather than other potential targets. It is to do something to the target, to act in respect of it, such as to run toward or away from it. Recall the simple identification rejected earlier: attention as selection of information for further processing. While the simple identification is too broad, James's characterization narrows the relevant selection, emphasizing selection *for the guidance of action*. James's description amounts to a correction to the simple identification and allows derivation of what I shall call the Common Conception:

> If a subject mentally selects target *Y* to inform acting (*A*-ing) on *Y*, that is, to deal with *Y*, then *S* attends to *Y*.

While in cognitive science, "action" often refers narrowly to motor movements, in this work, actions are the *things subjects do*, including not just moving their bodies but also performing mental actions such as reasoning, remembering, or making decisions. *Mental* selection is at the same explanatory level as the corresponding action description. Action and mental selection are attributed to the subject. So if a subject reaches for the visible cup of coffee, then the subject has visually selected a feature of the coffee to guide the reach. If the subject figures out the right conclusion from evidence, then the subject has cognitively selected some evidential feature to support drawing that conclusion.

We address persistent skepticism about attention by noting that cognitive science conducts experiments based on a shared methodology that presupposes the Common Conception. If so, the Common Conception is no more controversial than the assumptions of a shared experimental practice. This is to say, if one is committed to using the standard experimental paradigms for attention, one is committed to the Common Conception. In particular, the Common Conception provides a *normative* or *regulative condition* on experimental design: An experimental paradigm probing a specific form of attention will be methodologically adequate only if the paradigm ensures that attention is set on the required targets. One cannot study attention to a target type Y such as a feature or location without ensuring that experimental subjects are attending to instances of Y during the experiment. For example, one cannot study spatial attention if subjects are not attending to the requisite location in space, one cannot study feature attention if subjects are not attending to the requisite feature, and so on.

Experimenters impose a task structure to set attention in the desired way. Specifically, they define a task such that it is correctly completed only if the subject selects a requisite target to inform response. This is a normative ideal that an initial experimental design might fail to meet. If so, the task must be redesigned or else attention is not appropriately set. Alternatively, if the task has the right structure, then in doing the task successfully, the subject must attend in a specific way because the subject must select the requisite target in order to correctly perform the task. This is an uncontroversial methodological ideal that all experimenters of attention assume. Attention is set through task-relevant selection. We arrive at a conditional differently implemented across a variety of tasks:

> *Empirical Sufficient Condition*: If a subject mentally selects target *Y* to inform performance of experimental task *E*, then *S* attends to *Y*.

The empirical sufficient condition is the experimental expression of the Common Conception since experimental tasks are a subset of actions. Hence the empirical condition is entailed by the Common Conception.

If the argument from the logic of experimental design is correct, the logic of selection for task performance should fit actual paradigms. Consider standard experimental paradigms for attention and note the requirement for appropriate selection:

1. *Spatial cueing*: Subjects are instructed to discriminate a target that can appear at various locations while the subject maintains fixation, so correct performance is a correct report of target features (e.g., orientation). Cues for spatial location influence the selection of the target for report (see Chapter 4 for detailed discussion).

2. *Visual search*: Subjects are instructed to locate a specific target among an array of distractors and report whether the target is present or not (see Chapter 5 for detailed discussion).

3. *Delayed match to sample*: Subjects are given a sample stimulus which they must keep in working memory. A target array eventually appears and the subject must see if any of the targets match the sample. Subjects report yes or no.

4. *Dichotic listening*: Subjects verbally shadow one of two streams of words. In some cases, probes are introduced in the unattended channel to see if attention can be captured; this is determined by retrospective reports of said stimuli.

5. *Multiple object tracking*: Subjects are presented with a variety of motionless objects on a screen, and a subset of these objects are marked as targets (e.g., they flash). Subjects are required to track the targets as all the objects move; later, subjects are tested whether a given object was among the marked targets.

6. *Attentional blink*: Subjects are presented with a rapid serial presentation of numbers at fixation and are told to report when a *letter* appears. When a second letter appears too soon after the presentation of the first letter, the subject often fails to report it. Attention is said to blink. This presumes that in selecting the first target to report, the subject was deploying attention as required by task and that in failing to report the second target, the subject has failed to select it.

7. *Partial report of stimuli*: Subjects are presented with several rows of letters that are briefly flashed. In partial report, subjects are cued after array presentation to report a specific row. As the array is no longer present, the subject must select the letters as encoded in memory (*iconic* memory, Neisser (Neisser 1967); see retro cueing, Chapter 7).

8. *Inattentional blindness*: Subjects are given a task that involves attending to a specific target, such as counting the number of basketball passes by one of two groups throwing the ball between their members. A critical stimulus, such as a person in a gorilla suit, walks by with many subjects not noticing the gorilla. Subjects are said to be inattentionally blind to the gorilla because they are not paying attention to it, attention being paid to the basketball, as per task instructions.

In each paradigm, attention is set precisely by giving subjects task instructions that define targets to selectively respond to. For each of the tasks, we can derive a specific version of the empirical sufficient condition. For example, for multiple object tracking:

> *Multiple object tracking condition*: If a subject *S* visually selects targets in the set *T*, a proper subset of all presented objects *O*, to remember for later identification in the test phase, then *S* visually attends to the members of *T*.

Where the task is correctly performed, the subject has appropriately selected the target for response, so has appropriately attended. The above survey of many standard paradigms reveals that the empirical sufficient condition is the common thread. It expresses a methodological assumption concerning how to set the subject's attention, and it provides a schema for how to design new tasks.

In our formulation of the empirical sufficient condition, E is a variable for tasks. What precisely does "task" come to? Put another way, for any concrete task *e* that meets other methodological requirements, why is it that selection in *e* counts as attention? To capture the *generality* of the methodology, "task" means more than the finite set of experimental tasks already accepted by scientists; otherwise, no further experimental paradigms could be generated. Rather, the background conception that supports the generalization of methodology is that of selection for action, action in the general sense of *things that subjects do*. The relevant tasks in science are set by research interests, available subjects, and measurement technology. We are, in the end, interested in what people do. So, the methodological justification for any proposed experimental paradigm for attention is precisely that it tracks the Common Conception linking attention to the guidance of response in action.

We should work with the conception that we all agree on. This shared knowledge, what we all know, can be deployed to justify the construction of new experimental paradigms, namely new instances of the empirical sufficient condition. This gives us a direct response to the century's old complaint that we do not know what attention is. Emphasizing action in our logical frame

> *S*'s *m*-attending to *T* in doing *A* is *S*'s *m*-selecting *T* to guide her action *A*.

If we consider experimental tasks E as a subset of actions *A*, we have a more specific frame for cognitive science:

> *S*'s *m*-attending to *T* in doing *E* is *S*'s *m*-selecting *T* to guide her performance of *E*.

Finally, since each task E can involve distinct response R such as a movement for report which the subject is instructed to produce, the logical frame we will most often invoke is

> *S*'s *m*-attending to *T* to respond *R* in *E* is *S*'s *m*-selecting *T* to guide *R* in performing *E*.

Or more simply

> *S*'s *m*-attending to *T* for *R* is *S*'s *m*-selecting *T* to guide producing *R*.

To understand attention in a task E, we must specify the relevant R. We then fix the mistaken standard account as follows: attention is the subject's selecting a target for further processing *in generating a response* R *in respect of it* (added portion in italics).

One important function of the empirical sufficient condition is its role as a normative principle in experimental design and interpretation of data. We arrive at this conception of attention because it captures how one *should* structure a task in order to ensure that the subject's attention is properly directed. This principle sets a norm in experimental practice. Normative principles of this sort are not chiseled into stone tablets for lab display. They are learned through a practice that differentiates good from bad experimental design. So, it is compatible with the role of the empirical sufficient condition that one can find scientists who might seem to deny it, just as people can deny laws that, in fact, apply to them.

In uncovering a core assumption in experimental methodology, we have taken a step forward in explaining what attention might be. Despite this implicit agreement, one might persist in skepticism about attention so conceived. As we saw, complaints about attention are hard-wired, over a century old. Yet even if one is a hardened skeptic, the proposal suggests a route to unification. One reason to accept the proposal is that it works quite well. In my list of eight common experimental paradigms for attention, selection for action is a common thread. This is a discovery of the analysis. Even if we decide to assert that attention is other things, the bulk of what we study in science is attention as selection for further processing in guiding behavior. This position is no more controversial than the accepted paradigms, and it is self-defeating to be skeptical about attention in this sense and simultaneously to use those paradigms. Conceptually, this would be to deny that one has legs while using them to walk.

Hommel et al.'s (2019) paper "No one knows what attention is" suggests skepticism, yet none of their criticisms, which I think are correct, is inconsistent with the proposal defended here. Indeed, after criticizing contemporary accounts of attention, Hommel et al. advocate examining phylogeny and evolution to understand attention. They conclude:

> selectivity emerged through evolution as a design feature to enable efficient goal-directed action. Such selectivity became necessary as the action repertoire of the given line of organisms that led to humans increased. This means that selectivity is an emerging property arising from a myriad underlying processes, and the simple fact that humans (and other species showing selective attention) evolved the way they did, with selective attention being one of many byproducts, next to "selective intention" and "selective decision making."
>
> (p. 2298)

The idea expressed comports with James's description. Hommel et al. arrive at the need for selection for control of action through an illuminating route, evolutionary considerations regarding agents whose ability to deal with a complicated world necessitates selection to enable appropriate response to that world. That folk psychology, scientific methodology, and evolutionary considerations converge on the Jamesian description should give one confidence (see also (Krauzlis et al. 2014)).

Finally, the Common Conception provides a description of attention's function as being for the guidance of action and thereby establishes a functional theory of attention. The resulting condition provides an organizing principle for investigating the algorithmic level as well as its neurobiological implementation for a given task. This unification arises for a simple reason: the experiments that inform construction of algorithms, identification of neural correlates, and proposals for neural mechanisms are based on experimentally implementing the Common Conception in specific empirical sufficient conditions that set concrete tasks. That is, the relevant data are collected under that condition. In that way, the functional account connects all levels of analysis in the study of what is called top-down attention, attention set by performing specific tasks.

1.5 Proliferation of Attentional Selection

In Section 1.2, I noted an intelligible proliferation using the logical frame, S m-attends to T (cf. Henry Taylor (2023), who argues that attention is a "patchwork concept"). The Common Conception treats the values of S to be persons. Creatures with mind are the ones who attend as well as think, perceive, imagine, and remember. At the same time, the science of attention has identified a number of selective processes as attention. Thus, Donald Broadbent's (1958) filter and Anne Treisman's (1998) binding spotlight are historically important mechanistic constructs postulated to operate on sensory information streams, selecting representations in early perceptual areas for further processing. These are also identified to be attention. Notice that the values that Broadbent and Treisman posit for S are not persons but parts of persons, say parts of the brain or relevant perceptual system.

The *primary* level in which attention operates is that of the subject. I say primary because it is precisely people's attending that matters to us. We care very much whether our interlocutor is paying attention to us as we talk, our supervisor thinks of us when considering the best employee, our students are engaged in the lecture versus social media, and our children can focus adequately when studying. These and other subject-level forms of attention are why we study attention. Attention exists in that subjects pay attention. At the same time, science has identified or postulated a variety of selective mechanisms that explain subject-level attention. Yet many scientists take a further step of identifying these mechanisms as also being attention. Is such proliferating of attention sound?

One might respond as some do: call any selective process you wish "attention". It's just a word, after all. Even then, we should wonder why this laissez-faire attitude is theoretically adequate for cognitive science. This attitude amounts to endorsing word games. In any event, we should stop treating the central issue as a mere dispute about words. This is just to fall afoul of the use-mention confusion noted in Section 1.2. The problem isn't words but scientific inference about psychological phenomena. In raising the question of whether attention is a mechanism, we are talking about whether psychological theory correctly cuts nature at its joints. It is a substantial scientific inference to conclude that a specific mechanism, specified at a particular level of analysis, *is* attention. Such claims require justification. They are not to be established just by a play on words.

If we are searching for unity, we should set proliferation aside by focusing on the Common Conception, what we all agree on. Agreement is the best basis for a unified perspective. Proliferation of attention across levels of analysis distorts the unity that comes from shared knowledge. Instead, drawing on the Common Conception, we can organize different levels of analysis to understand what attention within a task comes to.

1.6 Fleshing out the Explanation of Attention

We can construct a complete explanation of what attention is centered on the Common Conception and, specifically, concrete empirical sufficient conditions. These give the functional theory of attention for specific tasks. Neural and behavioral data are collected during the implementation of those experimental tasks where the subject selects a target to guide instructed response. Similarly, algorithms and models are constructed to explain both the behavioral and neural data collected within that paradigm. This brings us back to my hypothesis: The fruitfulness of work over the last half-century is done not in the absence of a theory of what attention is but in light of a shared conception expressed by the Common Conception and its empirical offspring. Much of the research on attention over the last 70 years is tied to what we all know because we share the same methodology. That is why that work is unified and why, as more details are filled in, we understand attention as well as we understand any psychological phenomena.

That said, the focus on task suggests a cautionary approach, for it is not guaranteed that for a set of disparate tasks, we shall discover that they involve the same algorithms or neural implementation. This is certainly true for sensory forms of attention since auditory and visual attention do not share the same neural basis, though it would be a discovery that they share some of the same algorithms (as is claimed regarding divisive normalization, (Carandini and Heeger 2012); see Chapter 4.8). If algorithms are shared, then these can be multiply realized in different neural processes. Alternatively, we might find that similar tasks across different modalities are implemented in different algorithms.

We have a framework for organizing the empirical work to be surveyed in later chapters. This framework identifies attention as a phenomenon *to be explained*. To conceive of attention as what is to be explained is not to deny that a subject's attention makes a difference in having effects. Of course, it does. Where a *subject's* attention is a cause, it is in explaining her behavior, such as her drawing a conclusion, encoding a memory, or moving. These effects of attention are of central concern since what people do is of central concern. Attention can have profound personal and social consequences through the behavior that it guides (Chapters 11–13). We shall come to those issues at the end of the book, but in the next chapters, our goal is to understand what attention is as part of filling out the proposed Marrian explanatory frame to explain attention.

1.7 Summary

We will pursue a multilevel explanation of what attention is that is tied to specific actions guided by the agent's selecting a target to respond to. This functional account provides the initial step toward a functional theory, our parallel to a Marrian computational theory. The functional theory provides only a sufficient but not necessary condition for attention, yet in doing so, it identifies an empirically motivated starting point for connecting empirical work in psychology and neuroscience to attention as we experience it, what James aptly described. For example, we can begin with some defined task E that requires visual attention. This gives us the functional theory for visual attention vis-à-vis E: visual attention is visual selection of some target X that serves performance of E, namely guiding the response needed to correctly do E. We then canvass proposals for the algorithms that implement selection of X for task E and the representations that are needed. Moving to the level of neural implementation, we can then ask how the brain implements such algorithms and representations. Of course, work at each level will mutually inform and constrain the others. Ideally, at the end, we will have a comprehensive and unified explanation of one form of attention, namely visual selection of X for E. This can be iterated for other experimental tasks deploying visual attention, leading to a story across levels of analysis for each task for visual attention. One can do the same for other sensory and nonsensory modalities with the hope that we will identify commonalities and interesting differences in mechanisms, both computational and biological, across tasks and modalities. To do so, we need an organizing framework. James's description offers us one, and if it provides a Common Conception, then it takes no effort in beginning with it since we already endorse it. To make progress, we need only explicitly acknowledge the knowledge that we share.

Suggested Readings

Marr's seminal discussion of his explanatory scheme is given in his (1982, Chapter 1). It is mandatory reading of anyone interested in a concrete theory of explanation in cognitive science. The skeptical literature, in particular Britt Anderson's (2011) initial shot across the bows (see also (Anderson 2023)), is important. More recently, Bernhard Hommel et al. (2019) have sounded skeptical concerns. In fact, the points made in this chapter are broadly consistent with many of the central claims in those papers, albeit without the skeptical conclusion (see also Rich Krauzlis's perspective (Krauzlis et al. 2014, 2023)). Ruth Rosenholtz (2024) has recently discussed a "crisis" in attention.

2

ATTENTION AND ACTION

2.1 Attention as Selection for What?

The Explanatory framework proposed in Chapter 1 connects two of our questions:

Metaphysical: What is attention?
Function: What role does attention play?

In analyzing attention's function, we uncover what it is. We rejected the simple identification of attention with selection of information for further processing as too broad (Section 1.2). Instead, attention is selection for a specific purpose, namely to guide action. This narrower function is implemented in experimental paradigms, attention as the subject's selection of a target for responding in performing a task. The functional account, captured in the Common Conception, is not limited to experimental paradigms but covers the things that people do, from the trivial to the sacred. In this chapter, we provide an account of action which includes mental actions as "things we do in our head". The account coheres with well-established

DOI: 10.4324/9781003223450-3

ideas in cognitive science and clarifies attention's function by locating its place in the psychological structure of an action.

Descriptions of subjects attending are bound together with psychological descriptions of their behavior, including their remembering, imagining, reasoning, and moving in various ways. These actions are movements of mind and of body. At the same time, an agent's movements described at the functional level of analysis are constituted or realized by neural processes which themselves are described in the language of the algorithmic and neural levels of analysis. So, when a subject is attending, such as when listening to an interlocutor, thinking about a problem to solve, or reaching for a glass, the subject's brain is concurrently selectively processing action-relevant information to support that behavior. This rough distinction between descriptions of the *subject's* movements and descriptions of the *brain's* activity corresponds to distinct levels of analysis in the multi-level explanatory structure we aim to construct.

Section 2.2 introduces the Selection Problem that agents face. To act, the Problem must be solved. Section 2.3 introduces the notion of a *bias* needed to solve the Selection Problem. The solution is the action the agent performs. Section 2.4 applies the Common Conception to argue that attention is a component of every action. Section 2.5 connects bias and the Selection Problem to a computational mirror image in the *biased competition theory of attention*. On the latter, attention results from the resolution of neural competition by the brain in the control of behavior. Section 2.6 gives an influential implementation of the ideas of biased competition for the Stroop Task in a connectionist network. Section 2.7 reviews selection for action theories in psychology. Finally, Section 2.8 applies the distinction between automaticity and control to attention and action. We return to the automaticity of attention in later chapters.

2.2 Action and the Selection Problem

In ordinary contexts, the term "action" refers to *things that we do*. Cognitive scientists, especially motor control theorists, use "action" in a narrow sense to refer to bodily movements, namely "motor actions" such as reaching for an object, pressing a button to report, or shifting the eye to enable a better look. Yet this narrow sense leaves out many actions, including mental actions such as remembering, thinking, reasoning, and imagining. In this book, "action" will be used broadly to cover things that we do with our body and in our heads. Actions are movements of body *and* mind. Still, the generic description "the things we do" is too broad since pulling one's hand back automatically from a burning hot item is something we are said to do, yet intuitively, such reflexes are not actions. If so, actions and reflexes are distinct subsets of the general category of behavior that includes all the things we do. The kinds of actions we will discuss can, in principle, be done intentionally. They are subject to various normative descriptions and can be judged rational or not, skillful or not, morally upright or not, done with good reason or not, controlled or not, done freely or not, and so on. These normative assessments do not apply to reflexes which are never done rationally, morally, for a good reason, and as expressions of one's will.

Actions have a basic psychological structure. They are composed of the organism's generating a response, an output, in respect of its mentally registering a target, an input, such as the organism's perceiving or remembering it. We can represent the behaviors of such creatures as constituted by the *coupling* of inputs to outputs, of target registration to response (Allport 1987) In behavior, the content of the psychological input explains, indeed informs, the generation of the response. This process can be depicted as in Figure 2.1 in terms of a sequence of causal nodes with the node at the input stage on the left identifying a psychological state attributed to the subject, such as her perceiving or remembering the target, S, and the node on the right identifying a response at the output stage, such as a movement of mind or body (Figure 2.1).

Actions exemplify the following structure: an agent acts by responding in a particular way, guided by how she mentally registers the target. So an agent can respond by moving a limb guided by her perceiving or remembering the location of a physical object or by entertaining a thought in response to an initial thought. The reader can fit their favorite action

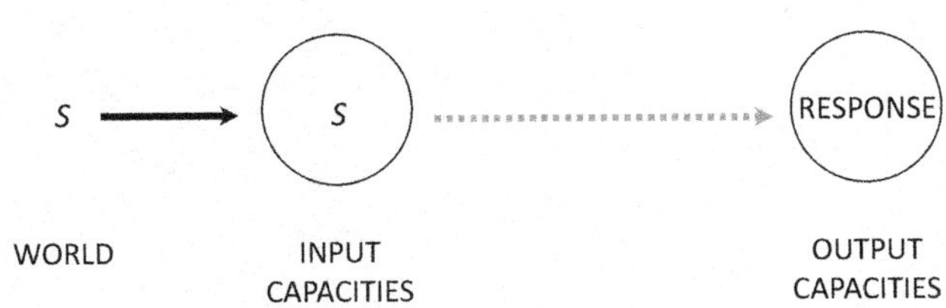

Figure 2.1 Input-to-output mapping given a stimulus S in the world that triggers an input capacity such as seeing S (left circle) that informs the production of a response (right circle).

to this structure by breaking it down to an input and output structure, including sequences of these couplings. That said, some reflexes exemplify an input-output structure such as a sudden, intense pain that triggers an involuntary scream. If so, the input-output structure depicted in Figure 2.1 will not distinguish reflexes from actions. We separate action from reflex by noting that action, not reflex, is a solution to a *Selection Problem*. For the current discussion, we invoke a weaker claim regarding the actions that cognitive scientists and philosophers care about. The actions done in the ebb and flow of life and those executed in the laboratory are solutions to Selection Problems.

What is a Selection Problem? Consider the problem faced by the donkey in the fable attributed to the philosopher, Jean Buridan. A donkey stands before two qualitatively identical bales of hay equidistant from it, one to the left, the other to the right. We can diagram the donkey's options, what it can do, in an *action space* that represents the two possible actions, things that can be done, namely eat the left bale (S1) and eat the right bale (S2) (Figure 2.2).

These action possibilities define a *Buridan Selection Problem*, a familiar structure to anyone ever paralyzed between two seemingly identical, desirable options. In the diagram, the left circles depict two visual inputs: the donkey's seeing the left bale and its seeing the right bale, two items in the world. We separate the visual experience into two psychological inputs since each can individually guide a response, namely distinct eating movements. The donkey's acting would be its "travelling" along one of the two possible paths (action options), so responding to one bale rather than the other by eating it. Where no path is taken, nothing is done. In the fable,

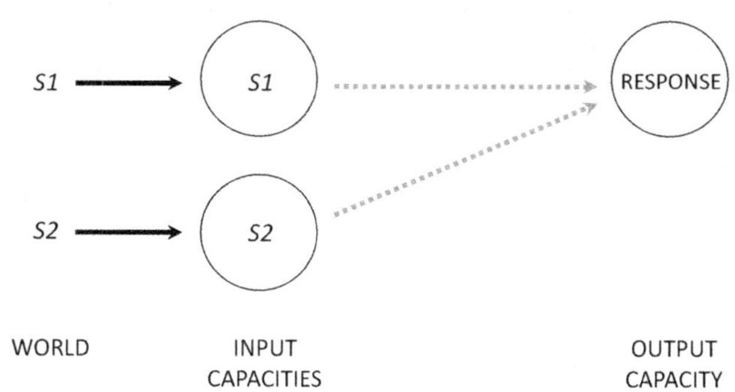

Figure 2.2 A 2 × 1 selection problem with two stimuli. *S1* and *S2* are targets in the world. They trigger the agent's mental registration of those targets (inputs, left circles), namely seeing them. Each visual experience can inform the response (output, right circle).

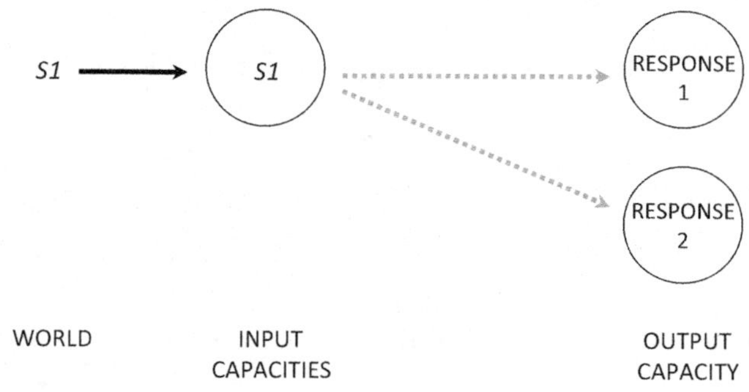

Figure 2.3 1 × 2 inverted Buridan Selection Problem.

the donkey, having no basis for favoring one bale over the other, remains paralyzed between the two targets. Taking no path, it starves.

The mirror image of the Buridan space yields another Selection Problem, a structure with one input and two responses (Figure 2.3). Perhaps the input is the perception of a predator (*S1*) and the responses are to flee to the left (*R1*) or to the right (*R2*). Again, with no difference between the two responses, the donkey has no basis for prioritizing one action over the other, does not flee, and again perishes. Philosophy is brutal.

These mirror images can be combined to yield the common *many-many version* of the Selection Problem (Allport 1987; Wu 2008, 2011a). That is, for every input there are typically many responses, and for every response there are typically many possible inputs (Figure 2.4)

For example, the donkey can eat either bale, commit the location of each to memory, fixate the eyes or a thought on each one individually, imagine eating one or the other, and so on. The Selection Problem leads to a

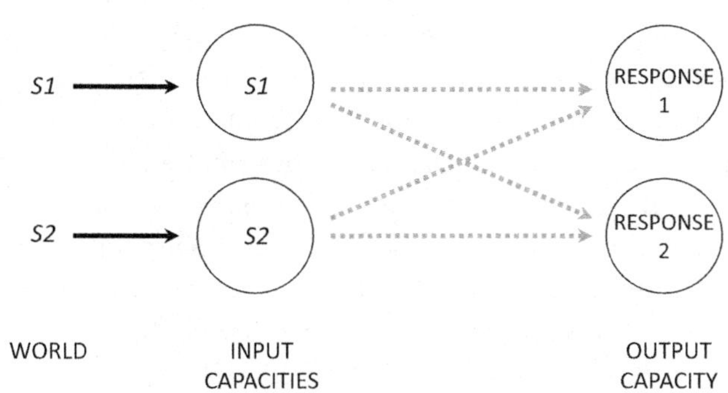

Figure 2.4 The many-many selection problem.

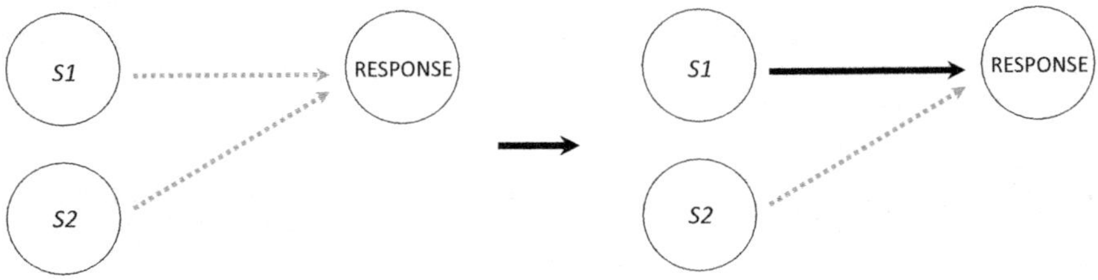

Figure 2.5 Selection as a transition from one action space to another, here from an action space indicating no action to one where an action is taken, namely responding to S1.

question some agents can pose to themselves: *What, among the many things that I can do, is to be done?* There is a parallel question that the brain faces as an organ that supports survival in complicated environments: what among the many things that can be processed is to be processed?

Note that "selection" is a technical notion in the theory. It does not imply *choice* such as when one selects clothing to wear. Rather, "selection" refers to solving the Selection Problem understood as the transition between the Problem as initially posed to its being solved when the agent acts (Figure 2.5).

Choice and decision as traditionally understood commonly play the role of *biases* that lead to selection that solves the Selection Problem. There are many biases. For example, an explicit decision to act in a specific way can bias an agent to perform the chosen action rather than another. If the donkey arbitrarily decides to eat one bale, then it acts decisively. Alternatively, a salient stimulus such as a bright flash can generate visual salience that biases, indeed drives, an automatic response. If the clouds part by divine intervention to illuminate one bale of hay, this captures the donkey's attention, and it moves toward the light. There are other biases beyond these "top-down" and "bottom-up" forms. (See Chapter 11.2 for a detailed list of biases.)

Given the Selection Problem, reflexes are behaviors that are *not* the result of solving a Selection Problem. Ideally, reflexive responses are guaranteed, necessarily triggered when an appropriate input is present. For example, if your hand touches a burning hot stove, you want there to be only one option: remove the hand! The input representing the heat would have only one mapping, namely to a withdrawal response. To guarantee avoidance of harm, there should be no other option. A *pure* reflex is a reflex that eliminates other possibilities to ensure that the requisite behavior necessarily happens (Wu 2018, 2023, Chapter 1). That is how reflexes ought to work but real-world reflexes are not pure so can fail. In contrast to reflexes, actions arise from a Selection Problem where there are no guarantees that anything will be done. Just ask the donkey—and bring him a bale when you do.

2.3 Bias and Solving the Selection Problem

Let us further examine biases by beginning with the agent's intending to act. When a subject intends to do something, she represents that action as to be done. In science, experimenters routinely manipulate intentions through task instructions. That is, an experimenter sets a subject's intention by instructing them on what to do, and a cooperative subject acquires an appropriate intention. If not, the experiment cannot be run. Intentions consequently function as a cognitive bias on the Selection Problem.

Alfred Yarbus provided a beautiful experimental demonstration of bias by intention where what the subject intends affects how she moves in an action space, here the space of possible eye movements across a constant visible scene. Yarbus presented his subjects with a painting of a dramatic domestic scene and asked them to perform various tasks. He then tracked their eye movements (overt visual attention) while they carried out his instructions and noted the following patterns in Figure 2.6 (see legend).

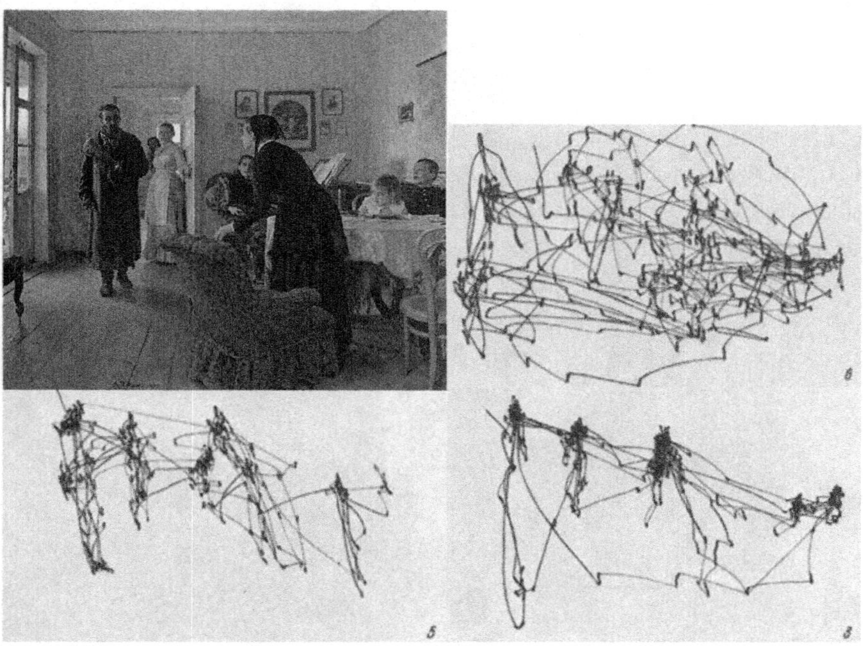

Figure 2.6 Yarbus's experiment, instructions as follows: (upper right) remember the position of objects and people in the room; (lower left) remember the clothes worn by the subjects; (lower right) estimate the ages of the subjects. Excerpts from Yarbus (1967) Figure 109, p. 174. Reprinted by permission from Springer Nature: Springer, *Eye Movements and Vision* by Alfred Yarbus (1967, 174, Figure 109).

Yarbus set his subjects' intentions through task instructions. Given a constant input, the painting, Yarbus measured visual attention through patterns of overt eye movement. By modulating intention through giving different instructions, Yarbus examined correlated effects on the eye. Distinct intentions biased visual search differently. Strikingly, the patterns of eye movements are intelligible given the subjects' more abstract intentions to carry out various tasks. For example, asked to remember the figures' clothes, the subject intentionally looks at each figure. Asked to estimate the painted subjects' ages, the eyes focus on the faces. While the subject did not intend to move the eyes in the specific way observed, the resulting pattern of movement in each panel makes sense given the operative intention to perform a specific task. Modulating intention through task instructions leads to different solutions to the Selection Problem in respect of the same target. We will discuss intentions in more detail in Chapter 6 when discussing the influence of working memory on attention, but for now, the basic point is that intention biases attention in action during experimental tasks.

2.4 Attention in Action

Given the Selection Problem, action is composed of an output response that is guided by a psychological input. It follows by the Common Conception that every action involves attention. After all, the condition states that attention arises when the mind takes possession of an object to deal with, that is to act in response to. Consider the Buridan Selection Problem. Let's say the donkey eats the bale to the left (*S1*). The solid line indicates that one of the two options is taken (solid versus dotted lines in Figure 2.7).

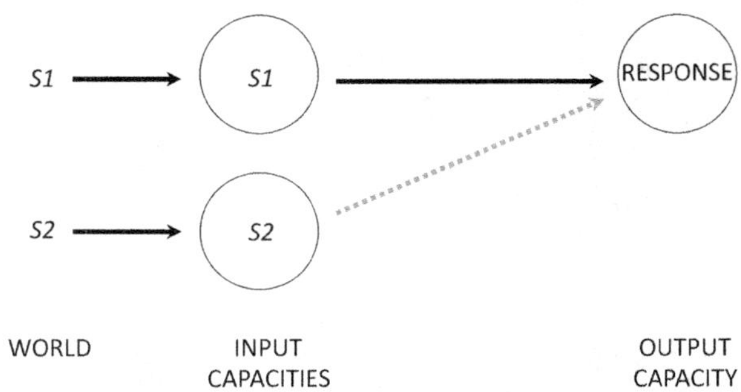

Figure 2.7 Solving the Buridan Selection Problem.

This satisfies the antecedent of the Common Conception: a subject's mentally selecting a target to deal with. The mind takes possession of an object to guide movement to it. In the diagram, one of the psychological inputs rather than the other guides behavior. The animal visually selects the left bale, withdrawing from the right, in order to deal with it. We depict the antecedent that specifies the mind's taking possession of a target with the arrow that connects the psychological input, a visual state, to the response, a movement. This represents the agent's visually taking possession of an object in order to inform a bodily response. Thus, the donkey visually attends to the left bale in moving toward it. Generally, in visually guided motor behavior, one visually attends to the target by fixating on it to guide movement. The point can be generalized to solutions to other Selection Problems. We thus derive attention's central guiding role in action. Attention is present at the core of action. For those who want to avoid controversy, we can again limit this thesis to just those actions of theoretical interest, and this is enough for the work we need to do in this book. Elsewhere, I have argued that attention is a necessary part of *all* actions (Wu 2018, 2023).

In our logical frame for attention (Chapter 1.4), S m-attends to T for R, we fill in m, T and R given a concrete action space for a specific subject s and how s solves the Selection Problem. The modality m of attention will be a function of the relevant biases and the psychological identity of the input that guides the response, the target T will be given by the content of that psychological input, and the response R will be the output required for the action performed. So, if the donkey decides to eat the right bale of hay, the bias is an intention and the input state is visual. So, the donkey s is intentionally-visually (m) attending to the bale of hay (T) to generate an eating response (R). We can similarly fill out S, m, T, and R for every action we care to analyze (the results for m will sometimes be grammatically awkward). The paradigm cases are the familiar ones where the mode, m, is identified with (a) a simple bias like intention or physical salience and (b) the psychological kind of the input state.

Attention holds for any solution to the Selection Problem in things we ordinarily do in the lab or world. Whenever such actions happen, there will be a prioritization of an input so that the input guides behavior. The point also applies to the *mirror image* Buridan case noted earlier where there is only one input, seeing the predator, and two outputs. The donkey in fleeing to the left takes possession of the danger to deal with it. If it does not, then again, death. In this case, we do not have withdrawing from potential input distractors, at least visible ones, but we have withdrawal from available outputs. In both Buridan Selection Problems, the fundamental expression of attention is when a psychological state selectively informs a response. In this way, attention is expressed in action.

Notably, our starting point is an *economical* account of attention in that if the Selection Problem identifies the basic components needed for action, it thereby identifies the components needed for attention. There isn't an additional attentional "spotlight" anywhere in the structure defining the Selection Problem. Put another way, there are no additional nodes needed in our causal structure that are identified as attention. What suffices is the input (here, vision), the output (here, motor response), and a bias, such as the intention to eat a specific bale or to run to the left. Attention arises so long as action is engaged when an input guides an output response (see biased competition, Chapter. 2.6).

Consider building an agent. Assume that we can build a system that can literally see and can move. This agentive system has a mind, and its movements are guided by what it sees, so the visual inputs inform the production of appropriate output movements. An engineer wants to build a sentient android rover to act on an alien planet, namely to collect rocks of certain kinds and to avoid certain threats. So, the engineer builds in a visual capacity that allows the rover to see rocks and threats. Movement capabilities are also added that allow the rover to translocate to and from relevant targets. The engineer avoids a Buridan agent by building in a control system encoding two goals: find rocks and avoid threats. This control system encodes (remembers) the system's current task, what the rover is to do. Given the information encoded, the control system functions as an intention to look for rocks and avoid threats (see working memory, Chapter 6).

When the robot finds a rock and moves toward it, it is acting in a way guided by visual attention to the rock, visual selection that guides movement to the target. When it avoids threats, visual attention is similarly deployed, namely visual selection to guide fleeing away from the danger. The engineer is entitled to attribute attention because her minded system satisfies the antecedent of the Common Conception. Notably, attention is present in this system without having to build a separate attention module distinct from the visual, movement, and control modules already in place. This is not to say that the engineer could try to build an "attention module", but for this system, it would be functionally redundant, an unnecessary extra node. Instead, securing attention in the agentive system does not require further engineering beyond building basic agency. We will make the same move in disputing the need to postulate an attentional spotlight in the brain (Chapter 4.4). This perspective is consistent with those who deny that attention is a distinctive mechanism ((Anderson 2011), (Krauzlis et al. 2014), see also the first objection in (Hommel et al. 2019)). What we get is an *economical* theory of attention where attention is not some further thing beyond the basic "components" of agency in input, output and bias.

Attention on the economical view is not an epiphenomenon. It is a causal factor in the following sense: the visual state that guides the response when the agent acts just is, or constitutes, the agent's visual attention to the target. That is, the agent's seeing, when it contributes to behavior, is the agent's visually attending, visually taking possession of the target to deal with. So attention causally influences by guiding response. The rover's response is causally guided by visual attention in being informed by the prioritized visual input. The economical perspective on attention might strike some as puzzling given how strongly we are in the grip of the spotlight metaphor. Yet getting attention "for free" is also a tenet in a core idea from neuroscience: *biased competition*. Biased competition is the neural-computational mirror of the Selection Problem.

2.5 Biased Competition

Robert Desimone and John Duncan (1995) presented a *biased competition* theory of attention. To contextualize this theory, note that *behavioral* competition is embodied in the Selection Problem between behavioral paths that vie for expression. Solving the Problem is resolving behavioral competition. In animals, resolution of behavioral competition is realized in the brain which faces a correlated *neural* competition in the processing of inputs and outputs.

Processing resources are limited in the brain of an agent confronting an informationally rich world. For example, visual stimuli compete for processing in an energy-limited brain. Unless neural competition over multiple stimuli is resolved, behavior will be undermined. The resolution of competition is not arbitrary but typically supports the agent's aims. In biased competition, *bias* is the factor that resolves neural competition. A potent bias is the agent's intention that represents the action to be done. Hommel et al. (2019) observed that processing

> selectivity emerged through evolution as a design feature to enable efficient goal-directed action. Such selectivity became necessary as the action repertoire of the given line of organisms that led to humans increased. This means that selectivity is an emerging property arising from a myriad underlying processes.
>
> (2298)

Neural competition parallels, indeed realizes, the action competition instantiated in the Selection Problem. The resolution of the subject-level phenomenon of the Selection Problem which yields action is constituted or realized by the resolution of the problem of neural competition. If the subject has to deal with multiple targets or responses, so does the subject's brain.

The biased competition model is presented as a neurocomputational model of attention. It seems to be an economical model of the sort noted in the previous section. Desimone and Duncan commented that

> the approach we take differs from the standard view of attention, in which attention functions as a mental spotlight enhancing the processing (and perhaps binding together the features) of the illuminated item. Instead. the model we develop is that attention is an emergent property of many neural mechanisms working to resolve competition for visual processing and control of behavior.
>
> (194)

Once competition is resolved via an appropriate bias, the resulting selectivity in the visual system yields attention (attention can "emerge"). The emphasis on the need to "resolve competition for visual processing and control of behavior" captures the action-oriented approach to attention in the Common Conception. Attention is explained by the appropriate selectivity demanded by agency to resolve competition. In doing so, we deal effectively with things.

Bernhard Hommel et al. aver that "No one knows what attention is", but their perspective is consonant with the one argued for here (Hommel et al. 2019). They advocate an approach that "synthesizes elements that actually correspond to real biological processes at both neural and functional levels" (2294). In particular, they consider the evolution of biological systems wherein attention is found through the need to "*select* between actions, such that one completely suppresses the other. This kind of selection could be accomplished through lateral inhibition that produces 'winner-take-all' dynamics" (2295). This characterizes the Selection Problem in competition terms. Finally, Hommel et al. invoke James's observation that attention "implies a withdrawal from some things in order to deal effectively with others." So, their final position is not skeptical. We know what attention is.

2.6 A Simple Implementation: The Stroop Effect

To emphasize that the economical approach is a familiar one in cognitive science, I note a well-known parallel distributed processing (PDP) model of the Stroop effect by Jonathan Cohen and colleagues (Cohen et al. 1990). My emphasis in citing this model is not to endorse the explanation of the effect but to demonstrate an instantiation of the economical view of attention, interpreting this PDP model as an implementation of biased competition. This also raises a central dichotomy of *automaticity versus control*.

In the Stroop effect, subjects are asked to name the color that a word is printed in, such as the word "dog" printed in red. Here, the correct response is to say "red". Notably, it is harder to report the color a word is printed in when the word's meaning is incongruent versus congruent with the printed color. For example, reporting the printed color of the word "red" is harder when it is printed in green relative to when it is printed in red. Reaction time is slower in the former case relative to the latter. An intuitive explanation is that subjects automatically start responding to the word and that this prepotent response is hard to suppress. In the incongruent case, the intention to execute the instructed task must provide a bias to overcome the natural tendency to automatically read the word. That is, *control* must be exerted to overcome a powerful *automaticity*.

Cohen et al. built a PDP network to model observed behavior in the Stroop Task. The details of the network need not concern us, for we are after the basic structure. The network consists of processing nodes that take as input either the printed word or the printed color, so a node for the colors, red and green, and for the words, "red" and "green". The outputs are two nodes corresponding to an utterance of "red" and an utterance of "green". A hidden layer of processing nodes is included, and each connection is given a weight. Since the utterance of "red" is strongly tied to the input node for the word "red", these connections have a higher weight which models the prepotent automaticity of word reading. In the incongruent condition, we end up with *behavioral competition* between the prepotent processing path for word reading and the task-relevant path for naming the color of the word. Finally, the model includes task nodes that encode the current task and that provide a bias that changes the weights of the relevant paths. The task nodes represent what the agent intends to do.

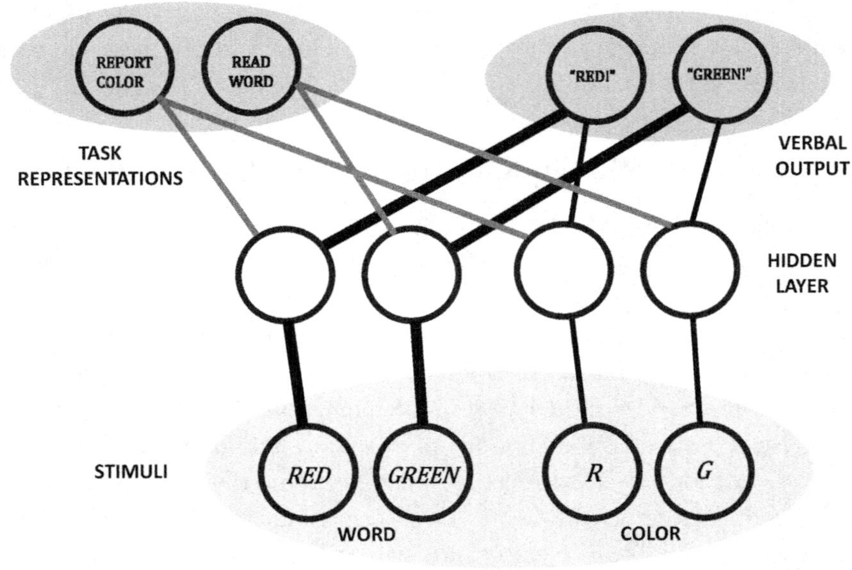

Figure 2.8 The connectionist architecture for the Stroop Task.

This architecture instantiates a Selection Problem and identifies four possible actions (the input-output mappings that would be mistakes are not indicated). The key point is that there is no node in the model for attention. Cohen et al. characterize attention in an economical way:

> given the task of naming the color [that a word is printed in], a person can exercise control by responding "red" to such a stimulus. In the model, this is achieved by activating the color-naming unit in the task layer of the network. This unit sends additional biasing activity to the intermediate units in the color pathway, so that they are more responsive to their inputs. In this way, the model can selectively "attend" to the color dimension and respond accordingly. It is worth emphasizing that the increase in responsivity of the intermediate units is achieved simply by the additional top–down input provided by the task unit... it does not require any special or qualitatively distinct apparatus. *The key observation is that attention, and corresponding control of behavior, emerges from the activation of a representation of the task to be performed and its influence on units that implement the set of possible mappings from stimuli to responses.*
>
> (p. 1254; my emphasis, cf. Desimone and Duncan 1995, p. 194, quoted earlier)

The economical view is not alien to cognitive science. Attention is implemented in the resolution of competition via solutions to Selection Problems. Accordingly, *attention is what we are trying to explain*. It is not the explainer. This is obscured by the pervasive view that attention is a special type of internal mechanism, an idea sharply expressed in the metaphor of a spotlight. This view is neither obligatory nor required (we reject it in Chapter 4.4).

2.7 Selection for Action: Original Psychological Accounts

The Common Conception can be characterized as a weaker version of the theory of attention as *selection for action* since it is implied by, but does not imply, that theory. The theory identifies attention with selection for action, while the Common Conception endorses only the sufficient condition. The label *selection for action* is due to seminal papers by Odmar Neuman and Alan Allport. Contemporary theories of attention since the 1950s have emphasized processing *capacity limits* as necessitating attention, leading to a conception of attention as selection that is required to avoid information overload. Neuman and Allport dissented from this assumption. They did not deny the presence of capacity limits. Neumann (1987) distinguished two notions of capacity limitation. First, capacity limitations are just the observed limits to performance during standard attentional tasks (see list of such tasks in Chapter 1.4). This notion of limitation is uncontroversial and precisely what the theory of attention must explain. Second, Capacity limitation, which Neumann intentionally capitalized, refers to the theoretical construct invoked to explain empirically observed capacity limitations in performance. Indeed, some identify attention with limited resources (Kahneman 1973). Neumann emphasized that "independent of all Capacity considerations, selection is evidently needed for the control of action. Organisms must constantly select what to do and how to do it" (374). Thus, the fundamental challenge that forces attention on the scene is

> how to avoid the behavioral chaos that would result from an attempt to simultaneously perform all possible actions for which sufficient causes exist, i.e., that are in agreement with current motives, for which the required skills are available and that conform to the actual stimulus situation.
>
> (374)

In other words, the Selection Problem rather than Capacity Limitations is the fundamental constraint necessitating attention. Put another way, even if the creature had no information processing capacity limitations, it must still solve the Selection Problem. It is the limit of agency that is fundamental.

For Neumann, two basic problems are raised by motor actions, understood as flexible, non-reflex motor behaviors: *effector recruitment* and *parameter specification*. Effector recruitment is connected to a concrete limitation, for an agent has only a limited number of effectors (body parts) to deploy. Moreover, deploying effectors involves basic skills that are applicable to different circumstances. To implement skills in concrete circumstances, an agent has to set specific parameters that allow their appropriate expression. In the case of perception-guided action, this involves drawing on relevant information from the environment to inform an appropriate response. Thus, a subject knows how to reach for objects, but to implement a reach for a specific object, the context will determine what is the appropriate reach, grip, trajectory, and force based on information about the object and the environment given the effector selected. To deploy an effector in specific circumstances, the precise parameters of the movement must be specified. For example, information from vision about object location, shape, texture, weight, and so on will guide (set parameters for) a reach-and-grasp movement with one's right hand. This guidance process can be ongoing throughout the movement.

Contemporaneously, Alan Allport (1987) presented a theory of attention as selection for action. He considered a basic case:

> Many fruits are within reach, and clearly visible, yet for each individual reach of the hand, for each act of plucking, information about just one of them must govern the particular pattern and direction of movements. The disposition of the *other* apples, already encoded by the brain, must be in some way temporarily decoupled from the direct control of reaching, though it may of course still influence the action, for example as representing an obstacle to be reached around, not to be dislodged, and so on. The same necessity of selecting, in respect of a given class of action performed by a given effector system, just *one* among a number of physically available objects to act upon appears to be essentially universal...Although the senses are capable of registering many different objects together, effector systems are typically limited to carrying out just one action of a given kind at a time. Hence the biological necessity, and the theoretical importance, of selection-for-action.
>
> (396–7)

Allport noted that

> the need for such a mechanism (of selective coupling and decoupling of perceptual and motor processes) arises directly from the many-many possible mappings between domains of sensory input and of motor output within the very highly parallel, distributed organization of the nervous system.
>
> (397)

This central but neglected insight provides the basis for both a philosophical theory of the nature of action (as developed by Wu (2011, 2023)) and an account of the nature of attention as selection for action.

Readers should separate the Common Conception from the theory of selection for action as endorsed by Allport, Neumann, and myself. The Common Conception commits itself only to the weaker claim that in standard experimental paradigms and most everyday actions, the form of attention at issue is selection for action. It allows for other conceptions of attention.

2.8 Automaticity and Control

We have focused on top-down attention biased by intention, yet much attention is not connected to an intentional task. For example, attention can be captured by salient stimuli such as a sudden loud noise or bright flash of light. Attention can be automatically pulled to the stimulus at the expense of a concurrent intentional action leading to distraction from the task.

We need a precise account of the distinction between automaticity and control. As Jonathan Cohen (2017) notes, this distinction "is one of the most fundamental and long-standing principles of cognitive psychology" (3). In an early paper that established spatial cueing paradigms as typically implemented in psychological experiments, Michael Posner et al. (1978) noted:

> One of the fundamental differences between processing modes is the distinction between exogenous, *automatic*, passive processes and centrally *controlled*, active, attended processes. While these processing modes usually appear as rivals in psychological theories, the persistence of the dichotomy undoubtedly arises in the fact that humans characteristically show both forms of processing. *Without "habits," which allow automatic processing, life would place intolerable burdens on the highest integrative levels; but without*

> *endogenous plans, which change the significance of input, the human system would hardly be as flexible as both casual observation and experimentation reveal.*
>
> (138, my emphasis)

Note the connection to behavior and the sharp division between types of processes. Conceptualizations of this dichotomy owe much to Walter Schneider and Richard Schiffrin's (1977) initial analysis. On automatic processes, they wrote:

> an automatic process can be defined...as the activation of a sequence of nodes with the following properties: (a) The sequence of nodes (nearly) always becomes active in response to a particular input configuration, where the inputs may be externally or internally generated and include the general situational context. (b) The sequence is activated automatically without the necessity of active control or attention by the subject.
>
> (2)

Automaticity is connected to the absence of control (or attention) by the subject. What then is control? "A *controlled process* is a temporary sequence of nodes activated under control of, and through attention by, the subject" (ibid.). Ignoring definitional circularity (the terms analyzed appear in the analysis), Shiffrin and Schneider characterized automaticity in terms of the absence of control and control in terms of attention.

To understand control, we must keep track of its logic: X controls Y. We must be strict about the value of the variables. Notice that Shiffrin and Schneider are explicit that both control and attention are attributed to the (experimental) subject. This renders both constructs as subject-level phenomena. Other notions of control not attributed to subjects are distinct notions of control. For example, in motor control theory, *forward models* and *comparators* function in explaining how the motor system controls bodily movements (Wolpert and Ghahramani 2000). While the motor system is part of the agent's brain, the agent herself is not computing forward models and comparing predictions and sensory data. The forward model/comparator structure underwrites a different notion of control at the level of computations by the subject's brain, computations in which the subject takes no part even if these computations partly constitute or realize the agent's performing a bodily action. Further, the subject-level notion of control in

Shiffrin and Schneider's account is conceptually tied to the concept of automaticity, a concept that does not have an explicit place in the motor control theory at issue. We must be explicit that the value of "X" in *agentive* control is tied to a subject. Further, we follow the tradition and link control to the absence of automaticity and vice versa.

The automaticity and control dichotomy, like the concept of attention, has had a rough history in cognitive science. When a definition of control (or automaticity) was proffered by appeal to some putative individuating feature F, such as slow processing, involvement of consciousness, voluntariness, and so on, an experiment would be done that showed that F could be found in automatic (or control) processes. After several rounds of explication and experimental refutation, theorists gave up on an analysis and resorted to characterizing the dichotomy in terms of sets of correlated features. For example, in an encyclopedia article on automaticity, Thomas Palmeri (2006) offers 13 pairs of features which differentiate automaticity from control. If we treat each pair as defining a dimension, then a process could be mapped in a high-dimensional space whereupon automaticity and control will be graded and multidimensional with no obvious way to separate the space into two kinds of processes. Still, Palmeri's characterization makes a common assumption. There are two *kinds* of processes: automatic and controlled.

Automaticity and control, as subject-level phenomena, characterize agency. The case of attentional capture shows that some of the things that we do such as orienting, we do automatically. We move our eyes to a flashing stimulus or turn our head toward a loud bang. If a distracting stimulus pulls our attention to it, we can exert control to counter (see Cohen et al.'s model of the Stroop effect, Section 2.6). Automatically acting in one way, we exert control by turning back to our task. This link to human agency suggests that we might explicate the notions in light of intentional agency.

An initial analysis ties control to acting with an intention. Intentions are an agent's representing an action to be brought about. These plans and their corresponding mental states can be expressed by reports such as *I intend to do* X or *I will do* X. Elizabeth Anscombe (1957) noted that while an action can be described in many ways, only certain descriptions capture how agents conceive of it. That is, an action is revealed as intentional only under certain descriptions. Thus, while Gavrilo Princip intended to assassinate Archduke Ferdinand, he did not intend to precipitate the First World War even if that was, in effect, what he did.

Begin with the *Simple Connection*: control implies the absence of automaticity and vice versa. This connection remains central in cognitive science in the separation of controlled processing from automatic processing. Yet if one looks at one kind of controlled process, namely intentional action, one finds substantial automaticity. You intentionally throw a ball, but many aspects of your throwing, such as its kinematics, your joint rotations, and the sequence of arm movements, are automatic. You don't intend to throw with that speed, rotation, or sequence of movements. They are not elements represented in your plan. However, your intentional throwing wouldn't be the action it is without your doing those things automatically, rotating your joints, moving with that specific speed, and so on. This raises an apparent inconsistency. Despite the Simple Connection's contrast between control and automaticity, intentional actions involve both. They provide a counterexample to the standard interpretation of the Simple Connection as finding two kinds of processes: automatic and controlled.

The putative paradox can be presented as an *inconsistent triad* of three putative truths. First, intentional action is a paradigm form of subject-level, agentive control, namely control by the subject when she acts:

1. An agent's intentional action expresses her control of what she is doing.

Yet every intentional action involves automaticity, for we do not, indeed cannot, control every aspect of that action, such as planning every parameter.

2. An agent's intentional action expresses substantial automaticity.

As noted, the Simple Connection remains central to characterizations of automaticity and control as *kinds* of processing. This is a way of understanding the Simple Connection:

3. Automaticity implies the absence of control and vice versa.

The three claims, under a natural interpretation, are inconsistent: If intentional action exemplifies control, then it entails the absence of automaticity, yet intentional action is pervasively automatic. Can we render these claims consistent?

I think (1) and (2) are truths of human action, so one might reject the Simple Connection. Yet the connection anchors empirical reflection on automaticity and given its perspicuity, it would be better to retain it. The resolution is to drop the idea that there is an interesting distinction between automatic and controlled types of processes. After all, intentional action is a subject-level process which exemplifies both automaticity and control. What we need to show is how a subject-level process can be both automatic and controlled.

A resolution is possible if one relativizes automaticity and control to properties of the process, say the specific parameters of a bodily action such as its kinematic properties but also higher-level properties, including relational properties such as what it causes. That is, control of a process is relative to specific features of that process and likewise for automaticity. Accordingly, automaticity, relative to a feature at a time, entails the absence of control of that feature at that time (and vice versa), yet a process can be both automatic and controlled in respect to different properties across time. That means that the analysis shows how automaticity and control in action are graded relative to the set of relevant features but also contrastive relative to a given feature at a time. I shall not give a detailed version of the analyses of control and automaticity (see Wu 2013a, 2023, Chapter 1). But the following biconditionals capture the essential idea and will suffice. We focus on *attention* as controlled or automatic.

(C) S's attending to X is controlled relative to its feature F if and only if S's attending to X having F results from S's intending it to have F.

Following Shiffrin and Schneider in defining *automatic* negatively as the absence of control, one derives:

(A) S's attending to X is automatic relative to its feature F if and only if S's attending to X having F is not due to control as per (C).

Consider visual conjunction search tasks (Chapter 5), where the target looked for is a red E. If the subject intentionally visually selects a red E, the subject's attention exemplifying the feature of *selecting a red E* (i.e., its being directed at that particular target) is controlled because that is what the subject intends to do. Similarly, if the subject has her attention captured by a suddenly appearing stimulus, then the feature of *selecting that stimulus* is automatic because the subject did not intend to select that stimulus. In both cases, the relevant feature F is the subject's selection having the target that it has.

The appeal to intention as the basis for explaining subject-level control is driven by the first truth where control is treated as a feature of the agent and not as a neural mechanism such as motor control computations in forward modelling. Intentional action (acting with an intention) is a paradigmatic form of control. On this point, there should not be controversy as it is part of what we take intentional actions to be. Cognitive scientists have conceptualized tasks and goals as the basis of control, so intention provides an intersection between philosophical concerns about agency and empirical concerns about understanding the role of task representations. The main question concerns what else one might include as the basis of control, such as various forms of knowledge. These are interesting issues that need further discussion.

With control fixed in this way, automaticity is revealed as having remarkably diverse sources, for they are the members of the complement of the set of sources of control. This means that emotions, learning, values, priming, desires, stimulus properties, and some memories—basically everything that isn't intention (and perhaps some types of knowledge)—are sources of automaticity. We shall return to automaticity multiple times in what follows since it will be important in explaining many interesting forms of behavior. The upshot of this section is that we can talk concretely about attention as controlled via intention and automatic attention in a way that fits the framework tied to biases in the Selection Problem and biased competition.

2.9 Conclusion

Attention informs action. When the Selection Problem is solved, the Common Conception of attention locates attention in that solution. Every action involves attention. If that is too strong, restrict the point to those actions with which we are theoretically concerned. These involve attention. Solving the Selection Problem requires a bias, so biases on action are also biases on attention. Understanding one phenomenon goes with understanding the other. As we deploy our explanatory structure, we aim to locate isomorphisms across levels, here biased neural competition in the brain as the reflection of biased behavioral competition in the agent's Selection Problem.

Finally, we introduced the concepts of automaticity and control by appealing to a specific bias, intention. Our account of automaticity and control resolves a paradox arising from merging truths about agency with a core idea in psychological theory, the Simple Connection. The intention as a representation of the task to be performed identifies what features of action are under the agent's control, the other features of the action being automatic.

This core idea will be crucial to understanding the relation between skill and attention and the norms of attention (Chapters 11 and 12).

Suggested Readings

A full discussion of the Selection Problem is given in Wu (2023). The original texts by Alan Allport and Odmar Neumann repay careful reading (Allport 1987; Neumann 1987). Desimone and Duncan's original account of biased competition is an important anchor to much later empirical work on attention (Desimone and Duncan 1995). A detailed critique of automaticity is given by Agnes Moors (Moors 2016). For philosophical discussions, see Wu (2013) and Fridland (2017). Christopher Peacocke (1998) has an important discussion of acting attentively not discussed in this chapter.

3

CONCEPTS OF ATTENTION IN COGNITIVE SCIENCE

3.1 Introduction

In this chapter, we discuss some important conceptualizations relevant to attention. We will separate those that apply to the algorithmic or neural implementation of attention from those that apply to attention as a subject-level phenomenon. Keeping track of distinct levels of analysis is crucial to constructing a properly integrated explanation of what attention is.

In Section 3.2, we distinguish between (a) biases on attention, (b) the mode of attention, and (c) the target of attention. Section 3.3 touches on the early versus late selection debate that was the first major controversy in contemporary attention research. We then shift to examining the idea of attention as a limited resource in Section 3.4 and its connection to *load* and task demands in Section 3.5. Section 3.6 considers two further common dichotomies: top-down versus bottom-up attention and pre-attentive versus attentive processing. Finally, Section 3.7 critically examines the idea of attention as selection for *perception*.

DOI: 10.4324/9781003223450-4

3.2 Attention: Bias, Mode, and Target

Let us focus on bias, mode, and target with respect to attention. The *target* of attention, T, and the *mode* of attention, m, are specified through the logical frame, S m-attends to T *for* R, which individuates different types of attention. So, let T be a letter that we are asked to detect in an experiment, say an "*A*". Detection requires that we select "*A*" to inform the report. Selection, however, can be subject to different *biases*. In Chapter 1.2, we explained bias in terms of its functional role: a bias shapes how Selection Problems are solved. Biases can contribute to the *mode*, m, of attention such as an intention as a bias that institutes *top-down* attention, one's attending as intended.

To see why keeping track of these distinctions is important, consider *temporal* attention. Since spatial attention targets space (T = *space*) and feature attention targets features (T = *feature*), it is natural to construe temporal attention as targeting time (T = *time*). So, what is it to pay attention to time? This is complicated. Consider waiting for a friend who is arriving on the 3:15 p.m. train. In what ways can we attend to time? Not through visual attention. Time is not visible, though proxies for time, such as the hands on a clock, are. So, there isn't visual temporal attention where the target is time (T = *time*) even if there is visual *object* attention to a timepiece (T = *clock*). So, time is not a target of the *visual* mode of attention.

Still, I am aware of time in a *cognitive* mode. I have to remember when my friend is arriving so as to be ready to locate her. In remembering that my friend arrives at 3:15 p.m., I am *cognitively* attending to time in that I represent the time conceptually in my plan: meet my friend at 3:15 p.m. So, even if visual attention is not (perhaps cannot be) directed at time as such, cognitive attention can be. A point in time (3:15 p.m.) can be cognitively attended to by being represented in intention. In this example, visual attention and cognitive attention have distinct targets, a clock and a point in time, respectively (Figure 3.1).

Cognitive attention to time, my remembering when my friend will arrive, can serve as a *bias* on visual selection. Given that my intended action is locked to a specific time, my intention biases visual attention to be directed at the clock in order to check what time it is, and as I wait, the intention prioritizes the clock so that I automatically check it periodically. Here, cognitive attention in memory directs visual attention by biasing visual selection. Put another way, visually, I face a Selection Problem in that there are many things I can look at to respond to, but given memory of my time-locked plan, the Selection Problem is solved in my visually selecting

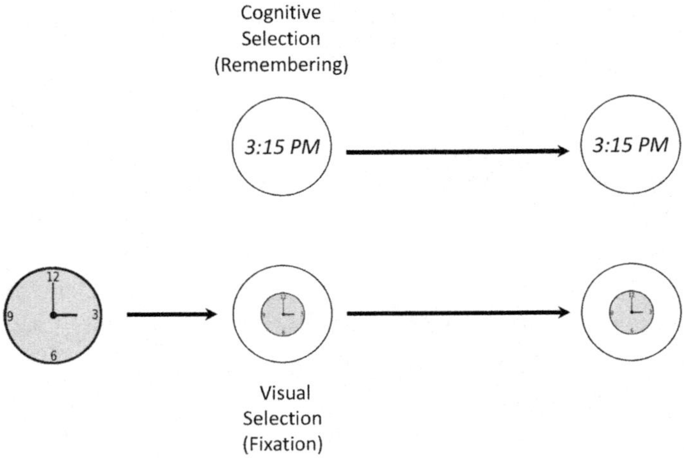

Figure 3.1 Cognitive Attention to a remembered time (top) and visual attention to a clock representing time (3 p.m., bottom). In this case, my eyes are fixed on the clock and my memory holds the arrival time in mind over time (3:15 p.m.). The depicted parallel selections of visual and mnemonic inputs are to maintain representations over time, such as keeping the clock in view and holding the time in memory. We select those psychological inputs to maintain them (response).

the clock to gain knowledge of what time it currently is. This solution to the Selection Problem is biased by my intention, my remembering that my friend arrives at 3:15 p.m. Accordingly, I visually focus on the clock rather than, say, my cup of coffee. We have a visual Selection Problem with clock and coffee as potential targets of visual attention (Figure 3.2).

With these distinctions established, note that the discussion of temporal attention in the empirical literature concerns the role of a *cognitive* representation of time, specifically *temporal expectations*. In that literature, expectations can be treated as beliefs that represent temporal structure in the environment, say representations of the probability that events will occur at specific times. Further, temporal cues that provide information regarding when something is likely to occur can lead the subject to update her temporal expectations. These expectations can affect (bias) attentional selection. We then need to keep separate two forms of attention distinguished by mode and target:

S visually attends to a clock.
S cognitively attends to a time.

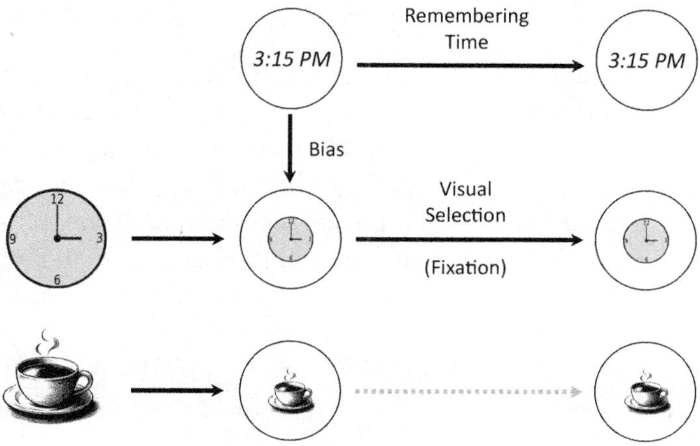

Figure 3.2 Cognitive Attention to a remembered time and visual attention to a clock representing time. In this case, I keep my eyes fixed on the clock because my memory maintains the arrival time as I wait, biasing where I look. As a result, I withdraw my eyes from the coffee (dotted lines from the input visual experience of the coffee). Coffee image generated by DALL-E.

Consider an experiment by Jennifer Coull and Kia Nobre (1998) that manipulated temporal expectations in a target detection paradigm. They provided subjects with a symbolic cue that indicated in which of two time points a subsequent target was likely to appear, namely either at a short time point t_1 (300 ms after the cue) or at a long time point t_2 (1500 ms after the cue). The target appeared for 50 ms at one of these time points, and subjects had to indicate target presence by pressing a key. Coull and Nobre observed reaction time benefits when the cue was *valid*; that is, when it correctly indicated the time interval for target appearance, versus when *invalid*, so when the target appeared in the time interval that was not cued (see op. cit. Table 2, p. 7429). In this task, the target of visual attention is an object (symbol): "X" or a "+". Time, however, is not the target of visual attention. Rather, time is represented in the temporal expectation, a cognitive representation updated given new information from the cue. This expectation functions as a bias on visual object attention for detection. So, temporal attention should be read not as identifying the target of visual attention but rather as specifying the content of the cognitive bias (see (Nobre and van Ede 2018) Box 1). If there is attention *to time*, it is *cognitive* temporal attention. In separating mode from target, the logical frame helps us draw important distinctions.

3.3 Early versus Late Selection

One of the first major debates regarding attention in contemporary cognitive science was the early versus late selection debate, beginning in the 1950s. This disagreement presupposed a division of early versus late stages in perceptual processing. In vision, early stages of processing concern basic visual features such as edges, orientation, color, and motion whereas later stages concern visual objects such as faces. In audition, early stages deal with basic audible features such as pitch or timbre whereas later stages process categorical features of sound, such as the identity of a voice or the syntactical properties or semantics of spoken language. A subject's ordinary awareness of items in the world depends on full perceptual processing of those items. That is, perception of an object as F, say as a face, as red, as semantically meaningful, and so on, requires that perceptual processing reach the F-stage. For example, in a neurologically intact individual, if visual processing of a face is in some way blocked before reaching a relevant face-stage, then the subject will be effectively prosopagnosic, face blind, until the block is removed. We can think of the relevant selection for such processing as *selection for perception* (Chapter 3.7). To perceive a target of type T, the stimulus must be processed up to an appropriate level. The central question then was this: at what stage in processing does attention engage?

This debate has its roots in Donald Broadbent's seminal book, *Perception and Communication* (1958). Broadbent drew on advances in the theory of information (e.g., Shannon (1949)) to propose a "fresh language" (35) and a "new set of descriptive terms" (36) for psychology. Information theory clarified the idea of specific capacity limits such as the limits on information channels (bandwidth) with mathematical precision. Such capacity limits motivate an account of the necessity of attention, conceived of as involved in information selection. Consider that information can flow at 10^7 to 10^8 bits per second along the optic nerve transmitting information from the eye (Itti and Koch 2001a). How can processing keep up with such vast input?

Assume that there is a limit to the amount of information that can be processed by any neural system. For example, given separate processing channels for each stimulus, one manifestation of limited processing capacity is that not all channels can be processed simultaneously. Since the organism should process important stimuli, the relevant information streams must be prioritized over others. This suggests a mechanism that ensures appropriate selection for further processing. If there is a bottleneck in perception at a given stage in processing given capacity limitations, then for any perceptual stage processing F that is after the bottleneck, for the subject to perceive the stimulus as F, the channel carrying information regarding F must be selected to pass through the bottleneck. Attention, on Broadbent's view, is the *filter* that selects information at the bottleneck so as to circumvent exceeding limited informational capacity. That is, attention is an information-processing mechanism of selection.

In pioneering work, Colin Cherry (1953) focused on auditory processing of language using a *filtering task*. Subjects were presented with multiple stimuli and asked to select some subset of them and ignore others. In the *dichotic listening paradigm*, two streams of verbal inputs are presented, and in a standard implementation, each verbal stream is presented to separate ears. Subjects then selectively shadow, namely verbally repeat, only one of the streams. This requires ignoring the words in the other, hence filtering them out. Cherry's basic finding was that when subjects attend to one stream, they miss a lot of content in the other. When queried about the unattended stream, subjects were able to report the gender of the voice given pitch but were unable to provide accurate answers regarding higher-level properties such as what was said.

Jon Driver (2001) noted that two questions were fundamental to theorists at that time: What conditions allowed people to effectively shadow the attended message? What do people typically know about the unattended message? (See also (Pashler 1998, 37), especially Chapter 2, for an overview.) On the first question, it was ascertained that substantial differences in the physical properties of the sounds between the two channels facilitated performance. For example, shadowing improved when the two auditory streams were coming from distinct rather than the same location. Shadowing was also aided by distinct acoustical properties between the streams such as presenting a low-pitch versus a high-pitch voice. In general, physical distinctness aided attentional selection of one rather than the other stream.

It is the second question, what happens to the unattended stream, that casts a long shadow over attention theory and the one we shall address. Notice that identifying a specific stream as attended versus unattended is set by the task instruction, consistent with the Common Conception (Chapter 1). So, the very probing of attention puts us on the familiar ground of selection to guide action, here auditory selection to inform verbal shadowing. In dichotic listening, the data suggested that while subjects could notice abrupt changes in lower-level physical properties of the unattended stream, higher-level perceptual properties like semantics (meaning) were typically missed.

Broadbent's *Filter Theory* of attention postulates that there is an attention filter that operates after processing basic perceptual features such as pitch and timbre in audition but prior to processing categorical features such as language and semantics. Specifically, the task-relevant target passes through the filter and is fully processed while other stimuli are blocked at an early stage. Given that the filter selects at an early stage, Broadbent's model is known as an *early selection* account.

Correct task performance requires selection of the task-relevant stimulus, but how is relevance distinguished from irrelevance if selection occurs at an early stage? After all, action relevance can be defined in terms of late-stage properties. For example, so long as we ensure that lower-level features are insufficient to distinguish the target category, task instructions that ask a subject to select the verbal stream of a specific *language* will force task-relevant selection to a late stage. How else can one detect, say, German from Dutch? While it might be possible to do "late stage" tasks by finding an individuating feature at an earlier stage (this is an empirical possibility), it seems a reasonable hypothesis that, for many actions, what is needed is *late selection*.

Early selection theorists hold that only a subset of processed stimuli are selected for processing that allows for more complete *awareness* of a given stimulus (i.e., awareness of higher-level properties). Late selection theorists do not disagree that selected stimuli are fully processed. A point of contention concerns the fate of unattended stimuli, specifically whether unattended stimuli are always blocked at an early stage or allowed to proceed to a late stage. Early selection theorists like Broadbent held that unattended stimuli are blocked early in processing with only relevant stimuli fully processed in perceptual systems. Late selection theorists held that all stimuli are fully processed but blocked at a post-perceptual stage. The fault line between these theorists concerns at what stage is processing of unattended stimuli blocked, if at all? It is worth emphasizing that, in this debate, we have the origins of the debate whether attention is a gate on phenomenal conscious awareness, an issue that comes into sharp relief in debates about *inattentional blindness* (Chapter 10).

In dichotic listening, evidence accumulated showing that quite a bit of semantics in the unattended auditory channel could get through. Drawing on the anecdote of the *cocktail party effect* where the mention of one's name in a nearby conversation is said to capture attention, Neville Moray (1959) found that when the subject's name appeared in the unattended channel, the subject was more likely to notice it: in Moray's task, subjects reported instructions expressed in the unattended channel when these were preceded by their name (33% of the time, Moray, op. cit. Table IV, p. 58). Moray concluded that "[i]t is probably only material 'important' to the subject that will break through the [bottleneck] barrier" (op. cit., 56; cf. (Bundesen et al. 1997)). This raises the question of how the system knows that unattended information is important.

Subsequently, Anne Treisman (1960) argued that "the selective mechanism in attention acts on all [stimuli] not coming from one particular source by 'attenuating' rather than 'blocking' them" (246–7). In one experiment, Treisman instructed subjects to shadow a verbal stream presented to one ear, say the right ear, while ignoring a second stream presented to the other ear. Unbeknownst to her subjects, Treisman swapped the verbal streams midsentence, so a sentence that begins in the right ear switches to the left and vice versa.

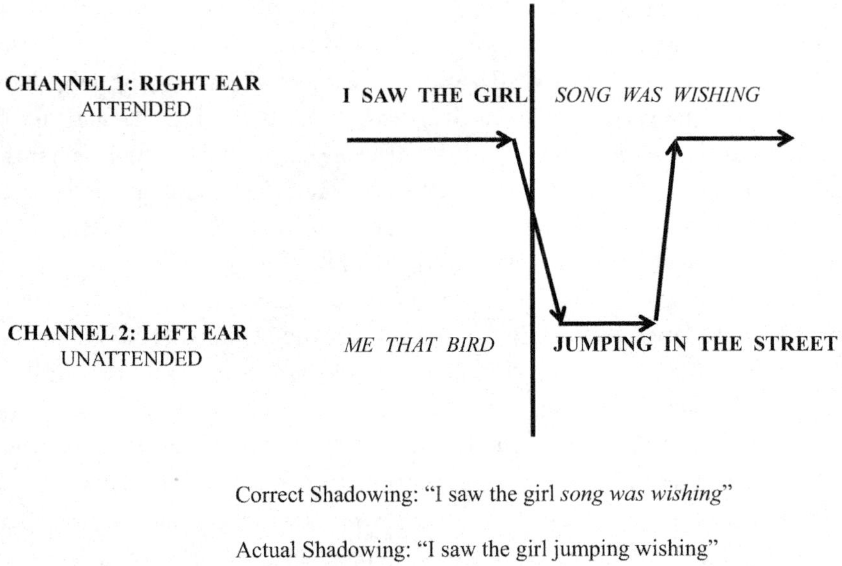

Figure 3.3 Two verbal streams are presented to each ear. One stream is rendered in italics, the other in bold. Normally, each stream is tied to a single ear, but Treisman changed channels mid-sentence so that the verbal streams switched ears. This switch point is indicated by the vertical line. Thus, the sentence "I saw the girl jumping in the street" begins in the left ear, which is the attended channel, but jumps to the right ear. Subjects were asked to shadow only one of the channels, so correct performance is just shadowing the words in a single channel. The arrows indicate what the subjects actually shadowed and, speculatively, suggested to theorists that the subject's attention jumps between channels despite task instructions.

Here, the sentence to be shadowed jumps from right ear to left, with the switch point indicated by the vertical line. To shadow correctly, however, the subject must continue to repeat the words on the right. In the example, the two sentences at issue are, first, "I saw the girl jumping in the street", which begins in the right channel but switches to the left after "girl", and, second, "me that bird song was wishing", which begins in the left channel but switches to the right after "bird". Correct shadowing would be enunciating the nonsensical "I saw the girl song was wishing." Surprisingly, the subjects shadowed "I saw the girl *jumping wishing*". It was as if attention shifted between the streams of each ear despite task instructions that locked subjects to one ear. This seems to require tracking higher-level linguistic properties. Further, subjects were *unaware* of doing this. Treisman reasoned that this intrusion of semantics from the unattended channel on the shadowing of the attended channel depends on contextual effects that continue to influence (bias) behavior since the word "jumping" rather than "song" is more probable given the preceding "I saw the girl…." It seems that unattended information remains available to influence behavior and is not completely filtered out. Assuming Treisman's explanation of why the subject jumps between channels, it seems that despite being unattended, the left channel must be analyzed to a higher linguistic level, including the statistics of word sequences. This means that information selected by the filter is not the only information being processed at higher stages. Treisman suggested that, since this unattended information is not being fully blocked, the filter is *leaky*: unattended information can get through the filter for higher-level processing.

Daniel Kahneman and Treisman (1984) noted a shift in the mid-1960s from early to late selection theories (Deutsch and Deutsch (1963), Norman (1968)). On late selection accounts, all stimuli are fully processed up to a categorical level of representation (e.g., semantic). Thus, relevant processing limits occur post-perceptually. Only at this late stage is an attentional mechanism needed in linking perception to response. That is, on a late selection theory, the limit on selection is not a limit on selection for perception but a limit on selection to guide behavior. There is, then, no early suppression of unattended stimuli and where late selection is observed, perceptual processing is not capacity-limited. J. Anthony and Diana Deutsch (1963) articulated an influential late selection view. They proposed that the processed stimuli are weighted in terms of importance, a bias, and that a simple mechanism ensures that "only the most important signals coming in will be acted on or remembered" (p. 84). If we take remembering to be an action (Chapter 6), then the Deutsch view is an implementation of selection for action. Questions about early selection aside, what is not in dispute in the early versus late selection debate is selection for action as embodied in the task, what the subject does to aid the experiment. After all, the standard paradigm driving the debate, namely dichotic listening, implements this condition.

We shall return in Chapter 10 to a version of the question of what happens to unattended items by asking whether we are in any way conscious of them. For now, we focus on whether unattended stimuli can influence task performance. Since unattended stimuli are defined by the task as task-irrelevant, where they capture attention, they induce *distraction*. As we saw with Moray's and Treisman's results, the unattended stimuli distract by pulling attention away from the instructed target. Such work probes the unattended channel as a source of distraction, something that can automatically engage response contrary to the agent's intention. Setting aside the question of conscious awareness, an important implication of the early versus late selection work is that it probes the possibilities of distraction. From this perspective, an early suppression mechanism would be of benefit in minimizing the possibilities for distraction since not every stimulus is fully process whereas the full processing of unattended stimuli increases the chances that attention is pulled off task, as in Moray's work on the cocktail party effect.

If we identify attention with a mechanism or process, a filter or filtering, then at least within the early selection theory, this process operates at an early stage in perceptual processing. Yet if so, it is *not* the subject who is attending in the sense of the subject filtering information. After all, the subject does not intervene in early sensory processing. Rather, part of the subject's brain filters. So, if we express Broadbent's account with our logical frame, namely that S *auditorily* attends to pitch, we equate this with S auditorily filters pitch for further processing by later auditory areas. The value of S, however, is not a subject but *part* of the subject, say part of the auditory system or some control system that modulates auditory processing. This contrasts with the Common Conception that takes the value of S to be subjects and not their neural parts. Accordingly, Broadbent's theory locates attention at levels below the functional theory for attention expressed in the Common Conception. His approach thereby proliferates attention, finding another type of attention in the postulated filter mechanism. Instead, we interpret the early selection account as identifying the *implementation* of a subject's auditory attention by a filtering mechanism in the auditory system. This filter contributes to explaining the *subject's* attention, namely their auditorily selecting an audible target for task performance. The filter mechanism is not attention. It is a selective mechanism that explains attention.

3.4 Resource and Capacity Limitations

Disputants in the early versus late selection debate agreed that selection is constrained by capacity limits to information processing. Attention as filter deals with those limits, so is distinct from them. As informational capacity is a limited resource, it is a causal factor or condition that interacts with the attention filter. It is then striking that some theorists *equate* attention with a limited resource. This idea is captured by the common attributions of *more* or *less* attention. Attention seems to be gradable, so attention itself *is* a limited resource. One can have too little of it or perhaps even exhaust attention.

Is attention a limited resource? To assess this, keep in mind two logically distinct claims:

Interaction: Attention is *modulated* by limits in resource R.
Identity: Attention *is* resource R.

Early and late selection theorists take the first option. Broadbent and others identify capacity limits in information channels as a fundamental constraint that necessitates attention. Attention is identified with the filter that deals with channel capacity limits. It is not identified with the channel capacity that imposes constraints on selective filtering.

If we accept Interaction, then the following fallacious inference is avoided: (1) there is a defined resource R; (2) R modulates/influences attention; therefore, (3) R *is* attention. Indeed, as (2) is a causal claim, then assuming causes and effects are distinct, (3) is false. Accepting it results in word salads since now "attention" in (2) and (3) have different meanings. This would lead to reading (2) as follows: *attention modulates attention*. Why court confusion?

We must remember that it takes a lot to establish identity claims ($A = B$) in science. Much of the evidence that we collect to support an inference to identity begins with various correlations. Identity is but one type of correlation, namely perfect and modally robust correlation. Yet how can experimentally observed correlations alone distinguish between A being a cause of B and *A* being B? As an empirical claim, the identification of attention with R must meet at least two significant conditions. First, we must identify R. Second, we must provide appropriate justification for why R should be identified with attention rather than being more weakly correlated with attention such as causal correlation.

One way to think of attention as a limited resource is to analogize it to resources that can be consumed like energy. Ulric Neisser observed, however, that "the metaphor of energy has never been very enlightening where cognition is concerned" (1967 p. 88). Daniel Kahneman's *Attention as Effort* provides a foundational treatment of the identification of attention with a resource. He notes:

> There is more to attention than mere selection. In everyday language, the term "attention" also refers to an aspect of amount and intensity. The dictionary tells us that to attend is to apply oneself presumably to some task or activity. Selection is implied, because there are always alternative activities in which one could engage, but any schoolboy knows that applying oneself is a matter of degree. Lulled into a pleasant state of drowsiness by his teacher's voice, the schoolboy does not merely fail to pay attention to what the teacher says; he has less attention to pay. A schoolboy who reads a detective story while his teacher speaks is guilty of improper selection. On the other hand, the drowsy schoolboy merely suffers from, or perhaps enjoys, a generally low level of attention.
>
> (Daniel Kahneman 1973, 3)

I suspect readers will find these reflections compelling, but what is the cash value of everyday language and dictionary definitions as constraints on a science of attention? Presumably, how we talk matters for science only if it reflects an accurate and informative epistemic source regarding psychological reality. We should not blithely assume that how we ordinarily talk or think about attention accurately reflects its reality. If such talk, as appealed to by Kahneman, is based on ordinary observations of behavior, then we should weight more substantially careful scientific observations of performance in controlled attention experiments. How the folk talk about attention might provide poor evidence for identifying attention with a resource.

Kahneman's account of attention as resource begins with *arousal*, a state of the subject for which we have behavioral correlates such as pupil dilation. Levels of arousal tracked in this way correlate with performance in attention tasks. Since arousal is a substantive notion in cognitive science, Kahneman's posit that a form of arousal, namely *effort*, is to be identified as attention is more firmly grounded than bare appeals to folk psychological language. Kahneman notes that

> voluntary attention is an exertion of effort in activities which are selected by current plans and intentions. Involuntary attention is an exertion of effort in activities which are selected by more enduring dispositions.
>
> (Kahneman op. cit. p. 4)

Kahneman uses "exert effort", "invest capacity", and "pay attention" synonymously. One can now work back to my question about what the folk have reliable epistemic access to. Perhaps a sense of effort could be something we are aware of. Presumably, at least some subjects are able to track the amount of effort they expend, such as high-level athletes who can shift their exertions or work rate to 50% or 100% effort and do so with reasonably reliable precision. So, an experienced runner can modulate their pace to different levels. Perhaps this involves accessing effort levels.

While I think there are issues to adjudicate regarding effort, I grant the first step for the sake of argument, namely identifying the relevant resource as a bona fide psychological entity that we can track: effort. I also allow, again for the sake of argument, that the subject can reliably track this resource and expresses said tracking when they talk about paying more or less attention. This leaves, however, the second step. Why *identify* effort with attention rather than take it as a resource that affects attention? Kahneman notes that his capacity model is meant to "complement" the selective information component of early and late selection theories. That is, Kahneman's model appeals to two distinct but complementary factors: selection and effort. Yet recall the two theses that we noted regarding attention, Interaction and Identity, namely that a resource limits or influences attention versus that a resource is attention. With these in mind, an alternative approach is to start with what is common, a subject's selection of a target to deal with. Kahneman does the same in the earlier passage. The next step will be to model how a distinct phenomenon, effort, affects the instantiation of one's selection of a target to act on. Here, it seems quite plausible as an empirical hypothesis that exerting more effort affects certain properties of attention. Yet on this alternative, attention itself is not gradable even if some of its properties are explained by the gradability of effort. The evidence and theoretical considerations support only the weaker Interaction claim, not the Identity claim. Attention depends on, though is distinct from, effort. We can then rewrite Kahneman's claim as

> voluntary attention is [dependent on] an exertion of effort in activities which are selected by current plans and intentions. Involuntary attention is

> [dependent on] an exertion of effort in activities which are selected by more enduring dispositions.

Identifying attention as a resource is neither theoretically nor empirically warranted.

This raises a challenge to those who want to claim, literally, that attention can be more or less. This is a resource conception, and it cannot be had for free since the Interaction position is a plausible, less committed alternative. The challenge to those who say attention *is* a resource is to provide an argument showing that there is a resource that is not causally correlated with attention but *is* attention. I suggest that we have no such argument. Until we give such an argument, talk of more or less attention is really talk of the gradability of certain features of attention, say as measured by reaction time and other performance measures.

3.5 Task Demands and Load

Kahneman and Treisman (1984) observed that the shift from early to late selection theories coincided with a shift in different types of experimental paradigms. Early work in audition involved filtering tasks where subjects were overloaded with task-irrelevant input. Later work focused less on filtering and more on target selection. This includes well-known paradigms like spatial cuing and visual search to be discussed in Chapters 4 and 5, respectively. Kahneman and Treisman argued that different experimental paradigms might tap into different mechanisms involving selection at different stages in processing. Thus, results favoring early or late selection might merely reflect choice of experimental task. The nature of the task affects the nature of the processing.

The *Load Theory of Attention* originally proposed by Nillie Lavie and Yehoshua Tsal provides a way of understanding processing changes that track the nature of the task (Lavie and Tsal 1994). Although Tsal became a critic of the account (Benoni and Tsal 2013), the theory has been consistently defended by Lavie (2005). Treisman (1969) suggested that "we tend to use our perceptual capacity to the full on whatever sense data reach the receptors" (p. 296). In contrast, Navon and Gopher (1979) proposed that when attention is engaged, it is affected by limited resources but need not deplete them. If so, what happens to the remaining resource?

Lavie and Tsal (1994) suggested that when the attended information channel does not exhaust available resources, remaining processing capacity is automatically apportioned to the processing of unattended channels. On their account, the critical factor is the *perceptual load* on the attended channel. (Later work also emphasizes *cognitive* load such as working memory capacity; I shall ignore that dimension here.) Under low load conditions, processing in the attended channel does not consume all resources, so unattended stimuli can be fully or more extensively processed. In contrast, under high load conditions, the attended channel consumes all available resources so unattended stimuli are not fully processed.

Load Theory predicts that early selection effects will be seen in high perceptual load conditions where all available processing is consumed by heavy task demands in the attended channel. For example, auditory filtering tasks in early work in the 1950s might be high-load, involving a large amount of information to be sifted through so that selection of task-relevant channels consumes all available resources, leaving none for full processing of unattended channels. In contrast, late selection effects will be seen in low perceptual load conditions where the system is not overloaded with information and additional processing resources are available for unattended channels. Under those conditions, perceptual processing is capacity-unlimited and each stimulus is fully processed.

The central insight is that the nature of the experimental task can affect whether early or late selection effects arise or, correlatively, early versus late suppression of unattended stimuli. In high-load cases, we get early suppression in the sense that there is no capacity to enable processing of unattended stimuli, while in low-load, there is capacity that enables further processing. More importantly, if early and late selection effects depend on the nature of the task, then it would be incorrect to tie the selectivity of attention down to a specific stage in processing (i.e., early or late). In both cases, attention is constant in that in performing the task correctly, the agent has attended to the task-relevant target. What changes is processing of unattended targets.

The rubric *Load Theory of Attention* suggests that attention is load, a limited resource, but the theory instead explains load's influence on attention. Load Theory answers the Properties and Relation questions:

Properties: What are characteristic features of attention?
Relations: How is attention related to other psychological phenomena?

Load theory identifies a causal relation between load and selection during task performance. The theory would be more accurately called, if less snappy, a Load Theory of Processing During Attention, especially with emphasis on processing distractors. The role of distractors is a major theme of attention research to which we shall often return. (See Chapter 6 on working memory and Chapter 10 on attention as gate.)

It is worth noting various objections to Load Theory, including by one of its originators. A serious concern is that the notion of perceptual load has never been adequately analyzed. It is a quantitative notion but has no quantitative analysis, say an equation that says what load is relative to other known quantities. The nature of load is left at a set of operationalizations such as manipulation of distractor properties. It will be important for the theory to answer the Metaphysical Question about Load (for a measured critical discussion, see (Murphy et al. 2016)). Regardless, the fact that different *task conditions* modulate whether the data generated are consistent with early or with late selection underscores Kahneman and Treisman's observation that the shift from early to late selection theories coincided with shifts in attentional paradigms (i.e., different tasks).

Let's return to one of the pressing questions: "What is processed in the unattended channel?" To get some conceptual control on the issues, we recast this question in three ways:

> What is accessed in the unattended channel?
> What is accessible in the unattended channel?
> What processing level do targets in the unattended channel achieve?

In respect of *access*, experimenters typically mean overt action, often report or movement that reflects using information. Given the Common Conception, experiments probing attention are designed so that subjects access the attended channel to guide task performance. In dichotic listening, the verbal stream is accessed to guide verbal shadowing which the experimenter can monitor and record. If the subject's name in the *unattended* channel captures the subject's attention, it thereby distracts her. Distraction is a form of unwanted access that disrupts access for the intended task.

In the early versus late selection debate, theorists were interested in what was *accessible* in the unattended channel, for they assessed whether the subject could later report its content. In Cherry's case, this involved probes after the trial and tests whether subjects remember what was in the unattended channel. Anything remembered is potentially accessible, could be accessed, for subsequent report. If the subject can remember aspects of unattended stimuli, then memory accesses that information to preserve it, keeping it accessible for overt response. Notice that it is important to keep track of the variables X and Y in the claims *X is accessed by Y* and *X is accessible to Y*. In Cherry's case, the verbal stream is *accessed by working memory* and is *accessible to report* but it is not, until explicitly probed, *accessed by report*.

We can also ask whether, independent of any connection to action (i.e., to access or accessibility), unattended stimuli are fully processed though fall short of being rendered accessible to memory or response systems. Imagine a sensory system that can complete its processing of all stimuli without making these results available to any further systems. In this scenario, even if the stimuli in the unattended channel are neither accessed nor inaccessible to behavior, sensory processing might be "late" in that it continues to the highest levels (see Chapter 10, endnote 2).

3.6 Common Dichotomies

Many common dichotomies regarding attention are not well defined. We have clarified one version of the dichotomy between automaticity and control (Chapter 2.8). In this section, we examine two common divisions: top-down versus bottom-up attention and preattentive versus attentive processing.

Talk of *top-down* and *bottom-up* attention individuates the mode m in our logical frame: S m-attends to T. Bottom-up attention is sometimes described as, or includes, *stimulus-driven attention*, *attentional capture*, *pop-out*, *exogenous* even *automatic* attention. These ideas are connected to a technical notion of *salience* in vision science (see Chapter 5.5). In contrast, top-down attention is often explained as *goal-directed* attention where the goal is part of the intended task, so top-down attention involves "cognitive" biases and is sometimes spoken of as *voluntary* or *endogenous* attention. Top-down and bottom-up attention can act at cross purposes, for bottom-up attention might disrupt top-down attention as when our attention is captured and pulled away from an intended task. (For the internal, non-sensory case, see discussion of mind wandering in Chapter 13.5.)

What counts as *top* and as *bottom*? There is general agreement that task representations such as the action represented in the agent's intention are one type of top-down bias on attention and that a computational notion of visual salience (Chapter 5.5) provides one type of bottom-up bias. Yet this leaves a host of other biases unaccounted for. Some advocate rejecting the top-down versus bottom-up dichotomy as exhaustive, noting that there are historical influences on attention as well, such as those tied to reward and learning through past experience (Awh et al. 2012).

In a well-known review of the neural substrates of "goal-directed" and "stimulus-driven" attention, Maurizio Corbetta and Gordon Shulman (2002) define top-down processing as "the flow of information from 'higher' to 'lower' centers, conveying knowledge derived from previous experience rather than sensory stimulation" (p. 201). Bottom-up processing concerns "information processing that proceeds in a single direction from sensory input, through perceptual analysis, towards motor output, without involving feedback information flowing backwards from 'higher' centers to 'lower' centers" (ibid.). Yet consider the case of emotion which can powerfully shape attention. Is attention modulated by fear bottom-up or top-down? What of emotions such as guilt or envy, which arguably involve beliefs and other cognitive attitudes yet distract from current intention and goals? Given the cognitive constituents of certain emotions, we might think that when these states influence attention, they are top-down biases. Yet envy and guilt can strike us suddenly, like a bright flash can grab our attention. So are emotions sometimes top-down, other times bottom-up? Once historical influences are allowed, things get murkier, as we must distinguish synchronic and diachronic dimensions.

In the absence of consensus regarding taxonomy, we might just appeal to a generic notion of a *bias*. We then go beyond a threefold division and focus on biases of interest, such as goals, stimulus properties (salience), emotions, reward history, and so on. This is just to allow m in our logical frame to range as broadly as theoretically advantageous. In doing so, we convey more information about the causal structure influencing attention. So, we drop dichotomies and trichotomies in favor of more informative descriptions.

In the first edition of this book, I distinguished between the top-down and bottom-up attention dichotomy from the controlled and automatic distinction (Wu 2014, Chapter 1.7). I am less sure about the utility of this move, but as some readers have found it helpful, let me review the proposal. My idea was to note that a key feature of bottom-up perceptual attention is that it is *initiated* by stimuli in the environment that grab attention. This leads to focusing on an occurrence, what triggers attention (slightly modified, Wu op. cit. p. 30):

S's attention to X is **bottom-up** if and only if S's attention to X occurs without influence from a non-perceptual psychological bias as necessary for its occurrence.

S's attention to X is **top-down** if and only if S's attention to X requires the influence of a non-perceptual psychological bias for its occurrence.

On top-down, a subject *intends* to pay attention in a certain way, such as to focus on a specific object. Selection occurs because of the intention, a non-perceptual psychological capacity. Where perceptual attention happens without the influence of non-perceptual biases, attention is bottom-up, such as when attention is captured by a loud bang. As analyzed, any non-perceptual psychological system counts as part of the "top". So, motor influences on perceptual selection would count as top-down. This is stipulative, but let's work with it.

This raises the question of how to relate the top-down/bottom-up distinction to the control-automaticity distinction. I do not think they are coextensive since the latter, as analyzed in Chapter 2.8, is exhaustive and the former is not. The former distinction, based on the above biconditionals, concerns how attention *initiates*. The latter concerns the features of attention across its duration. If so, this leads to four combinations:

(1) Top-down, controlled attention

(2) Bottom-up, automatic attention

(3) Top-down, automatic attention

(4) Bottom-up, controlled attention.

(1) and (2) are familiar categories. You tell me to follow the man in the fedora, and I attend to him. My attention to him is top-down because I initiate attention given my intention to follow your instructions, and I would not have done so otherwise. It is controlled because given my intention to keep my eyes on that person, my attention has the feature of being directed at that person over time. In general, intentional attention fits with (1). On (2), a loud continuous sound pulls my attention to it. This capture of my attention occurs independently of any top-down influence, so it looks to be bottom-up. Given that I don't have any relevant intentions, many of the features of captured attention might be automatic though perhaps not for long. I hear the sound and subsequently intend to figure out where it is coming from, so attention thereby takes on a controlled aspect. It is sustained according to my intentions. Pop-out in visual search might also seem like a case of bottom-up, automatic attention, but this is controversial (see contingent capture of attention, Chapter 6.7). It seems likely that no process instantiates (4) since the causal processes imputed by each dichotomy

operate at cross purposes: bottom-up attention requires a stimulus-driven initiation contrary to any intentions, but control requires the influence of an intention. At best, attention might be bottom-up and automatic but quickly *becomes* controlled once intentions kick in to sustain attention to the stimulus.

What of top-down, automatic attention? Category (3) seems odd, but recall Yarbus's experiment (Chapter 2.3, Figure 2.6). Choosing the panels where subjects were tasked to remember what the people in the picture are wearing, the pattern of eye movements makes sense given the subjects' more abstract intentions to carry out instructions. To remember the clothes, the subject intentionally looks at each figure. This intention need not be an intention to move one's eyes in any specific way, but the resulting pattern of eye movements is intelligible given the intention in question: the eyes gravitate around the people without spending time on the objects. The specific pattern of eye movements happens automatically and is not itself intended. As the pattern is not controlled, it is automatic. At the same time, the subject's looking at the painting in this way was initiated due to an intention, so top-down, overt attention with this pattern would not have occurred without the subject having the requisite goal, so attention is top-down. Thus, while the idea of top-down automatic attention might seem contradictory, it is not. That we can categorize the phenomenon Yarbus observed suggests that the initial analysis is theoretically useful. My present position, however, is that while dichotomies can be useful, we should focus on describing as precisely as possible the nature of the bias that sets attention.

A second influential dichotomy is between *attentive* versus *preattentive* processing. This has deep roots in contemporary work on attention as a mechanism (see Neisser's discussion in Chapter 4 of his (1967)). *Any* account of perceptual attention that treats it as an internal mechanism endorses this distinction. After all, unless the attentional mechanism engages at the sensory receptor such as the retina, there must be a point where we have processing before the attentional mechanism kicks in, hence also processing after that mechanism. This identifies preattentive and attentive processing. Thus, Donald Broadbent spoke of an attentional filter to deal with informational bottlenecks and Anne Treisman of attention as a spotlight needed to glue features together to generate object representations (Chapter 5.3). Processing before filtering and binding is preattentive. The dichotomy has less play in the neuroscience of attention, but if one were to identify top-down modulation of initial sensory processing as attentional modulation, a description many neuroscientists use, this implicitly divides neural processing into preattentive and attentive processing. The empirical claim requires identifying a concrete mechanism and locating its influence in the path of information processing.

How does this fit with the Common Conception? If there is to be a distinction between preattentive and attentive processing, then it is the difference in the neural processing that implements the subject's attending, her selecting a target to respond to. Making this clear allows us to take on *mechanistic* distinctions deployed in the early debates about attention. For example, perhaps there is a mechanism that integrates separate perceptual feature representations to bind them into object representations, as posited by Anne Treisman and Garry Gelade's Feature Integration Theory (Chapter 5.3), but it is not the subject who attends to feature representations constructed in early vision so as to pull them together to form object representations. Those representations in the visual system are not accessible to the subject. Her task is not to do anything with them. Rather, she enters the scene when she sees an object, but this is explained by the visual system's processing of objects, including binding of sensory features.

3.7 Attention as for Perception

The previous points about preattentive versus attentive processing speak against the identification of attention as *selection for perception* as opposed to selection for action. If we think that attention is a subject-level phenomenon, then the problem with characterizing attention as selection for perception is that selection for perception applies to a level of analysis *below the subject*.

Assume that attention for perception is a claim about a subject-level phenomenon. Perception is also a subject-level phenomenon, such as the subject's seeing. If attention is selection for perception, then a subject selects something in order to be able to perceive it. That is, the subject has a role to play in order to perceive. This seems to get things backwards, for it requires that to enable perception, before perception occurs, the subject has to select something. But that is not how perception works. It is enough, say, that our eyes are open. With regard to perceptual attention, perception comes first. Of course, there is selection for perception in the brain, beginning with retinal selection of specific optical information that provides input into further processing that ultimately generates perceptual awareness. This is, however, selection at the brain, not subject, level, so none of this neural processing is itself attention even if some theorists label it "attention".

Selection for perception—that is, neural selection for perceptual processing leading to the subject's seeing—is not itself a subject-level phenomenon but explains it.

There are interpretations that make true the claim that a subject can select for perception. Here is one way, and readers can come up with others. One aspect of peripheral vision in primates is that it is subject to visual crowding which we can describe as the subject's failing to see crowded objects distinctly (Levi 2008; Whitney and Levi 2011; Rosenholtz 2016). Readers can examine the effect by fixating on the center of this page and covertly attending to words in the periphery which will appear as a visual jumble. Assuming that crowding defeats a "clear view" of the object, then one solution is to foveate the objects in question, namely to bring them into the center of the visual field by an eye movement (saccade). We can then say that overt visual attention is for object perception in that in bringing a peripheral object onto the fovea, the subject allows the object to escape crowding. This makes true the claim that this form of visual attention is for visual object perception given the informational limitations due to the physiology of the human eye. That said, this is not what proponents of attention as selection for perception have in mind. Rather, they treat the selection at issue as being part of the neural basis of a subject's perceiving, so attention's function is for the generation of perceptual experience. The alternative is that we can acknowledge selective processing for perception such as Broadbent's filter or Treisman's spotlight, but deny that this is attention, the subject's selection. Rather, these selective mechanisms for perception contribute to the implementation of attention.

3.8 Conclusion

There is the ever-present danger that despite the admonishments against the use-mention confusion in Chapter 1.2, the conceptual points discussed in this chapter will be set aside as unimportant, mere word games, simply semantics. Yet how we conceptualize things in carving the world up for thought determines the cogency of our questions, of the explanations that provide the answers, and of the resulting theory. Clear conceptualizations shape the content of our hypotheses and the meaning of counterexamples. They frame how we design experiments and interpret the data obtained. Serious consequences should not be shrugged off by poorly informed complaints of word games and mere semantics. That attitude is why Groos's worry a century ago gets repeated today. We have the tools to settle those complaints, and we should. Failure to take seriously the conceptual domain has led to the rampant proliferation of poorly analyzed terms and fallacious arguments. In particular, the continued extension of the term "attention" is a stylistic reflex that amounts to a sloppy way to characterize the rampant selectivity inherent in neurobiological, computational, psychological, and behavioral systems. Selection is everywhere. Attention is not. To equate attention with selection does not serve science.

As an antidote, we have traced a clear conception of attention long ago articulated by William James who gave voice to what we all know. Further, that basic idea is echoed in a methodological condition in the design of experimental paradigms that probe attention. Because the cognitive science of attention relies on the results from these paradigms, the common starting place for discussion of what attention is should begin with the Common Conception. Where we disagree, we should fall back to this agreed-upon conception. It is a well-grounded way to achieve consensus.

Suggested Readings

Temporal attention is a new area of active research. A detailed overview is given by Kia Nobre and Freek van Ede (Nobre and van Ede 2018) and more recently by Rachel Denison (Denison 2024). An accessible overview of the early versus late selection debate is given by Harold Pashler (1998, Chapter 1). Daniel Kahneman introduces his theory of attention and effort in his (Daniel Kahneman 1973). The limitations of the top-down and bottom-up dichotomy are clearly enunciated by Edward Awh et al. (2012). An interesting list of attentional phenomena that might not fit traditional categorizations smoothly is given by Sarah Shomstein and colleagues in (Shomstein et al. 2023).

4

VISUAL SPATIAL CUEING

4.1 Introduction

In this and the next chapter, we review the science of attention focusing on two well-studied phenomena: visual spatial attention with cues and visual search. There are many excellent reviews of these phenomena out there. Our approach is different. In each case, we build a multitiered, integrated explanation of attention that is organized by beginning with a clear conception of the task via the Common Conception. Along the way, readers will be exposed to salient empirical work at the behavioral, architectural, computational, and neural level. The goal is not completeness but rather to show how things hang coherently together and thus how much has been achieved. Systematic integration is the upshot of this and the next chapter.

Spatial cueing is itself a large topic, so this chapter's focus is on spatial visual attention biased by *indirect* cueing such as an arrow that points to a location where a target may or may not appear. Such *symbolic* cues can carry spatial information that reduces uncertainty regarding target location. Drawing on the Common Conception, we begin with an initial functional theory of visual spatial attention as follows:

DOI: 10.4324/9781003223450-5

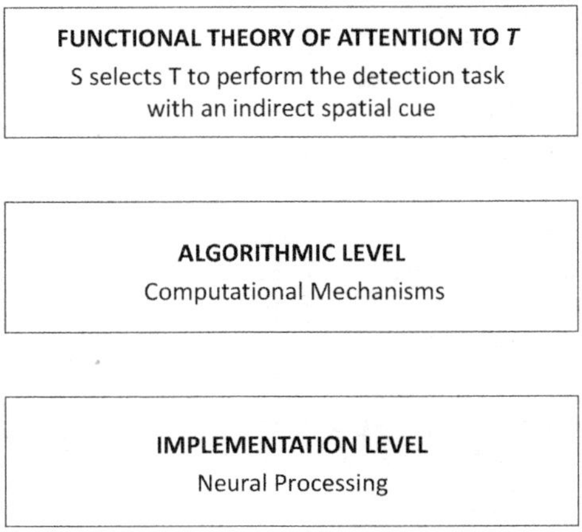

Figure 4.1 Marrian Framework for indirect spatial cueing.

(A) If a subject S visually selects T to perform the detection task using an indirect spatial cue, then S visually attends to T.

Further analytical progress is gained by specifying concrete values for T, the targets of attention. The intuitive structure of the task suggests three targets: (1) attention to the cue (T_1), (2) attention to a location (T_2), and (3) attention to the target at that location (T_3). Accordingly, we have

1. Visual selection of the cue to guide updating expectation

2. Visual selection of a location to guide a preparatory response there

3. Visual selection of the target to inform instructed report.

Accordingly, each corresponding empirical sufficient condition provides a component of the functional theory (three "sub-functional" theories).

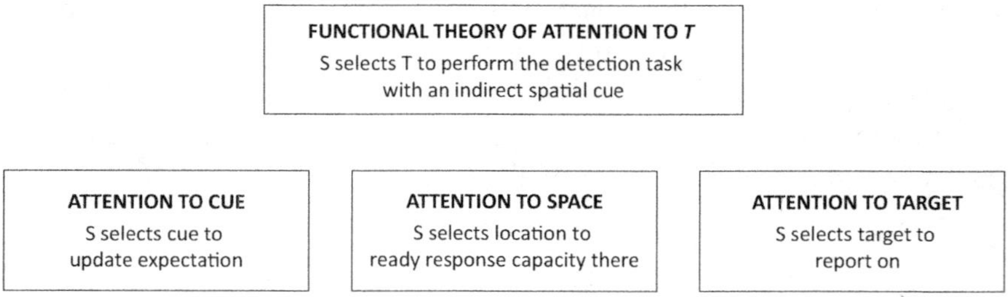

Figure 4.2 The three-part computational theory.

This explanatory structure provides a frame to fill in. We will move from left to right. After an overview of visual spatial cueing in Section 4.2, Section 4.3 examines the first movement of attention to the cue in order to update the subject's *expectation* (belief). Theorists often talk of the subject interpreting the symbol as part of processing that directs spatial attention. Once expectation is in view, Section 4.4 begins discussion of spatial selection, arguing that the spotlight is an unnecessary mechanistic appendage and should be eliminated. Section 4.5 introduces a systems neuroscience perspective, linking two neural networks relevant to understanding cue validity. Section 4.6 considers the nature of the response informed by spatial selection, examining the premotor theory of attention. In Section 4.7, we briefly look at selection of target for report focusing on signal detection and perceptual sensitivity. Finally, Section 4.8 examines algorithms that partially explain the correlated neural activity observed during spatial cueing. Although many details remain to be added, the goal is to unite different levels of analysis in explaining spatial attention.

4.2 The Visual Spatial Cueing (Posner) Paradigm: Preliminaries

Michael Posner and colleagues did much to establish spatial cueing as a central experimental paradigm (e.g., (Posner et al. 1980)). As Richard Wright and Lawrence Ward (2008) note, the paradigm has three elements. First, subjects maintain fixation to ensure that attention is deployed *covertly*, so independently of eye movement (*overt* visual attention). Second, subjects are asked to detect or discriminate targets. In a standard implementation, these targets appear in one of two locations, say equidistant left or right of fixation. Finally, subjects are cued, gaining information regarding the location of the upcoming target. A *valid* cue indicates the actual target position, an *invalid* cue does not. The primary behavioral measures are reaction time and response accuracy. The valid and invalid cases are as given in Figure 4.3.

Subjects are instructed on *target* types and how to respond to them, are informed which *locations* targets can appear, and are presented with the *conditional probabilities* of target location given the cue. The task structure involves three notable selections for response:

1. Selection of the cue to interpret and update expectation
2. Selection of a specific spatial location to ready a behavioral response to it
3. Selection of the target for report.

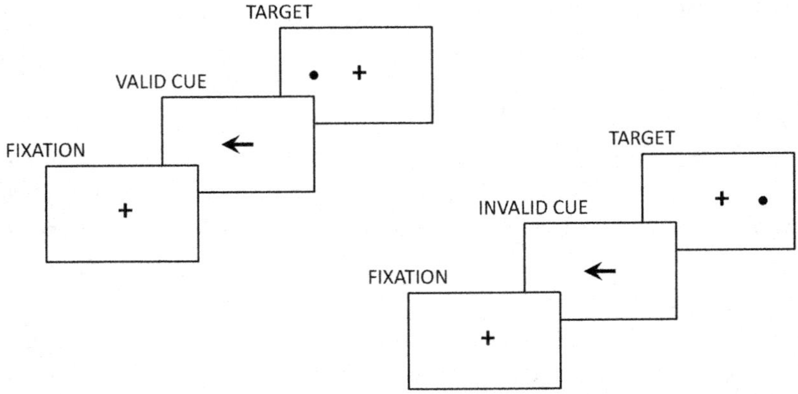

Figure 4.3 Posner Indirect Spatial Cueing with valid cue (left side), the arrow indicating the actual location of target (dot), and with invalid cue (right side), the arrow indicating the incorrect location.

Notably, attention in spatial cueing involves more than spatial attention. Cues and targets are task-relevant and also attended to during task performance.

Attention to the cue is the first step. If the subject fails to pay attention to the cue, then it will not influence performance. Cues lead to spatial prioritization, often captured by a spotlight metaphor: the subject preemptively shifts the spotlight to the cued location selecting it to "highlight". There are *direct* and *indirect* cues. A direct cue appears at or near one of the potential target locations. Indirect cues such as an arrow refer to one of the potential target locations. The subject interprets the cue to establish a *context-specific expectation* regarding target location in that trial. This updating alters how the subject prioritizes the relevant locations. Cue *validity* is another important factor. Valid cues correctly indicate target location, while invalid cues do not. Cue informativeness is manipulated by changing the conditional probability of a target appearing at a location given the cue type, say a cue that is 80% valid, 20% invalid. The cue's informational content varies with cue probability.

Reaction time and accuracy are consistently affected by cue validity. Three conditions are relevant: (1) a valid cue, (b) an invalid cue, and (c) a neutral cue. Neutral cues might be an uninformative signal at central fixation. Reaction time decreases (subjects are faster) and accuracy increases (subjects make fewer mistakes) in valid cueing relative to invalid cueing. When compared with neutral cues, valid cueing *enhances* performance, with reaction time and accuracy improving relative to neutral cues. In contrast,

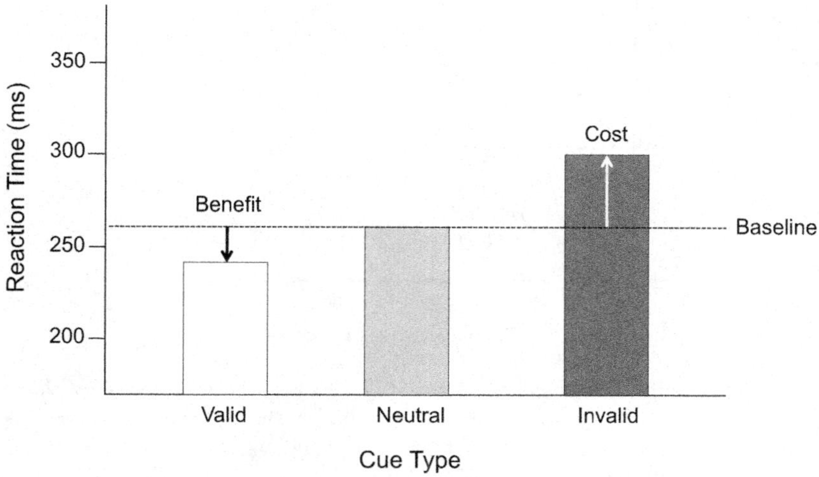

Figure 4.4 Reaction time cost and benefit in Posner spatial cueing. Adapted from Figure 2.6, Wright and Ward (2008), p. 20.

invalid cueing incurs a *cost* in performance relative to neutral cues, with reaction time and accuracy suffering (Figure 4.4).

In indirect cueing, the manipulation of validity has a clear effect on performance, but direct cues enhance performance *independently of cue validity.* As John Jonides noted: "Peripheral cues maintain their attention-capturing property even when subjects do not particularly expect their occurrence. That is not true of central [symbolic] cues: Their effectiveness in causing attention shifts is directly related to subjects' expectations about their occurrence" (Jonides 1981, 200). Researchers conceptualize indirect cues as engaging "voluntary" or "goal-directed" attention. For example, if subjects are told to *ignore* the cue, the facilitatory effect disappears in indirect cues (Jonides op. cit. Experiment 2) but is only partially attenuated in direct cues (Lambert et al. 1987), suggesting that the latter effect is *automatic*.

Direct and indirect cueing also have different time courses. By changing the time between cue and target presentation, the *target* or *stimulus onset asynchrony*, we observe the following difference between the two types of cues (Figure 4.5). The facilitatory influence of direct cues quickly engages and quickly drops off. If the target is presented too long after the direct cue, no facilitatory effect occurs. Indeed, there is a negative effect, a repulsion from the cued location termed *inhibition of return*. In contrast, the facilitation by indirect cues takes time to build up and can be sustained, suggesting a type of control present in indirect cueing that is absent in direct cueing.

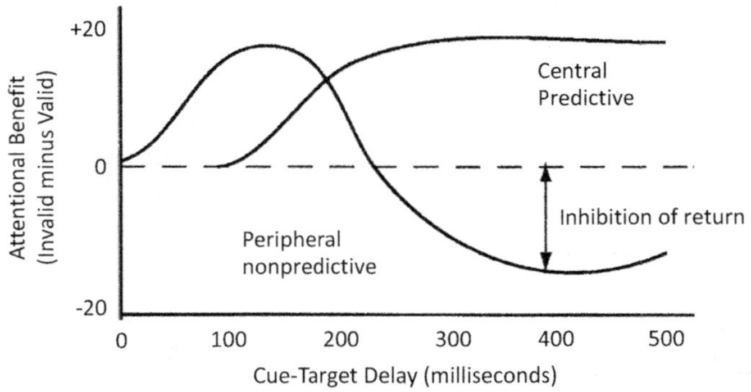

Figure 4.5 Time course of the benefit in performance of direct versus indirect cues. Note that the peak effect for direct, peripheral cues occurs earlier than that for indirect, central cues. Reprinted from Vecera and Rizzo (2003) "Spatial Attention: Normal Processes and their Breakdown." Neurologic Clinics 21: 575–607 with permission from Elsevier.

4.3 Expectation

The explanatory framework depicted in Figure 4.2 identifies three components of the task. As an action, task performance is subject to a spatial cueing Selection Problem. The first task we isolate is updating expectation. Let's depict the subject's visual experience of each potential target location as a node in an action space; each visual input can be mapped to an instructed response, say pressing an F key for the left target, the K key for right. The input nodes, L and R, in Figure 4.6 stand for the subject's visual experiences of locations L and R during the experiment. For ease of exposition, we will also treat those capacities as capable of representing the target T if it occurs at L or R.

The inputs to the Selection Problem identify task-relevant locations, the outputs task-relevant movements. This depicts the functional level describing the subject's potential behaviors in performing the task (the perspective

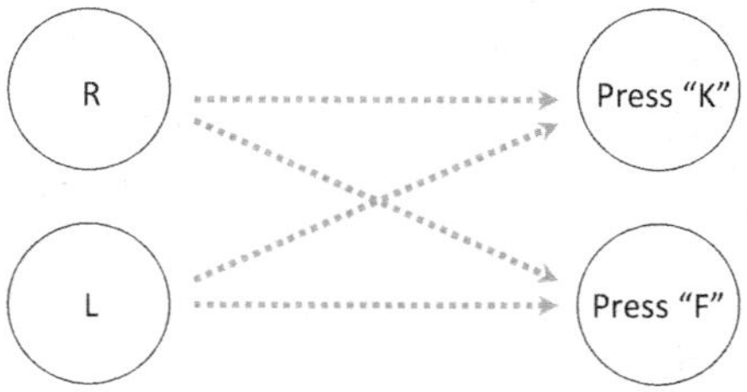

Figure 4.6 Selection Problem in spatial cueing during fixation with "L" and "R" denoting spatial locations where the target can appear. Correct responses are when the visual input informs the output via the horizontal connections. Diagonal connections yield an incorrect report.

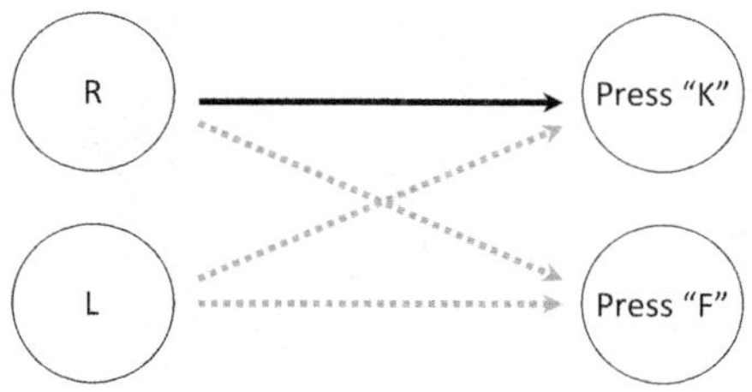

Figure 4.7 Solving the Selection Problem by responding to R. In this case, the input experience of R guides the production of the output response, pressing K.

of the top box of Figure 4.2). The four dotted arrows indicate input-output couplings that constitute different actions, two correct, two incorrect. For example, the subject on seeing R can visually guide a response, namely correctly pressing K (Figure 4.7).

Now consider the fine-structure of spatial cueing (recall Buridan's donkey facing two potential targets, Chapter 2.2). At the beginning of a trial, the subject prioritizes L and R over other visible locations as task-relevant (for ease of exposition, I ignore the fixation point). This reflects the initial bias due to the subject's intention to report a target occurring at either L or R, her conception of the task at its most general level (in Chapter 6, we discuss this biasing as *preparatory attention* and vigilance). Note that, at this point, there is no differentiating L from R as both are equally likely target locations.

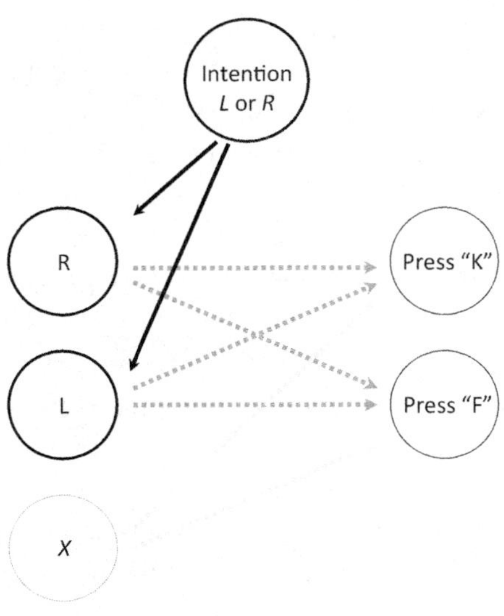

Figure 4.8 The intention identifies L and R as task-relevant, whereas any other location X is not task-relevant. The biasing effect of intention is indicated by a difference in the boldness of the circles around L and R versus X.

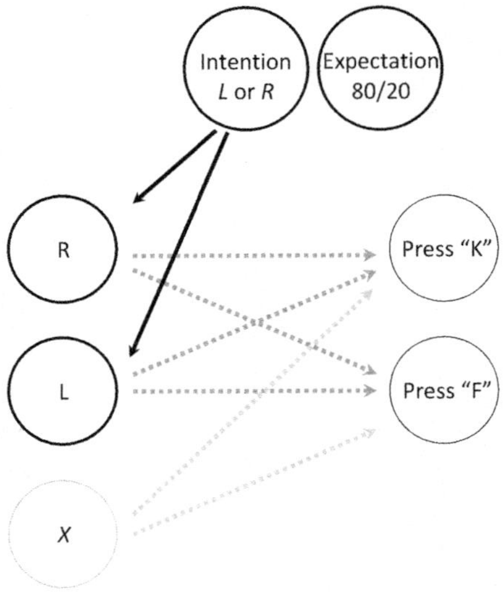

Figure 4.9 Expectation regarding cue probability. Since this knowledge concerns the cue, it does not yet bias spatial representations to prioritize one over the other.

Now, given that the subject knows that cues will be 80% valid and 20% invalid, this being part of the information she is given in instructions, this sets an expectation (belief) about the general statistics of the task. Yet until a specific cue is presented, this general expectation does not differentiate R from L in this experimental trial. We can add the general expectation regarding the cue into our picture, though it does not shift the bias to one target location over another (Figure 4.9).

The influence of expectation on attention comes with the presentation of an actual cue in a trial, the appearance of an arrow pointing in a specific direction. This cue changes the structure of the Selection Problem. Consider an arrow that points to R. The arrow provides additional information (reduces uncertainty) about likely target location. Given the cue, the target will probably be at R. If the subject fails to attend to the cue, she will be inattentionally blind to it (Chapter 10) and fail to update her expectation. In contrast, by attending to it, interpreting the significance of its direction, the subject updates her general expectation to a specific one, from (general) expecting that the target will occur at either R or L *across trials* to (specific) expecting that the target more likely will occur at R than at L *in this trial*.

So visual attention initially engages in visually selecting the cue to inform statistical updating of expectations. The subject selects the arrow to infer a

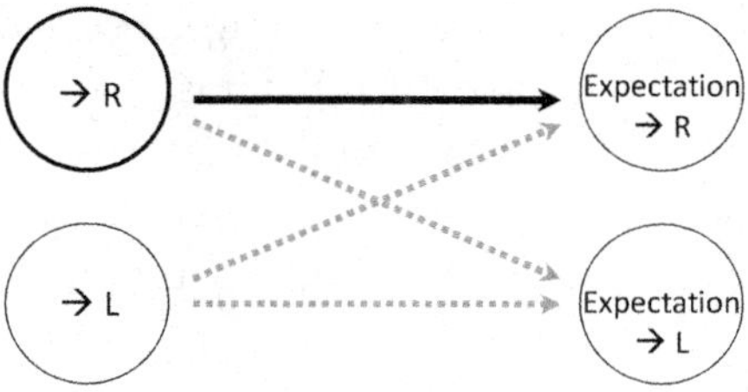

Figure 4.10 Updating expectation once a cue is observed. In this case, given the cue that points right, the subject now forms an expectation regarding R as the probable target location. This expectation, an updated belief, is the response output of visually selecting the cue.

conditional probability. The result is a new expectation (bias) that favors R over L, prioritizing R (Figure 4.10).

So, while the intention, based on the original task instructions, does not favor R over L, the updated expectation does. We can speak of an increased vigilance for R, a readiness to attend to the target should it appear there. (Think of being told which of two doors the birthday guest is likely to open for a surprise party.) The expectation in Figure 4.11 functions like a spotlight.

This first movement of attention, made salient by the Common Conception, brings forward expectation as an important factor explaining task performance (recall our discussion of temporal expectation and temporal attention

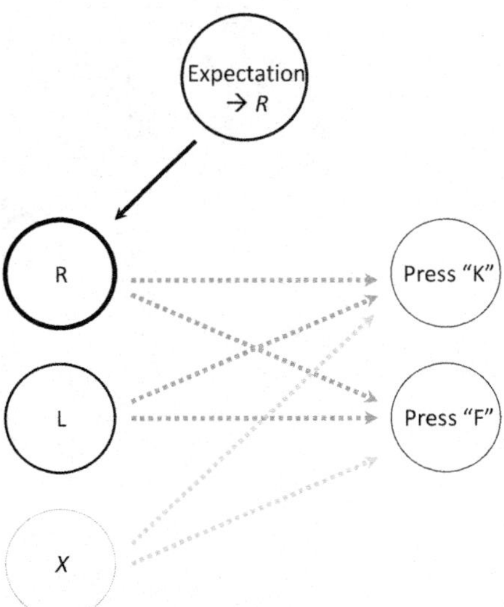

Figure 4.11 Specific knowledge about the difference between L and R in terms of likely target appearance is acquired when the cue appears, here an arrow pointing right. This prioritizes R over L as the likely target location.

in Chapter 3.2). There is more to say regarding expectations at other levels of analysis such as algorithmic and neural, but it is enough for our purposes to highlight that it is an important part of the first deployment of attention to the cue. We now move to the second movement of attention, namely to space. This leads us to spatial attention. It also brings us to the *spotlight*.

4.4 A Spotlight of Attention?

The spotlight metaphor captures the common assumption that attention is an *internal mechanism* and that implication is what we shall focus on. There is nothing wrong with metaphors in science as ways to capture ideas, but in the end, we should opt for mechanistic precision. In this section, we shall examine the spatial bias provided by the updated expectation as a basis for *eliminating* the need for positing a spotlight.

If we speak substantively of the spotlight (i.e., a mechanism), then in the cueing paradigm, expectations, given a cue, preemptively direct the spotlight to relevant locations in advance of the target's appearance (Figure 4.12).

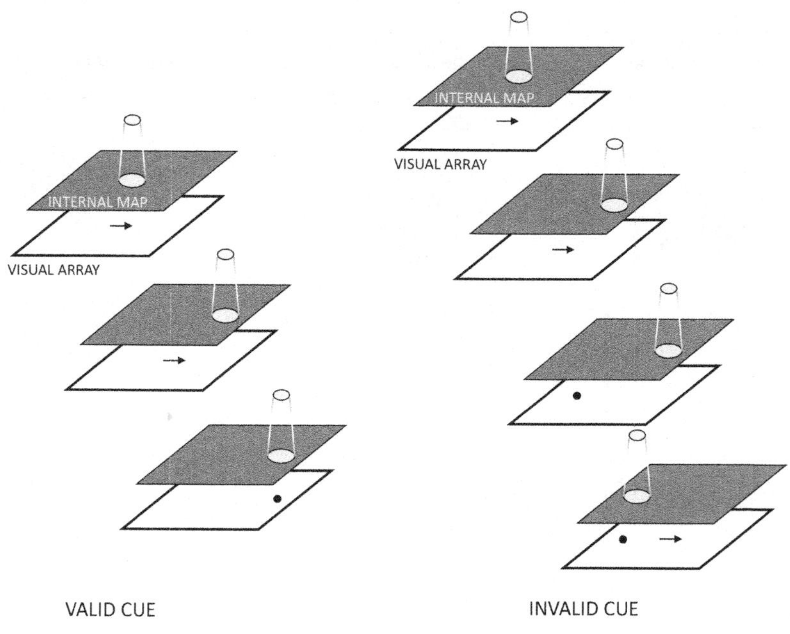

Figure 4.12 The spotlight of attention in valid and invalid cases. The spotlight is an internal mechanism that operates over an internal representation of visual space, an internal map (cf. saliency map). The visual array corresponds to the visible field, the external world (e.g., the screen on which stimuli are projected). Redrawn from (Wright and Ward 2008, 21).

The resulting modulation of processing explains reaction time benefits in valid cueing and costs in invalid cueing.

Here's the question: given that the expectation is itself prioritizing one of the two locations as being likely task-relevant, why the need for an additional spotlight component? Christopher Summerfield and Tobias Egner note that "the behavioural and neural consequences of such probabilistic cueing are typically attributed exclusively to the effects of attention, even though this procedure also engenders perceptual expectations, as well as their fulfilment or violation" (Summerfield and Egner 2009, 403). Further, "the behavioural effects of expectation and attention are superficially identical; both attended and expected stimuli are detected and recognized more readily than unattended or unexpected" (Summerfield and Egner 2009, p. 405). If attention and expectation are distinct phenomena, we have two causal factors that explain observed behavior. The spotlight model holds that attention is the primary determinant of behavioral improvement. Accordingly, expectation's role would be to shift the spotlight of attention, so it functions as an indirect cause of behavior, mediated by attention.

What is the difference between expectation and attention? Christopher Summerfield and Floris de Lange have proposed tying expectation to the *probability* of the occurrence of an event and tying attention to the *task-relevance* of the event: "a stimulus can be conditionally probable or improbable, irrespective of whether it is relevant or irrelevant for behaviour" (Summerfield and de Lange 2014, 751). But consider this distinction in terms of the two biases in spatial cueing we have noted: intention and belief (expectation). Task-relevance is set by the intention which identifies a cue and two locations as relevant. Cue probability is represented in the expectation, first in a general way and then, with concrete cues, in a more specific way. In the cueing paradigm, however, cue probability and task-relevance converge, for cue probability concerns the probable location of the *task-relevant* stimulus. Nuttida Rungratsameetaweemana and John Serences call this a "conflation" of expectation and attention in the experiment (2019, 181). It is possible to make expectation and intention *orthogonal* to each other (Wyart et al. 2012), but this requires a different task than standard spatial cueing where intention and expectation both deal with task-relevance. The point is that, in spatial cueing, we cannot fully disentangle expectation from task-relevance.

Conflation raises a philosophical question: is expectation, a belief, *incorporated* into one's conception of the task? Do expectation and intention merge? The subject's initial intention is to detect a target at one of two locations, but given the cue, knowing which of these two is more likely to be the target location, the statistical knowledge can be incorporated into the subject's conception of the task. On this proposal, the expectation becomes part of the intention.

Setting the question of how expectation and intention are related aside, the point is that we have identified crucial factors that bias task performance. These roles would seem to render the spotlight unnecessary. After all, the "spotlighting function" is just that of a bias. If so, then we already have two biases that seem to do the work required, the subject's intention and expectation, two constructs that must be on the table to capture the subject's cognitive background, her knowledge of the task structure, and her knowledge of the cue probabilities. So consider the conditional expectation given the arrow pointing to R (Figure 4.13).

On the standard spotlight view, the expectation first shifts the spotlight mechanism of attention to R to modulate processing of R for task (Figure 4.14). What is clear is that the architecture of attention in Figure 4.14 is more complicated than that of Figure 4.13. Nature does not have to take the simple path, but empirically, why think that there is an extra mechanism as in Figure 4.14? Take any evidence for the attentional spotlight. Why isn't that just evidence for the underlying circuitry needed to connect expectation to the visual input capacities? Rather than argument by metaphor, what empirical data establish a third factor, the spotlight, that mediates between the biases already postulated?

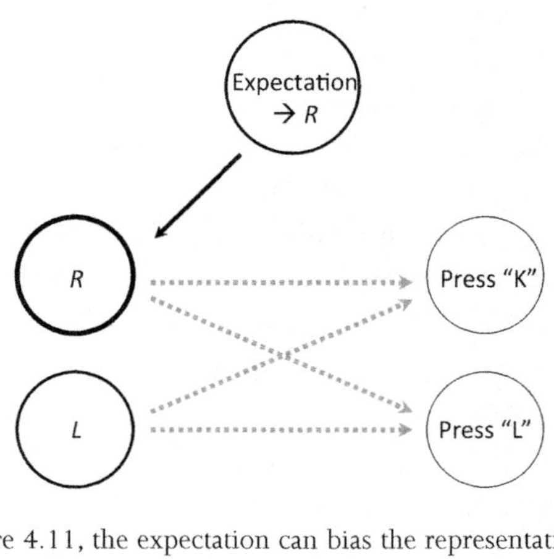

Figure 4.13 As in Figure 4.11, the expectation can bias the representation of R given that the cue indicates R.

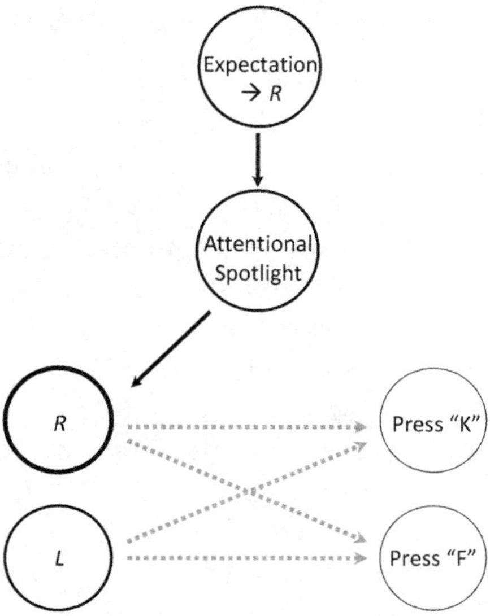

Figure 4.14 On the traditional picture, the spotlight mechanism changes the representation of R. As the spotlight must be directed to the cued location, the expectation biases the spotlight which then affects the representation of R.

Recall Britt Anderson's exercise where we cross out the word "attention" without explanatory loss (Chapter 2.2). Where expectation is the indirect cause influencing behavior through the direct cause, attention, would anything be lost if we crossed out attention? After all, expectation has to shift attention to the correct location, so couldn't expectation directly influence processing at that location? Erasing the attentional spotlight in Figure 4.14, we get Figure 4.13 with no clear explanatory loss. If we opt for simplicity, the mechanism of Figure 4.13 should be our starting point. This comports with Desimone and Duncan's (1995) deflationary proposal that eschewed the spotlight and took attention to arise after resolution in biased competition (Chapter 2.5). It also agrees with implementation of top-down attention in the PDP model of the Stroop Task (Chapter 2.6). The deflationary account does not do away with emphasizing mechanisms as informing the explanation of attention (see Figures 4.1 and 4.2). The spotlight is a metaphor capturing prioritizing mechanisms, but these are retained in Figure 4.13 without having to add an unnecessary appendage, a spotlight of attention.

4.5 Neural Systems of Attention

We have been examining expectations given a specific symbolic cue which points to the likely location of the target. Yet sometimes, the cue is invalid in that the target appears at the other position. Given validity versus invalidity, let us drop down to the implementation level and note an influential picture of neural attentional systems (see the influential framework of Michael Posner and Steven Petersen (1990, see also Petersen and Posner, 2012)).

Based on the work of Maurizio Corbetta and Gordon Shulman using functional imaging in humans, some theorists have identified two attentional networks: a dorsal and a ventral attention network (Corbetta and Shulman 2002). On this parcellation, the dorsal network is a frontoparietal system that includes the posterior parietal cortex with areas such as the intraparietal sulcus (IPS) and the superior parietal lobule (SPL) playing notable roles as well as the dorsal frontal cortex including the frontal eye field (FEF). A ventral network includes the temporoparietal junction (TPJ), the ventral frontal cortex, and other areas (Figure 4.15). Interestingly, some have argued that macaque monkeys lack a ventral attentional network (Patel et al. 2015).

Within this framework, the dorsal network is linked to top-down attention exemplified by indirect spatial cueing tasks. Initially, the ventral network was conceptualized as a "circuit breaker" that was sensitive to salient events and so subserved bottom-up attention (Corbetta and Shulman 2002). On this view, the ventral network alerts the dorsal network that task-irrelevant but salient stimuli should be considered. Based on later work, Corbetta and Shulman revised the circuit-breaking conception, suggesting that the ventral network collaborates with the dorsal network in tasks such as spatial cueing (Shulman and Corbetta 2012). Where the dorsal network processes goals and expectations to influence selective processing, the ventral network serves to reorient the system to task-relevant targets in unattended locations, as with invalid cues. (Figure 4.15 (c))

Elaborating these functions within the indirect spatial cueing paradigm, the dorsal network would be active during response to valid cues while additional contributions from the ventral network will engage when a target appears in an invalid location. That is, the ventral network serves to *reorient* the dorsal system to task-relevant objects in unexpected locations. Indeed, *salient* distractors seem to engage the dorsal and not the ventral system. Highly salient but irrelevant stimuli do not engage ventral network activation, while relevant stimuli of low salience do. Irrelevant stimuli can engage the ventral network if they share some features with relevant stimuli (Serences et al. 2005). We will return to some of these issues concerning when distractors distract in Chapter 6.7 in discussing the *contingent capture of attention.*

In general, when task-relevant attention is engaged, there seems to be a cascade of signals originating from prefrontal areas, including prefrontal cortex

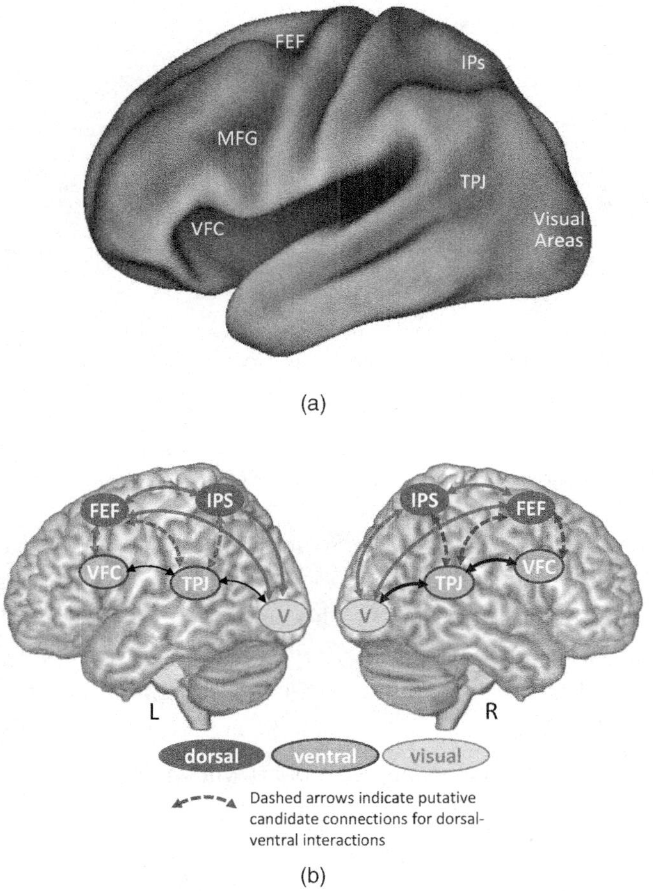

Figure 4.15 (a) Anatomical map of notable cortical areas viewed on the left hemisphere (corresponding regions also appear on the right). FEF: frontal eye field; IPS: intraparietal sulcus; MFG: middle frontal gyrus; VFC: ventral frontal cortex. (b) Elements of the dorsal and ventral attention systems. FEF: frontal eye; IPS: intraparietal sulcus; TPJ: temporoparietal junction; V: early visual cortex; VFC: ventral frontal cortex. I am grateful to Simone Vossel for providing the original figure, reproduced from Vossel, Simone, Joy J. Geng, and Gereon R. Fink. 2014. "Dorsal and Ventral Attention Systems: Distinct Neural Circuits but Collaborative Roles." *The Neuroscientist* 20 (2): 150–59. https://doi.org/10.1177/1073858413494269. Reproduced through Creative Commons Attribution 3.0 License from Sage Publications.

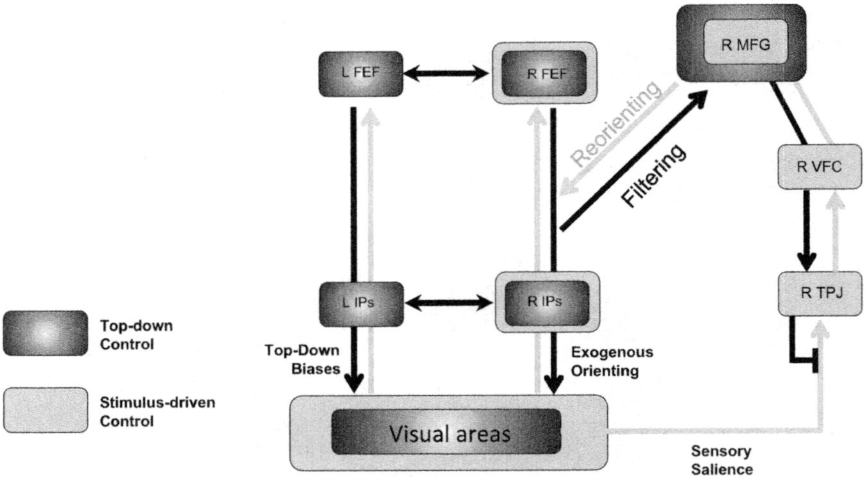

(c)

Figure 4.15 (Continue) (c) Interactions of the dorsal network (dark gray) and ventral network (light gray). Here, a reorienting to a signal is depicted, such as occurs in invalid cues. Dorsal regions IPS and FEF bias visual areas and via a filtering signal through the ventral network via MFG and then restrict ventral activation to behaviorally relevant stimuli. While the ventral network reorients the dorsal network, the latter biases stimulus-response selection as needed for the Selection Problem. Figure adapted from (Corbetta et al. 2008).

(PFC) and FEF that influence the lateral intraparietal area (LIP), as well as visual areas such as the middle temporal area (MT) and area V4. This fits a general conception of control that has the anchor of control in prefrontal areas, influencing visual processing more posteriorly, so moving toward the back of the head. We can then situate this at the implementation level as follows:

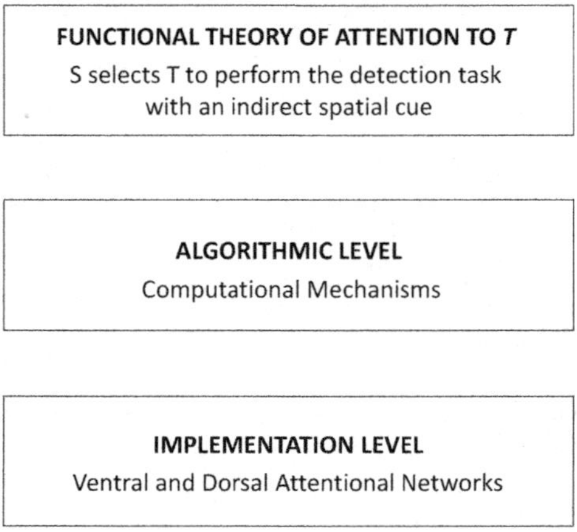

Figure 4.16 Fleshing out the Marrian Framework for visual attention to update expectation.

Strictly speaking, the activity of the network is engaged when the target appears, so this activity would be the implementation of the third movement of attention in Figure 4.2, but Figure 4.2 points to additional phenomena relevant to the implementation level in Figure 4.1. Note that we can split the functional characterization into two conditions, namely where attention engages given when the cue is valid and where attention initially incorrectly engages when the cue is invalid. In each case, the neural implementation will involve different parts of the networks just discussed.

4.6 Spatial Selection for Motor Preparation: The Premotor Theory

Let us move on to spatial selection in the task, the second movement of attention (Figure 4.2). The empirical sufficient condition demands that we specify the relevant response for spatial selection since as per our logical frame, attention is selection of a target to produce response R in task performance (Chapter 1.4). What is this response? The metaphorical answer would be this: Spatial attention involves shifting the attentional spotlight. Yet we have eschewed the spotlight in favor of concrete empirical posits.

We have examined the influence of expectation as a factor that induces a spatial bias. This suggests that a first step in spatial attention might be vigilance, a preparation to attend to targets at a specific location. Spatial vigilance reflects a phenomenon we are all familiar with. Consider waiting for the surprise guest to arrive at the front door. That said, if vigilance is a preparation to visually attend, it is not itself attention. Rather, if spatial attention is engaged, it should involve a specific response guided by visual selection of location R. Vigilance, in contrast, involves only a readiness or preparation to respond. We can represent the difference as follows:

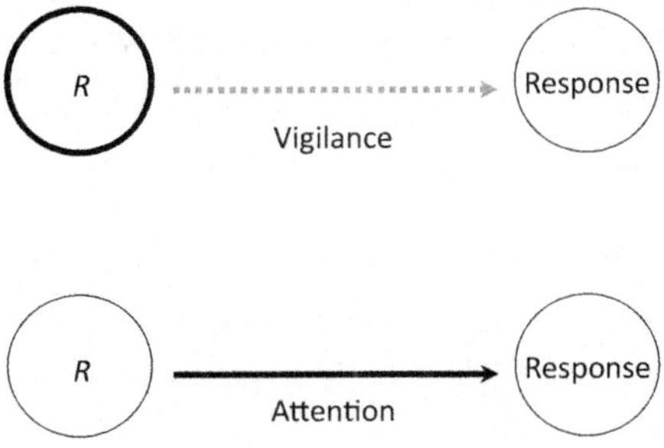

Figure 4.17 Vigilance versus Spatial Attention. The former is readiness to attend but not yet attention. The latter is attention engaged, selecting a spatial location, R, to inform a response.

We might call vigilance expectation-based "priming", but the present issue is that an adequate conception of visual spatial attention must identify the response. Consider *overt* visual attention as a clear case of visual spatial attention in that there is an obvious response, the eye movement, a saccade to a location R so that the subject fixates on it. Accordingly, the subject's visual selection of location R guides a saccade to R.

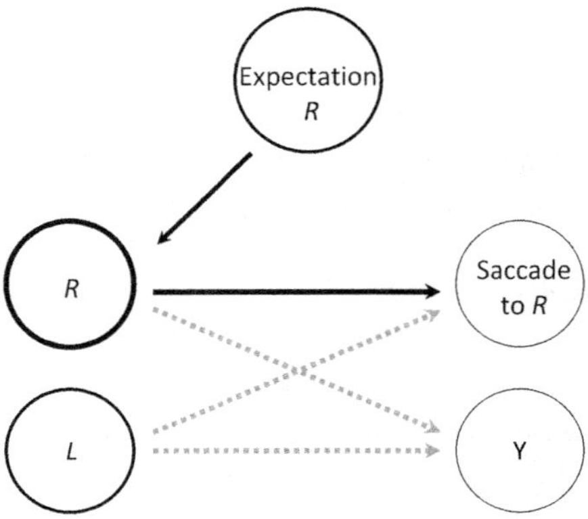

Figure 4.18 Expectation regarding R biasing overt visual attention to R.

Here, we have more than vigilance to R. We have attention proper in selection of R to program a saccade to R. This suggests a relevant response for *covert* attention to R where there is no eye movement. In covert visual spatial attention, the response can be *motor preparation* to move the eye. This is distinct from vigilance because, in that case, the preparation can be just in sensory representations. To make the proposal concrete, however, we must say more about what this preparatory response is. One proposal for what this response might be is given by the *Premotor Theory of Attention*. This theory aligns overt and covert attention as follows: where the response in overt attention is an actual eye movement, in covert attention the response is *preparation* of an eye movement. The circuitry responsible for generating overt attention is also that for generating covert spatial attention. Raymond Klein (1980) suggested that

> When attention to a particular location is desired, the observer prepares to make an eye movement to that location; the oculomotor readiness...has the effect of enhancing processing in or from sensory pathways dealing with information from the target location.
>
> (262)

Klein spoke of this as the *oculomotor readiness hypothesis*. Later, Giacomo Rizzolatti (1994) and colleagues proposed the Premotor Theory. Klein and Lawrence (2012) suggest that the oculomotor readiness hypothesis and the Premotor Theory "both propose that the process of preparing to move the eyes...*is* the mechanism by which endogenous covert spatial attention is engaged" (15). I focus on the more widely known Premotor Theory.

The Premotor Theory invokes a *spatial pragmatic map*, conceived as implemented by neurons with specific properties. Visual neurons have *receptive* fields that correspond to a region of space S such that if an appropriate stimulus is presented therein, the neuron will "fire", generating action potentials (spikes). These neurons carry information in their activity regarding stimuli in their receptive fields. Oculomotor neurons have motor *response* fields that correspond to a region of space such that a motor output toward that region is correlated with the neuron's activity. Some neurons have visual and motor properties, firing either when a stimulus is placed in S, triggering its visual receptive field, or a movement is directed toward S, triggering its motor response field. Such neurons code both a motor and visual spatial map of S (i.e., a spatial pragmatic map).

Rizzolatti et al. (1994) note three central tenets of the Premotor Theory:

1. The mechanisms responsible for spatial attention are localized in the spatial pragmatic maps.

2. Spatial attention is a consequence of the facilitation of neurons in the spatial pragmatic maps. This facilitation depends on the preparation to perform goal-directed, spatially coded movements.

3. Different spatial pragmatic maps become active according to the task requirements. (239–40)

A simple construal of the Premotor Theory for visual spatial attention holds that if spatial pragmatic maps do double duty as action and spatial representations, then when the subject intends to execute the represented action, this activates the action representation in the spatial pragmatic map. But since these representations are *spatial* pragmatic maps, the activation of the action representation of necessity activates the spatial representation. We can explicate overt and covert visual spatial attention using spatial pragmatic maps. We have overt attention when the spatial pragmatic maps are expressed in an overt eye movement to R that is guided by the visual

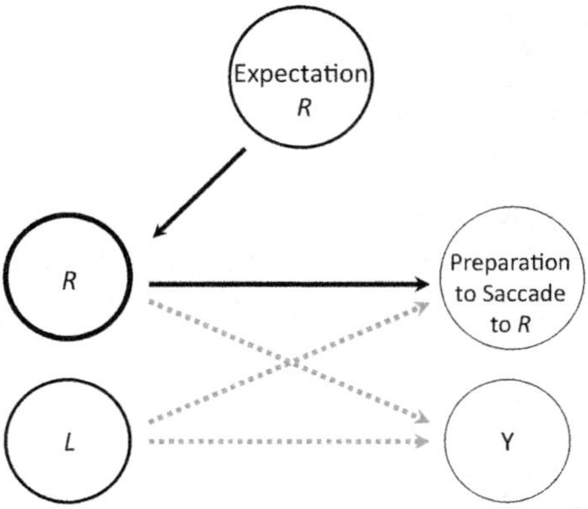

Figure 4.19 Expectation biasing motor preparation of saccade to R. Compare with Figure 4.18.

representation of R. We have covert attention when the same map is active but only sufficient to *prepare* an eye movement. Here, an eye movement is not generated. In this case, the output is a readiness to move (Figure 4.19). On the Premotor Theory, we have covert visual spatial attention in spatial cueing when there is a motor preparation to generate an eye movement to R. Is there evidence for actual motor preparation?

Consider two formulations of the Premotor Theory: the *identity* and the *causal* versions (I leave out constitution formulations). The former holds that preparing an eye movement to R *just is* visually attending to R for the systems in question. This has an implication regarding neural implementation, namely that the neural circuits for preparing an eye movement to R just *are* the neural circuits for visual spatial attention to R. Identity seems to be what is intended in the classical statements of the Premotor Theory.

The causal formulation is weaker, presenting necessary or sufficient conditions or both.

Sufficiency: If there is preparation to move the eye to R, this is sufficient to cause visual covert spatial attention to R.

Necessity: There is visual covert spatial attention to R *only* if there is preparation to move the eye to R.

Both versions of the Premotor Theory have implications regarding neural implementation. The top-down network of visual spatial attention in primates involves several areas: the FEF in the frontal lobe that connects to the lateral interparietal area (LIP) as well as to other visual areas including area V4. FEF is also connected to a subcortical structure, the superior colliculus (SC), which is necessary for generating saccadic eye movements (for an overview, see (Munoz 2002)). SC is also necessary for the implementation of attentional effects since inactivating SC can block attention even if the standard neural signatures in cortex remain, such as changing the strength of response (gain modulation; see (Zénon and Krauzlis 2012) for a powerful demonstration of this). Notably, stimulating FEF neurons with a sufficiently strong electrical current can generate saccadic movements.

Tirin Moore and Mazyar Fallah (2001) collected evidence that FEF supports covert attention. In their experiment, while a monkey fixates on a central point, stimulation of FEF neurons with a strong enough current generates a saccadic eye movement to its response field. Moore and Fallah then had monkeys perform a change detection task: to release a held lever when a target changed in luminance. The target was not at the fixation point but within the response field of a recorded neuron. Stimulating FEF neurons at lower current levels that did not generate eye movements, Moore and Fallah observed that detection task performance was enhanced when FEF stimulation occurred while a target was present in the neuron's response field, the location to which the eye would have moved at higher currents. So activating an FEF neuron whose motor field is at R facilitates target detection at R. While stimulation at lower currents did not induce a saccade, it led to attention-like effects on neural activity and performance. This is consistent with Sufficiency. Stimulation at FEF in the conditions at issue seems sufficient for covert attention to R (for parallel work in humans, see (Ruff et al. 2006)). The idea is that the neural machinery for saccadic movement was activated sufficiently to lead to signatures of attention but without generating a saccade. This is a "premotor" effect.

Later work suggested that electrical stimulation of FEF neurons with a motor field at location R induces attentional effects in neurons in other visual areas whose receptive fields are at R. Moore and Katherine Armstrong (2003) found that stimulation of FEF neurons at levels insufficient to induce a saccadic eye movement did increase the response of V4 neurons whose receptive fields overlapped the FEF response fields. Thus, stimulation of FEF neurons led to changes in V4 neuronal activity, an effect often taken as a neural correlate of attention, a change in neural gain (e.g., response intensity). Interestingly, stimulation of FEF neurons whose motor fields did *not* coincide with the V4 neuron's receptive field led to suppression of the response of V4 neurons whose receptive fields are at R. These effects in V4 were observed about 40 milliseconds (ms) after stimulation at FEF, consistent with FEF being the source of the changes. This provides support for causal sufficiency on the assumption that microstimulation of FEF at low currents induces motor preparation for a saccade.

Can we draw stronger conclusions? The identity formulation entails that the neural substrate for motor preparation of an eye movement is the substrate for visual spatial attention. Against this, Pierre Pouget et al. (2009) argued that the FEF neurons that influence V4 as in the Moore and Armstrong results are *anatomically distinct* from the FEF neurons that play a role in eye movement. Specifically, the relevant FEF neurons for each circuit reside in different layers of the cortex, those for movement in excitatory pyramidal neurons in cortical layer 5, while those targeting V4 reside largely in layers 2/3 (the cortex has six layers). That said, the point might not be decisive since the neurons in each layer might be interconnected (for Pouget et al.'s response to this worry, see op. cit. p. 11). There are arguments that the current body of evidence speaks against the identity formulation of the Premotor Theory (Smith and Schenk 2012). The causal formulation, however, is left open, and further work is needed to decide whether it is correct. Thus, it might be that some of the mechanisms of spatial attention involve circuits tied to preparing eye movement.

To summarize, since visual spatial vigilance does not entail visual spatial attention (Figure 4.18), we have canvassed responses that must engage when spatial attention is deployed. The Premotor Theory provides one answer: visual spatial selection informs motor preparation in covert visual spatial attention. Readers disinclined to the Premotor Theory might consider alternate output responses. As it stands, the second part of the Marrian explanation of indirect spatial cueing is that the subject selects a spatial location to prepare a response to that location or to initiate a state of vigilance to that location. We have fleshed this out in terms of motor readiness linked to the neural substrate of saccadic eye movement, with emphasis on the roles of FEF and V4 in spatial attention as neural implementation. This suggests the partial Marrian structure in Figure 4.20.

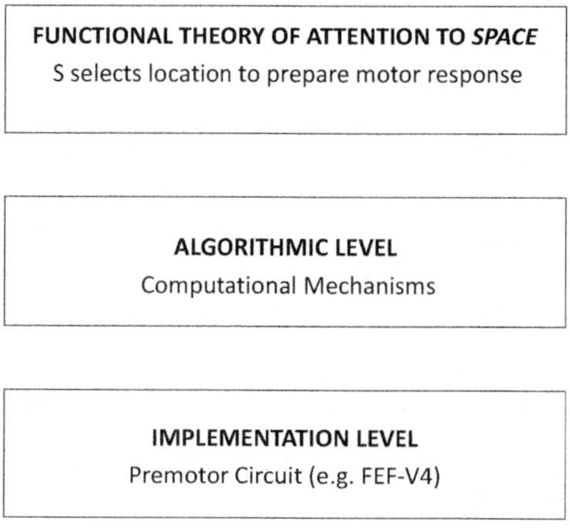

Figure 4.20 Partial filling in of the explanatory framework for covert visual spatial attention.

4.7 Facilitating Target Detection

Let us now consider attention to the target, the third movement of attention (Figure 4.2). There are a variety of possible mechanisms explaining enhanced target detection (e.g., (Lu and Dosher 2009)). One is that attending to a location increases spatial resolution at that location leading to better detection of spatial features. Yaffa Yeshurun and Marisa Carrasco provided evidence for this effect by predicting, and demonstrating, that attention can impair performance in contexts in which increased spatial resolution is *disadvantageous*, namely in certain forms of texture discrimination (Yeshurun and Carrasco 1998). The consequences of visual spatial attention are extensively reviewed by Carrasco (Carrasco 2011). We discuss some of her research in Chapters 10.3 and 10.4.

Another way that attentional targeting can be improved is by improving signal-to-noise ratio. These issues are dealt with comprehensively in signal detection theory (SDT). We will operate with an intuitive sense of the theory (Green and Swets 1966; Macmillan and Creelman 2004). In spatial cueing, increased accuracy is one observed behavioral outcome. The subject will be more often correct than not when they pay attention versus when attention is directed elsewhere. In SDT, correct reports are *hits*. One way of being inaccurate, making a mistake, is reporting that the target is present when it is not, a *false alarm*. Under certain assumptions about the signal and noise distributions, hit and false alarm rates allow one to calculate two important factors on detection behavior: the subject's perceptual *sensitivity* and their response *criterion*. In effect, sensitivity is a measure of the difference between signal and noise distributions (specifically, the distance between the means of the distributions relative to their standard deviations). The criterion is a decision threshold that determines when the subject will report that a target is present in response to the activity of the perceptual sensor at issue. Notably, sometimes, when the signal is absent (no stimulus), noise in the activity of the sensor will cross the response threshold. If the subject then reports that a target is present, they give a false alarm.

Increasing sensitivity aids performance by separating signal from noise. Let's consider the criterion, specifically *conservative* versus *liberal* criteria. Imagine a jumpy airport security inspector with a liberal detection criterion for danger when examining the X-ray images of luggage during security screening. In light of their criterion, the liberal inspector will respond to every ambiguous image in the X-ray, such as a comb oriented in an odd way, as a danger (weapon). Consequently, they will flag the innocuous luggage for further screening, hence a false alarm. If you're in a hurry, this is not the agent for you. On the other hand, if you are afraid of hijackings, liberal criteria might set you at ease. The over-zealous inspector evinces a higher hit rate ("Phew!") but also more false alarms ("No! That's a comb! I'm going to miss my flight!"). In being more likely to respond to a signal, they are also more likely to report a hit when there is just noise and no (dangerous) signal. In contrast, a conservative criterion leads to less checking since the inspector will stop luggage only if there is *clearly* a danger. This means that said inspector will false-alarm less frequently but at the cost of fewer hits. Finally, note that given no shift in criterion, with an increase in sensitivity, increased hit rate can come with a *decrease* in false alarms (this is illustrated in Figure 2c (Luo and Maunsell 2019)).

Thomas Luo and John Maunsell speak of sensitivity and criterion as *components* of attention. Let us situate this proposal within the Marrian account we are elaborating for target detection. The task begins with the deployment of visual representations responsive to the target. The activity of this representation, or its neural substrate, is noisy, and sometimes it will be active when no stimulus is present. If the subject responds when this is the case, we have a false alarm; if the subject responds to the representation when there is a stimulus that triggers it, we have a hit. This provides the behavioral data that SDT unpacks for us in terms of sensitivity and criterion as factors that explain the patterns in the agent's response.

SDT provides an algorithmic, or at least formal, description of the underlying computations explaining certain aspects of target detection behavior. What of a potential neural implementation? Luo and Maunsell gathered evidence that the typical changes in neural activity in visual area V4 under conditions of attention were associated with shifts in sensitivity and not criterion (Luo and Maunsell 2015). In contrast, they found activity correlated with sensitivity and criterion in the lateral prefrontal cortex (Luo and Maunsell 2018).[1] The behavioral, formal, and neural approaches line up nicely in filling out the Marrian explanatory structure of what attention is, in this case that part of task performance that involves visual attention to a target at a location for detection report (I leave fleshing out the Marrian structure to readers as an exercise). In the next section, we continue examining lower levels of analysis that might apply to all three parts of our Marrian explanation: attention to the cue, to space, and to the target for report.

4.8 Algorithmic Components and Neural Implementation of Attention

In the previous sections, we noted the correlation between activity in neurons in visual area V4 when the animal is paying attention to a target to which the neuron is responsive and changes in the animal's perceptual sensitivity. How might we model those changes? Consider biased competition as connected to the Buridan Selection Problem (Chapter 2.2), namely a subject facing multiple, qualitatively identical stimuli with no basis for choice. This competition between action possibilities at the behavioral level is mirrored in neural competition at the brain level. Kia Nobre and M. Marsel Mesulam explain the latter as driven by

> the limits of perception [that] arise because of the inherently competitive organization of perceptual systems. Through the visual hierarchy, convergence of inputs from afferent areas leads to increasingly complex receptive-field properties with increasingly lower spatial and temporal resolution. At downstream areas, such as the inferior temporal (IT) cortex, multiple objects or attributes can fall within the receptive field of the same neuron. Averaging the response across all the stimuli impinging on the receptive field would conflate the coding of the various stimuli and abolish discriminability. To be informative, the neuron should respond according to one of the multiple competing stimulus sources. To be adaptive, the neuron should respond according to the most relevant stimulus source.
>
> (Nobre and Mesulam 2014, 106)

They mean *behavioral* relevance (op. cit. p. 106). Further

> the sites and temporal characteristics of modulatory mechanisms are likely to be highly task-dependent, and to be influenced by the specific types of features that need to be discriminated and the number of competing response tendencies that need to be handled for accurate task performance.
>
> (op. cit. p. 109)

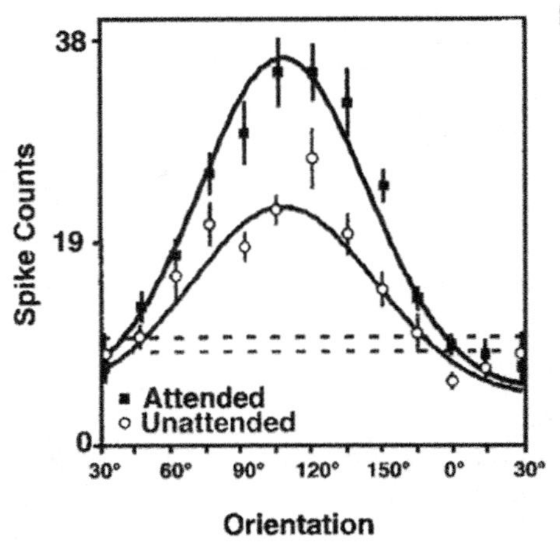

Figure 4.21 V4 neuron under conditions of attention and inattention. Reprinted from *Neuron* 23 (4) C. J. McAdams and John H R Maunsell. "Effects of Attention on the Reliability of Individual Neurons in Monkey Visual Cortex." 23 (4): 765–73, 1999 with permission from Elsevier.

We are going to examine the computational implementation of biased competition in the *divisive normalization* model of attention (better: model of neural modulations during attention) as a model of top-down modulation by intention and expectation. These two will be understood to influence processing via the "attention field" (see below). To begin, consider a basic neural effect, here as observed by Carrie McAdams and John Maunsell (Figure 4.21). The figure plots the response of a V4 neuron to a Gabor patch in its receptive field at various orientations. Note that for each orientation, the neuron responds differently between the unattended and attended conditions (the difference between the two curves). This is *multiplicative gain*, a type of modulation of the neuron's response to an input. One can analogize this to turning up the intensity of a signal, like turning up the volume.

On its own, nothing in the difference between these curves entails attention. An exercise I do with neuroscience students is to withhold the figure legend and ask them to explain why the neuron might show different activity in two conditions. A number of explanations can be offered, but consider a simple one: appropriate changes to the intensity of the stimulus at each orientation, literally modifying the gain of the external signal, can affect the internal gain of the neural response. To rule out alternative explanations, we need additional premises. In McAdams and Maunsell's case, they set the animal's attention through the task. Specifically, they manipulated the animal's attention by training it to perform a task with a cue that indicated that the stimulus within the neuron's receptive field either (a) is task-relevant and so to be acted on or (b) is not the target, with the task-relevant stimulus located outside the receptive field. This manipulation is just implementing a specific empirical sufficient condition set by the task: directing the animal to select specific targets in different locations in order to respond to as trained. In this way, the animal's attention is set.[2]

Divisive normalization computations implemented by neural processing (Carandini and Heeger 2012) institute biased competition. A number of different models of divisive normalization have been presented but let's focus on the model by John Reynolds and David Heeger (2009). Notably, their core figure models a computational solution to a familiar problem, the Buridan Selection Problem: two qualitatively identical targets. (For other normalization models of attention, see (Lee and Maunsell 2009; Boynton 2009)).

In Figure 4.22, imagine the investigator recording the activity of neural populations in area V4. The stimuli are two Gabor patches (orientations) presented equidistant from the point of fixation in the *Stimulus Array*. As the

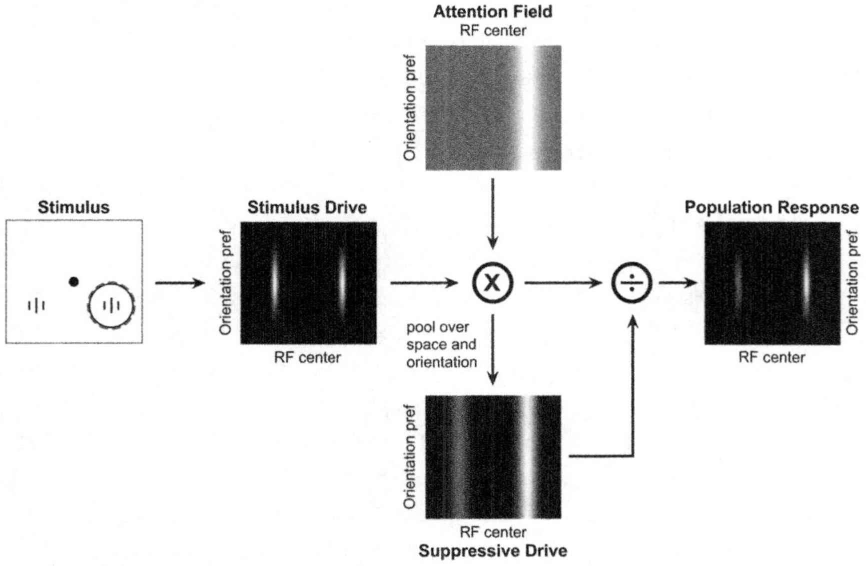

Figure 4.22 Reynolds and Heeger Model of Divisive Normalization. Reprinted from *Neuron*, 16 (2), John H. Reynolds and David J. Heeger. "The Normalization Model of Attention." 168–85. 2009 with permission from Elsevier.

stimuli are qualitatively identical, we have a Buridan Selection Problem (Figure 2.2; cf. locations L versus R at the beginning of a spatial cueing task). Given this, the population response of all the relevant V4 neurons does not differentiate between the two stimuli, as represented by two identical vertical bars in the *Stimulus Drive*. These bars represent the activity of neurons whose receptive field is responsive to either the left or right location and which evinces different tuning, namely different responses across the orientation dimension. We can imagine that like Buridan's donkey, the subject in this experiment initially has no basis for choice. Correlatively, the activity of the animal's brain, as represented by the Stimulus Drive, does not yet differentiate L and R beyond spatial location. Recall as well our depiction of the Selection Problem in indirect cueing (Figure 4.6 above). So the Buridan property at the behavioral level when confronted with identical stimuli is mirrored at the neural level.

In this experiment, the animal ultimately acts on R because they receive a cue indicating R (cf. Figure 4.3). This is depicted in Figure 4.22 as a *direct* cue, a cue at the target location, but it does not alter the present point to think of R as indirectly cued. The result of cueing is that the brain shifts its response. If the subject attends to R, the brain must also select R. This is seen in the output *Population Response* that depicts an increase in the activity of neurons responsive to R relative to their activity in the Stimulus Drive, while neurons responsive to L decrease in activity relative to their activity in the Stimulus Drive. We can locate McAdams and Maunsell's gain-modulated V4 neuron within this figure. Its activity in the unattended condition is given as one of the points in the bar on the right in the Stimulus Drive, while its increased activity in the attended condition is given as one of the points of the bar on the right in the Population Response.[3]

Why do the animal's behavior and correlatively the neural modulation shift? Buridan's donkey moves when it acquires a bias, such as a cue from the farmer to eat the right and not left bale that leads to the animal deciding (intending) to eat the right bale. In the present case, the imagined subject receives a cue to respond to R and consequently acts on R. Let's assume that the cue is 100% valid and so eliminates uncertainty about the target location. The information in the cue changes the animal's thinking, for now it intends to act on R and/or its expectations regarding the target location change to focus on R. This provides the source of the top-down bias both on behavior and, necessarily, on the animal's brain and so provides a model for the top-down bias of expectation and intention discussed earlier.

In the model, the bias from intention/expectation is implemented in what Reynolds and Heeger call the *Attention Field*. (see Figure 1 in Carandini and Heeger (2012) where the field is labeled "Attention/Attentional Gain Factors".) In addition, the model identifies a source of suppression of neural response in the *Suppressive Drive* which we can understand as competition for representational resources between neurons responsive to R and other visual neurons such as those responsive to L. This is the divisive normalization (division). Focus, however, on the Attention Field. Again, let us assume that the cue is 100% valid so the subject in this case knows that the target will be at R. The animal updates their expectation or intention to act on R. This shifts the animal's behavior, how it solves the Selection Problem, but it also shifts perceptual processing in visual areas. We might interpret the Attention Field signal as part of the representation of the target's location in the animal's task representation (intention and expectation), implemented as a spatial bias to the location of R (right bright vertical bar in the Attention Field). I intend to act *there* (R), or I expect the target to be *there*. In either case, the animal is ready to respond to (is vigilant for) the stimulus in order to perform the instructed task. On this proposal, there is no spotlighting beyond the biasing signal from the intention or expectation. Those suffice to resolve competition, putting the subject in a better position to act on intended or expected targets. We can then begin to explain the third movement of attention using the explanatory framework of Figure 4.1.

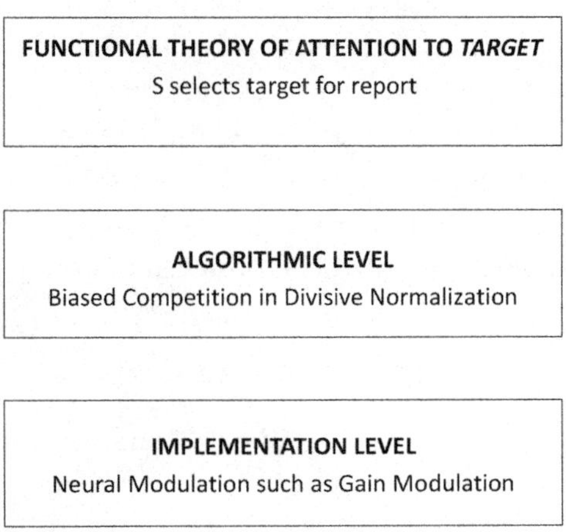

Figure 4.23 Partial filling in of the explanatory framework for visual attention to the target.

What we have, then, is a link between the functional description of attention as selection to guide behavior in a Buridan case, one we mapped out in general terms earlier. The Buridan case is given a concrete implementation in spatial cueing where, at the beginning of the experiment, two locations are equally likely to contain the target. A cue provides a bias that shifts the agent's orientation toward a specific location, and when the target appears there, the agent acts. The resolution of competition (the behavioral possibilities in the Selection Problem) has as an algorithmic correlate in the divisive normalization computation where a bias likewise resolves neural competition. This resolution leads to changes in information processing that we can draw on to explain the agent's performance. The critical point is that these different levels of analysis are unified by the empirical sufficient condition that provides the initial functional structure of the task with respect to which we map the algorithmic and neural details in a unified explanation that answers the question, what is attention in this task?

4.9 Conclusion

Our goal was to review some of the empirical and theoretical work using one of the key attentional paradigms to show how the results can be integrated into an explanation of attention. The key is to elaborate the structure of the task and the role of selection, attention, therein. This structural posit regarding how the task is performed, as implemented in the paradigm, connects work at other levels of analysis. Analyzing performance in indirect spatial cueing, we identified three stages of attention as well as relevant computational algorithms and correlated neural activity that might serve as the neural substrate for algorithms and the subject's performance. Much relevant work has been left out, and the explanatory structure is incomplete. Yet enough has been laid out that the unity of the noted achievements of the science of attention is clear. What the Common Conception allows us is a way to integrate these experimental and computational achievements in a unified picture.

Suggested Readings

Wright and Ward (2008) provide an excellent and accessible overview of orienting and attention. For an overview of historical work on attention, see Hatfield (1998) and Mole (2011), who discuss psychological work on attention pre-1950. Tsotsos (2011, Chapter 1) presents a nice overview as well. A succinct account of the psychology of attention from the 1950s onwards is provided in Driver (2001). Pashler (1998) is a monograph discussion of similar terrain. Alan Allport (1993) raised questions about attention as a mechanism, and similar questions have been raised by Britt Anderson, Rich Krauzlis, and Bernhard Hommel et al. (Anderson 2011; Krauzlis et al. 2014; Hommel et al. 2019) (see also recent update by Anderson (2023) and Krauzlis and colleagues (Krauzlis et al. 2023)). Sabine Kastner and Kia Nobre's edited collection provides a comprehensive overview of all aspects of attention by some of the key figures in the field, including their own reviews (Nobre and Kastner 2018). Marlene Cohen and John Maunsell (2011) provide a nice overview of many of the modulations in neural activity correlated with attention. Marisa Carrasco (2011) provides an overview of 25 years of research on visual attention and overlaps with Alan Allport's earlier skeptical article on the mechanisms of attention (Allport 1993). Thomas Luo and Maunsell review SDT as identifying components of attention (Luo and Maunsell 2019).

Notes

1 For interesting work on these issues in the subcortical structure, the superior colliculus, see work of Richard Krauzlis and colleagues (Lovejoy and Krauzlis 2010, 2017; Zénon and Krauzlis 2012).

2 There are other neural effects seen while animals deploy attention. Aside from multiplicative gain, there is also *contrast gain*, which can roughly be understood as a shift in sensitivity (see (Reynolds and Heeger 2009)). We focus here on gain modulation.

3 Note that not all visual neurons exhibit normalization (Lee and Maunsell 2009; Ni et al. 2012). For those that don't, one can think of their response as an answer to a stricter question: is my preferred stimulus in my receptive field? Where the preferred stimulus is present, the neuron fires strongly, even if there are non-preferred stimuli present as well. A non-normalization neuron's response to multiple stimuli is not the weighted average of its response to each stimulus individually. Indeed, non-normalization neurons do not show the effects of attentional modulation that normalization neurons do. Normalization is also not restricted to attention. Matteo Carandini and David Heeger (2012), for example, argue that normalization is a "canonical neural computation", one that is computed throughout the brain. Normalization, then, might be a fairly ubiquitous feature of neural computation, including its specific role in biasing selective processing for behavior (i.e., attention).

5

VISUAL SEARCH

5.1 Introduction

"Visual search" in cognitive science names an important experimental paradigm. In typical implementations, subjects move their eyes to search for defined targets. In this chapter, we survey some key results and models. The discussion is selective and certainly not exhaustive. Our aim is to begin the project of elaborating an integrated explanation of what this form of attention is.

We will focus on two instances of selection for response in typical visual search:

1. Selection of a target/location to move the eye to in order to fixate the target/location.

2. Selection of the targeted item to decide whether it is a target or a distractor, for (potential) report.[1]

We can state two corresponding empirical sufficient conditions to articulate a functional theory of attention in visual search:

A. If the subject visually selects a target/location to guide the eye to fixate in visual search paradigms, the subject is visually attending to that target/location.

DOI: 10.4324/9781003223450-6

B. If the subject visually selects an item at a location to decide whether it is a target or distractor, for potential report, the subject is visually attending to that item.

Intuitively, subjects move the eye, or shift attention, to locations with potential targets. Subjects must then make a decision about the identity of those targets. These conditions help link algorithms and models of information processing to possible neural implementations in visual search. We shall deal with each stage separately since visual search can be done covertly (i.e., without eye movement). There can be visual search tasks for which the first empirical sufficient condition is not applicable.

In Section 5.2, we discuss standard behavioral data in visual search. Sections 5.3 and 5.4 explore two well-known theories of visual search due to Anne Treisman and Jeremy Wolfe respectively. Those sections focus initially on (2), and so on the processes needed to select targets for decision making. In Section 5.5, we introduce an algorithm for computing saliency and priority, leading to saliency and priority maps that contribute to explaining eye movement and shifts of spatial attention. This emphasizes (1). Section 5.6 canvases some data regarding the neural implementation of these maps. Since visual search defines its target by features, Section 5.7 examines feature attention and its neural basis pointing to the role of feature templates in working memory. Finally, in Section 5.8, we examine complications for classical explanations of search due to the properties of the human retina as argued for by Ruth Rosenholtz.

5.2 The Visual Search Paradigm: Behavioral Data

A standard search task requires subjects to locate a target amid a set of distractors. The number of items in the visual array gives the *set size*. There are two experimental conditions: arrays with *target present* and those with *target absent*. The subject reports whether a target was present or absent (*yes* in the first condition, *no* in the second). Consider targets defined by a single unique feature. For example, one might look for a red T against a set of green Ts where color is an individuating feature identifying the target as red versus the green distractors. In these situations, the target is a *pop-out* (Figure 5.1).

In *conjunction search*, targets are defined by multiple features, such as a green T target in a mix of brown Ts and green Xs as distractors. One cannot locate the target on the basis of a single feature. After all, the target is green, but it shares this feature with distractor Xs; the target is a "T" but it shares this

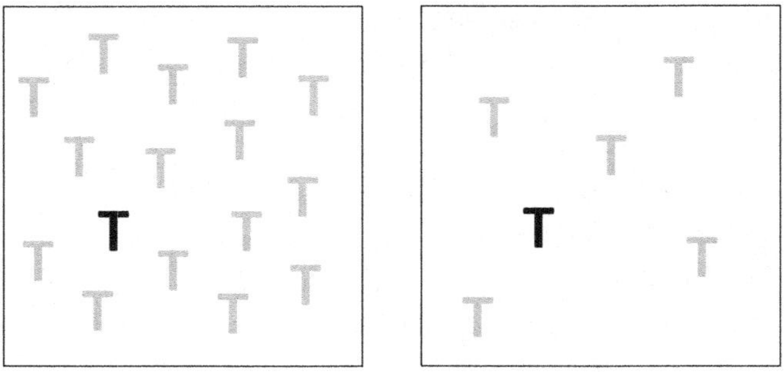

Figure 5.1 Pop-out. The black "T" pops out even when set size increases.

feature with distractor brown items. To identify the target requires locating the conjunction of green and T (Cf. Figure 5.2).

A standard performance measure is reaction time, how long it takes the subject to make a report. The classic finding is that where targets are defined by a unique feature, search time is largely unaffected by set size. So the red "T" *pops out* among green "T"s no matter how many green "T"s are present. Plotting reaction time relative to set size, the slope is about zero (i.e., reaction time is nearly constant despite increasing the number of distractors). On the other hand, where the target is not defined by a unique feature, slope is affected by set size. A slope between 20 and 40 ms/item is commonly observed for reporting target present, while a slope of 40 to 80 ms/item is observed for terminated search where the report is target-absent. That is, there is a 2:1 ratio of slope values in target-absent versus target-present arrays. The thought is that on average, where the target is present, one will find the target half-way through a sequential search. If

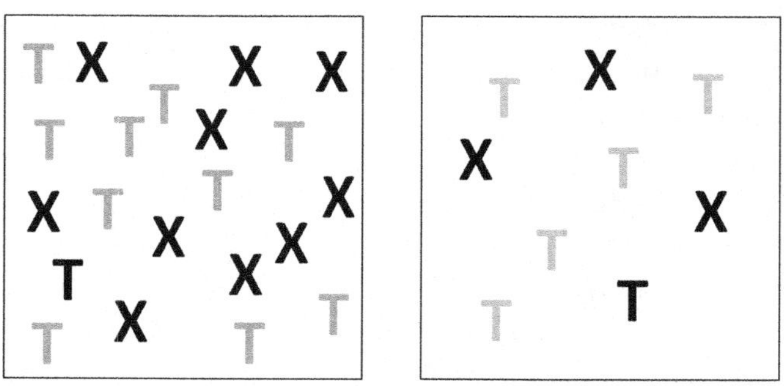

Figure 5.2 Conjunction Search is more difficult as set size increases. Here, find the black "T" among gray "T"s and black "X"s. Perhaps it feels like you are sequentially looking at each symbol to decide if it is the target, a *serial* search.

search requires the sequential deployment of a spotlight, *serial* search, then the internal spotlight moves faster than the eye, which generates perhaps two to three saccades/second. This and other data led to Anne Treisman and colleagues developing the Feature Integration Theory of Attention.

5.3 Feature Integration Theory of Attention

In its initial version, Feature Integration Theory (FIT) treats visual object recognition as a constructive process where basic visual features like color, shape, and motion are processed in separate feature maps ((Treisman and Gelade 1980); for an informative, detailed assessment, see (Quinlan 2003)). The visual system *binds* features to form object representations. Visual object recognition involves two stages: a *preattentive* feature detection stage and an *attentional* binding stage.

Treisman and Gary Gelade (1980) write that in FIT:

> features are registered early, automatically, and in parallel across the visual field, while objects are identified separately and only at a later stage, which requires focused attention. We assume that the visual scene is initially coded along a number of separable dimensions, such as color, orientation, spatial frequency, brightness, direction of movement. In order to recombine these separate representations and to ensure the correct synthesis of features for each object in a complex display, stimulus locations are processed serially with focal attention. Any features which are present in the same central "fixation" of attention are combined to form a single object. Thus focal attention provides the "glue" which integrates the initially separable features into unitary objects. Once they have been correctly registered, the compound objects continue to be perceived and stored as such. (98)

Using our logical frame, *S m-attends to T to respond R*, the attentional spotlight can be captured in this way where T = features represented in feature maps and R = binding for object representation:

> *S* selecting features at location *L* in visual feature maps in order to bind them for representing objects is *S* attending to these features.

The modality m is visual since we are examining visual processing. Since attention selects from feature maps, the postulated process is internal to the

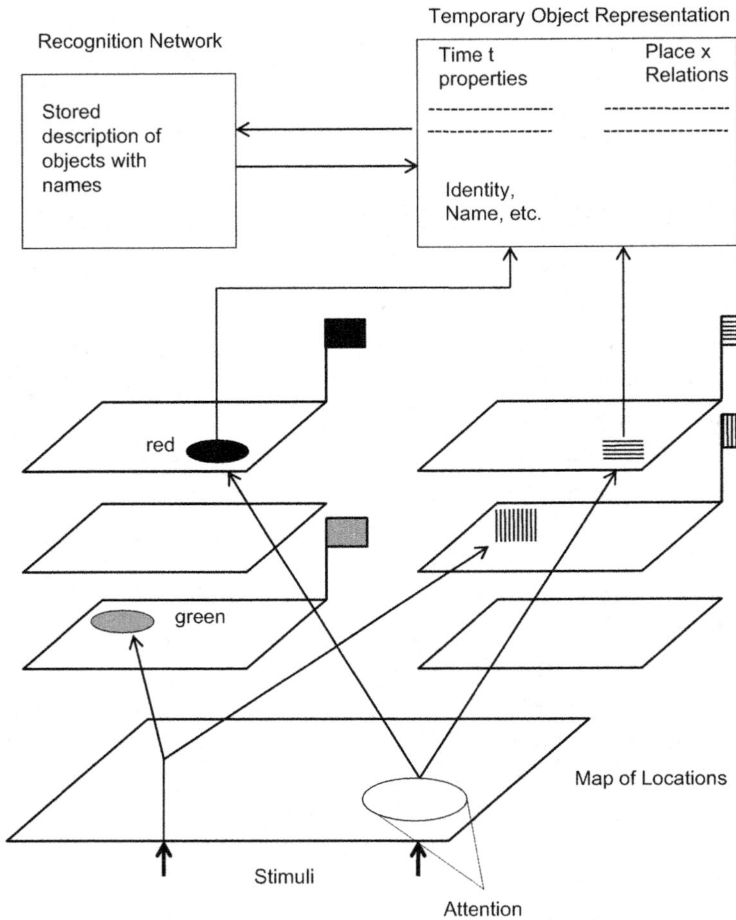

Figure 5.3 Feature integration theory. Redrawn from Treisman (1998). The spotlight of attention focuses on a location represented in a spatial map that does not code features. Features are coded in separate feature maps which give information that the feature is present (the 'flag' in the feature map) and information about the location of the feature. Attention to a location then selects certain features to be bound into an object representation which can then be compared with stored information or used in other tasks.

visual system. What then is the subject *S*? It doesn't appear to be the experimental subject, the person. After all, they do not select features in visual feature maps to create visual object representations. Indeed, they have no idea that there are such internal maps. Rather, part of their brain does so, specifically a mechanism, a spotlight. So let *S* = spotlight, the internal mechanism at issue where the spotlight is something *in* the subject (the subject ≠ the spotlight). Attention in FIT is a spotlight mechanism visually selecting features for the purpose of binding. Effectively, attention is selection for object representation (this is a mechanism that implements the function of selection for perception; Chapter 3.7).[2]

FIT holds that processing of features happens concurrently or *in parallel* without capacity limitations. This is a preattentive stage because it occurs prior to the involvement of the attentional spotlight. The attentive stage begins with the serial deployment of the spotlight binding features to yield object representations that are stored in *object files*. Note that the attentional spotlight is required for correct binding. Unattended features could be bound, but the absence of attention can lead to *illusory conjunctions* of features (Treisman and Schmidt 1982). Treisman's preferred model prioritizes an initial *master map of locations* which identifies where feature discontinuities are located but does not specify *which* feature is *where*. (Treisman (1998) noted that one of her versions of FIT has feature maps feeding into a master map of locations.) The attentional spotlight initiates the identification of features at the location it targets, retrieving content from feature maps. "Locations in the feature maps are made available to control responses and conscious experience only through their links to those locations in the master-map that are currently selected by the attentional 'spotlight'" (Treisman 1998, 203). Note that Treisman modified FIT over time, and substantive discussions of her theory should include later elaborations (Treisman 1998, 2006).

In conjunction search, attention must be deployed serially to one location at a time in order to verify the conjunction of the targeted feature. In search for a unique item, "an item with a highly distinctive feature tends to 'call attention' to itself; this is the basis of the 'pop-out' phenomenology" (Treisman 1998 226). Pop-out will result from the relevant feature map modulating the master map so that the spotlight is pulled to the pop-out location. One might be able to identify the presence of a unique feature without binding if the relevant map *flags* the presence of the feature. There are separate feature maps for each hue. If a target is uniquely red, the feature map that represents the red dimension will flag the presence of red. Here, an attentional spotlight is not needed to bind features (Treisman 1998, 1296). One question is whether the scanning of the flag is done by the spotlight or by some other selective mechanism, and if so, what is that mechanism's relation to attention? Is it another type of attention?

The 2:1 observed slope ratio in conjunction search led to the postulation of a serial attentional spotlight. However, subsequent data from various labs, including Treisman's, suggested a more complicated story. Pop-out effects, a flat search slope, are seen for some feature conjunctions (first reported by (Nakayama and Silverman 1986)) and indeed even for a case of triple conjunction search ((Wolfe et al. 1989), experiment 9). Furthermore, not all searches exhibited a 2:1 slope ratio (Wolfe 1998). One response is to allow for parallel and serial *aspects* of search. Consider as an estimate that object recognition processes needed to identify a target proceed at a rate of 100 ms/item. Yet reaction time in visual search suggests target processing at 20 to 40 ms/item. How can this be? Wolfe and colleagues have used a carwash metaphor as a heuristic (Moore and Wolfe 2001). Like entry into a typical carwash, only one item can enter the object recognition system at a time, this capacity limit providing the rate-determining step in processing. Once an item is the object recognition system, however, recognitional processing happens in parallel just as multiple cars can be washed in a carwash even if only one car can enter at a time.

FIT's importance in the history of the theory of attention is hard to overstate. It gave rise to an active research program across many labs as visual search became one of the primary paradigms used to study visual attention. It was subsequently modified by Treisman and other labs, and an important development was Jeremy Wolfe's model of *Guided Search*.

5.4 Guided Search

We noted that conjunction search can have shallower search slopes than predicted by a serial process. Wolfe and colleagues suggested that feature search can be *guided*. He provides an intuitive example (Wolfe 2021a). Consider the earlier figure used to demonstrate conjunction search (cf. (Egeth et al. 1984)):

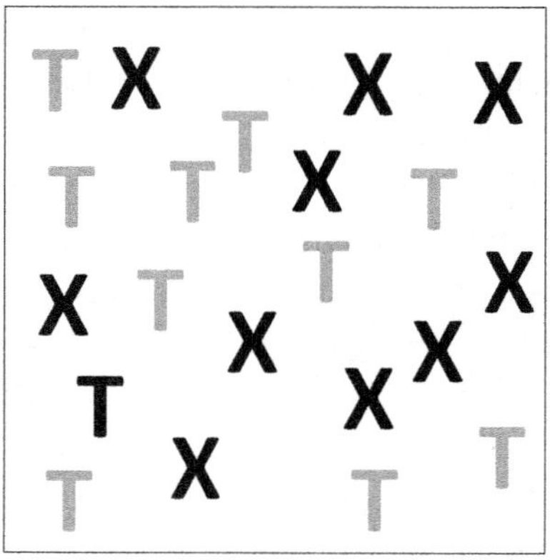

Figure 5.4 Conjunction search guided by knowledge that only the black letters can contain the target so that the gray letters can be ignored.

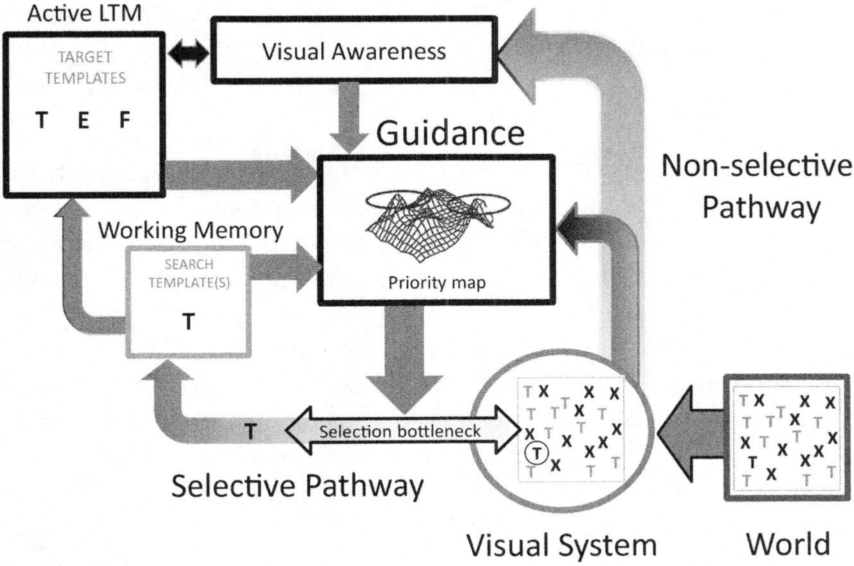

Figure 5.5 Guided Search 6.0. A subject in this experiment might be given three potential letter targets: black T, E, F. These are stored in active long-term memory (LTM). A cue, for example, might tell the subject that a "T" is the target for this trial. The basic features of "T", such as *black*, *horizontal*, and *vertical*, become the search template stored in working memory. These features guide (bias) computation of the priority map. This figure, a representation of part of the model, is adapted from Figure 3 in (Wolfe 2021). I am grateful to Jeremy Wolfe for providing the figure and permission to adapt it.

As Wolfe points out, you can focus your search on the black figures if you were informed antecedently that the target is black. That is, knowledge of the relevant color can guide search to be more effective.

Wolfe and colleagues developed a *Guided Search* model incorporating guidance by features. The most recent version is Guided Search 6.0 (Figure 5.5). Guided Search 6.0 identifies two important branching processes: a *selective pathway* and a *nonselective pathway*. The selective pathway incorporates many of the ideas in FIT, updated to account for new data. The guided part of visual search involves a bias on selection, due to a dynamic *priority map* that updates over the time of search. We discuss such maps in the next section. Visual search is also constrained by a capacity limitation, one that necessitates attention:

> There are capacity limits that require that many tasks can only be performed on one (or a very few) item/s at a time. Notably, for present purposes, this includes object recognition. Selective attention, as used here, refers to the

> processes that determine which items or regions of space will be passed through the bottleneck.
>
> (Wolfe 2021, 1064)

This assumption is one that Wolfe shares with Treisman, who implemented this capacity limitation in the binding process effected by the attentional spotlight (Wolfe 2012, 102). Wolfe also speaks of selective attention as the process that selects items to pass through the bottleneck, but in Guided Search 6.0, the factor depicted as biasing that process is the priority map and not an attentional spotlight. It is not clear that Guided Search 6.0 needs to postulate an additional factor called "attention" beyond the priority map (cf. our discussion of the Attention Field as spotlight in divisive normalization models, Chapter 4.8). Eliminating attention as an internal causal factor is consistent with the core of Guided Search 6.0 as a model of attention in visual search, ultimately of target selection for decision making. As we shall see in the next section, on most computational conceptions of the priority map, the map does not represent features. It is a spatial map, and the resulting bias on selection through the bottleneck must also be spatial. So features at the prioritized locations are escorted through the bottleneck to inform object representation processing.

Consider now the nonselective pathway. For example, some processing of the visual scene is part of the nonselective pathway. This processing is quick and seemingly without capacity limitations. The relevant scene properties are sometimes referred to collectively as the *gist*, a concept that has been explicated in different ways (for discussion, see (Koehler and Eckstein 2017, 1177–79)). Aude Oliva and colleagues have discussed gist as including "all levels of visual information—ranging from low-level features (e.g., color, contours) to intermediate (e.g., shapes, texture regions) and high-level information (e.g., activation of semantic knowledge)" ((Oliva 2005, 251); see also the pioneering work of Mary Potter (Potter and Levy 1969; Potter 1976)). Michelle Green and Oliva (2009) demonstrated that, in a forced choice task, subjects who were asked to report (yes/no) whether a briefly presented image belonged to a feature category could in some circumstances achieve 75% accuracy with as little as a 19-millisecond (ms) presentation of the image, in this case judging whether the stimulus depicted a natural environment (op. cit., Table 2, p. 468). Across the two types of categories they tested, namely *global properties* such as naturalness and navigability, and *basic-level features* such as being a desert, forest, and mountain, the mean maximum duration of stimulus presentation where there were *no* classification errors was 100 ms. Clearly, observers can rapidly extract diagnostic properties of a scene from very brief presentations.

We can incorporate the role of gist in the computation of priority in Guided Search. Consider a case presented by Antonio Torralba et al. (Torralba et al. 2006) as part of their model of generating a *scene-modulated saliency map* (see their Figure 1, p. 767; this is effectively a priority map). Imagine walking down a street with stores displaying gaudily colored signs. The elevated signs being so colorful are the most salient items. Yet you are looking for a friend. The ground level is the likely location of a pedestrian, unless your friend is a sign cleaner, so your eye movements linger on that lower part of the scene (Neider and Zelinsky 2006, Figures 1 and 2). Salience in terms of the prominence of features does not on its own explain your search. Torralba et al. note that knowledge of the scene structure along with statistical knowledge of where items relevant to the task are likely to be located can be integrated to bias search toward the street and not the signs.

Guided search, then, is biased search rooted in two distinct processing pathways. Since the spirit of FIT is accommodated within Guided Search 6.0, we can place the latter in our explanatory structure. Here, we will situate Guided Search as explaining the subject's selecting a target for decision regarding whether it is a target or distractor, by comparing it to the target template in active long-term memory:

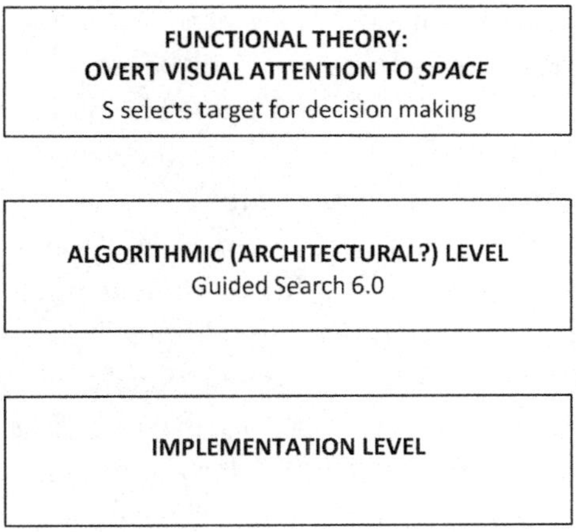

Figure 5.6 Fleshing out the explanatory framework for visual selection for decision making.

Note that Guided Search is not an algorithm but an architecture that links a variety of algorithms in describing the flow of information during visual search. Accommodating it requires inserting an "architectural" level into the threefold explanatory structure that we began with (see Figure 6.1). By organizing the details we have surveyed thus far, we begin integrating different levels of analyses to answer the question of what attention in visual search is. In the next sections, we situate an element of Guided Search at the algorithmic and neural levels, namely the priority map computation and its neural implementation.

5.5 Saliency and Priority Maps

In vision science, saliency and priority maps can explain eye movements and shifts of attention across a scene. For this reason, we will shift focus to the other aspect of visual search, namely selection that programs shifts of the eye, or of attention, to putative target locations. Nevertheless, the ensuing discussion also adds detail to the explanatory structure in Figure 5.6, since it elaborates the priority map invoked in Guided Search. We begin with saliency maps. "Salience" is a tricky term because its ordinary use refers to targets that are or should be noticed (Chapter 12.3). In the *ordinary* sense, an item is perceptually salient to a subject precisely because the subject notices it or is pulled to notice it. Used in this sense, "salience" applies to anything that we attend or can attend to: the color of a hat or of someone's skin, the sadness apparent on a face, the face itself, a disturbing thought, or the subtle negative meaning of a gesture.

In cognitive science, "salience" has a narrow technical meaning tied to the concept of a *saliency map*. In this sense, only *locations*, not features or objects, are salient. This restriction is not always noted by philosophers drawing on this work, but it is a crucial difference with the ordinary notion. An algorithm for computing visual salience was initially presented in a foundational paper by Christoph Koch and Shimon Ullman (Koch and Ullman 1985) and implemented more fully by Laurent Itti, Koch, and Ernst Niebur (1998) (for an accessible review, see (Itti 2007); for a deeper dive, see (Laurent Itti and Koch 2001a)). The saliency map as a computational construct assigns a scalar value to a location, what we will refer to as its *salience value* (for a different approach, see (Bruce and Tsotsos 2009); for a comprehensive review of the state of the art up to 2013, see (Borji and Itti 2013)).

On many models, the saliency map can be represented as a spatial map with peaks at each location where the height indicates the salience value of that location. For example, the Itti and Koch algorithm takes individual *visual feature maps*, such as for color or intensity, as input and computes the *conspicuity* of each location L with respect to that feature by comparing the feature value at L with a set of neighboring locations along the relevant dimension. This is done at various spatial scales. For example, the algorithm takes a visual map of intensity and identifies the brightest location as the most conspicuous relative to its contrast with the intensity values at nearby locations. The *conspicuity maps* generated by each feature map are then normalized and combined to establish a saliency map which assigns a salience value for each location (Figure 5.7).

The visual saliency map has been used to predict saccadic eye movements that are driven by visible features of the environment. The eye moves to L because the saliency map marks L as having the highest peak. The saliency

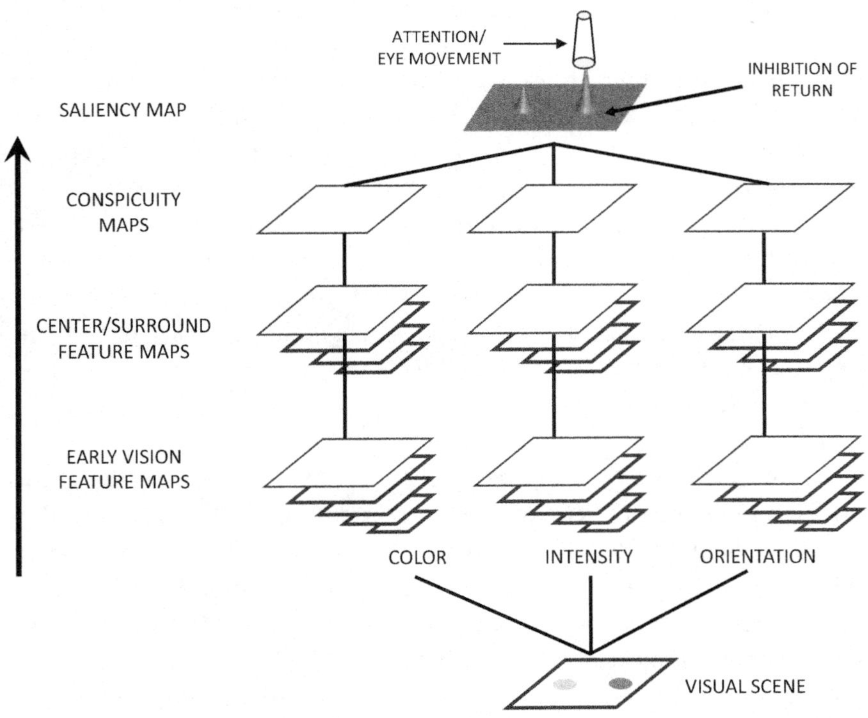

Figure 5.7 Salience Computation. The visual scene is analyzed in separate feature maps corresponding to different visual channels. The computation is executed over various spatial scales (feature maps of different sizes). This results in a *conspicuity map* for each feature dimension. Conspicuity maps are the inputs to constructing a single featureless saliency map of locations. In this case, the darker item is the most salient item, and there is a corresponding peak on the saliency map. The eye or attention moves to that location based on a winner-takes-all computation. An inhibition of return mechanism inhibits attention/the eye from returning too quickly to the selected location. Drawn after Itti, Koch, and Niebur (1998). Thanks to Shawn Willett for contributing a key part.

map explains saccades in bottom-up overt visual attention. This bottom-up account ignores task-relevance, relying only on information about features in the visual input. It is stimulus-driven. Programming where the eye moves to next is explained by a *winner-takes-all* mechanism that identifies the location with the highest peak on the map as the location to which the eye is to move. To ensure that the mechanism does not perseverate, constantly oscillating between the two most salient locations, the algorithm builds in an *inhibition of return* mechanism to ensure that the next highest peak will be the target of the subsequent eye movement. At each fixation, the information is transferred to a *central representation* for further processing, say to determine the identity of targets at that location.

Strictly speaking, only *locations* are represented as salient in the saliency map. A theoretical challenge is to avoid equivocating between "salience" in the narrow technical sense with "salience" in the broad ordinary sense where *any* target of attention can be salient. The claim that a face is salient has no meaning in a saliency map because that map is *featureless* and, presumably, *objectless*: the "saliency map only computes bottom-up information and has no notion of what an object is" (Elazary and Itti 2008, 12). Let us stipulate that a signal is feature- or object-*silent* when it provides no information about features or objects. (It is *agnostic* regarding features and objects (Veale et al. 2017).) The peaks of the saliency map are feature- and object-silent. Given these peaks, one has information about where the eye will likely move next, but one can only guess what features or objects are at that location.

Jeremy Wolfe (1994, 238), fn. 6) suggested that while the saliency map does not represent objects, "in an array of items [objects], activation will be higher at the items than in intervening blank space. Objects and locations will be, in effect, the same thing" (ibid.). So, a location is salient in the narrow sense because the object at that location is salient in the broad sense (cf. (Henderson and Hayes 2017, Figures 1 and 2)). The correlation, however, is not perfect. Lior Elazary and Laurent Itti (2008) computed the salience of locations on photographs where salient objects had been labeled by human observers ("salience" in the ordinary sense). In this case, "the saliency map showed a 43% chance of finding a labeled object within the first predicted location and over 76% chance within the third predicted location." Itti and Koch (2001b) trained their algorithm to more closely align the output of a saliency map to highlight locations of salient (ordinary sense) objects such as pedestrians on a city street (op. cit.) or military vehicles in an isolated landscape (Laurent Itti and Koch 2000). This involved using supervised learning to increase the weight on relevant feature maps that were correlated with the broadly salient objects. These computations veer toward what are called *priority* maps.

Even if the correlation between narrow and broad salience were perfect, the saliency map remains feature- and object-silent, so there is still work to do by action systems since task-relevant information beyond locations must be selected. The agent's goal in a task is often to respond to features or objects, not just to space. Spatial attention leaves work to be done for feature and object attention. In respect to guiding overall behavior, the saliency map identifies a relevant area for further analysis. In the Itti and Koch model, non-spatial targets at the salient location are passed on to a *central representation* (Itti and Koch 2000, p. 1491). Further selection mechanisms then focus on features or objects, such as to aid task processing.[3]

Does salience apply to other modalities? There is work on auditory salience that draws on similar ideas (Kayser et al. 2005). To the extent that a sensory modality with spatial content is subject to bottom-up attentional capture, saliency maps might also apply. Still, we can speak of thoughts and memories as salient in that they can trigger responses, but a cognitive saliency map is not obviously spatial, so the extension of saliency maps to certain cognitive domains is not obvious. The same issue arises with respect to sensory modalities that are not strongly spatial, such as olfaction.

We have noted that there is a general notion of a bias needed to solve the Selection Problem and the saliency map can function to clarify one type of bias that resolves the Problem in respect of determining eye movements given the visual world. That bias, in the pure bottom-up case, is driven by properties of the stimulus as processed in the relevant perceptual system through construction of a location-based saliency map. Yet there are many types of bias that also influence behavior. Eye movements are sensitive to task, expectation, gist, and so on, and so biases go beyond narrow salience (cf. visual search in radiology, Chapter 11.6). Consider Yarbus's experiment again:

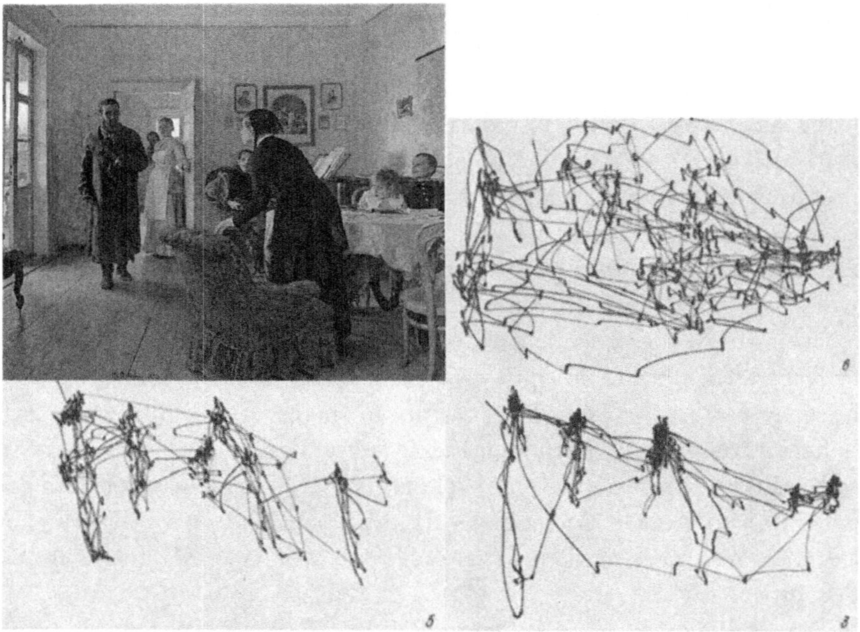

Figure 5.8 Yarbus figure reprinted from Figure 2.6.

These saccadic visual search movements are automatic in that the agent does not intend to produce a specific saccade or the overall pattern of the movements. At the same time, the pattern of movements is modulated by intention. As these task-sensitive automatic movements cannot be explained just by the saliency map, theorists have appealed to a *priority map*. The priority map computes not only over sensory information in feature maps—the priority map can be understood to take the saliency map as one of its inputs—but also over task-relevant information and much more. (Confusingly, in the literature, "saliency map" is sometimes used when priority maps are intended.) Among additional inputs for computing a saliency map noted by Rebecca Todd and Maria Manaligod (2018) are statistical learning, semantic associations, reward, and affective salience. Further, bodily states like hunger or thirst, representational states like memories of various sorts, beliefs or desires, and historical effects like priming also have an effect. No doubt, there are others (Shomstein et al. 2023).

Like saliency maps, priority maps are said to be featureless. Yet, arguably, some priority maps cannot be feature- or object-silent if "we tend to think of a priority map as the final common map for guiding attention" (Bisley and Mirpour 2019, 109). After all, task-relevance is often locked to specific features or objects as task instructions indicate that agents should respond in a certain way to them. A map that indicates that a location contains something of high priority does not tell us what to respond to at that location, such as if there are overlapping features or objects. To attend appropriately to non-spatial targets requires additional information. Accordingly, the priority map construed as feature- and object-silent cannot be the final map for guiding attention in many tasks. Otherwise, all that would be selected are locations. In any event, to maintain conceptual clarity, it is best to restrict the technical notion of salience to the original conception of the saliency map and to use "priority" to pick up the content of the priority map. This terminological regimentation is not always observed in the literature and this is partly, I suspect, because "salience" has a broad ordinary usage that is hard to bracket from technical discussions.

5.6 Neural Substrates of Saliency and Priority Maps

Let us turn to the neural implementation of saliency and priority maps. Biological data have identified various potential neural substrates of such maps in visual areas, including the lateral intraparietal area (LIP) and the superior colliculus (SC), all known to be involved in the generation of eye movements and visual spatial attention.

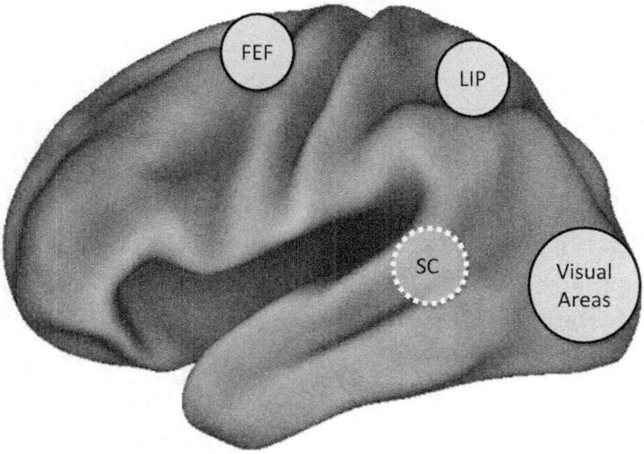

Figure 5.9 The frontal eye field (FEF), lateral intraparietal area (LIP), and the superior colliculus (SC). Note that SC is subcortical and so should be understood as underneath the depicted cortex.

Given the assumption that saliency and priority maps are featureless, there are specific constraints on their neural implementation, clearly summarized by Heiko Stemmann and Winrich Freiwald:

> For an area to be considered a priority map, it must match a number of criteria: for an area to encode the location of attention, it must have spatially confined RFs [receptive fields] tiling the visual field. For the area to encode the attentional focus of an object, its cells should exhibit little feature selectivity and high visual responsivity, thus being able to encode attention to a wide range of stimuli. Furthermore, the area should exhibit strong attentional modulation, and ideally, the strength of this modulation should be independent of stimulus properties.
>
> (Stemmann and Freiwald 2019, 23798–99)

Let us restate these conditions as concerning the *implementation* of attention and related constructs. A neural implementation of the visual priority map will (a) cover the entire visual field, as it is a map of all visible space (receptive field *tiling* of the visual field); (b) be general and so responsive to anything visible that is present at a location that can be assigned priority; and (c) have a graded response that is independent of stimulus type, namely feature dimension or object identity. We should add to (c) that this response should correlate with the salience or priority of the target. Interestingly, Stemmann and Freiwald argue that regions of the posterior inferotemporal cortex exhibit these properties. This is striking since the brain regions most commonly associated with priority maps are in other areas such as LIP and SC (Figure 5.9).

To what extent does LIP or SC fit the neural criteria noted? I will focus on (c) and divide that condition into two necessary conditions. The first is that the activity of the neural substrate should scale with priority as given in the peaks of the priority map. The second is that this priority representation should be the same for any two stimuli X and Y that are of the same priority, say when they are equally task-relevant. That is, neural response should scale not with feature dimension but with priority. If neurons fail to show this feature *invariance*, then that activity will not be an implementation of priority maps in the sense that we are currently discussing.

Consider one study that we can interpret as probing the neural substrate of a saliency map. Puiu Balan and Jacqueline Gottlieb (2006) provide evidence that LIP neurons respond similarly to changes of stimuli in their receptive field, that area of space to which they respond to appropriate stimuli. This includes both *increases* and *decreases* of luminance as well as a change in color at equal luminance, the appearance of a frame around a stimulus, and radial motion (see Figure 4a, p. 9245). Intuitively, these changes will affect the saliency map since they were task-irrelevant changes whose function in the experiment was to distract the subject. Roughly, equivalent salience of the different stimuli is reflected in a similar response in the recorded LIP neurons to each. Further, the fact that the LIP neurons responded in the same way to increases and decreases along the same dimension suggests that these neurons can be appropriately invariant to the feature values, here along the intensity dimension. This evidence suggests that the neurons in question respond in a way that is consistent with their being a neural implementation of the computational construct of a saliency map.

A second structure that has been implicated in encoding salience is the SC. This is a subcortical structure that is shared across vertebrate species. In a striking experiment, Alexandre Zénon and Rich Krauzlis (2012) showed that inactivation of SC disrupted the deployment of covert visual attention even though standard cortical neural signatures of attention were still present. Measurements from cortical activity on its own would suggest that the animal subjects deployed covert attention, yet selection for response was disrupted. The animals' ability to perform the attention task was severely degraded even though their cortices showed signatures of attention. The experiment provides evidence that the SC is necessary for the normal engagement of covert visual attention. Accordingly, the cortical modulations correlated with attention are not sufficient for attention. A natural picture is that SC and cortex must work together to enable visual attention.

The SC has been argued to be a neural substrate for the computational construct of a saliency map. The structure tiles the visual field and shows visual responses to items therein. There is also evidence that the SC can represent stimuli in a *featureless* way. Brian White et al. (2017) examined activity in the SC while their animal subjects watched videos of natural scenes. They observed that neurons in the *superficial* layer of the SC which receives only sensory inputs generated responses that were largely independent of what feature was present in the neuron's receptive field (op. cit. Figure 6). This is not to deny that SC neurons can exhibit feature sensitivity (reviewed in detail in (Hafed et al. 2023)), but it is compatible with that fact that some colliculus neurons can function as a saliency map. A *priority* map in SC would need to integrate task-relevant signals among other inputs, and the superficial layer, receiving only sensory inputs, would not be a plausible neural substrate for encoding priority since it would not receive the requisite inputs. One possibility is that the deeper *intermediate* layer of the SC which does receive goal-related inputs could serve as the substrate of a priority map, but whether these cells also exhibit featureless response to priority is to be determined.

To flesh out the Marrian account regarding shifting the eye to scrutinize specific locations during search, we can ask why does the eye select those locations to process for the task? Saliency and priority maps provide an algorithmic description of what the brain might do to answer that question, intuitively by marking locations as salient or as having priority. These models are implemented in a complicated cortical and subcortical network. An initial explanatory structure, incorporating the details discussed in this and the last section, is as follows:

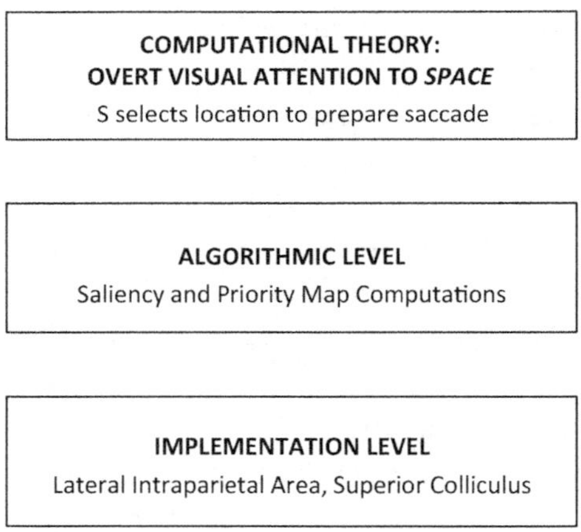

Figure 5.10 Partial filling in of the explanatory framework for spatially directed eye movements (cf. Figure 4.20).

5.7 Feature-Based Attention

Visual search targets are often specified in terms of feature or feature combinations, such as color or shape or both. Given that subjects visually select features to report on, visual search will depend on visual attention to features. In the past sections, we have focused on spatial attention in saliency and priority. In this section, we consider attention tied to features. One area of study in the neuroscience of attention is *feature-based attention*. We'll speak simply of feature attention. To support feature attention, the brain must select features for behavior. This is distinct from spatial attention. A notable contrast between feature attention and spatial attention with respect to neural activity is that while visual spatial attention is correlated with the modulation of visual neurons whose receptive fields respond to the selected location, visual feature attention is correlated with the modulation of feature-responsive neurons *across visual space*.

For example, Narcisse Bichot, Andrew Rossi, and Robert Desimone (2005) recorded from visual area V4 in monkeys trained to perform a visual search task. In one case, monkeys were presented with the cue at fixation specifying the target feature, such as shape or color. For example, a cue might indicate a red object the shape of which would be task-irrelevant in a color selection trial. Once the cue disappears, the monkey performs visual search over an array of various shapes of different colors, one of which is the target identified by the cued color red. The key case is (a) when the animal is fixating on a distractor, (b) where the target falls within the recorded neuron's receptive field, and (c) when the animal moves its eyes *away* from the target. The animal fails to notice the target even though part of its brain, specifically a V4 neuron, registers the target within its receptive field.

Consider the case where red is the target color, and we record from a V4 neuron that prefers red in that it fires more strongly for red relative to its response to other colors such as green. In the illustrative case where the animal fails to notice the targeted red object that falls within the neuron's receptive field, the animal moves its eyes in another direction. Since spatial attention is thereby moving away from the target, we should not expect the neuron to show modulation of the sort correlated with spatial attention. Nevertheless, Bichot et al. observed that, despite the absence of spatial attention in its receptive field, the V4 neuron's response to the preferred color is stronger when the stimulus is task-relevant (i.e., is the target) than when it is task-irrelevant (i.e., is a distractor). Neurons also showed the same differential response to task-relevant targets versus task-irrelevant distractors when the target is defined by shape. The alteration in neural response to a feature was present even though the subject failed to notice it. Since the animal is presumably shifting spatial attention away from the receptive field, the neuronal correlates of feature attention just noted can be disconnected from spatial attention.

In a study with humans, John Serences and Geoffrey Boynton (2007) observed that even when there was no stimulus present in the visual neuron's receptive field, it showed modulated activity tied to the targeted feature. Serences and Boynton had their subjects observe random dot motion stimuli and report when motion in one of two directions slowed down. Crucially, the set of dots in each motion direction were co-localized and so spatially superimposed. Two potential target locations, one on each side of fixation, were relevant. Subjects received a cue as to which of the locations they should spatially attend to (spatial attention) and which of the two motion directions they should monitor to detect a motion-slowing event (feature attention). While the subject was attending to one location, the other location might also contain (distractor) motion stimuli or no stimuli at all. Neural activity was tracked by functional magnetic resonance imaging (fMRI). The authors reported that even if there was no stimulus in the unattended location, information about the task-relevant motion direction could be decoded from neurons responsive to the unattended location. They suggested that decodable neural activity reflects the influence of feature attention to spatially unattended, empty locations of the visual field.

Feature attention is important for visual search, but some comments are called for. The logical frame, *S m-*attends to *T for R*, is useful for clarifying what feature attention involves. Specifically, what is the relevant modality of attention in feature attention? In the Serences and Boynton result, the neural activity that is decodable need not be a response to a visible feature in the unattended location for sometimes the location has no feature. If so, the subject is not, indeed *cannot* be, visually attending to a target feature that is not there. Yet the neural activity in the unattended location carries information regarding the feature since we can decode feature identity from the noted activity. In what sense, then, does feature attention modulate relevant neurons across the visual field? At the very least, the observed activity cannot be the basis of *visual* feature attention at that location since, again, there is no feature at that location. Speaking simply of feature-based attention leaves the modality unspecified, but if the modality cannot be visual, what then is it?

Given points to be made regarding working memory in the next chapter, we propose that if the observed feature-based, non-spatially localized activity "across the visual field" instantiates attention, the mode of attention is the subject's *cognitively* attending to the feature. Specifically, such attention is the subject's holding the target feature in memory. Correlated neural activity in visual areas observed in the absence of a visually present feature constitutes the subject's inclination or readiness to visually attend to said feature, should it appear (cf. the discussion of temporal attention and expectation in Chapter 3.2). This reflects the subject's keeping the target in mind, namely remembering it. Thus, the Serences and Boynton observation might be of the neural substrate of *visual working memory*, namely memory of the task-relevant feature. The memory capacities deployed need not be anchored to just one spatial location but can spread to others, for one's working memory concerns a feature (general) and not a feature-at-a-location (specific). So, in visual search, if sensitivity to features, measured in neural response, is enhanced across the visual field, this could be the neural basis of the agent's memory of what feature is task-relevant ((Wolfe et al. 2011) Box 1).

5.8 Search and the Biological Limitations on Primate Vision

We began the survey of visual search by suggesting a concrete picture of how the agent performs the task, including visual selection of objects for decision. Yet we must be open to the possibility that our conception of task performance is incorrect. In this final section, we consider this possibility.

At a fixation, many objects in a search array are in peripheral vision. Crucially, processing is not the same across our retina. It is natural to think that, in standard search arrays, each stimulus is represented as a distinct object. Highest acuity, however, is at the fovea. The distribution of rods and cones leads to differences in processing of color and space among other features across the visual field. Further, there is a greater number of neurons in visual cortex devoted to processing the fovea versus the periphery, what is termed the *cortical magnification factor* (Dow et al. 1981). This leads to differences in how we experience the world, two of which we shall illustrate here.

Fixate on the "A" on the left (Figure 5.11). In the first row, while maintaining fixation, compare the fixated "A" with the "A" in the periphery which you must covertly attend. Notice the difference in how the two "A"s appear. Now, in the second row, again keeping your eyes fixed on the left "A", compare how the peripheral "A" appears in it versus your experience of the first row's peripheral "A" when you fixated on the left "A" in that row. Reflect on these appearances. Move now to the third row and covertly attend to

1 A A

2 A X A X

3 A XAX

Figure 5.11 Crowding move the page relative to your eye to test where effect is strongest.

the peripheral "A", maintaining fixation on the third row's left "A". Striking isn't it? Reflect for a bit before reading the next paragraph.

What the example illustrates is both (1) the loss of acuity (row 1) and (2) the phenomenon of visual crowding (row 3, (Pelli 2008; Levi 2008; Whitney and Levi 2011; Rosenholtz 2016)). In crowding, information is lost in the sense that uncertainty increases. You are less certain, based on visual evidence alone, that the center symbol in the letter triplet is an "A" in row 3.

So, at a given moment in visual search, one might be foveating one of the items in the display, while many of the other items are located in the periphery at various distances from fixation. What difference might this make to search? Consider a model proposed by Ruth Rosenholtz and colleagues. Research on visual crowding has identified *windows of integration* where visual information in a given region of the visual field is pooled. These windows get larger as one moves from the fovea to the periphery. The three-letter triplet that forms a crowded display does not appear as composed of three distinct objects. Rather, the visual system captures the triple and the relevant regions surrounding it in terms of *summary statistics*. (For a demonstration of different encoding strategies for a search display, see (Rosenholtz et al. 2012a, Figure 1) and (Rosenholtz 2016) for a thorough discussion of peripheral vision.) The idea is that the visual system compresses information and, in doing so, keeps information that is likely important for behavior and discarding what is likely unimportant. Compression reduces overloading processing capacity limits.

This suggests that we might think of processing in visual search not as operating over a representation of a field of distinct objects. Rather, many of the items in the search array will fall within a window of integration and be subject to crowding. The limits of peripheral visual processing and the phenomenon of crowding will undercut the availability of many stimuli in the periphery as *distinct* objects. Peripheral vision and the automatic selection of summary statistics impose important constraints on understanding human visual search.

Guided Search 6.0 accommodates these factors by invoking a nonselective pathway that operates over summary statistics and whose output can guide selection via a priority map. Rosenholtz offers an alternative approach. On her account, visual search involves distinguishing *patches* that correspond to windows of integration across the visual field. Given the constraints on peripheral processing, the relevant computation for visual search is not whether the next object to be fixated is a distractor or target. This assumes that peripheral objects are distinctly represented. Rather, the question is whether a given patch, which encodes summary statistics of a peripheral region, likely contains a target or not. Thus,

> rather than thinking about the similarity between a single target and a single distractor [in conducting visual search], we should be thinking about the similarity between peripheral patches containing a target (plus distractors) and those containing only multiple distractors. After all, that is the visual system's real task as it confronts a search display.
>
> (Rosenholtz et al. 2012b, 4)

Consider a computational process over visual patches. If one patch is more likely to contain the target than the other, then the subject should move to the former patch. If the two patches are not distinguishable with respect to the likelihood of containing the target, then there is no basis for choice beyond choosing one or the other to continue search. The constraints imposed by the limits of peripheral vision become the primary constraints on the efficiency of visual search given loss of acuity and crowding. The model predicts that search will be more or less difficult if the target-containing patches are more or less discriminable from patches that do not contain the target.

To test their account, Rosenholtz and colleagues used a *Texture Tiling Model* of processing in peripheral vision (Rosenholtz et al. 2012a, 2012b). This model treats visual processing in the periphery as computing over patches as pooling regions. These regions are overlapping "tiles" that cover the visual field, the tiles growing larger with eccentricity (distance from the fovea). These tiles instantiate windows of integration in the model. On the Texture Tiling Model, a key constraint on performance is not the discriminability of individual stimuli construed as distinct objects but rather the discriminability of the patches. If so, the model predicts that visual search performance will correlate with patch discriminability.

Rosenholtz and colleagues took classic visual search arrays and isolated patches therein, separating those which contain the target from those which do not. They used a texture algorithm to generate "mongrels" that preserve the summary statistics of the patches. Subjects were tasked with discriminating between plus-target and minus-target patches. The hypothesis is that visual search difficulty will track the discriminability of these patches. Rosenholtz et al. observed a strong correlation between search performance on some common search arrays and patch discriminability. (For other tests of the model, see (Rosenholtz et al. 2012a), Figures 8 and 10 and associated experiments; for in depth discussion, see (Rosenholtz 2020).) Interestingly, the Texture Tiling Model predicts the visual search results that motivated developing basic assumptions of FIT built into the idea of a selective pathway. The argument against standard models is that the early results do not favor FIT and Guided Search *over* the Texture Tiling Model. If central properties of visual search can be explained by the non-selective pathway, does this render the selective pathway otiose or, at least, reduce its role in explaining core aspects of search? If so, Rosenholtz suggests that this is a way of "living without attention" (Rosenholtz 2024). Alternative models such as Rosenholtz's challenge our understanding of task performance. We began with a functional model of visually selecting targets for decision and report, but we must keep in mind alternative accounts of task performance which can prompt rethinking how the attentional function is carried out.

5.9 Conclusion

Visual search is a pervasive part of our lives. We look, and we look for things. In the history of modern attention research, visual search is a core paradigm to probe visual attention and related phenomena. We have provided a necessarily partial survey of salient results in the field, organizing them in a Marrian explanatory framework that is centered on providing an explanation of what selection is for, namely reporting the presence or absence of a target in an array often by moving the eye to each putative target location. What is clear is that while much has been accomplished, controversies remain and much work remains to be done. This work can, however, proceed with a clear explanatory framework, beginning with a Common Conception of attention, that organizes research at different levels of analysis in mutually informative ways. This provides a foundation for thinking about visual search in real-world contexts where attention, skill, norms, and implicit bias will come forward (Chapters 11 and 12).

Suggested Readings

The literature on visual search is overwhelming. Anne Treisman has provided a variety of overviews, and she (2006) provides a comprehensive statement. A variety of responses to her work as well some of her seminal papers are collected in (Wolfe and Robertson 2012). A two-issue memorial collection on her work was edited by Jeremy Wolfe (Wolfe 2020a, 2020b). Wolfe (2012) provides a brief intellectual biography connecting Treisman's model to his development of guided search, and he (2021) presents Guided Search 6.0 in detail. He also provides a general overview of visual search (Wolfe 2020c). Ruth Rosenholtz provides an overview of peripheral vision (2016) and her texture tiling model (2012a).

Notes

1 We can be inattentionally blind to targets at fixation in the sense of failing to notice them (Mack and Rock 1998).

2 We can run a contradiction argument with the Common Conception (Chapter 1.2), for if we are concerned with the *subject's* attention as selection of a target to generate an eye movement, then this is not the same as the visual system's selection of a feature to create an object representation. Plausibly, the latter can be part of the explanation of the former. Given her methodology, Treisman implicitly endorses the Common Conception, so her postulating attention as being a spotlight *proliferates* types of attention. For her, there are two kinds of attention: the subject's and the visual system's selections. Yet unless proliferation here is merely verbal, an extension of the use of "attention", we need an argument that attention (the phenomenon) is a spotlight.

3 There has been work to broaden the saliency map to allow responsiveness to objects. Alexander Russell et al. (2014) constructed a saliency algorithm that would incorporate Gestalt grouping principles. This identifies visual *proto-objects* yielding *proto-object based saliency* (see also (Uejima et al. 2020)). Proto-objects are "relatively complex assemblies of fragments that correspond to localized structures in the world" (Rensink 2000, 22). Francesco Orabona et al. proposed a proto-object based model of visual attention drawing on Gestalt grouping principles leading to "proto-objects defined as blobs of uniform color in the image" (Orabona et al. 2007, 200). Dirk Walther and Koch (2006) adapted the Itti, Koch, and Niebur saliency model to allow identification of "proto-objects" using the saliency map *as input*. Relatedly, John Henderson et al. proposed a *cognitive relevance theory* to explain eye movements where the saliency map provides an input into parsing a visual scene "to generate a visuospatial representation that includes a coding of potential object locations and their spatial layout" such that "as soon as a figure-ground representation coding object regions has been generated, saccade target ranking based on cognitive relevance can be applied to it" (Henderson et al. 2009, 854).

6

ATTENTION AND MEMORY IN ACTION

6.1 Introduction

What is the relation between memory and attention? In this chapter, we focus on *working memory* and its relation to attention. Examining working memory helps us understand the intimate relation between intention and attention. Mark D'Esposito and Bradley Postle noted that "the functions that we label attention, intention, and retention [memory] may be treated identically by the brain" (D'Esposito and Postle 2015, 121). Perhaps *identity* is too strong, but intention, attention, and memory are tightly intertwined. This chapter illuminates these interconnections.

What is working memory? Klaus Oberauer asserted that

> there is a broad consensus on what the term *working memory* refers to: The mechanisms and processes that hold the mental representations currently most needed for an ongoing cognitive task available for processing.
>
> (Oberauer 2019, 223)

DOI: 10.4324/9781003223450-7

If we revise the description to speak of the subject's *maintaining* contents for task, Oberauer's description fits the Common Conception of attention. In working memory tasks, the subject selects a target by remembering it to inform cognitive tasks. Holding something in mind in working memory tasks, mnemonically selecting it for response, is *cognitive* attention. Consider remembering a sequence of numbers, say "4621", and then transforming it by adding one to each place (i.e., adding 1111). One retains and manipulates numbers in working memory. A common architecture of working memory construes it as containing (1) storage buffers for the active maintenance of memoranda where these contents can be modulated by (2) an executive control system.

One thing to keep in mind is that working memory neither is something the subject does nor is attributed to the subject. This is different from attention. While subjects can be said to attend to things, we do not speak of them as "working memorizing" things. Rather, a subject remembers things for a task or *for work*. This is implemented by the subject's subpersonal working memory system. Thus, we should keep descriptions firmly at the appropriate level of analysis. Remembering for work is cognitively attending to a target (functional level of analysis), and cognitive attention is implemented in a working memory system (algorithmic or "architectural" level of analysis).

Let us consider the relation between *perceptual* attention and memory. The first questions to address are formulated as follows:

- How does the subject's perceptual selection of target for response, in attention, bear on remembering for work?
- How does remembering for work bear on the subject's perceptual selection of a target for response (i.e., attention)?

In effect, the questions can be understood as concerning the relation of two modes of attention:

- How does perceptual attention bear on cognitive attention?
- How does cognitive attention bear on perceptual attention?

Provisionally, we can say that remembering for work is realized in working memory just as perceptual attention is, perhaps, realized in biased competition. We can change levels by stating correlated questions of interest to cognitive neuroscientists (we will not answer these):

- How does biased perceptual selective processing of target for response bear on working memory?
- How does working memory bear on biased perceptual selective processing of a target for response?

In Section 6.2, we discuss a subject's remembering an item *for work*, namely for action. Section 6.3 discusses working memory as the subpersonal substrate of memory for work. Section 6.4 connects memory for work and working memory by discussing the latter's role in maintaining plans of action and Section 6.5 details working memory's role in controlling attention. In Section 6.6, we deploy these insights to explain certain attentional phenomena such as vigilance, sustained attention and preparatory attention. We discuss the debate regarding *contingent capture* in Section 6.7 including whether memory for work is needed for items to capture attention.

6.2 Remembering for Work

We often remember things for doing work. We remember someone's phone number to dial it or write it down. This action involves selecting what is remembered to inform response. Such memory-based selection instantiates a type of cognitive attention. Memory-based actions such as recalling, remembering, keeping in one's head, holding onto an idea, and so on, are, as actions, solutions to Selection Problems. They involve some or all of three stages: *encoding*, *maintaining*, and *responding* (*accessing*). Consider a mundane working memory behavior, intentionally remembering a nine-digit American telephone number: (101) 497-8560. Encoding occurs when you hear the numbers to memorize, namely when you auditorily select the heard numerals to form a memory.

Auditory Perception (1014978560) ⟶ Memory Encoded (1014978560)

Once you have the sequence in mind, you actively maintain it, perhaps repeating it in your head in inner speech (in the *phonological loop* (Baddeley and Hitch 1974)). We might represent the action of maintaining the phone number in this way:

Memory Encoded (1014978560) ⟶ Memory Encoded (1014978560)

Finally, you dial the number, and so the memorized sequence selectively informs the production of finger movements.

Memory Encoded (1014978560) ⟶ Dialing (1014978560)

Each stage of remembering (encoding, maintaining, and recalling) identifies something you do intentionally. In the last two cases, we have the mind's taking possession of a remembered item to deal with. Since memory provides the subject-level input, attention is based on cognition (memory inputs), so the last two steps involve cognitive, mnemonic or memory-based, attention. Remembering for work in its different phases deploys either perceptual attention in encoding or cognitive attention in maintaining and recalling.

While our focus will be on working memory as the basis of remembering for work, the structure of mnemonic actions applies to recollecting declarative memories such as *episodic* remembering of past episodes or *semantic* remembering of facts. Specifically, when a declarative memory is recalled from long-term memory, it enters into working memory (see Cowan model of working memory, Figure 7.4; Section 7.3). When we remember events and facts, declarative memory informs encoding of working memory, is maintained over time, or informs further responses such as reasoning or verbal report. In every case where our actions draw on what we remember, we solve a Selection Problem in that specific memoranda rather than others inform our response.

The category of cognitive attention, broadly construed, should not be controversial. In psychology, an influential conception of attention in memory invokes the idea of *internal* attention contrasting it with perceptual attention as *external* attention (Chun et al. 2011). The spatial metaphor is potentially misleading. In remembering a past event or a fact, I am still attending to the world (this is also emphasized by Oberauer (2019, 223), fn. 2). So, at the level of content, remembering and perceiving are typically external in being world-directed. If there's a sense in which they are "internal", it is that both rely on psychological representations, realized in the brain, as a basis for attention. Yet if memory-based attention is internal in relying on internal representations, so is perceptual attention. In light of this, rather than internal versus external attention, we should speak, broadly, of *cognitive* attention versus *perceptual* attention.

The relation between working memory and cognitive attention is not causal but something like constitution, realization, or implementation. Working memory processing constitutes the agent's cognitive attention to what is being actively remembered. This fits a Marrian frame for cognitive attention (see also (Oberauer 2019) p. 7ff). Accordingly, in invoking working memory as the substrate of a subject's remembering an item for work, we explain cognitive attention by setting the act of remembering above the architecture of working memory at different levels of the Marrian explanatory structure. Remembering for work, unpacked into the three phases of encoding, maintaining and accessing, express a functional theory, while working memory is the lower level implementation of those phases. Since the working memory construct is an information processing architecture, we might speak of an *architectural* rather than an algorithmic level. This would be a *fourth* level in the explanatory structure:

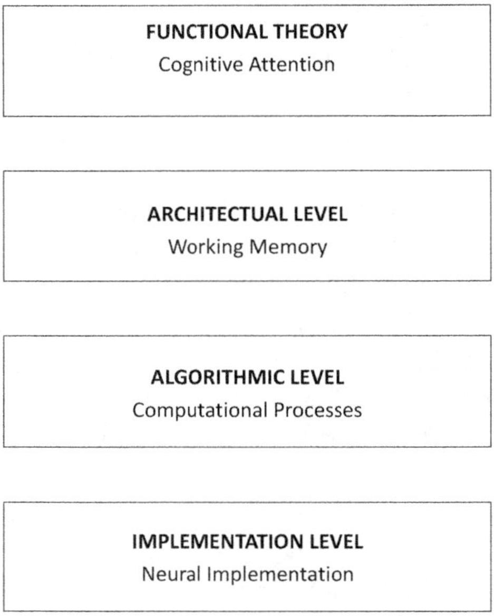

Figure 6.1 Adapted Marrian structure where working memory is the substrate of cognitive attention. We have added an "architectural" level.

Consider a working memory paradigm, the *retro-cue task* (Landman et al. 2003; Griffin and Nobre 2003). In a typical version, an array of items such as different shapes are presented to be remembered. During the *delay period* after the array is extinguished and before the subject must recall the array to perform an instructed response, a cue is presented that indicates one or a subset of the remembered items. For example, consider a memory-based change detection task (see Figure 6.2). The subject is presented with a circle of differently oriented rectangles to retain in memory. To do the task, the subject encodes the array and maintains it. During the delay period, the subject receives a spatial cue indicating one of the objects as a likely target during the response phase. The subject is then presented with a test array of the same number of shapes where the object corresponding to the cued location might or might not have changed in orientation. The subject reports whether there is a change (see change blindness, Chapter 10). As with spatial cueing (Chapter 4), cue validity influences performance. Valid cues facilitate performance while invalid cues induce a cost. (For a systematic review of retro-cueing, see (Souza and Oberauer 2016).)

During the delay period, the subject remembers a specific array rather than other items. So the subject's cognitive attention remains selective, thinking about a specific train of memoranda versus other possible

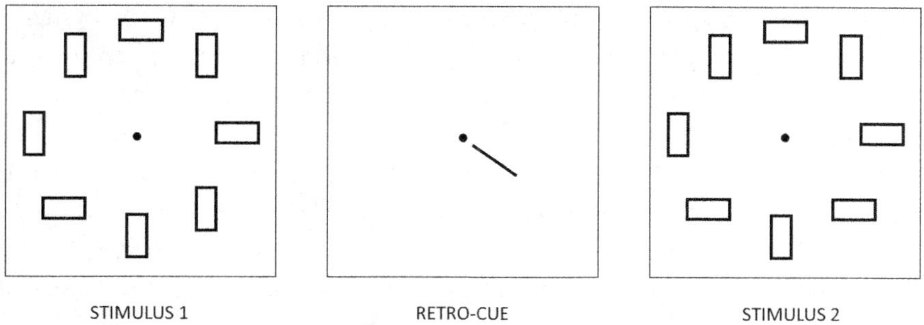

Figure 6.2 Retro-cue paradigm. Panel 1 shows the first stimulus array. Panel 2 is the retro-cue after the presentation of the first stimulus, indicating the location on the bottom right. Panel 3 is the second stimulus array with a change at the cued location. This figure was drawn after the task in Landman, Spekreijse, and Lamme (2003).

memoranda. Next, the cue allows her to prioritize specific memoranda among the totality of what she holds in mind to guide task performance in the test period. Dropping to an implementation level, the shift in working memory explains the modification in the subject's cognitive attention at the subject level, a shift in what the agent focuses on to selectively guide behavior. With the cue, the agent's memory focuses on specific parts of what she remembers. Retro-cueing parallels the Selection Problem in spatial cueing, so we can repurpose that basic architecture for working memory (Figure 4.9), assuming (a) only two items, R and L, in working memory; (b) an intention to remember both for work; and (c) an expectation from the cue that R is the one that we shall ultimately act on:

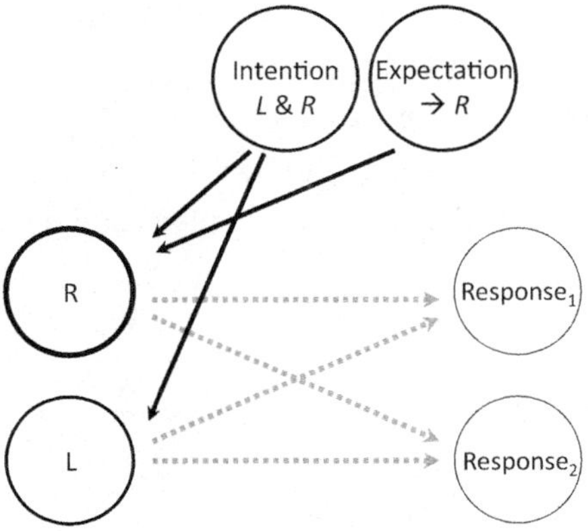

Figure 6.3 Retro-cueing with an intention to hold two targets active in memory and an updated expectation, based on the retro-cue that R is task-relevant. Compare with Figure 4.9 in spatial cueing.

In cognitive science, a common conception of this shift in working memory maintenance in light of the cue is that attention, construed as an internal mechanism, modifies the agent's working memory store. Attention is an internal mechanism that manipulates working memory representations. Since retrocueing is the memory analog of visual spatial cueing discussed in Chapter 4, we can ask, as we did in that chapter, whether an internal spotlight (i.e., some attentional mechanism) is needed to explain alterations in memory processing or whether constructs already in place, such as expectation, might be sufficient to account for the changes. After all, if the agent's expectation (belief) about cue probability and relevance is detailed enough to point internal attention to a specific location in the store, why can't the expectation directly bias processing? On this picture, it is not attention, as internal mechanism, that affects working memory processing. Rather, expectations bias this processing.

6.3 Working Memory

Working memory has broad application. Adele Diamond lists some of the tasks that psychologists take to be dependent on working memory:

> Doing any math in your head requires WM [Working Memory], as does mentally reordering items (such as reorganizing a to-do list), translating instructions into action plans, incorporating new information into your thinking or action plans (updating), considering alternatives, and mentally relating information to derive a general principle or to see relations between items or ideas. Reasoning would not be possible without WM. WM is critical to our ability to see connections between seemingly unrelated things and to pull apart elements from an integrated whole, and hence to creativity because creativity involves disassembling and recombining elements in new ways. WM also enables us to bring conceptual knowledge and not just perceptual input to bear on our decisions, and to consider our remembered past and future hopes in making plans and decisions.
>
> (Diamond 2013, 143)

Working memory informs other actions besides cognition. Dialing a phone number just entered into memory is a working memory-guided *bodily* action. Working memory informs mental and bodily action. Given the expansive cognitive roles ascribed to working memory (Engle 2002, 19; Baddeley and Logie 2012, 28–29; Miyake and Shah 1999, 446; Unsworth 2016, 3), Nelson Cowan worried that "allowed to blossom, [such expansive accounts] can include so much of cognition that, taken at face value, the definition may admit all active, complex thought processes as WM" (Cowan 2017, 1162).

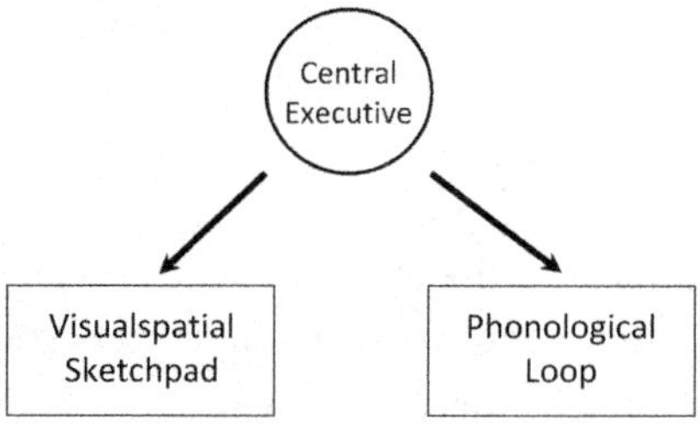

Figure 6.4 Basic structure of the original Baddeley and Hitch model, indeed most models, with two types of components: (1) a central executive and (2) various stores. In the original model, there were two stores: a visuospatial sketchpad and a phonological loop.

Arguably, the most influential model of working memory is due to Alan Baddeley and Graham Hitch (1974). Their original presentation posited two memory stores, the *visuospatial sketchpad* and the *phonological loop* (Figure 6.4), and an important line of research has focused on working memory *capacity*. A common value for working memory capacity is about four *chunks*. A chunk can be a sequence of symbols organized into a unit, such as *chunking* the letters "I", "B", and "F" into "FBI", an acronym for a law enforcement agency in the United States. In this way, three individual letters can be chunked into a single acronym, allowing the agent to efficiently retain three letters as one chunk.

The contents of the stores and their maintenance and transformation are regulated by the *central executive*. Baddeley commented on this component as follows:

> In the interests of simplicity and tractability, we assumed that the executive was purely a system for attentional control, and did not itself have any storage capacity. It was able to focus attention against potentially distracting irrelevant information, to switch attention between two or more stimulus sources or actions, to divide attention in order to perform two concomitant tasks, and finally to interface with LTM [long-term memory].
>
> (Baddeley 2002, 247–48)

The central executive does not exert such executive control arbitrarily. It operates according to plan, yet any plan that regulates the stores must also be actively maintained. Where is this plan stored? If the central executive does not contain the plan yet acts according to it, then something else must direct it according to plan. That plan must be remembered and stored somewhere else such that this distinct element controls the central executive which then modulates the stores according to that plan. But then there is another executive system. Does it store the plan or is it controlled by another executive module, leading to a possible regress? This regress is stymied if the controlling system contains the plans needed to organize appropriate control. But if so, perhaps the central executive itself must be involved in storing the plan, including task instructions (Wu 2023, Chapter 3).

The working memory architecture instantiates the agent's remembering for work and hence cognitive attention to memoranda. Remembering for work, the deployment of cognitive attention, is at the subject level. So, if one is remembering a phone number to write down, to tell a friend, or to dial it, each plan has a different outcome anchored on the remembered phone number. Freek van Ede and Kia Nobre speak of working memory as "the maintenance and manipulation of information over short periods of time to guide adaptive behavior" ((van Ede and Nobre 2023, 138), see also (Myers et al. 2017a)). Memory guidance in this context means the control of behavior. In his description of the central executive, Baddeley characterizes its function as for *attentional control in multiple domains* (for a detailed philosophical discussion of these issues, see Buehler (2022a, 2022b)). "Attentional control" is, however, an ambiguous term. Does it mean control of attention or a type of attention that exerts control?

The operation of the central executive cannot be independent of the agent's plan. I argued that the executive operates according to a plan that it retains. But plans bring us into the domain of intention. In the case of the phone number, the plan is to remember *that sequence of numbers*. At the personal level, one's cognitive, memory-based, attention is of the sequence of numbers *to remember*. This suggests the following possibility: the subpersonal basis of the intention as representation of planned action, here to remember a sequence of numbers, is (i) the executive system that stores the action to be executed and (ii) the buffers that store the numerical sequence that are the targets of the plan. Accordingly, the precise numbers stored are not independent of the plan but are its targets. One is planning to respond not to any old phone number but to the specific one maintained.

This connection to plans and intention might seem odd to some working memory theorists where the focus has been on measuring working memory capacity, such as the size of the stores (Cowan 2012). Yet Baddeley (1996) emphasized that the central executive controls attention to a target while suppressing distractors, and in his model of working memory (Figure 6.5), Nelson Cowan makes explicit a role in setting attention to specific targets in the working memory store where the store contains activated long term memory (LTM) representations (see also (Oberauer 2002, 2009)).

On the current proposal, working memory serves memory for work. Remembering as something the agent intentionally does results from solving the Selection Problem in respect of prioritizing one memory over others. This suggests the following parallel between the agent's Selection Problem and the underlying working memory architecture as proposed by Cowen (Figure 6.6).

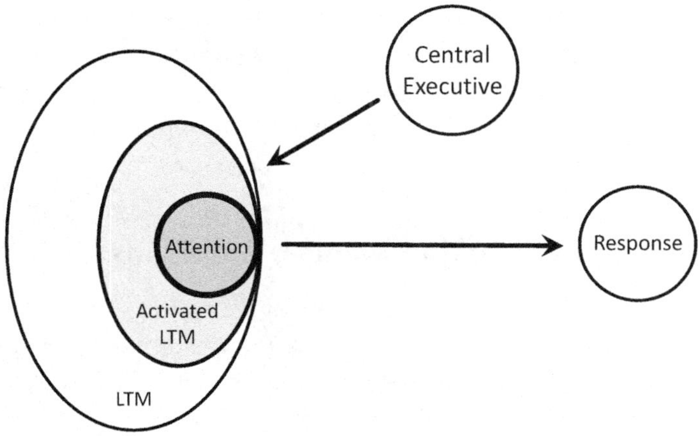

Figure 6.5 Cowan model.

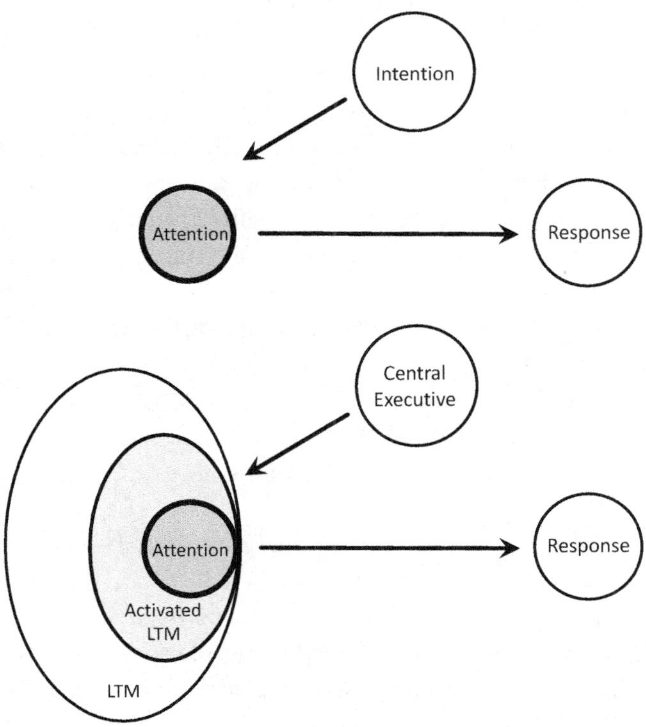

Figure 6.6 Cowan model as a reflection of the Selection Problem. LTM: long-term memory.

A natural hypothesis is to take working memory as giving the dynamics of maintaining and updating one's plans. Specifically, research on working memory explains how one type of bias, an intention or plan associated with executive functions, yields appropriate attention, namely selection of appropriate targets that inform relevant response.

6.4 Working Memory and Plans

Task instructions set a subject's intention to act in the experiment. If the subject does not agree to the instructions, there is no point in doing the experiment. So appropriate intentions are necessary for successful behavioral experiments. To carry out the instructions, the subject must *remember what to do*. If she forgets the instruction at the experiment's beginning, her performance will no longer aid the experimenter. The postulated amnesia (forgetting) undercuts experimentation (it also undercuts coherent agency, see (Wu 2023, Chapter 4)). Tasks must be remembered and maintained throughout the experiment, and maintaining a plan is the subject's intending to carry it out.

The central executive regulates memory stores *according to plan*. This suggests the following functional merger: The plan implemented by the central executive must not be separate from the plan implemented by the subject's intending to act. For when the agent carries out her intention as planned, there is not a *separate* step of the central executive kicking in to keep up with the agent. Similarly, the central executive is not leading the agent who must keep up by forming a similar plan. Rather, the agent's carrying out her intention is *constituted* by the central executive initiating the plan. The two levels line up constitutively (Figure 6.5).

This connection between intention and working memory was clearly articulated when George Miller, Karl Pribram, and Eugene Galanter introduced the concept of working memory as memory *for the retention of plans*:

> The parts of a Plan that is being executed have special access to consciousness and special ways of being remembered that are necessary for coordinating parts of different Plans and for coordinating with the Plans of other people. When we have decided to execute some particular Plan, it is probably put into some special state of place where it can be remembered while it is being executed. Particularly if it is a transient, temporary kind of Plan that will be used today and never again, we need some special place to store it. The special place may be on a sheet of paper. Or (who knows?)

> it may be somewhere in the frontal lobes of the brain. Without committing ourselves to any specific machinery, therefore, we should like to speak of the memory we use for the execution of our Plans as a kind of quick access, "working memory." There may be several Plans, or several parts of a single Plan, all stored in working memory at the same time. In particular, when one Plan is interrupted by the requirements of some other Plan, we must be able to remember the interrupted Plan in order to resume its execution when the opportunity arises. *When a Plan has been transferred into the working memory we recognize the special status of its incompleted parts by calling them "intentions".*
>
> (Miller et al. 1960, 65) (my emphasis)

The function of actively holding a plan to guide its execution is an executive function, a central feature of all models of working memory.

The action as specified in task instructions is initially schematic, abstract. For example, subjects might be verbally instructed to remember *red* objects that will subsequently appear. This color concept underspecifies the specific shade of red to act on. Accordingly, when a specific stimulus appears, the strategic subject sharpens their plan to remember not a generic red target but *those* specific burgundy (red) targets. That is, concrete stimulus instances become the targets of the agent's intended task. The plan is updated to reflect new information. So the subject moves from a general intention to remember *red* objects (category) to a specific intention to remember *those burgundy* objects (specific instances of red). The same updating was seen in indirect spatial cueing and expectations (Chapter 4). Such updating can be captured as a type of practical reasoning:

1. I intend to act on red objects as per task instructions.

2. This burgundy target is red.

3. I intend to act on this burgundy target.

If the burgundy target disappears during a delay period, maintaining the intention formed in step (3) amounts to remembering for work, retaining a plan focused on a specific target. Nicholas Myers et al. (2017) argue that when working memory is geared toward affecting behavior, the relevant representations are not just activated but transformed into an action format. For example, when a retro-cue is presented, it functions like a pointer for establishing (2) in the practical inference: *that* remembered target is the one (likely) to be tested. Accordingly, the agent can make their plan more specific. At the level of working memory processing, "the reformatted representation of the cued WM stimulus is now part of the task set. Therefore, the task set has become more specific and much simpler" (Myers et al. 2017, 453).

Again, this line of thought might be jarring to some since working memory is often introduced by talking about *spans* of symbols, not plans. Yet plans are updated as the working memory stores are. Return to the subject's practical reasoning as she elaborates her plan, updating it with new information. She incorporates specific targets into her plan (intention) and so shifts from a general intention to act on red targets to a specific intention to act on this red (burgundy) target. The latter is stored in memory as part of fine-tuning the plan remembered. The stimulus the subject remembers as a target is not separate from what she plans to do. She plans to act *on that target*. Accordingly, the plan and the incorporated target are now objects of cognitive attention, the agent's remembering to act. Let us now return to an earlier question:

- How does perceptual attention relate to cognitive attention?

Here's one answer. By perceptually attending to a target, the agent modifies her remembered plan. Perceptual attention shifts cognitive attention, namely in making the action representation more precise. If the encoding of a target deploys visual attention, then we can say that visual attention changes cognitive attention by introducing a stimulus which the agent responds to by remembering it as part of forming or modifying her plan. The agent's intention to act, her cognitively attending to her planned action, changes.

When we intend to act, we cognitively attend to the planned action by actively remembering it. The remembered plan is modified, often by perceptual attention to incorporate relevant targets that are consequently remembered as part of an updated plan. The machinery of working memory helps us understand this subject-level dynamic movement of mind where perceptual attention shifts cognitive attention in plan updating. Yet as we have argued earlier, intentions (plans) set perceptual attention. This brings us to the other question:

- How does cognitive attention relate to perceptual attention?

6.5 Working Memory and the Control of Attention

Span tasks are used to measure working memory capacity (Conway et al. 2005). One span task is *simple span* as exemplified in remembering a telephone number. *Complex span*, however, is the preferred way to measure working memory capacity, in part because it shows stronger correlation with measures of fluid intelligence to which working memory is postulated to contribute (Engle et al. 1999; Fukuda et al. 2010). Complex span interweaves two tasks that agents perform, namely (1) a sequence (simple) span task and (2) an additional task such as assessing the grammaticality of sentences or the correctness of mathematical statements. Consider *operation span*, in which subjects retain a span of numbers presented sequentially where, after each numeral, an arithmetic statement is presented that must be assessed as correct or not (e.g., $(2*4) + 1 = 11$) (Turner and Engle 1989). In these tasks, the subject must remember one sequence while making judgments about arithmetic statements. Both tasks draw on working memory but must be segregated to minimize interference. Given that task instructions set cognitive attention, complex span tasks require agent to divide cognitive attention and update plans.

Complex span seems to measure more than just how many units can be retained in a working buffer. It assesses the control of attention across interleaved tasks. Consequently, many theorists treat working memory as a capacity for executive control of attention. Thus, Andrew Conway et al. note

> a clear distinction between the traditional concept of short-term memory capacity (STMC) and WMC [working memory capacity]. STMC is thought to reflect primarily domain-specific storage, whereas WMC is thought to reflect primarily domain-general executive attention.
>
> (Conway et al. 2005, 771)

Randall Engel notes that

> the tasks used to measure WMC [e.g., complex span] largely reflect an ability to maintain information in the maelstrom of divergent thought. Tasks measuring fluid intelligence largely reflect the converse of that—the ability to think of something that may be important at the moment, but when it shortly proves to be unimportant or wrong, to disengage or unbind that information and to functionally forget it... *both abilities rely on the ability to*

> *control attention to do the mental work necessary to either maintain information or to disengage from information.*
>
> (my emphasis) (Engle 2018, 191)

Baddeley emphasized that

> the central executive clearly reflects a system concerned with the attentional control of behavior, with subsequent developments almost certainly depending on parallel developments in the study of attention and the control of action.
>
> (Baddeley 1992, 559)

The control of attention to guide behavior begins with cognitive attention to a plan and updating plans given new information. As noted earlier in discussing retro-cueing, registering new information, the agent's cognitive attention to the planned action is made more specific. The subject's challenge in complex span experiments is to maintain two distinct tasks in a dynamic dual-task situation and to execute each task with minimal interference from the other. The capacity for executive control is reflected in the ability to maintain and execute distinct plans. This brings us back to Figure 6.5, which depicts a functional convergence between the agent's intention and the executive system of the working memory architecture.

In earlier chapters, we emphasized how intention sets perceptual attention in guiding planned action. Leveraging research on working memory, we explain further how intention (cognitive attention to task) sets perceptual selection of a target for response. This allows us to illuminate three phenomena related to attention: vigilance, sustained attention, and preparatory attention.

6.6 Vigilance, Sustained Attention, and Preparatory Attention

In intentionally performing an action, such as pressing a button when I see a target stimulus in an experiment or remembering to turn right instead of left to go to the market before heading home by car, my intention puts me in a position to succeed. I have to be appropriately *vigilant* for relevant signs or cues, but that can be hard work. N. K. Mackworth (1948) demonstrated this in the *vigilance decrement*. Mackworth investigated deteriorating performance over time by radar operators detecting critical signals such as an enemy aircraft. He had air force cadets monitor a single black "clock hand" on a white surface that rotated a full circle in 100 equally spaced jumps. Occasionally, the pointer would move twice the typical distance, and subjects had to report such rare jumps. They did this mind-numbingly dull task for two hours. Not surprisingly, Mackworth noted a drop in performance over time measured as an increased failure to report the target double-jump (the number of *misses* increased). This vigilance decrement is often characterized as a failure in *sustained* attention.[1]

Like attention, the nature of vigilance is debated. Some theorists identify vigilance as a distinct form of non-selective attention (e.g., Robbins (1998)). Oken et al. (2006) highlighted three meanings of "vigilance" in the empirical literature: (a) sustaining attention to a task, (b) attending to potential threats, and (c) "the arousal level on the sleep-wake spectrum without any mention of cognition or behavioral responsiveness" (1885). I am going to focus on (a) and (b) as these involve selection and can be linked in an illuminating way through considering plans (working memory) and attention.

We have discussed the agent's attention to her task *T* as constituted by her cognitive attention to task where such attention is her intending (remembering) to perform *T*. Failing to sustain cognitive attention is failing to keep the intended action in mind. Forgetting is one such failure (I forgot I was doing that!). So, at the extreme, a failure to sustain attention to task by Mackworth's subjects is their momentarily losing track of their task, perhaps because their mind was distracted while wandering. Temporary amnesia can explain a failure to engage with task-relevant stimuli. Failure of vigilance as failure to sustain cognitive attention to task means momentarily forgetting or losing track of what one is doing, with corresponding changes in the operations of working memory. That said, the agent's failing to maintain cognitive attention is compatible with the agent's maintaining visual attention to the hand, such as their staring dumbly at it. Yet, given cognitive failure, the agent fails to visually attend to, so report, the jump even while visually attending to the hand.

Perhaps talk of amnesia is too strong. To see how cognitive attention might fail without wiping one's plans from mind even temporarily, consider failure of perceptual attention due to a failure to maintain vigilance for a target. When Mackworth's subjects miss the jump, they fail to visually notice it. Visual attention is not engaged. If we construe vigilance as the subject's *readiness to attend* to important stimuli, the sign of a vigilance decrement is expressed as a failure to notice critical targets. Perhaps the failure is explained if one's memory of the task and targets is not functionally at the fore perhaps because one is distracted. In this case, memory of one's plan is in some sense less active and so fails to prepare visual attention to intended targets when they appear. This suggests an interesting intersection between cognitive attention to task in intention and perceptual attention: cognitive attention readies perceptual attention. In intending to act, one is ready to visually attend to the targets of one's action. This readiness to attend explains a familiar type of vigilance such as waiting for the guest of honor at a surprise party or being ready for threats in a dangerous situation. (For discussion of different functional working memory states, see (Muhle-Karbe et al. 2021).)

Bernhard Hommel (2000) suggested that intention is a *prepared reflex* (for a philosophical discussion of this idea, see (Wu 2008)). To understand one implementation of such reflex, focus on intentional visually guided action. One way to implement a prepared reflex is that intention readies visual selectivity to guide action-relevant response. Before the target appears, intention sets a readiness for appropriate visual attention to targets of that kind. So, when the honored guest appears through the front door, at the right time, everyone shouts, "Surprise!", so long as one is not distracted or has forgotten the task. When we intend to act on a target not yet present, the intention readies us to act by readying us to attend appropriately. The intention to act on T makes us perceptually *attuned* to, specifically vigilant for, T. Consequently, when T appears, it drives attention and the intended response.

Such vigilance in light of intention is characterized in cognitive neuroscience as *preparatory attention* (Stokes 2011; Battistoni et al. 2017), a link also presaged by a connection between target templates in working memory and neural preparatory activity as posited by biased neural competition (Chapter 2.5; (Desimone and Duncan 1995)). For example, in recording from single neurons in object-sensitive inferotemporal (IT) cortex, Leonardo Chelazzi et al. observed increased baseline firing of neurons during the delay period after they were stimulated by a cue that presented the upcoming target, such as a face (Chelazzi et al. 1998, Figures 3 and 4). They note:

> This maintenance of cue-specific activity throughout the delay period could be evidence of the 'bias' in favor of the cells representing the target stimulus, as predicted by the biased competition model. A related possibility is that the activity during the delay is part of the mechanism for maintaining the memory of the cue.
>
> (2922)

In these experiments, the cue image is also later the target image, and the authors note that preparatory activity (vigilance) can also be conceptualized as working memory maintenance.

Similar preparatory activity during a delay period was observed using functional magnetic resonance imaging (fMRI). Mark Stokes et al. (2009) used an auditory tone to cue their subjects to detect either an "X" or an "O" present against background noise. Note that in contrast with the Chelazzi et al. experiment with macaque monkeys where the cue was also the target stimulus, with humans, the cues were "abstract", a tone whose association with specific visual stimuli is set by task instructions. The target letters, "X" or "O", were present in 25% of the experimental trials, a non-target letter was present in 25%, and no target was present in the remaining 50% of trials. The region of interest for imaging was the lateral occipital complex (LOC), which is a shape-sensitive area in the visual cortex. Stokes et al. focused on the delay period before target presentation. Univariate analysis revealed the same level of LOC activity during the delay period understood in this experiment as the period between the auditory cue and the visual presentation of the cued stimulus (this interval was between 0.5 to 14.5 seconds after the cue). Think of univariate analysis as that which leads to coarse descriptions of brain areas "lighting up" in fMRI images. In contrast, multivariate pattern analysis (MVPA), which detects patterns of activity in the fMRI signal, uncovered shape-specific activations in population activity in LOC: "preparatory attention specifically activated the same neural subpopulations that were active during corresponding visual stimulation" (p. 19571; also Figure 3A). That is, the neural representational capacities exercised during visual experience of targets are activated during the delay as the subject gets ready to respond to the same targets. This delay period activity was positively correlated with behavioral performance (see also (Giesbrecht et al. 2006, Figure 4)).

Maurius Peelen and Sabine Kastner (2011) obtained evidence for preparatory activity for higher-level categories in object-selective cortex (OSC). They had their subjects search for either people or cars in pictures of never-seen-before natural scenes. Subjects were given a symbolic cue, a letter or number, to indicate target category. Thus, subjects were cued only for the general category but had to search for novel instances. Using MVPA, Peelen and Kastner detected category-specific responses in OSC. These responses correlated positively with detection accuracy and negatively with reaction time, providing evidence that preparatory activity was correlated with improved behavioral performance (see Figure 4, p. 12127; cf. (Muhle-Karbe et al. 2017)). Some work using disruptive transcranial magnetic stimulation of regions exhibiting preparatory activity generated performance decrements, although these effects tend to be small. (See (Reeder et al. 2015, Figures 4 and 5); cf. similar studies discussed by Yaoda Xu (2017) in the context of sensory recruitment, discussed next.) The evidence canvassed suggests that intention/working memory sets vigilance implemented in preparatory neural activity before visual targets appear.

Techniques for decoding information in neural activity has demonstrated that working memory memoranda can be decoded across the brain (Christophel et al. 2017). For example, in visual working memory tasks where the targets to be retained are visual stimuli, investigators have been able to decode the contents of working memory across visual areas, sometimes as early as primary visual cortex (V1; (Serences et al. 2009; Harrison and Tong 2009)). This finding is striking since much of the early focus on working memory maintenance emphasized activity in prefrontal cortex. Given an increasing number of studies demonstrating activity in sensory areas correlated with memory maintenance, some have advocated a *sensory recruitment* account of working memory storage (D'Esposito and Postle 2015a). John Jonides et al. (2005) suggest that "the same brain regions that are involved in encoding information are those that are maintained in a temporarily active state while that information is retained for short intervals. That is, these same areas mediate working memory" (p. 2). On this view, sensory cortices provide the "first site of working memory storage" (p. 3).

Following the two options noted by Chelazzi et al., we can ask whether this correlated activity is the basis of working memory storage or of vigilance in the sense of preparatory attention to the task-relevant targets stored in working memory. Are we looking at the neural substrate for cognitive attention to a target or for preparation of visual attention to it—that is, sensory recruitment for memory maintenance of target or sensory recruitment for preparing perceptual attention to it? An initial argument against sensory recruitment for memory storage is that if one assumes that the visual areas at issue are *the* substrate for the memory store, then disruption of activity in those areas should induce amnesia. The consequences of amnesia on behavior should be substantial. Given the Mackworth result of a vigilance decrement, amnesia, even if temporary, should lead to strong behavioral effects, a failure to notice. In a critical review of the sensory recruitment account, Yaoda Xu (2017) notes that many studies that disrupt processing in early visual areas yield small behavioral effects, and this is prima facie inconsistent with induced amnesia where we would expect to see larger failures in performance (recall the small effect obtained in (Reeder et al. 2015, Figures 4 and 5)).

Still, it will be hard to disentangle the two possibilities given a tight conceptual link. As I have argued (Wu 2023):

> The two positions [early visual areas as the substrate of memory storage or as that of preparatory attention/vigilance] are strongly linked. Assume that early sensory activity is part of the neural basis of maintenance. Since by hypothesis, those representations were activated during sensory encoding when the target was first perceived, they are also ready to be efficiently redeployed once the target appears again after the delay period. Maintenance activity is also preparatory. Similarly, if we think of the activity as preparatory, the basis of the agent's being vigilant, this activity results from an intention which maintains specific targets in mind to guide future action, a mnemonic function. In principle, this activity enables decoding of mnemonic content from sensory areas even if these areas are not necessary for maintenance. Delay period activity reflects, informationally, the targets of intention. The ecumenical position consistent with the data is that delay period activity amounts to a readiness to attend and reflects, in the sense of allowing decoding of, remembered targets for task. This activity is maintained by the subject's intending to act.
>
> (p. 114; cf. Stokes (2011, 1425))

As Mark Stokes notes, focusing on visual short-term (working) memory (VSTM): "The contents of VSTM are pre-selected for task-relevance, therefore maintenance-related bias should optimise perception accordingly" (op. cit., 1426). We have a convergence on the following point: when the subject maintains and updates a plan, this can be instituted in preparatory activity in relevant visual areas. Such activity can facilitate the subject's visual attention to remembered task-relevant targets. So, whatever we decide about sensory recruitment for memory maintenance, all positions can allow that the correlated activity can bias subsequent perceptual attention and modulate task performance.

6.7 Contingent Capture

The connections that we have drawn are theoretically fruitful. For example, they illuminate debates about attentional capture. Think of attentional capture as a purely passive mental movement where something *grabs* attention, disrupting other forms of attention such as task-oriented attention. For the past several decades, there has been a debate about the limits of attentional capture and what allows for it (there might be a rapprochement

(Luck et al. 2021)). One influential view is that attentional capture is *contingent* on task. This is not to deny that attention can be captured by completely task-irrelevant stimuli, and we return to some of these issues when we discuss inattentional blindness in Chapter 10. Yet the surprising dependence of distraction on task speaks to the general picture developed in this chapter of how intention controls perceptual attention by setting a readiness to attend, preparatory attention, or vigilance.

Work on inattentional blindness indicates that intentional action yields insensitivity to salient distractors (Mack and Rock 1998). Salient items like a random visible gorilla can fail to capture attention (Simons and Chabris 1999). James noted that selection to deal effectively with things involves withdrawal from distractors. That said, distractors sometimes win. While some subjects stay on task, ignoring distractors that fail to grab attention, others get pulled off task, attention being captured (Conway et al. 2001; Colflesh and Conway 2007). This difference can be correlated with working memory capacity, an indicator of a capacity to control attention.

Captured attention can disrupt or impair task performance. A fire alarm suddenly blaring breaks one's concentration. Social media pulls on attention as one works, and one succumbs by checking one's feeds. Attentional capture is often described as involuntary, but to keep to a technical vocabulary, we say that capture is automatic in the precise sense defined in Chapter 2.8, an agent's attention being captured by a stimulus is automatic since the agent did not intend to attend to that stimulus. Yet there are cases where we want attention to be captured by notable stimuli, especially when these are potentially task-relevant or of more general interest. How do agents find a balance between staying on task, blocking distractors, while remaining sensitive to, hence ready to attend to, potentially significant distractors?

There has been a venerable debate about the precise parameters of attentional capture in the visual domain. Steven Yantis and John Jonides initially hypothesized that *abrupt-onset stimuli*, such as a letter that suddenly appears, always capture attention (Yantis and Jonides 1984; Jonides and Yantis 1988). This is analogous to a fire alarm in the auditory domain, a sudden auditory burst, though perhaps not quite at the same intensity. Yantis and Jonides tested a specific conception of automaticity in attention based on an "intentionality criterion": "an automatic process is not subject to voluntary control: Attempts by a subject to prevent an automatic process from proceeding are not successful" (Yantis and Jonides 1990, 122). Given their experiments drawing on spatial cueing, we can understand the tested criterion as implying that even when one is intentionally performing a task, attentional capture by task-irrelevant abrupt onsets can occur. Interestingly, Yantis and Jonides found that rather than an abrupt-onset stimulus always breaking through task performance, attentional capture was modulated by task. Specifically, in a spatial cueing paradigm, the effect of abrupt-onset stimuli on reaction time was significantly modulated by cue validity which depends on the subject's expectation and understanding of task. In the case of cues that were *100% valid* (i.e., where the cues always indicated the upcoming location of the target), modulation by abrupt-onset stimuli relative to non-onset stimuli was effectively eliminated (op. cit., Experiment 2). They concluded:

> The visual attention system is evidently prepared to give high priority to abrupt onsets when in diffuse attention mode. This is adaptively sensible, because onsets usually signal novel stimulus information, and this information may often be perceptually important. At the same time, the system delays the potentially distractive influence of abrupt onset when other task demands have led to highly focused attention-also adaptively sensible.
>
> (133)

I suggest an alternative to their invocation of diffuse attention. Instead, one could say that agents are more susceptible to attentional capture when the target location is more uncertain given cues that are less than perfectly (100%) valid. The observed dependence of attentional capture on higher-level states was further explored by Charles Folk, Roger Remington, and colleagues. They formulated the *contingent involuntary orienting hypothesis*, or as they sometimes say, *contingent capture* thesis:

> a given stimulus will capture attention only if it matches an attentional set, and cases of automatic capture of attention by salient stimuli are the result of tasks that implicitly encourage an attentional set that favours these stimuli.
>
> (1)

We can connect the concepts of *task set* and *attentional set* to intention and vigilance as a propensity to attend. Task sets can be understood as representation of the action to be performed, including specification of task-relevant targets at a certain descriptive grain, represented in the agent's plan. Attention sets can be understood as the readying of the subject's attention, often set by the agent's intention but, as we shall see, subject to automatic biases as well

(Chapter 11). An important contingency is where the attention set matches elements in the task set. When it does, attention can misfire in being captured by task-irrelevant targets that share features to intended targets.

Like Yantis and Jonides, Folk and Remington used a spatial cueing paradigm. In Folk, Remington, and Johnston (1992), the contingency of attentional capture was demonstrated by a distinctive spatial cueing paradigm. Subjects maintained fixation on a central box surrounded by visually equivalent boxes forming an array in a "+" shape (top, bottom, left and right). In the initial "cue" display, the cue(s) appeared abruptly, a cue for a box being four small circles centered on each side of the box. Two cue displays are relevant: abrupt-onset cueing in that a single cue (white circles) appeared around one of the four peripheral boxes and a color cue in that one cue (red circles) appeared with three other cues (white circles), with each surrounding one of the four peripheral boxes (Figure 6.7).

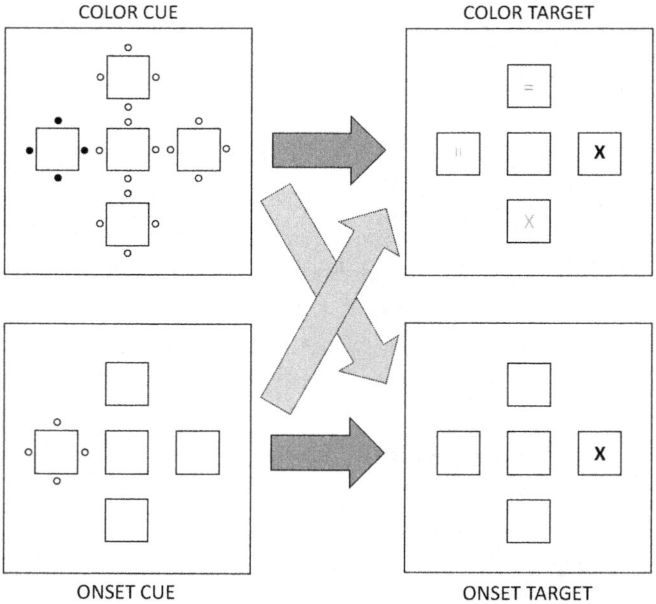

Figure 6.7 When searching for a red target (top right box; black "X" is the red target), only cues that match the target color capture attention (top left box, black dots surrounding box represent "red" dots), observed as slowing down of reaction time since in this case, the capturing cue amounts to an invalid cue. If the target was an onset (only) target (bottom right box), the color cue does not capture attention. Dark, thick, horizontal arrows connecting left and right boxes show cases of contingent capture. Similar points hold for when the target is an onset rather than colored target. Figure drawn in black and white with black symbolizing red. Figure redrawn from Theeuwes, Olivers, and Belopolsky (2010).

In the former case, the cue is salient because it is a unique abrupt onset, the only such stimulus in the display; in the latter case, the cue is salient because it is a unique, distinctive color, red versus white. In the test phase, subjects were tasked with either locating an object that was uniquely colored among distractors or detecting a single abrupt-onset target. Folk et al. observed that the initial cues seemed to capture attention only if the cue matched a feature of the targeted object. This was inferred due to changes in reaction time relative to neutral cues, with an increase in reaction time suggesting that the cue captured attention. For example, if the task is to locate a red object, then red distractors but not abrupt onsets capture attention because they match the attentional set. The intention to locate red objects predispose subjects to notice red distractors over abrupt onsets. Similarly, if the task is to locate an abrupt onset, then such cues, but not uniquely colored cues, captured attention. The task seems to attune subjects to be predisposed to attentional capture by specific stimuli that match the task set.

As per our definitions, attentional capture by a stimulus S, the cue, is automatic in respect of being captured by S because the subject did not intend to attend to S. The case of contingent involuntary orienting raises an interesting mixed case, for it looks like attentional capture is contingent on task set but the task set is what the subject intends to do. Isn't capture the result of an intention and therefore controlled?

There is a normative dimension to intention. The content of intention specifies the form of correct or incorrect performance. If you ask a friend to grab your red backpack in another room, they would fail the task if they bring back a red pillow. The intended target is specified to a finer degree, a red X and not a red Y (for all $Y \neq X$). Your friend's protest that you asked for something red (which is true) is hollow. You asked for a specific red thing. Yet what if there are two red backpacks in the other room? Here, the problem is not your friend but your instructions, for in bringing back a red backpack, your friend correctly executes your instructions even if you had something more specific in mind, one red backpack rather than the other.

The same happens in the lab. Experimenters, in giving task instructions, sometimes discover that their instructions are not specific enough. The subject follows the letter of the instructions but does something incorrectly, such as undertaking a different way of doing the task than the experimenter intended. A solution is to make the instructions more detailed to rule out mistaken implementations. Partial matches are not fulfillments of the intention. Rather, they are a misfiring of control (just like our friend

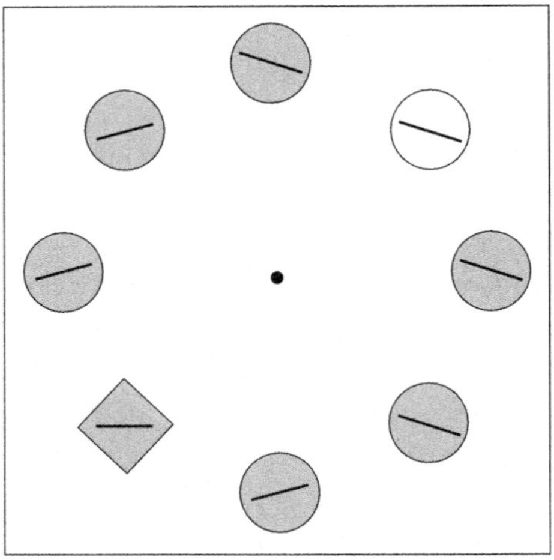

Figure 6.8 Additional singleton paradigm where subjects must report whether the line is vertical or horizontal in the *unique shape*, namely the diamond in the bottom left of the figure (figure based on paradigm in Theeuwes (1992)). An additional singleton, here the white circle in the top right, is added. Theeuwes reports that the singleton increases reaction time and so seemingly succeeds in grabbing attention.

misfired with the red non-backpack). Control can misfire as in cases where working memory leads to task-irrelevant attentional capture (Olivers et al. 2011), a phenomenon related to contingent capture.

The strong reading of contingent capture is that it is always paradoxically driven by the subject's intention to perform actions on specific targets. In contrast, Jan Theeuwes argues that attentional capture by a task-irrelevant stimulus is possible. There is *non-contingent* capture. For example, even if intention sets vigilance to explain some cases of contingent capture, sometimes the bottom-up signal is sufficiently robust to overcome other biases. Salience in the narrow sense of a saliency map can drive non-contingent capture.

Theeuwes engaged the debate with Folk and Remington with a new paradigm: *the additional singleton paradigm* (Figure 6.8). In this paradigm, subjects were asked to search for a target defined by its being a unique shape, such as a diamond among circles of the same color. Color is task-irrelevant. So a subject might search for a green diamond among green circle distractors. As in other visual search tasks, the unique object is a *singleton*. Subjects were instructed to judge the orientation of a line within the target shape singleton. Notably, in some conditions, one of the distractor shapes was differently colored, such as a red circle among green circle distractors. Here, there is an "additional singleton", a red shape among green shapes. In this condition, reaction time increased relative to displays where all shapes were the same color, suggesting that the salient additional color singleton grabbed attention. Since color is *task-irrelevant*, Theeuwes argued that this demonstrated non-contingent attentional capture. This effect disappeared when the additional singleton was not salient in the sense of the saliency map, such as a yellow circle among green circles.

The debate might be heading to a resolution with the model in Figure 6.9 proposed as a way of integrating extant results. Working memory, presumably the representation of the action and targets that we have associated with the contents of the agent's intention, plays a role in the computation of a priority map (i.e., goals; there is also an emphasis on historical bias that we shall return to in Chapters 11 – 12; cf. Guided Search, Chapter 5.4).

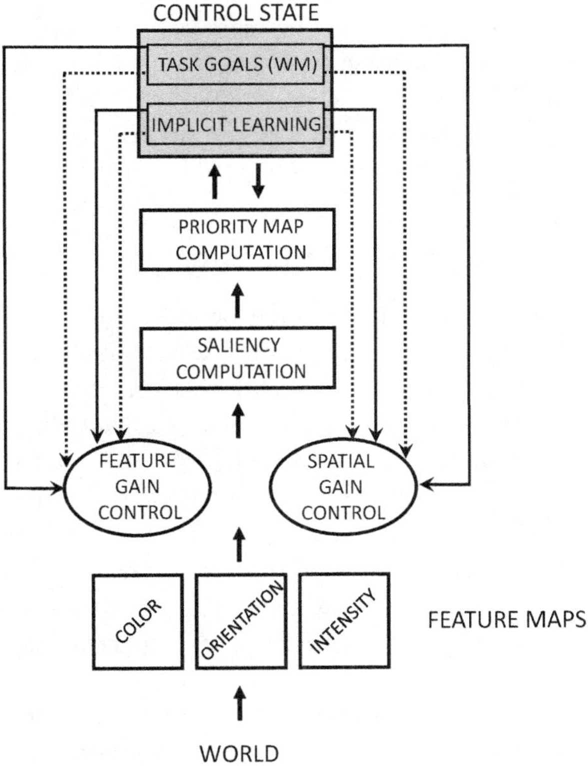

Figure 6.9 Proposed Common Control Framework to accommodate extant findings. Note the role of working memory, as well as what is acquired by implicit learning, as a bias on attention via the priority map. Solid downward arrows indicate a positive bias, dotted downward arrows indicate a negative influence. Figure redrawn from Figure 1 of (Luck et al. 2021).

The basic idea is that various biases shift the computation of the saliency and priority maps by changing the activity (gain) of feature and spatial representations.

The central point is that intention can set the parameters of attentional capture. If the content of intention is tied to working memory, contingent capture suggests that working memory might sometimes induce attentional capture or distraction as per contingent capture. (For reviews, see (Soto et al. 2008; Olivers et al. 2011); for behavioral evidence, see (Olivers et al. 2006) and (Soto et al. 2007, Figure 1); for more discussion of similar studies in the context of intention, see Wu (2023), Section 3.4.)[2] The discussion in this chapter emphasizes that given an intention to act on specific targets, agents are ready to attend to those targets, sometimes similar distractors, when they appear. This preparation to attend is what we have been calling vigilance or more broadly *attunement* (Chapter 12.4). Vigilance emerges from the intersection of intention (working memory) and perceptual attention. In the context of intentional behavior, cognitive attention to an intended action constituted by the agent's intention to so act, an intention as memory for work subserved by working memory, prepares perceptual attention that can be efficiently engaged when the intended target appears.

6.8 Conclusion

This chapter has looked at the relation between attention and memory focusing on working memory. Keeping levels of analysis straight, the issue concerns how to understand the relation between a subject's attention and intention through examining the underlying cognitive architecture of the working memory system. Critically, it is important to distinguish perceptual from cognitive attention. In the perceptual-to-cognitive direction, we focused on memory encoding, a familiar action in remembering: our memories are often based on what we perceptually attend to. What is more interesting is the cognitive to perceptual direction. Here, the working memory construct helps organize disparate concepts within a general notion of executive modulation by the agent's representation of her planned action. Thus, to act coherently over time, the agent must remember what she is doing. She must sustain cognitive attention to her task. Failure to do so leads to various decrements in performance, one being the vigilance decrement, a failure to perceptually attend to task-relevant targets. We connected this to a failure of preparatory attention or vigilance due to memory failure in the neglect of one's plans. Interestingly, intention can also misfire in that one's perceptual attention is captured by seemingly task-relevant but actually task-irrelevant stimuli as in contingent capture. The framework we have deployed now in multiple domains helps us see a commonality between contingent capture and working memory–induced distraction. We can thereby set attention and working memory together in a familiar structure, the agent's solving a Selection Problem by her intending to act.

Suggested Readings

My own thinking about the connection between intention and working memory as discussed in (Wu 2023, Chapters 3 and 4) is inspired by Miller et al.'s (1960) *Plans and the Structure of Behavior*. Denis Buehler has written a number of informative articles on the central executive and the control of attention in action (see among other papers, (Buehler 2018b, 2022b)). Carolyn Dicey Jennings also has a recent discussion of mental control and attention (2022). As with attention, there are many reviews of working memory, an immense area of research. For a recent overview of the Baddeley and Hitch model within the context of short-term memory research, see (Baddeley et al. 2019). For an overview of standards and targets for working memory research, see (Oberauer et al. 2018). Nelson Cowan provides a monograph treatment of working memory capacity (Cowan 2012). Klaus Oberauer has written a conceptual analysis of attention and working memory (Oberauer 2019). On the debate about contingent capture, see Luck et al. (2021) and the articles in that issue. On the sensory recruitment account, see (D'Esposito and Postle 2015), and for a philosophical deployment of the thesis, see (Carruthers 2015). Yaoda Xu argues against the sensorimotor account in various articles (Xu 2017, 2020), and there are many replies, including (Gayet et al. 2018; Scimeca et al. 2018; Iamshchinina et al. 2021). For questions about working memory as a psychological kind, see (Gomez-Lavin 2020).

Notes

1 Recent work deploys different paradigms done in shorter periods of time. For example, in the sustained attention to response task (SART), subjects must monitor a sequence of rapidly presented numbers, hitting a key to report every number except for a less frequently occurring "3" in which case they must *withhold* a key press. A vigilance decrement can be demonstrated in a block of trials lasting only five minutes. Note that SART differs

from the Mackworth task in that response to the infrequently occurring digit requires *suppression* of an automatized response. Some have argued that SART does not measure sustained attention (Dang et al. 2018).

2 Nachshon Meiran et al. speak of *intention-based reflexivity* (Meiran et al. 2012). They argue that "the mere representation of a plan in ALTM [activated long term memory] provides a sufficient condition for its reflexivity" (p. 4), namely inadvertent attention to task-irrelevant stimuli. They suggest that when instructions are remembered, there is a transformation of the instruction from a declarative to procedural representation. That is, subjects are not just remembering the plan. They are doing so in order to implement it (see (Brass et al. 2017) for a review). Thus, there is a difference between subjects who are merely remembering the instructions so as to be able to repeat it and those who intend to implement the instructions. (Recall the suggestion by Myers et al. (2017) that working memory contents are transformed into an actionable format.).

7

THE METAPHYSICS OF ATTENTION

7.1 Introduction

In this chapter, I discuss the theories of four philosophers in the Anglo-American tradition who have published books on attention. This is a narrow focus. A number of younger philosophers who have published articles on attention are not discussed. I ignore the history of attention theory and the Continental tradition (for some discussion, see (Jennings 2020, Chapter 2)). Further, I bypass work on Buddhism and attention with a notable omission of Jonardon Ganeri's book *Attention, Not Self* (Ganeri 2017). The discussion that follows uses published monographs in the analytic tradition as a cutoff for inclusion.

We discuss the work of Christopher Mole (Section 7.2), Sebastian Watzl (Section 7.3), Carolyn Dicey Jennings (Section 7.4), and Wayne Wu (Section 7.5) in the order of the publication date of relevant monographs.

DOI: 10.4324/9781003223450-8

7.2 Attention as Cognitive Unison

Mole's (2011) account emphasizes attention as *attentiveness* as a feature of action, namely the *manner* in which the agent's activity unfolds. Accordingly, he presents his theory as an *adverbial* account of attention (see (Mole and Henry 2023) for a recent discussion). In this book, a central question is the metaphysical question:

1. What is attention?

In contrast, Mole prioritizes the question:

2. What is it for something to be done attentively?

Mole emphasizes (2) over (1) given his stance against identifying attention as a process.[1] He argues against the sufficiency of empirically specified processes as follows, here focusing on feature binding in Treisman's Feature Integration Theory:

1. If attention is a process, then, for all events *x* and *y*, if *x* and *y* instantiate the same process, then if either one of them is an instance of attention, the other is too.
2. There are some events that are instantiations of the feature-binding process and that are instances of attention.
3. There are some events that are instantiations of those same feature-binding processes and that are *not* instances of attention. Therefore,
4. Attention is not a process (adapted from Mole, 2011, 46; for Mole's recent detailed defense of this argument, see (Mole 2023)).[2]

One can replace "process" with "neural mechanism" and in place of feature-binding substitute an appropriate mechanism. Mole does not consider neural mechanisms explicitly, but here is one possibility. In Chapter 4.8, we discussed divisive normalization as a computational account of various neural modulations observed during processing of targets in attention tasks, including different ways that neural signals (gain) shift (Reynolds and Heeger 2009). The hypothesis is that divisive normalization provides a fundamental computation realized in neural processing for attention. At the same time, divisive normalization has also been dubbed a *canonical* neural computation (Carandini and Heeger 2012):

> Normalization was developed to explain responses in the primary visual cortex and is now thought to operate throughout the visual system, and in many other sensory modalities and brain regions. Normalization may underlie operations such as the representation of odours, the modulatory effects of visual attention, the encoding of value and the integration of multisensory information.
>
> (51)

For example, divisive normalization occurs on the human retina where we argued that there is selectivity without attention (see Carandini and Heeger op. cit., 52–3). One can run Mole's argument against divisive normalization in respect of sufficiency by inserting this point at premise (3): there are instances of divisive normalization that do not entail attention. Attention then cannot be *identified* with divisive normalization.

A natural rejoinder would be that there are specific deployments of divisive normalization that yield attention, and the neural mechanism-based metaphysics will appeal only to these deployments. Fair enough, but what is the additional ingredient that renders certain deployments attentional? One possibility is that neuroscientists will find a neural property that renders certain instances of divisive normalization as "attentional". But what is this property? A simple answer is provided by empirical sufficient conditions: the relevant instances are those deployments of divisive normalization that explain selective processing guiding performance of specific tasks. This underscores the central role of task performance in making sense of neural activity as attentional (Wu, n.d.).

Let's return to some of the details of Mole's landmark discussion. Mole notes that whenever one performs a task, one brings to bear various capacities that are deployed in *unison* to serve the task, like the members of a well-rehearsed orchestra playing a symphony. Acting attentively is just using one's resources in this unified manner. This leads to a *simple* account of acting attentively:

Simple unison: A subject S performs task T attentively if and only if S's performance of T displays unison.

The problem with this proposal is that *all* tasks come out as performed attentively: resources used to guide any task are brought together to serve that task (see Mole, p. 64). Yet some actions are done inattentively.

Mole's theory differs from the simple account of unison in two ways. First, he restricts the relevant resources to specific *cognitive* resources. Second,

Mole's account is presented in *negative* terms. It defines what must *not* happen if there is to be attentive performance. This yields *cognitive unison*:

> Let α be an agent, let τ be some act that the agent is performing, and call the set of cognitive resources that α can, with understanding, bring to bear in the service of τ, τ's 'background set'.
>
> α's performance of τ displays cognitive unison if and only if the resources in τ's background set are not occupied with activity that does not serve τ. [I have replaced "task" with "act".]

This is complicated, but the central idea is that for an action to be performed attentively, every relevant cognitive capacity is put to work to aid the action, or, if not aiding the action, it is *not* put to work in the aid of any other action. One can appreciate the essential feature of the account without explicating the central ideas but a few words about (a) cognitive processes, (b) the background set, and (c) the notion of understanding. The theory explicates cognitive processes in connection to the agent's propositional attitudes such as beliefs, desires, and intentions. Specifically, cognitive processes operate over representations that can determine the content of the subject's propositional attitudes. Thus, in doing sums, one calls on cognitive processes of relevance to arithmetic, and these processes put one in a position to think about, ponder, or recall numerical operations. The set of cognitive processes that can serve an action form the *background set* for that action. These are capacities that the subject can deploy with *understanding* in that the agent can articulate what she is doing, how she is doing it, and for what reason. Such understanding plays a specific causal role: it controls and guides behavior. Thus, in completing an academic paper, the agent can describe, explain, and justify what she is doing, thus expressing understanding that guides action. In sum, an action is done attentively when all the relevant cognitive capacities that constitute the action's background are deployed by the agent with understanding to serve the action, or, if those capacities are not deployed, they are not deployed to serve any other action.

For Mole, unison entails that "the resources in τ's background set are not occupied with activity that does not serve τ" (51). This requires "the *absence* of any irrelevant processing" (70). There are, however, two ways that the absence of irrelevant processing can be achieved. First, *all* the members of the background set are clicking in sync, working toward the same task. Second, *some* of the members are working toward a task while the others are dormant. In both cases, irrelevant processing is absent. Mole, however, notes that "the cognitive resources of a normal waking brain tend to find something to occupy them, and so one can typically expect there to be some processing going on in any given resource" (70). Where processes in the background set are dormant, there is the danger of their being distracted, siphoned off to task-irrelevant processing. If so, the required unison would be abolished.

Contrast Mole's proposal with a *positive* version of cognitive unison that maintains that it is enough for cognitive unison that *some* of the relevant capacities are deployed in unison for the task. Thus,

> α's performance of τ displays cognitive unison if and only if *at least some* of the resources in τ's background set are occupied with activity that serves τ.

Distraction, namely the siphoning off of some of the members of the background set, is not a threat to positive cognitive unison so long as other members of the set are operating in unison to serve a task. In general, attentive performance seems less *fragile* on the positive account than on Mole's negative account, for on the latter, if just a single member of the background set gets distracted on matters that are task-irrelevant, performance is no longer attentive. No such consequence follows from the positive theory.

In fact, Mole's theory can be put in positive terms: to say that no member of the background set is serving tasks other than the targeted task is to say that if any member of the background set is serving a task, then it is serving the targeted task. Rather, the difference between the two versions is best stated in terms of quantification. (Mole speaks of this as the difference between *absolute* and *threshold* accounts of unison.) Fragility varies with quantification, namely whether cognitive unison existentially or universally quantifies over the background set, whether the theory requires some or all of the members of the set to be operating in unison. On the universally quantified theory, unison is fragile: one bad apple spoils the lot. Existentially quantified accounts can allow for bad apples, to a point.

Mole's main objection to the existential account is that it seems that (nearly) *all* tasks will be attentive (personal communication). For any task will involve unison in the existentially quantified sense: there will be some number of capacities deployed for that task. Since one must allow for inattentive tasks, this seems to be a *reductio* of the existential account. In response, one might opt to speak of degrees of attentiveness and inattentiveness. One is more or less attentive, and to the extent that one can individuate the capacities that belong in a background set, one can speak of more attentiveness when more of the background set is involved in the action; less attentiveness when less is involved. The same goes for talk of inattentiveness. This leads to an objection to Mole's universally quantified version of the theory, for strictly speaking, it does not allow for partial or divided attention. Mole is aware of this worry, noting ways in which his version of cognitive unison can make sense of talk of partial attention. Still, he emphasizes that just as something that is only partially built fails to be built, something that is only partially unified fails to be unified.

If one thinks that there is partial attention, then this might give one reason to prefer the existential formulation of cognitive unison. But it is worth raising a different question: is there an interesting notion of partial attention, of attention itself being more or less?[3] We have already raised questions about theories of attention that identify it with a gradable resource. Even if we reject that view, perhaps attention could be scaled in other quantitative terms. It is certainly true that ordinary speech treats attention as gradable, but is this something a theory of attention should take on board? Can attentional gradability be given a firm basis?

In the climactic gun fight in Sergio Leone's *The Good, the Bad and the Ugly*, the three gunslingers stand equidistant from each other along the circumference of a large circle, poised to shoot. The camera cuts between each individual's face and, as the scene drags on, focuses directly on each individual's eyes that rapidly flick from one opponent to the other. What would be the best strategy for each gunfighter? Rather than always having to take their eyes off one opponent, they might divide attention to each, perhaps by covertly splitting their attentional spotlight. I surmise that, instead, each would feel more confident in shifting attention back and forth rather than dividing it. Why? Because in dividing, there is a *cost*. One should give undivided attention to each opponent. In dividing, one is *less* attentive (on this, see (Mole 2011, sec. 4.11–12)). This can be seen in slower reaction times, which in the case of your typical duel at high noon is literally life-threatening. It is reaction time decrements that provide evidence for less attention.

In Chapter 3.4, we questioned whether attention itself is gradable. It is one thing to point to a property of behavior, such as reaction time, as gradable, another to infer that the underlying capacity, attention, is gradable. Mole's opponents treat attention as a process, but processes themselves are not gradable, though some of their properties and consequences can be. Combustion as a process is not more or less, though there can be more or less things that combust and more or less energy or smoke that is produced. We noted that partial attention poses a potential challenge to some unison accounts, but process theories might founder as well on partial attention. What is a partial process? One defense of Mole's theory of cognitive unison involves denying that attention comes in degrees.[4]

7.3 Attention as Structuring Mind

Watzl (2017) has presented a Priority Structure View of attention that emphasizes the notion of priority: "Attending consists in regulating *priority structures*" (70). In particular, a subject's attending is their undertaking an activity that has two relevant aspects: *guidance* and *priority*. A subject attends to T when they are *guided* to put a mental state that represents T at the top of a priority structure. Guidance is tied to guiding subject-level states, such as an intention. A priority structure is a hierarchical ordering of a subject's mental states, and Watzl explains the various relations that organize priority structures. The constituents of priority structures are "parts of the subject's mental life and not part of the world around her" (75). The mental phenomena at issue are largely *occurrent* phenomenon, "what is currently going on with the subject; what is currently on her mind" (76). This seems to rule out belief in the traditional sense but includes belief contents that are actively being thought (recall the capital of France right now!). The role of attention in guiding action is important. Watzl claims that his account provides the better explanation of the role of attention "in organizing the mind so as to allow for flexible action" (74).

Watzl provides formal accounts of the various relations that can hold between elements of a priority structure. A basic idea is that of *weak priority*: *x* has weak priority over *y* if and only if *x* has at least as much priority over *y* (79). Watzl recognizes that this is circular, so the entry point must be that one has an intuitive grasp on the idea of "at least as much priority". Given that Watzl's definitions trade on a basic understanding of ordinary notions of priority, his formal definitions can be taken up by any theory of attention that draws on priority.

What then is it on Watzl's view for a subject S to be attending to an object O? S is attending to O at a time t is S's regulating a priority system such that a psychological part that is intentionally directed at O is of top priority in the priority structure at t (83). S's regulating this system is guided, say by S's intention to attend to O. So, to visually attend to O is to regulate the priority structure so that one's seeing O is at the top of that structure. Finally, Watzl enters a distinction between active and passive guidance. Active guidance can involve the standard motivational states that guide intentional action. Passive guidance also involves subject-level states. These states are *psychologically salient* because they present attentional commands (115). This attentional command has the form: put *x* on top of a priority structure! (115).

Watzl's functional account of attention has compelling parallels to the experience of attention. In functionally prioritizing mental phenomena, there is often a corresponding phenomenal prioritization. In particular, attention imposes a center-periphery structure on consciousness: "the center-periphery structure of consciousness is never the object of conscious attention. It *is* our conscious attention" (184). This leads to his formulation of *phenomenal structuralism*: "Complex experiences are structured by attention so that some of their parts are more central than others" (184). Akin to his account of weak priority, Watzl also formulates a relation of weak centrality in consciousness (192), this leading to corresponding phenomenal structure of peripherality (Watzl 2017, Chapter 9.5). The phenomenal descriptions, especially of a center-periphery structure, are intuitive, but does introspection accurately support these claims? (Compare (Wu 2019) for comments on introspection of center-periphery structure and Chapter 8 on introspection.)

In outline, Watzl's account draws interesting parallels between the functional role of attention and the role of attention in consciousness. A worry one can raise is that his view makes attending too internally directed. To bring this out, consider Watzl's example of a fire alarm that grabs your attention. "In the case of the experience of the fire alarm the command is (roughly): put the experience of this fire alarm at the center of your field of consciousness!" This rings phenomenally off-key (Wu 2019). My experience of the fire alarm is that of a command, namely "Get out!" On Watzl's view, attention seems to be inwardly directed, focused on regulating a mental priority structure. Yet, in alarm cases and more mundane situations, attention is outwardly directed. If the alarm does anything with respect to our attending, it is not to encourage us to do mental bookkeeping but to search for an escape route. We can put the objection in terms of highlighting two dependency relations:

Outside-In: In attending to *X* in the world, my internal states regarding *X* are prioritized.

Inside-Out: In attending to my internal states regarding *X*, I prioritize *X* in the world.

All views can agree with outside-in, that given one's attending to an external object, the mind takes on a particular structure. Indeed, this has to be a commitment, *supervenience*, of every theorist of attention who endorses the mind's dependence on the brain. It is a further step to say that the attending to an external object begins with the agent's acting on their mental states, that attention is inside-out. The challenge to the Inside-Out approach is that it inverts the dependency (Mitchell 2022, 15–16). Note that Watzl's view is a narrow form of selection for action in that the targets of selection are relevant mental states or prior priority structures selected to inform restructuring of a priority structure. Consequently, one can ask why one should restrict the activity of attention in this way. These points are not decisive objections but bring out the distinctiveness of Watzl's account of attention as structuring the mind.

7.4 Attention as Prioritization by a Subject

Carolyn Dicey Jennings (2020) defends the idea that attention is the mental prioritization or selection *by a subject*. This is part of exploring "the existence of the self through the subject of attention, or that which directs attention. Directing attention is a central role of the self" (36). In her book, Jennings works with three "working definitions of attention" that she takes to be "roughly equivalent": that attention is "a process of mental selection by a subject", that attention is "the prioritization of mental and/or neural processing on the basis of the subject's current interests", and that attention is "selection that is informed by top-down biasing mechanisms" (p. 167).

An important thesis is that "the existence of an emergent self with its own causal powers is the best explanation of the phenomenon of top-down control in attention" (35). This subject directs attention, exerting control over attention (38). Attention is something that the subject can control in diverse ways. For example, attention as something the subject controls can "do the work of applying [a] rule to incoming perceptual stimuli" (57), "brain activity at a macro scale [can use] top-down attention to control brain activity at a micro scale, according to the current task of the subject" (58), that "the true role of attention in perception…[is] the role of providing facticity to raw particulars by linking those particulars to the "space of reasons" (97), "providing sensory input with a structure that is useful to the subject" (ibid.), "attention is any process of mental or neural prioritization that takes account of the subject's current interests or tasks" (114), "attention provides meaning for sensory input, making it informational for us" (ibid.), and "transforms sensory input into an organized perceptual field, with layers of meaning" (115). In looking at the neural data, Jennings writes that the subject is "illuminated as macro-scale patterns of brain activity, which control micro-scale patterns of brain activity through the feedback of attention" (59) and thus the subject "has an effect on the prioritization of neural processing" (75).

Jennings gives multiple characterizations of attention, but given that she makes a notable effort to invoke a self to give a distinctive account of mental causation, part of the distinctiveness of her account is its appealing to a subject of attention who manipulates attention to induce various forms of prioritization according to the subject's interests. (For her discussion of attention and mental control, see (Jennings 2022).) The weight put on the subject as a source of causal influence is one way that Jennings's view is distinguished from Watzl's, though both make central the notion of guided prioritization.

Jennings underscores the subject's direction of attention, and it seems that if this is to be a distinctive contribution, it says more than the basic view of subject causation we are all committed to when we say, for example, that a subject pays attention as they intended to. Jennings's approach sees the neuroscience as best characterized as supporting the idea of the subject as distinct mental cause. She writes that the "mental is defined in terms of scale" (55) where the scale at issue is cashed out in terms of different types of neural oscillations, different frequency bands, observed in the nervous system. Jennings's proposal is that the oscillations are more than neural correlates of some behavioral measures of mental processes. Rather, the neural marker, and its scale, individuates certain mental properties. "So long as both our psychological and our neural description occur at a scale that is not reducible to that which is describable by local causal factors, then the causal power in question will be mental" (56). Further, she argues:

> In my view...the source [of mental causation] is emergent macro-level patterns of brain activity. Insofar as these are patterns, they have some unity, and so I am inclined to call them a self. Thus, this picture is one of not only mental causation, but mental causation by a self.
>
> (58)

The last remark responds to a query by Watzl, who asks why we should favor Jennings's seemingly inflationary account of the self over what we can call the basic idea of mental causation. After all, we have appealed to a subject's intentions as organizing task-relevant processing, including neural processing, and to the extent that what the subject intends influences what they do, in intending, subjects are causal sources of action. Why make a stronger claim (cf. (Prinz 2022))?

As we have seen, other theorists have been keen to understand *automatic* attention, and it is a striking feature of Jennings's account that she seems to deny it. To capture the different ways that attention can be shifted, Jennings deploys the subject's *interests* as influencing attention's direction. This allows her to capture many shifts of attention. Jennings's denial of automatic attention results from her reflection on skilled and habitual behavior. Here, theorists such as Wu and Ellen Fridland (2014) are apt to describe skilled and habitual action as involving automatic attention. In contrast, Jennings advocates a type of automatic selectivity, *strategic automaticity*, which does not involve attention. Jennings suggests that in habits, attention is "almost universally thought to be missing" by scientists working on these behaviors (144 and passim; cf. 175 and passim). Jennings is right that theorists of habit often say that attention is absent, but deploying these claims might beg present questions. If the disagreement concerns the status of different forms of attention, that issue cannot be prejudged in theoretical discussions of skill, and as we shall see (Chapter 11.3), theorists of attention allow for attentional habits and skills.

What seems uncontroversial is that in acquiring skill and habits, top-down attention is reduced, and so the agent has less need for guidance by task representations and instructions encoded in working memory. As we learn skills and acquire habits, we need to think and remember less. It does not follow, however, that as top-down attention is reduced, attention dwindles, then disappears. An alternative is that attention becomes automatic. An alternative reading of the habit and skill literature that maintains appropriate neutrality is that it emphasizes that *one* form of attention is reduced in a familiar way, say in practice obviating the need to concertedly attend to instructions as one executes the action being learned.

The previous points concern interpretation of the empirical literature which is not essential to Jennings's argument. Rather, her main move is driven by the phenomenology of skill or fluid performance, what she calls *conscious entrainment*. This is the experience of being "completely engrossed in one's task or activity and not thinking about oneself, one's surroundings, one's past, or one's future" (p. 150). Jennings's example is that of being engrossed in drawing a live figure (pp. 147–8).

> I suddenly "woke" mid-drawing as though from a dream. I had been lost in the moment, but I was now suddenly aware of myself. While I knew that the moment before I had been conscious, the structure of that experience was unlike what I was now experiencing. I had lost my sense of self, which was now present again. I had felt deeply connected with the model and my drawing, which now felt separate from me. I had been drawing with ease, but felt that continuing would require effort.
>
> (148)

I will not discuss the phenomenology of conscious entrainment in detail, but readers are encouraged to examine Jennings's discussion (Jennings op. cit. Section 5.4.2; also (Jennings 2015)). For present purposes, let us grant that Jennings has the phenomenology right. She is drawing a live figure so that her drawing movements are guided by her visually selecting certain features of the model. As she draws, she looks, visually taking the model in, in a fluid, effortless way, tightly coordinating her looking with her drawing strokes. Why isn't this attention that is automatic integrated in a way in her behavior that does not require concerted thought? Jennings suggests that in affirming automatic attention, one is introducing a "new" category of attention (fn. 18, p. 145) for there is a "presumed opposition of attention and automaticity" (181). Instead, she concludes that the phenomenon involves *focus* rather than attention where in skilled behavior, such focus amounts to "strategic automaticity" (182). So, in her entrained experience of drawing, Jennings is focused without attending. The proposal presents a different conceptual framework for understanding the bounds of attention in skilled and habitual behavior.

This is a distinctive view worth exploring. Here, I will note one theoretical cost. In discussing skill, Jennings denies that the automatic eye movement data from Yarbus, often cited by Wu and Fridland (2014) in discussing skill, illustrate attention. In doing so, Jennings's approach contrasts not just with those philosophers but with a long-standing empirical line of investigation on *looking*, a basic form of human attention. It is looking that Yarbus probes in his pioneering use of eye tracking, and the data reveal instances of overt visual attention. Wu and Fridland (and Yarbus) can agree with Jennings that looking is strategically automatic, but it is strategically automatic *attention*. A response to Jennings's approach is that it distorts a basic visual attentional phenomenon by denying that automatic looking is automatic overt visual attention.

The cost ramifies, for the proposed contrast undercuts the uniformity of explanations of overt visual attention in terms of *priority maps* which are computed by integrating various biases (see Chapter 5.5). These maps provide an explanation of eye movements within a visual scene, and while the inputs to computing a priority map can include the subject's interests in Jennings's sense, these inputs also include factors that are distinct from the agent's interests, including implicitly learned statistics and associations (see Chapter 11). To segregate some eye movements as attention because they are driven by interests and others as not attention because they are driven by biases distinct from the agent's interests introduces a theoretical distinction where vision scientists have not found need for one. This is not necessarily an objection, for a philosophical theory can be revisionary. Readers are invited to adjudicate this disagreement.

7.5 Attention as Selection for Action

We discussed the important connections between attention and action, rooted in James's articulation of the folk conception of the function of attention. All of the views thus far agree that attention plays an important role in agency, though they need not agree that this exhausts the essential function of attention. The *Selection for Action* account holds that a subject's attention to T is the subject's mentally selecting T to deal with. The cognitive science of attention implements an entailment of this position across numerous experimental paradigms (Chapter 1.4). The empirical approach, expressed in the Common Conception, does not entail the metaphysical position, so readers can reject selection for action as identifying what attention is while allowing that selection for action is the primary form of attention studied in cognitive science.

To review some salient aspects of my (Wu's) version of the theory (see discussion of Allport and Neumann in Chapter 2.7), attention is a subject-level phenomenon that is constituted by the machinery of agency needed to solve the Selection Problem. An input, the agent's taking things in a modality such as perception or cognition, that is the agent's having a perceptual or cognitive experience, constitutes attention in that modality when the agent responds guided by how she takes things to be. So, if the agent moves in some way toward an object seen, where the movement is guided by that seeing or the memory of it, then that seeing or memory of the object constitutes the agent's visually or cognitively attending to it (respectively), namely visually or cognitively selecting it for guiding response, a movement of mind or body (for a defense, see (Wu 2023)). Guidance can involve what Allport speaks of as coupling and Neuman as parameter setting (Chapter 2.7). A simple idea is that we visually attend to a feature because that feature, what it is, is needed to set the parameters of a response such as the programming of an appropriate grip to grasp the target or the application of an appropriate concept in generating a report about the target.

This is an economical or deflationary account of attention because once one has built in capacities to respond on the basis of appropriate mental inputs, attention comes for free. To speak of a subject's attention is to capture the selective guidance of a response by the agent's taking things in some way. In that respect, attention gives a functional description of a process of guiding action, namely where the intentional content of the input state explains the properties of the resulting response. Of the views considered in this chapter, Selection for Action is, I believe, the metaphysical account that coheres most directly with the cognitive science of attention since, as argued in earlier chapters, the science builds on the same functional structure in constructing attentional paradigms.

Selection for Action is taken to be easily refuted by simple cases, and this has blocked recognition of the virtues of the theory. Philosophers have provided a host of simple counterexamples to sufficiency, that a subject's selecting a target to guide a response in acting is the subject's attending to that target. They attempt to identify cases of such selection where attention is absent. Let's consider some notable challenges. Watzl writes:

> consider coming home and switching on the light in a familiar room. Again, you might be peripherally conscious of switching on the light (as well as being peripherally conscious of the switch). Furthermore, you are selecting the light switch as the target of your bodily action. But again, in a case like this, your act of switching on the light might be so automatic that your attention need not be focused on the light switch.
>
> (Watzl 2011, 154)

The case is underdescribed. It seems to assume that the automaticity of the action speaks against attention (cf. Jennings, Chapter 7.4), yet automatic attention is a pervasive part of agency, as we will see in Chapter 11. Watzl also speaks of focused attention, and perhaps here he means that one need not be aware of directing attention. That is, however, a typical feature of automatic attention. It does not show that attention is not deployed unless the question of automatic attention is begged. In a similar vein, Denis Buehler has suggested the following:

> We can imagine [an agent] exiting the metro, his attention entirely devoted to reading a newspaper. He has the intention to walk home. Unless he encounters obstacles, the individual need not attend to what he is doing. Yet he acts, and exercises agential control over his movements [including selection for action]. These points seem intuitively obvious.
>
> (Buehler 2019, 2130)

A point's being intuitively obvious does not cut any ice in psychology, and the assertion that the agent need not attend seems again to beg the question regarding automatic attention. Readers can adjudicate the disagreement. (For further discussion, see (Wu n.d.).)

We have already observed that empirical sufficient conditions provide the central lever by which scientists manipulate attention in the lab. The general sufficient condition is provided by James's description as an expression of folk psychology. It is an important question whether all cases of such selection for action amount to attention. No doubt, someone will come up with another problematic case. The point here is that many putative counterexamples in the literature discount automatic attention or simply assume that the folk intuitions or introspective judgments that yield the examples accurately track psychological reality. This is far from clear and should not be merely assumed. (See discussion of the accuracy of introspective attention in Chapter 8.)

The other challenge to selection for action concerns its necessity for attention: that where there is attention to a target, that target is selected to guide action. Attentional capture presents a potential counterexample to necessity. Can selection for action allow for fully automatic attention, and thus:

> If *S*'s attention is captured by *X*, then *S* selects *X* for performing action *A*.

The answer is yes, but attentional capture is automatic selection so:

> If *S*'s attention is captured by *X*, then *S* automatically selects *X* for performing action *A*.

Remember that "action" captures things we do, including mental actions. Automatic selection of X for action is, of course, a type of selection for action. Given the definition of automaticity given in Chapter 2.8, to say that the selection of X is automatic is to say that selection of that target is not intended. Yet that is precisely what happens in attentional capture, at least initially: the capture of attention involves the capture of action.

Attentional capture is driven by cases where there are sudden changes in one's mental state in respect of an object (or feature): a loud sound or a sudden shift in the pitch of a current sound, a swooping bird, a fragrant smell, a pleasurable memory, a twinge in one's calf, or a disturbing thought. One thereby moves from not having any mental states directed at the object (which has not yet appeared) to having a mental state directed at that object. Yet since none of the imputed mental states directed at the object on its own entails attention, being in a mental state is compatible with not paying attention, something else must be added for attention to appear. For example, in the perceptual cases, the appearance of a sudden stimulus yields only the perceptual registering of a change, a transition from not perceiving an object to perceiving it. But the perceptual registering of a change does not entail that one attends to the object at issue. In general, there can be alterations in a subject's mental states without these alterations engaging attentional capture. Something else is needed to allow for attention, but what? Proposal: selection for action. The input state must be coupled to a response of some kind. (Compare with Buehler (2018a), who seems to require that the theory must specify a specific kind of response.)

This proposal that selection for action transforms the mere registering of change to attention fits with the psychology of attentional capture, namely that it is tied to an orienting response (Wright and Ward 2008). This suggests an action that is automatically driven by the suddenly appearing stimulus, an input-output coupling that can be contrary to the subject's current intention. What captures attention always engages a response: you move your body toward the object, orienting toward it; you think about or remember it; you explore it with other senses. In such cases, the resulting actions are automatic, at least initially, because none of them is intended. If this automatic response yields information that is goal-relevant, control can kick in. One subsequently intends to explore the object further. Attentional capture gives way to controlled attention.

Similarly, thoughts and images can also pop into your head as an object pops into your sensory field. The same considerations apply here as well, though in the mental case, there can be a small distance between input and output. The first point is that the flash of a thought is no different from the flash of a change in perception. Both yield alterations in what is given in one's mental states that do not necessitate attention. It is only when thought and perception engage with the mind in a further way that one moves toward attention. Thus, consider the flash of a thought that leads one to ponder it further. An embarrassing image of last evening's faux pas might involuntarily flash in one's head, but if the thought amounted to nothing more than that, no attention emerges. There is just the fleeting image. It is only when that image engages further activity, when one ponders it, maintains it (e.g., in working memory), laments it, or just sustains the image over time as one internally cringes, that attention emerges. In attentional capture, attention enters the scene when the item that does the capturing not only alters the shape of one's mental states but engages a response. Otherwise, there is only the mental registering of a change.

What is there to say for Selection for Action? Readers should recognize its overlap with the Common Conception. On the question of the "easy" refutations, my response is that the cases already presume substantial points about when and how attention works or about the adequacy of our access to it. These are not matters that can be merely assumed. Thus, like the three previous theories, Selection for Action should command one's consideration. Given its easy integration with the cognitive science of attention, I would suggest that it should be the starting point for philosophers interested in attention.

7.6 Conclusion

The goal of this chapter is not to settle the metaphysics of attention but to give readers a sense of four approaches in a set of rich discussions that mark the reemergence of attention as a topic of philosophical inquiry. Metaphysics aside, to do substantive work with attention, one does not have to settle the metaphysics. As argued in earlier chapters, the Common Conception as the overlap between cognitive science and folk psychology suffices for most theoretical projects. This is not to say that metaphysics does not matter. Rather, neutrality about the metaphysics does not mean neutrality about a substantive picture of what attention is in philosophically and empirically important contexts.

Suggested Readings

The books discussed here are Jennings's *The Attending Mind* (Jennings 2020), Mole's *Attention is Cognitive Unison* (Mole 2011), Watzl's *Structuring Mind* (Watzl 2017), and Wu's *Movements of the Mind* (Wu 2023). Jonardon Ganeri's *Attention, Not Self* (Ganeri 2017) discusses Buddhist theories of attention in the Pāli philosophical tradition. Denis Buehler has written several papers on attention, and a notable emphasis is the role of the central executive in explaining a subject's attention in action (Buehler 2018b, 2022a, 2022b). Adrienne Prettyman has discussed diffuse attention (Prettyman 2023). Philipp Koralus (2014) has presented an erotetic theory of attention.

Notes

1 Some years ago, Alan Allport argued against a broader mechanism-based metaphysics using a version of multiple realizability (broader in that he did not limit himself to neural mechanisms). He wrote:

> most contemporary theories of information processing in general, and selective attention in particular, view attention as some sort of causal mechanism. However, even a brief survey of the heterogeneity and functional separability of different components of spatial and nonspatial attentional control prompts the conclusion that, qua causal mechanism, *there can be no such thing as attention*. There is no *one* uniform computational function, or mental operation (in general, no *one* causal mechanism), to which all so-called attentional phenomena can be attributed. (1993), 203).

Allport's argument can be simply stated:

1. "The evidence…indicates that, in implementing visual-attentional selectivity, a number of qualitatively *different* mechanisms are involved" (202).
2. So the evidence is that there is no unitary mechanism that is or constitutes attentional selection.

Allport's argument is an empirical one. He takes the support for the first premise to be derived from experimental work.

2 Mole argues against sufficiency by drawing on the phenomenon of *hemispatial neglect* where subjects are thought to be unable to attend to specific portions of visual space, often the left side due to lesions in right parietal cortex. There are striking cases where neglect patients show

responsiveness to information that they cannot report. John Marshall and Peter Halligan (1988) presented a neglect patient, P.S., with pictures of two houses. The central difference between the two houses was that, in one, a fire can be seen emanating from the left side that is subject to neglect. P.S. explicitly reported no visual difference between the two houses, yet when prompted to choose between them, she chose the one that was not burning. Similar results have been obtained with other patients where they evince sensitivity to information from the neglected portion of space. The subject cannot attend to the relevant region of the picture, yet the suggestion is that some feature binding of elements allows for a "sense" of the fire. If so, attention is absent but feature binding is present; hence, attention can be dissociated from feature binding.

3 As we shall see, in the empirical study of attention and consciousness in Chapters 9 and 10, it is often claimed that we can be conscious of items outside of attention. Sometimes, the claim is that there is consciousness outside the "near absence" of attention, implying presumably that there remains at least the possibility of residual attention.

4 Philipp Koralus's *erotetic theory* of attention offers an alternative adverbial account to Mole's cognitive unison theory (Koralus 2014). The central idea is that we can think of perception as a way of interrogating the environment and attention as connected to answering those questions. Thus, when I look for my keys, perception aims to answer the question: where are my keys? Attention is a way of focusing one's attempts to answer that question. This suggests an interesting way to conceive of the function of attention in performing a task, namely to aid answering of task-relevant questions. Koralus invokes the semantics of interrogatives.

In modeling the relationship between questions and answers in natural language, it has been recognized that in order for something to count as a fully *congruent* answer to a question, what the putative answer is "about" has to match what the question is "about." In English, stress patterns aid matching, while other languages like Japanese include special grammatical particles to mark the relevant distinctions. For example, reading the italicized word with appropriate stress, "*Adam* philosophizes" is an appropriate or congruent answer to "Who philosophizes?" while "Adam *philosophizes*" is not a congruent answer although it is a congruent answer to a different question: "What does Adam do to make the world a better place?" The erotetic theory emphasizes the following two features: (a) the set of possible answers that individuate a question and (b) the contribution of focus marking in determining congruent answers.

Like Mole, Koralus emphasizes tasks. Let us take as the basic case for the erotetic theory situations where agents monitor the performance of their task so as to query whether the task is completed. This task monitoring can be modeled by a set of questions for the agent. In visual search for a red square, monitoring task completion will involve the question: *where is the red square?* This question determines a set of answers that specify the *completion conditions* for the task, namely propositions identifying the possible location of the square: {red square is at p_1, red square is at p_2...}. Now, most tasks are complex, involving subtasks, each with its own completion conditions. For complex tasks, agents will need to monitor subtasks as well, each tied to its own question and set of possible answers that fix its completion conditions. In reaching for a mug, certain questions seem appropriate to assessing completion: Where is the mug? Is the arm on the right trajectory toward the mug? Is the grip being prepared of the right sort? Such monitoring need not be explicit or conscious.

To do a task attentively is to be sensitive to the answers to the questions set by a task. Thus, to visually search for one's keys attentively is to be sensitive to target location, one of the answers to the question set by the task: where are my keys? The problem, however, as we noted in the semantics of questions, is that not all answers are congruent. To aid congruency, attentional focus plays the same role in attentive action as focus does in interrogatives. Both help to determine congruent answers. Doing a task attentively, then, involves the agent's being sensitive to congruent answers to the questions posed by the tasks. More simply, attention helps to get us to the right answers.

8

ATTENTION AND INTROSPECTION

8.1 Introduction

We need to understand how we introspect conscious experience since introspection provides the primary data for building theories of consciousness. Yet we do not have agreed-upon ways of assessing the adequacy of introspective data, and this in part because we don't understand introspection adequately as a psychological phenomenon. Introspection involves attention, so our focus will be on *introspective attention* of conscious, phenomenal, perceptual experience. The term "introspective attention" suggests that attention is turned inward as perceptual attention is turned outwards. Yet this characterization is theoretically loaded. I opt for a neutral understanding of introspective attention as *attention that informs introspective response* such as judgements, thoughts, or reports about experience. Specifically, given an experience E and an introspective response R, introspective attention is the subject's selection "of" E to inform R. I draw on a robust theory of attention to explain introspective attention of phenomenal consciousness.

DOI: 10.4324/9781003223450-9

In Section 8.2, we begin with Simple Introspection of conscious perceptual experience where attention is constituted by the experience examined. Challenges for Simple Introspection are raised in Section 8.3. Complex introspection that involves multiple attentional channels is introduced in Section 8.4, and challenges raised by it are examined in Section 8.5. The direct model of introspective attention is discussed in Section 8.6.

8.2 Simple Introspection

We begin by adapting an idea from Gareth Evans (1982), who suggested that we can introspect perceptual experience by reusing the psychological machinery for generating a perceptual report based on that experience. For example, to report that there is a visible feature or object T, we visually select T to inform *observational* report: there is a T (there's the red target; there's a bear)! We can also draw on those same visual-cognitive capacities to inform an *introspective* report: I *see* T (I see the red target, the bear)! When we introspect experience, we begin by doing what we would normally do in providing an observational report of the presence of T but rather than invoking the observational concept, T, we instead deploy the experiential concept *see*-T. So, rather than producing the report "(There's) a bear!" we instead report, "I *see* a bear!" This shift is effortless. We often use "see" in observational reports: I see a fire, the keys, the bear. The report is introspective because it is about one's *seeing* T.

Generally, we elaborate on the quality of our visual consciousness of the world with detailed descriptions of what we see. Each of these introspective responses tracks a parallel perceptual report that we could have made. The introspective and perceptual responses begin by deploying the same perceptual-cognitive capacity. So, where I introspectively report seeing a brown thing, a furry thing, a bear, a large bear, with big teeth, I begin by doing what I would do in generating the observational report that there is a brown thing, a furry thing, a bear, and so on. In both cases, we extract information about the visible object by deploying visual attention. Visual attention is visual selection of T to inform either a perceptual or an introspective response. Specifically, visual attention to target T guides application of the concept T in perceptual observation or application of the concept *see*-T in introspection. We can diagram both movements as in Figure 8.1.

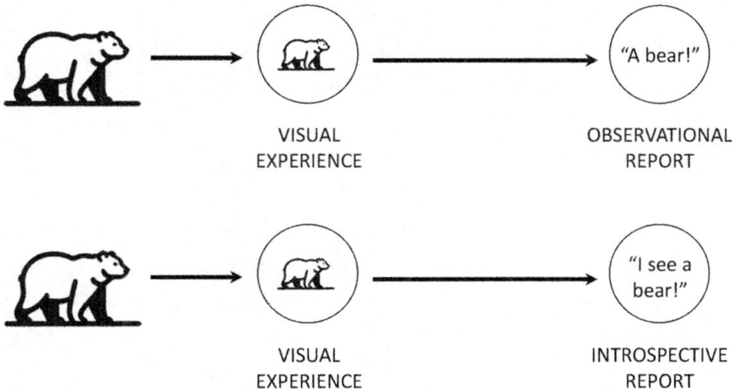

Figure 8.1 Observational versus Introspective report where the visual experience selectively informs the report response. Bear drawn by DALL-E.

Visual attention to T, visual selection of the bear for report, anchors both conceptual responses. Because the visual experience of T is the basis of the introspective report, there being just this *single* information channel that guides (informs) response, we have *simple* introspection.

This model suggests concrete proposals about the reliability and accuracy of introspection. Introspective reliability is a function of the reliability and accuracy of perception in the relevant context, something we can measure. Consider the interchangeability of reporting that there is a T and that one sees a T. Given the shared psychological basis in the input visual experience, if the first report is accurate, so (likely) is the second. After all, if the first is accurate, this means that one did see the T. If, in that instance, one had instead generated an introspective report informed by that experience, then the introspective report that one sees the T would also be correct for it would be based on the subject's actually seeing T. In this case, the reliability and accuracy of introspection is based on the reliability and accuracy of perception.

Is simple introspection really introspection? Simple introspective attention in this case is visual attention. Visual attention is directed at the world, but isn't introspective attention turned inward at the mind? This suggests a linguistic-conceptual objection to the Evansian proposal as getting the directionality of introspective attention wrong. Recall, however, that we imposed an ecumenical reading, affirming a neutral depiction of introspective attention as attention that functions to guide introspective response. This avoids making contestable assumptions about the nature of the psychological machinery of introspective attention at the outset of debate. If Evans's proposal captures psychological reality, it is not to be gainsaid by how we talk.

There is more to explore about how to assess introspection in these domains, but one might wonder what use is simple introspection? At best, it only tracks the homely forms of consciousness in basic perception. We will consider more difficult cases later, but simple introspection shows that it is possible to model introspective attention in a way that leads to concrete proposals regarding introspection's reliability and accuracy. One thing the model emphasizes is that, to probe experience, we use a psychological machinery that is well investigated in perception science, namely the use of perceptual attention in guiding diverse responses which include all manner of bodily and mental movements. Among these responses is the ability to deploy the conceptual repertoire needed to talk about experience. What we gain is a scrutable psychological capacity where introspection is built on capacities which we understand.

Gilbert Harman observed:

> When Eloise sees a tree before her, the colors she experiences are all experienced as features of the tree and its surroundings. None of them are experienced as intrinsic features of her experience. Nor does she experience any features of anything as intrinsic features of her experiences. And that is true of you too .... Look at a tree and try to turn your attention to intrinsic features of your visual experience. I predict that you will find that the only features there to turn your attention to will be features of the tree. (1990, 667)

Harman voices the *transparency observation*: that attempts to introspect phenomenal properties of consciousness lead attention to the external world. This is a good description of simple introspection. The transparency observation has been used in arguments against qualia theories of phenomenal consciousness where qualia are special, possibly nonphysical, properties of experience. It has also been invoked in favor of representationalist theories of consciousness where phenomenal properties are explained by the experience's representational properties (see especially (Tye 2000)). There are genuine questions, however, whether the transparency observation can support such arguments (Martin 2002; Kind 2003; Siewert 2004; Stoljar 2004; Molyneux 2009). I shall, however, sidestep these broader debates and focus on something explicitly raised in Harman's transparency observation: the role of attention. Harman makes a prediction: "Look at a tree and try to turn your attention to intrinsic features of your visual experience. I predict that you will find that the only features there to turn your attention to will be features of the tree." The claim is that attention as used to generate introspective reports locks on to the external world, consistent with the model of simple introspection. Does the transparency observation establish simple introspection? The problem is that the observation is based on an introspective report, but the accuracy of such reports is under debate. To assume introspective accuracy begs the question.

8.3 Challenges for Simple Introspection

Simple introspection raises a host of questions. First, introspective knowledge is regarded as epistemically superior to, more reliable than, perceptual knowledge, yet simple introspection appears to obliterate that advantage. Since the model identifies introspective attention with perceptual attention that informs introspective response, at best, introspection looks like it can be no better than perception. Perceptual capacity in a specific context seems to set the upper bound of introspective performance in that context.

Relatedly, sometimes one has vivid hallucinations, experiential states that appear clearly to have phenomenal character, yet there is no corresponding object in the world. When one is visually hallucinating pink elephants, there are no pink elephants to see, hence to visually attend to. Consequently, perceptual reports that there are pink elephants are reliably incorrect in hallucination. Still, the report that one is visually experiencing a pink elephant seems to be accurate. Introspective and perceptual accuracy come apart in that introspection is accurate while perception is not. This is counter to the prediction of the simple model which links together the reliability of both.

Consider the cellphone buzzing hallucination that many people experience: one feels one's phone buzzing in one's pocket, reaches for it, and realizes there's no phone! Let's imagine that this somatosensory hallucination is continuous, that one's cellphone feels to be buzzing over a period of time. So, after discovering that nothing is in my pocket yet still feeling, disturbingly, a tactile buzzing, I report that I am undergoing a somatosensory hallucination. Let us stipulate as per common opinion that introspection here is accurate but perception is not. Yet note that one reason that the subject generates an introspective report that they are hallucinating is not just the somatosensory experience but also the acquired perceptual knowledge that there is no phone in the pocket. So, introspection in this case draws on two channels: their present experience of the buzzing and their acquired knowledge that there is nothing in their pocket. Given the two information sources, they can accurately note their hallucination. Such introspection, however, is no longer simple. It goes beyond the sensory channel, drawing on additional knowledge. We will cover such *complex* introspection in the next section.

Yet can I not just directly be introspectively aware of the phenomenal properties associated with hallucinating a pink elephant? I attend to those qualitative features of my experience simply and directly. This response relies on the *direct model of introspection* to be discussed in Section 8.6. I only note here that the direct model is inflationary in positing an additional form of attention that can be turned inward. Alternatively, there are theoretical positions that can explain the introspection of phenomenal features of hallucination within the simple model. I have in mind *representationalist* accounts of phenomenal experience where the phenomenal properties of perceptual experience are explained by the representational content of those experiences. The qualitative features of experience are identical to or supervene on the content of experience. Often, representationalist theories endorse the transparency observation, leveraging it as an argument for their theory of consciousness (Tye 1995; Dretske 1995). I take no stand on this theory except to note that once a thesis about the metaphysics of consciousness is introduced, we can combine it with the simple theory of introspection to explain how yoking the basic capacities deployed in perception and in introspection can deliver the result that, sometimes, perception is reliably inaccurate while introspection is reliably accurate.

Debates about introspection are often intertwined with metaphysical accounts of consciousness. Consider a different theory of phenomenal character associated with some versions of *relationalism* (Fish 2009). Relationalist theories appeal to the world that the subject is aware of to explain introspected phenomenal character. In a strong version, the phenomenal character of experience just is the perceptible character of the objects experienced. So the phenomenal character associated with seeing shape is explained by the shape seen. On this view, given that there is no perceptible target in hallucination, there is no phenomenal character corresponding to the report. That means that an introspective report that one is having a specific qualitative character in hallucination is *false*. Introspection is mistaken. Admittedly, many theorists of consciousness think this result is, to put it politely, insane. Yet the insanity objection cannot be based on introspective reports since the reliability of those reports is a point of contention between the theories. In contrast, the relationalist holds that subjects are wrong in introspecting hallucination (for more discussion on this clash, see (Wu 2023, Chapter 7)). The neutrality we have undertaken identifies introspective reports of hallucination not as an uncontroversial data point but as a critical point of contention.

There is more to say here, but that is the point. There are substantive debates to be had once we think seriously about the structure of introspective attention and move beyond intuition and assumption to elaborate realistic psychological models. In the next section, I consider the more common form of introspection deployed in science and philosophy: complex introspection.

8.4 Complex Introspection

If simple introspection relies on only one information channel anchored in perceptual experience (Figure 8.3), complex introspection is not simple in that it relies on more channels. Let me begin with a basic example of reliably accurate complex introspection to illustrate its structure.

Readers who wear corrective lenses will be familiar with optometric exams, but for those who do not need vision corrected, this is roughly how it works. One goes into the doctor's office and is seated so that the head is comfortably held in a fixed position. Letters of different sizes (or Landolt figures in Europe) are projected on the wall, and one is asked to read them with glasses off. If one's vision needs correction, say one can't see letters of a certain size clearly, the doctor tests various lenses. So let's say you're observing an "E". The doctor puts $lens_1$ in front of your eyes and then $lens_2$, asking you which is better. This prompts you to introspect blur in your visual experience and assess which lens is less blurry (or, correlatively, more clear). The doctor takes your introspective report at face value and proceeds with comparing further lenses until you are unable to detect a difference between the two lenses.

The basic test is built on simple introspection. You observe the "E" right now under $lens_2$ and compare it with your memory of "E" under $lens_1$, effectively a working memory task in that you have to retain memory of "E" as previously seen to compare with "E" as currently seen. Your judgment

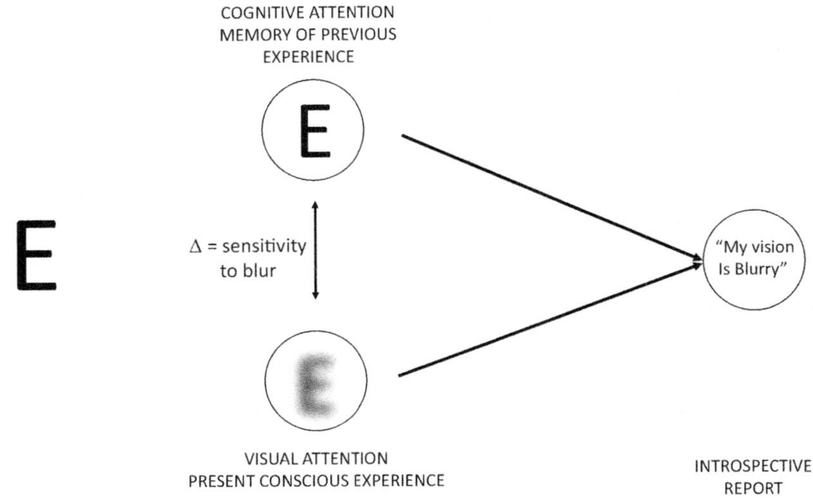

Figure 8.2 Complex introspection involving the memory of one's experience of the "E" in the world (left side) under one lens and then comparing this memory with one's present experience of an "E" under a less powerful lens. The contrast between these two cases, and the sensitivity to the difference in spatial acuity, leads to a complex introspective judgment that one's vision is blurry.

of blur here is relational and introspective. It is relational because you are comparing present and remembered experience, and it is introspective because it is your visual experience that is blurry, not the letter. So, given the role of the mnemonic channel in addition to the perceptual channel, we have non-simple (i.e., complex) introspection. In this case, there is an additional cognitive channel that informs introspective report. We can diagram the matter this way (Figure 8.2).

There is more to say (Wu 2023, Chapter 7), but my goal is to emphasize the basic structure of complex introspection as drawing on *multi-channel* attention. In the blur case, we draw on two channels: visual attention in present experience and cognitive attention in past experience as remembered. We can also give an indirect argument for the accuracy of introspection in that accurate optical refraction depends on accurate introspective report of blur, so the fact that many of us have corrected vision provides evidence for the introspective accuracy of complex introspection of blur in optometry contexts.

That said, the deployment of further channels in complex introspection can increase noise relative to signal. For example, consider theory-ladenness in the sense of a theorist's prior commitment to a specific account of the phenomenology of a particular domain. This commitment is embodied in the theorist's belief about what the experience is like. Let's say that this belief is incorrect. In a context when the theorist is introspecting the experience in question, it is possible that their incorrect belief informs their complex introspective report of that experience. They report what they *think* rather than what they experience. Since, by hypothesis, the two diverge, the introspective report is false for being theory-ladened (Cova et al. 2021). Someone not saddled with the incorrect belief might render a different introspective judgment when having the same type of experience.

This raises the difficult question of how to decide which complex introspective reports are correct. In the case of simple introspection, we have a way to probe the basic perceptual channel on which it is built through psychophysical methods. So, in contexts where perception is reliably accurate, we can reasonably infer that subjects with normal psychological capacities will also simply introspect in a reliably accurate way (this isn't guaranteed). With complex introspection, however, the first step in validation is to enumerate the various sources that inform introspective report. That is, we must identify the further forms of attention that guide introspective response. This amounts to constructing hypotheses about how introspection works. For many forms of consciousness, the introspective data is hard to assess until we know how it was generated. Accordingly, we must build models to address introspective reliability and accuracy. We turn now to a hotly debated case, the question of consciousness and cognitive accessibility.

8.5 The Challenges of Complex Introspection

In this section, we examine one debate in the theory of consciousness, whether phenomenal consciousness requires attention or cognitive access. Ned Block (1995) distinguished *access* consciousness (A-consciousness) from *phenomenal* consciousness (P-consciousness). Block characterized A-consciousness as follows (in the version printed in N. Block 2007, 168):

> A state is A-conscious if it is poised for direct control of thought and action. To add more detail, a representation is A-conscious if it is poised for free use in reasoning and for direct "rational" control of action and speech (The "rational" is meant to rule out the kind of control that obtains in blindsight.).

Access conscious representations are poised for access in the sense of being *accessible* for use by action systems (with "action" broadly construed). When such representations are, in fact, used, they are *accessed* in action, say to guide report or other movements. So the central notions are *access* and *accessibility*, but these must be deployed with care. One of Block's early examples of P-consciousness without A-consciousness is the following:

> Suppose that you are engaged in intense conversation when suddenly at noon you realize that right outside your window, there is—and has been for some time—a pneumatic drill digging up the street. You were aware of the noise all along, one might say, but only at noon are you consciously aware of it. That is, you were P-conscious of the noise all along, but at noon you are both P-conscious and A-conscious of it.
>
> (Block, 2007, p. 174)

How does the access/accessibility distinction apply in this context? Certainly, before one notices the drilling, one doesn't access it in that it does not guide or prompt a report of the sound. Were one to make a report, one accesses that information to guide behavior. Block also points out that you might realize that the drilling has been going on for some time. This realization calls upon information from memory, but until the memory is recalled, it is only accessible to but not yet accessed by report capacities (see discussion by Jesse Prinz (2012); also Dehaene and Naccache (2001)). Yet there is a further dimension, for imagine that as the buzzing occurs, your perceptual system registers the sound. There might be a further step between registering the sound in perception to its being accessible for encoding in memory. It is possible to have perceptual information about the drill without this being accessed by or accessible to memory. This leads to two further distinctions: (a) perceptual representations of the drill that are accessible to working memory but short of being actually accessed by (encoded in) working memory and (b) perceptual representations that are not even accessible to memory. The challenge is that the notions of access and accessibility can be used to describe different points in processing. One must be explicit about which point is intended lest confusion ensue. So, in every case, the logical frame is X *is accessed by/accessible to* Y. To keep things clear, one must always specify the values for X and Y.

Given discussion in the literature on cognitive access, four stages are salient:

1. Perceptually registered, inaccessible but potentially accessible to memory

2. Perceptually registered, accessible to but not yet accessed by memory

3. Encoded in, accessed by, memory, and accessible to but not yet accessed by behavioral systems

4. Accessed from memory to guide behavior such as report.

In our logical frame, *X is accessed by/accessible to* Y, Y identifies a system to which information from X is sent, say Y is working memory or the reporting system. So, in (1), perception is only potentially accessible to working memory; in (2), perception is actually accessible to working memory; in (3), perception is accessed by working memory but only accessible to behavior systems; in (4), working memory is accessed by behavior systems.

Is access consciousness necessary for phenomenal consciousness? Distinguishing access from accessibility leads to the following claims:

(A1) Subject S is P-conscious of X only if X is accessed by S.
(A2) Subject S is P-conscious of X only if X is accessible to S.

Here, the values of X are what one can be P-conscious of. Which stage of processing is at issue? What is typically intended is that X is accessed or accessible to S implies that X is accessed by or accessible to S's working memory. Since the concepts at issue are subject-level, namely the subject's being conscious, then X is accessible to/accessed by S's working memory entails that X could be/is remembered for work (action). If access is tied to attention (i.e., X is accessed in the relevant sense only if S attends to X), we derive a *Gatekeeping* view (Chapter 10): consciousness, here access consciousness, of X entails that S attends to X, say to encode in memory. Since accessibility is defined as potential access, Gatekeeping entails the possibility of attention to X. (A1) and (A2) can then be used to derive the following Gatekeeping theses:

(GK_{A1}) Subject S is P-conscious of X only if S attends to X for working memory (i.e., to remember for work).
(GK_{A2}) Subject S is P-conscious of X only if S *could* attend to X for working memory (i.e., to remember for work).

Consider theorists who focus on the role of *access* in consciousness, hence on (A1). If one were inclined to think that *actual* report of a stimulus (verbal or some relevant behavior) is a necessary condition for phenomenal consciousness, then one would unpack (A1) as requiring that phenomenal consciousness arises only when processing reaches stage (4), thus not just that X is accessed by (encoded in) working memory, but further is accessed by action systems such as in generating actual reports. It is not clear that anyone holds this view. Most hold that reports or relevant behaviors provide evidence for phenomenal consciousness but are not necessary for consciousness. If these theorists endorse (A1), they will only require access in terms of stage (3) as necessary for phenomenal consciousness. This includes many proponents of the *Global Workspace Theory* of consciousness where the workspace is a cognitive architecture that broadcasts, makes accessible, information to action systems. A related interpretation of (A1) is that encoding in working memory determines the content of consciousness. Versions of (A1) can be weakened to a corresponding version of (A2). Thus, one can hold that phenomenal consciousness requires access by working memory (encoding) or only accessibility to working memory (Prinz 2012). Finally, those who deny that phenomenal consciousness implies access or accessibility will claim that one can have perceptual consciousness without reaching any of stages (2)–(4). To return to (1), this position holds that there can be perception that is not accessible to working memory yet is phenomenally conscious. It is not clear that anyone holds this view.

I will focus on (A1) formulated in terms of working memory: phenomenal consciousness requires that the contents of consciousness are accessed by (encoded in) S's working memory. Working memory access is a necessary condition on phenomenal consciousness. This can also be stated in terms of entry into the Global Workspace. In contrast, the *Overflow* thesis denies (A1). Thus, there can be phenomenal consciousness of X even if X is not encoded in working memory. If report relies on working memory, there will be cases where subjects are phenomenally conscious of X yet cannot report X because they have not made X available to memory systems that support report. But why think that subjects who cannot report X because X has not been made accessible to working memory are phenomenally conscious of X? Introspective reports have provided putatively relevant data.

In 1960, George Sperling published, "The information available in brief visual presentations" (Sperling 1960). Sperling's question was: how much does one see in a glance? To answer this, he presented visual stimuli to subjects for very brief durations. To report what they saw, subjects must deploy working memory of perceived stimuli. Sperling's goal was to determine the informational capacity of what is seen and whether this is tied to memory capacity. He recognized, however, that if memory for report is limited, then attempts to report everything that was seen, *total report*, can never exceed the capacity of memory for report, working memory. Accordingly, he pursued a *partial report* paradigm: the subject is directed to report only part of what was seen.

Sperling presented subjects with stimuli containing a number of numerals and letters (from 3–12) in various configurations. When his subjects were asked to give a total report of the identity of the letters flashed, they were able to report 4.3 letters on average (experiment 1, p. 6). This estimate was stable across changes in stimulation durations from 0.015 to 0.5 seconds (experiment 2, p. 6). In his third experiment, Sperling shifted to partial report where subjects were required to report no more than four letters from a stimulus display. Consider then a presentation of 12 letters in three lines arranged top to bottom, with four letters per line (Figure 8.3).

Sperling used a tone, a retro-cue, after stimulus presentation to indicate randomly which line subjects were to report. He assumed that if subjects used the tone to tap into a specific part of a memory representation of the array, namely that corresponding to the cued line, then by taking the number of letters reported in partial reports and multiplying it by the number of lines in the array, he could obtain an estimate of the total number of letters that were seen (for critical remarks on this assumption, see (Phillips 2011)). Doing this, Sperling found the number of letters reported to be on average 9.1, about three of the four letters in each line. In other words, using partial reports, what was accessible—and presumably seen—was measured to be about 9 letters; using total reports, what was remembered was measured to be about 4 letters. So the visual memory capacity as measured in partial report exceeds measured working memory capacity. The effect is called *the partial report advantage* and lasts for about 300 ms after the stimulus is removed, the *stimulus offset*.

Sperling provided evidence that (a) what is seen, in the specific sense of information processed by the visual system, can persist after stimulus offset; (b) it can be accessed in report as in the partial report paradigm; and (c) the

7 I V F

X L 5 3

B 4 W 7

Figure 8.3 One of the arrays used by Sperling.

content of what is seen exceeds the content of what Sperling spoke of as *immediate memory* (i.e., working memory). What is accessible after stimulus offset can be dubbed *visual persistence*, and Ulric Neisser (1967) named this *iconic memory*. If iconic memory reflects conscious perception, then its phenomenal capacity exceeds the capacity of working memory. This suggests that there is phenomenology that overflows what is cognitively accessed by working memory.

Is the persistence associated with iconic memory phenomenal? Here, introspective data has been adduced. On the conception of Gatekeeping that opposes Overflow, access of perceptual content by working memory is a necessary condition on phenomenal consciousness. That is, a subject is phenomenally conscious of X only if X is accessible to action (report) systems (i.e., X is accessed by, encoded in, working memory and, in that sense, access-conscious). On this account, a subject is phenomenally conscious of X if and only if they are access conscious of X.

To dispute this, Overflow theorists provide introspective reports. For example, Block reports his experience of a partial report experiment: "I am P-conscious of all the letters at once, that is, jointly, and not just as blurry or vague letters, but as specific letters (or at least specific shapes)" (Block 1995, 244). The report suggests that one is phenomenally conscious of *specific* letters, presumably some of the identity of letters that one cannot report when later probed. These letters identified as such fail to be encoded in working memory.

Others claim that subjects undergoing the partial report paradigm make introspective reports supportive of Overflow. Yet as noted in the first edition of this book (2014), there were to my knowledge no systematic assessment of relevant introspective data at that time and of reports of overflow phenomenology:

> [this claim] is one that defenders of overflow often raise (see also Burge, (2007)), yet it is unclear how much weight one should give to it. The claim is largely anecdotal. For example, Block (2011, 570) notes Bernard Baars observation that "subjects – and experimenters serving as subjects – continue to insist that they are momentarily conscious of all the elements in the array." Yet Baars seems to be reporting Sperling's own observations here, not independent studies that provide clear empirical support for the first point....what is needed but currently lacking is a systematic study of subjects' reports about their phenomenology in partial report paradigms.
> (193)

Since then, Florian Cova, Maxence Gaillard, and François Kammerer (2021) have collected relevant introspective data. In their experiment, they reproduced Sperling's total report condition using a 12-letter array and systematically collected introspective reports regarding what people see. Let us connect their data with the model of complex introspection.

Notice that the reports collected in Sperling-type paradigms are not exactly introspection but *recollection*. That is, the subject reports from their memory of a recently past visual experience rather than basing the report directly on that experience. What is missing is the perceptual channel as an attentional source, so strictly speaking, we don't have introspection of experience. To simplify, I assume that working memory directly and accurately reflects the content of visual experience of the Sperling array. It preserves at least part of what would be introspectively accessible if the experimental subjects were to immediately introspect their experience. All parties to the debate can agree on this. What they disagree on is whether the working memory content exhausts what was phenomenally seen.

Do subjects give introspective reports that affirm Overflow? Take the assertion that one nevertheless sees the specific identity of the letters that one fails to report. These identities are not in working memory and unless they are a guess, they must have a source. What then is the source? This is not obvious, and the structure of complex introspection forces us to canvas concrete options:

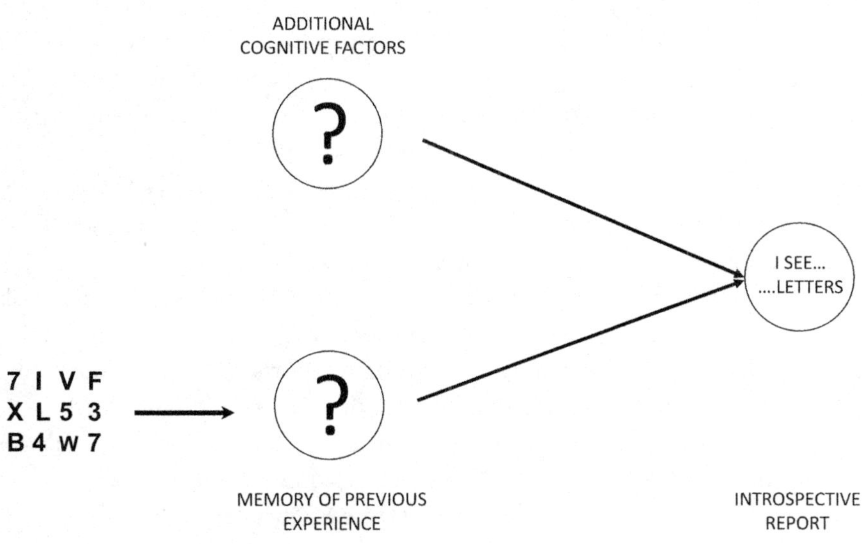

Figure 8.4 Complex Introspection in the Sperling Partial Report experiment. The question marks indicate that it is in dispute what precisely is remembered about the previous experience and what are the additional cognitive factors that influence introspection as to the number and identity of the letters seen (the ellipse in the output indicates the possibility of a variety of answers).

One possible source is the theorist's belief in Overflow. Introspection influenced in this way will not aid Overflow theorists since it implies theory-ladenness. Theory-ladenness of this sort must be ruled out if introspective reports are to provide neutral data in the debate. Accordingly, while Block has contended that to deny the introspective reports of seeing specific unreported letters is to attribute to subjects that they are under an introspective illusion, there is a different reply, namely that they are just telling us what they believe. The belief could be false, and the experience not have the reported features. The influence of the theoretical belief presents a serious potential confound and, as far as I can tell, has not been ruled out. Introspective confidence that introspective reports are not theory-ladened would not settle the issue.

Even ordinary subjects who might not have confounding theoretical beliefs about consciousness often overestimate their visual capacity. This is what makes inattentional blindness so surprising (Chapter 10). So, in introspection in partial report, many subjects might have a belief in a capacious visual capacity, namely that they can see quite a lot in a glance. Further, given the experimental instructions, subjects *know* that the arrays that they are presented with contain twelve letters. The hypothesis is that when asked to assess whether they saw all the letters even though they can report only a subset, a subject might automatically (i.e., unintentionally) draw on prior belief and knowledge. Indeed, in difficult perceptual conditions, we use prior knowledge to our advantage to settle on a judgment about what is there. This might involve an automatic inference: I saw four letters clearly, plus I saw a structure (now insert knowledge) that was made up of eight additional letters and (now insert belief about visual capacity) I am able to see lots, so, yes, I saw more letters than I can report. In this case, introspective report draws on three sources: (1) working memory of the limited number of items previously seen, (2) knowledge of the contents of the array as specified in task instructions, and (3) belief about visual capacity. This yields an empirically plausible hypothesis about how introspective reports seemingly supportive of Overflow might be generated, explaining that support away.

In light of these points regarding complex introspection, the data on subjective reports obtained by Cova et al. are quite interesting. First, after each block of 20 trials under the total report condition, they ask subjects the following two questions:

Q1: In general, did you feel like you saw all the letters displayed on the screen?

Q2: Think about what you experienced during the block that just ended. Which of the following statements best describe what you experienced when the letters were displayed on the screen?

- I felt like I saw all the letters in detail and was able to identify them at this time.
- I felt like I saw all the letters in detail but without necessarily being able to identify them and tell which letters they were at this time.
- I felt like I saw all the letters but not in detail: I just saw where they were and that they were letters.
- I felt like I saw most letters but not all.
- I felt like I saw only a small part of the letters.
- I felt like I saw nothing.

Answers to Q1 allow an initial categorization of whether subjects' coarse characterizations are consistent with Overflow or not. That is, the initial prediction is that the report that denies seeing all the letters is inconsistent with the claim that one is "conscious of all the letters at once, that is, jointly, and not just as blurry or vague letters, but as specific letters" (Block 1995, 244).

Interestingly, there is a shift in introspective responses after each of three experimental blocks. After the first block (20 trials), subjects answered Q1 yes/no at 22/78%, yet after the third block, the same subjects answered Q1 at yes/no 50/42% (we shall assume that this change is statistically significant). If introspection is a simple readout of experience and the reports are accurate, this would suggest that perception is changing across the experiment. Subjects see more of the letters with more experience in the task. Alternatively, if introspection as deployed in the experiment is not simple but draws on cognitive sources, then the change in answers to Q1 might reflect a shift in the influence of different factors that inform the correlated introspective reports, including updating belief during the experiment and increasing dependency on prior knowledge. On this account, how cognitive attention is deployed changes over time. Introspection in this case is not simple, and we should not treat it as if it is.

A second issue is that if subjects answer "yes" to the question of whether they see all the letters, then one might expect the same subjects to also answer yes to one of the first three options in Q2, which explicitly specify seeing all the letters. However, 50% of subjects answering Q2 after the first block affirm seeing all the letters in some way, over twice the number of subjects who claim to see all the letters in Q1. That is, we should expect those and only those who said yes to seeing all the letters in Q1 to be those who said yes to the "all letters" prompts in Q2. This illustrates how different ways of probing experience can lead to different responses. It might be that some subjects are confused by the more detailed wording of Q2, but if they change their introspective reports, what is the basis for their generating a different judgment? This is abundantly interesting.

One final point about the introspective reports. The Overflow theorist might object that the report in question isn't the right probe to assess Overflow. What is wanted is the subject's report of their experience on a *specific* trial, but what is actually requested is the subject's attitude about experience *across the block*. This requires subjects to synthesize a general description of (some subset of the) 20 individual experiences. One way the subject could do this is to recall the last trial and extrapolate from that, something like induction from a single (recent) case. Another way is that the subject "averages" over the individual trials that remain available in memory (but see Study 2 using the paradigm of Landman et al. (2003) for trial-by-trial reports). This points to the difficulty of interpreting introspective data. We cannot get a handle on the Overflow versus Gatekeeping debate, including the data from Sperling-type experiments, without getting a handle on how complex introspective reports in this domain are generated. There are too many possibilities regarding what could be happening. We should not make blind assumptions.

Complex introspection is complex both in terms of its architecture and in terms of the implications of its deliverances. Much of the introspective data of interest to the theory of consciousness is generated by complex introspection. A cognitive architecture helps us parse the different ways that an introspective report might be generated, each way potentially changing how we should understand the report and its significance for debates about the nature of consciousness. Introspection itself should be a primary target of explanation in the theory of consciousness.

8.6 Introspection and Direct Attention

A popular conception of introspection is that it involves *direct attention* to consciousness. This can be characterized as a form of simple introspection but not in the way discussed. Direct attention posits a form of attention which is in some ways alien from the forms of attention studied in science. Let me float two points at the outset: that the form of attention at issue is a theoretical posit, not grounded in empirical work, and that if it exists, its deployment appears to be in special cases of introspection. (For a recent discussion of "inner eye" views of introspection and the model discussed here, see Adriana Renero (2019).)

Brie Gertler (2001) and David Chalmers have presented accounts of direct introspective attention.[1] For both theorists, attention allows one to think about those phenomenal features in a unique and immediate way. Gertler spells out her account in terms of *phenomenal state introspection* (PSI):

> S introspects her occurrent phenomenal state token *a* with phenomenal character *F* if and only if S has an occurrent mental token *b* which is such that
> 1. *a* is embedded in *b*;
> 2. *b* refers to *F*; and
> 3. 2 is true partly in virtue of 1 (Gertler 2001, 307).[2]

This account provides a metaphysical and semantical framework for introspection that can be spelled out in more explicitly psychological terms by adding attention: When a subject attends to an experience, *a*, exemplifying phenomenal feature, F, so as to form a judgment *b* about that phenomenal character, then the judgment *embeds* the experience as a part. So, if I attend to my visual experience of a red rose and specifically the visual phenomenal character associated with seeing red, the resulting judgments about that experience can embed the exemplification of the phenomenal character as a part. A complex mental state results where the judgment refers to the embedded phenomenal character. Gertler also emphasizes that it is embedding that enables *direct* reference to F. (Hence, clause (2) in PSI might be helpfully rewritten as "b directly refers to F" since the embedding also explains the referential *directness*.)

Directness in light of embedding emphasizes a distinctive first-personal aspect of introspective attention. For example, one might make judgments about another person's pain states by neuroimaging, namely looking at the person's brain activity. Similarly, you could image your own brain and in that way get evidence regarding your mental states. Gertler considers a case where a brain scan reveals that one is in a neural state N which, for argument's sake, is necessarily correlated with mental state M. Accordingly, one can on the basis of the neuroimage form the judgment that one is in M. This judgment is formed in an indirect way that depends on perception of the scan image. An external observer has the same kind of access to the mental state via neuroimages. If such access is indirect, one can define direct access negatively in terms of a contrast with the indirect route to M provided by perception.

It would be better to provide a positive characterization of direct access. Attention, perhaps, is oriented directly at the relevant internal property. Gertler's positive proposal is to appeal to embedding. When a judgment embeds its referent in light of attention, this allows for a distinct relation between the judgment and what it refers to such that reference failure is *impossible*. That is, if reference to some phenomenal feature is a result of embedding it, the phenomenal feature referred to cannot fail to be there. In that sense, reference failure is impossible. This provides a contrast to perceptual-based, indirect forms of reference as in the neuroimaging case. Embedding allows for a contrasting direct form of reference.

Embedding is not a causal relation but secures reference by *constitution*, namely in making the referent literally part of the referring state. In this way, embedding makes available direct ways of thinking about phenomenal features. Gertler conceives of the resulting phenomenal concepts as demonstrative concepts. On her view, phenomenal demonstratives differ from perception-based demonstratives in that attention is directed at phenomenal features. While both types of demonstratives depend on attention, there is, again, a critical contrast. Many perceptual demonstratives require a descriptive component to secure reference, say an accompanying sortal term (that *cow*):

> When we perceptually demonstrate something, we use an implicit descriptive component so long as we presume that the referent must be something to which we stand in an appropriate causal relation. And this presumption is always present in perceptual demonstration.
>
> (Gertler 2001, 315)

Phenomenal demonstratives, however, secure reference independently from either descriptive mediation or the use of ordinary means of demonstration, such as pointing. Rather, attention to phenomenal features is sufficient for securing demonstrative reference to those features. Gertler speaks of these demonstratives as *pure* (phenomenal) demonstrative concepts.

Chalmers's account shares many of the same structural features as Gertler's. One possible difference is that Chalmers takes attention to explain embedding while Gertler does not, at least not explicitly (Chalmers's suggests this reading, fn 15, p. 169). On Chalmers's account, embedding (clause (1) in PSI) and reference (clause (2) in PSI) have a common basis in introspective attention. So PSI can be fleshed out in light of Chalmers's proposal of the role of attention in this way: attention to a phenomenal feature is sufficient for embedding it in a judgment, a constitutive relation that allows for a distinctive sort of direct reference to that feature, one where failure of reference is not possible. Chalmers refers to the resulting phenomenal concepts as *direct* phenomenal concepts.[3] Since Chalmers's proposal is compatible with Gertler's framework, I shall assume that both Gertler and Chalmers accept that introspective attention explains embedding. As subjects of conscious experience, we can attend to those experiences in a direct way such that our distinctive first-personal judgments about them have a high level of accuracy, perhaps even infallibility.

Anna Giustina has further developed such "acquaintance" views. She argues that introspection provides for a nonconceptual form of knowledge by acquaintance of the phenomenal state where the direct awareness of that state is what makes it a constituent of the resulting introspective knowledge (Giustina 2022). Like Gertler and Chalmers, she assumes that introspective attention can be deployed directly on conscious experience (Giustina 2021), but she differs from them in taking introspective attention to necessarily alter the *salience* of the introspected experience (this necessity is at least nomological; (Giustina 2023)). On her account, salience is tied to a *structure* of conscious experience that exemplifies a phenomenal foreground and background: X is in the foreground of consciousness if X is attended to. So a phenomenal experience is in the foreground of the structure of consciousness if it is (introspectively) attended to. If correct, then any act of introspection will alter the introspected experience by changing consciousness's overall foreground-background structure (see Watzl (2017) for a detailed discussion of this idea). This imposes a demand on an acquaintance view to accommodate the change in salience.

Giustina's emphasizes a relation of interdependence between the state introspected and the resulting introspective knowledge of that state, what she calls their mutual integration. Introspective knowledge by acquaintance depends on the conscious experience that is introspected since it is constituted by that experience. At the same time, the conscious experience depends on introspection as it is altered by introspection. The experience's salience changes as a result of being introspected. Notably, the phenomenal feature altered is only an accidental property. So an experience, individuated by a distinct essential phenomenal property, remains the same experience, typed by being of a certain kind, even though its salience changes during introspection (Giustina 2023). The reality of these changes imposes constraints on and challenges to an account of introspection. One thing to flag is how to understand the attribution of foreground-background to consciousness, and we shall discuss such *phenomenal* salience in detail in the next chapter.

8.7 Conclusion

We have two basic structures for introspective attention. One captures the idea of introspection as the mind's turning inward on itself by attending to conscious experiences directly. The other builds introspective attention on attentional capacities of which we have an expansive empirical understanding. On this view, attention can be directed outwards in a way that informs reliably accurate judgments about one's experience.

It is possible that each process is correct in different domains, so there need not be a question of compatibility. Perhaps introspection is diverse in its forms (Schwitzgebel 2012; Kammerer and Frankish 2023; Franco 2024), so we can build a big tent in thinking about its exemplars. My interest in probing the architecture of introspection as a psychological capacity is tied to concerns about the adequacy of introspective data for building informative theories of consciousness. For too long, we have assumed that introspective reports are reliably accurate. This assumption is often unwarranted. Instead, we need to understand the structure of introspection and leverage that structure to assess introspective reliability and accuracy. To do this, we should begin with an empirically adequate understanding of attention.

We illustrated this initial engagement by examining introspective data regarding Overflow and Gatekeeping in respect of Sperling's partial report paradigm. Though we did not resolve the challenges, having a cognitive architecture of introspection raises specific questions and identifies clear lines for further investigation. Seeing clearly how an empirically scrutable form of attention might contribute is an important first step.

Suggested Readings

Liz Irvine (Irvine 2012a, 2012b) and Maja Spener (2024) discuss assessing introspection and its data. Eric Schwitzgebel raises a variety of challenges for "naïve" introspection (Schwitzgebel 2011, 2012). An informative collection of essays on introspection is edited by Declan Smithies and Daniel Stoljar (Smithies and Stoljar 2012). Brie Gertler reviews these issues in a volume for this series (Gertler 2011). Jorge Morales (2024) applies signal detection theory to introspection. A recent discussion of introspection has centered on a target paper by François Kammerer and Keith Frankish (2023) with many commentaries by philosophers who work on introspection.

Notes

1 For a more recent statement, see Gertler's (2012) as well as her overview on self-knowledge (2011) in the New Problems of Philosophy series. Gertler speaks of both accounts as *acquaintance* theories, evoking Bertrand Russell's idea of knowledge by acquaintance (Russell 1910).

2 Slightly adapted (replacing Gertler's "content" with "feature"). This is, in fact, the *preliminary* version of PSI, and Gertler later adds a fourth clause. As that clause raises complications that are not necessary for our discussion, I will omit considering it here.

3 Chalmers does not characterize the phenomenal concept made available by introspective attention as a *demonstrative* concept. He agrees that attention to phenomenal features can make available demonstrative phenomenal concepts but that these are distinct from direct phenomenal concepts. In part, this distinction is due to differing semantic analyses of the concepts but also to a test for cognitive significance. (For discussion of the semantic analysis that appeals to a two-dimensional framework, see (Chalmers 2009, Chapter 8).) We can understand the test roughly as follows: if the identity claim X=Y is not trivial, then it is cognitively significant, and if it is cognitively significant, then "X" and "Y" are different concepts. Take now a phenomenal demonstrative concept for phenomenal feature red, $this_R$, and a direct phenomenal concept for the same feature, R. Chalmers claims that $this_R = this_R$ and $R=R$ are not cognitively significant (unsurprisingly) but that $this_R = R$ is. So we have two distinct concepts where R is not a demonstrative concept. In the end, the issue between Chalmers and Gertler on this point seems terminological. It is likely that Chalmers's direct phenomenal concept aligns perfectly with Gertler's pure demonstrative concept. It is not clear to me, however, that $this_R = this_R$, $R=R$, and $this_R = R$ differ.

9

ATTENTION AND PHENOMENOLOGY

9.1 Introduction

William James emphasized that "focalization, concentration, of consciousness are of [attention's] *essence*" [my italics]. The metaphor of an attentional spotlight echoes James's talk of focalization and concentration. The link to consciousness suggests two different answers to the Metaphysical Question. The first yields a phenomenal conception of attention: attention is *a distinctive way of being conscious*. There is a distinctive phenomenology of attention. The second yields a Gatekeeping account of attention, discussed in Chapter 10: attention is *for consciousness*.

Some speak of attention as *highlighting* (Campbell 2002) or *foregrounding* its object (Watzl 2017). As with James's descriptions, these metaphors are suggestive but illusive. Consider as a concrete example the following illusion by Peter Tse (2005).[1] Fixate on the central dots in the right panel. While maintaining fixation, shift covert attention to any of the three overlapping disks. Introspect on your visual phenomenology. Do not read the next paragraph until you decide how to describe your experience. Write it down.

DOI: 10.4324/9781003223450-10

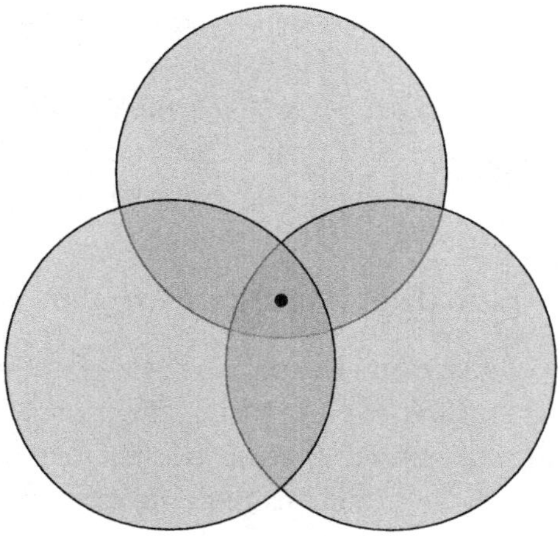

Figure 9.1 Fixating on the central circle, shift attention covertly between the three circles. Adapted from (Tse 2005).

Some subjects report that attending to a disk makes the disk appear darker relative to the unattended disks. Did you experience this? If you didn't, now do the task again. If you experience it now, is that because you have been told what others experience?

Let us go with the standard interpretation. Attention changes the phenomenology where talk of highlighting, focalization, or foregrounding seems apt. It is a further question whether there is a distinctive attentional qualitative character, something that characterizes attention itself rather than its effects. Consider our logical frame: *S m-attends to T for R*. We might take the value of "m" to be consciousness. Indeed, theorists often invoke the idea of consciously attending to T. What do they have in mind? For example, we might distinguish between consciously *visually* attending to T from consciously *auditorily* attending to T. Do these different forms of perception share the same "attentional" phenomenal character? If so, how should we capture that sameness? For example, talk of highlighting is overly metaphorical, but it is related to a perceptual quality, namely qualitative intensity which arguably has a neural correlate (Morales 2023). If conscious perceptual attention to T involves an increased in the apparent sensory intensity of T, would the same kind of intensity phenomenology be found in other forms of conscious attention such as conscious cognitive attention like active thinking?

We begin in Section 9.2 by asking whether attention is necessarily conscious, confronting data supporting the conclusion that attention can be unconscious. Section 9.3 examines empirical work by Marisa Carrasco providing evidence of changes in visual experience when visual spatial attention is deployed. Philosophical perspectives on attention-based changes in experience are considered in Section 9.4. Finally, Section 9.5 considers various proposals for a general phenomenal feature tied to conscious attention.

9.2 Unconscious Attention

If consciousness is of attention's essence, then there cannot be unconscious attention. It is hard to think of cases where attention is unconscious since salient deployments of attention seem inextricably tied to conscious experience. How might one demonstrate that there are cases of unconscious attention? If attention is essentially conscious, this seems to entail the following sufficient condition:

> Sufficiency: If *S* *m*-attends to *T*, *then S* is phenomenally-*m*-conscious of *T*. So, if one visually attends to T, then one is visually conscious of T.

Experimental work suggests that this conditional is false. There is unconscious attention. The arguments for unconscious attention are empirical and draw on the Common Conception. Consider work by Robert Kentridge et al. (1999) with the blindsight patient GY. Blindsight patients are said to lack visual phenomenal experience of certain stimuli in their visual field due to damage in primary visual area V1, the first area in cortical visual processing. For example, damage to the left primary visual area (V1) will lead to a blind field in the right hemifield (i.e., the right visual field). (Left hemisphere cortical visual areas process the right side of visual space, the *contralateral* side, while the right hemisphere processes the left side of visual space.) This blind field can be of different sizes and can be mapped by investigating whether subjects *miss* targets presented in the blind field. Blindsight patients will deny seeing those targets, so there is behavioral and introspective evidence that they are blind.

The damage to V1 accounts for the blindness in blindsight, so why attribute sight? Blindsight patients still have some access to visual information from the blind field. This information is perhaps carried in preserved subcortical visual pathways, such as via the superior colliculus, that bypass V1 and connect to later cortical visual areas such as V2, V3, V4, and MT (see (Weiskrantz 1999) for a discussion of these areas in relation to blindsight). Accordingly, this information is in some way available to patients, as revealed when they are forced to guess about items in their blind field which they deny seeing. Strikingly, their guesses can be accurate, significantly above chance. They can visually detect the presence of targets as well as some of their features. Blindsight patients have access to relevant visual information even if not, apparently, through normal phenomenal experience. After all, they vigorously deny that they see the objects about which they are "guessing".

The gist of Kentridge et al.'s work is the use of the Posner spatial cueing paradigm with GY (see Chapter 4). Kentridge et al. showed that GY demonstrated the standard cueing advantages and costs that are taken to signify spatial attention in normal subjects. In GY's case, the relevant space cued is in the blind field. This provides *prima facie* evidence that GY can deploy spatial attention to location L without apparent visual phenomenal experience of L or items therein. Some conclude that GY exhibits attention without consciousness. GY selects the reportedly unseen target to inform his response. Similar experiments have also been conducted with neurologically intact subjects (Jiang et al. 2006; Kentridge et al. 2008a; Norman et al. 2013). Accordingly, there is empirical evidence that attention can be deployed to unconsciously seen targets; in that sense, attention can be unconscious. This data suggests that consciousness is not of attention's essence in that attention to target T is not sufficient for conscious awareness of it. Blindsight patients can select a target for response but deny seeing the target.

Jesse Prinz (2012) has objected that the cueing paradigm tests *spatial* attention, but the relevant form of consciousness is of an object (see gatekeeping conditionals, Chapter 10.2). That is, the sufficiency claim to be tested is

(A) If S attends to object O, then S is conscious of O

not

(B) If S attends to location L, then S is conscious of O at L.

For example, one might be looking at the location where one's keys are and yet not be aware of the keys, not an uncommon occurrence. Prinz claims that the cueing paradigm probes only spatial, not object, attention and so does not satisfy the antecedent of (A). One can disagree. We noted in Chapter 4 that spatial cueing also involves attention to the target which the subject must report. The subject must attend to the object in order to report on its presence. In reporting on the presence of a *target*, GY attends to an object that he reports not consciously seeing.[2] So the data does seem to speak against sufficiency.

A second case for unconscious attention draws on work regarding the dorsal visual stream in the cortex of primates. The dorsal stream was characterized as the *where* stream by Leslie Ungerleider and Mortimer Mishkin (1982) and was postulated to serve visual spatial awareness. David Milner and Melvyn Goodale (1995) later argued that the dorsal stream is for action that can be independent of conscious awareness. One of the subjects they worked with, DF, has a lesion largely localized to the ventral stream, affecting a region called the *lateral occipital complex* crucial for processing object form. Consequently, she acquired visual agnosia (Farah 2004) as an inability to see visual features such as shape and orientation. Strikingly, while she was unable to report whether a pen was held vertically or horizontally, she could grab the object with fluid accuracy. Given DF's reporting not seeing shape and orientation along with her ability to respond accurately to those features, it was argued that her vision for action as implemented by the dorsal stream must be unconscious. Since DF is able to selectively respond to spatial features of objects to grab them, she visually attends to those features. Hence, she unconsciously attends to those features.

Later work in neurologically intact individuals suggested similar conclusions (for a deductive argument for unconscious vision based on this data, see (Wu 2013a)). Some blindsight patients also show preserved visuomotor abilities in respect of objects they deny seeing, though their movements often reflect a hesitancy that tracks their introspective report (de Gelder et al. 2008). DF is notable in that, to casual observers, her movements appear normal. DF visually selects targets she attests to not seeing, dealing effectively with them.

In each case, an argument for unconscious visual attention is initially plausible (Clark 2001). Roughly, if there are cases of accurate visually guided behavior such as reaching for an object that is served by the dorsal stream, then such vision for action is unconscious. (For doubts about this claim, see (Wallhagen 2007; Mole 2009, 2013; Wu 2020b).) Since visual guidance in these actions involves the subject's visual selection of shape or orientation to guide a movement, we have visual attention to those features for action. So visual attention for action, served by the dorsal stream, is unconscious. Attention does not imply consciousness.

The subject's introspective reports that they cannot see are generally accepted as accurate. In Chapter 8, we made the case that introspective reports deployed in theoretical arguments must be validated. In clinical contexts such as dealing with subjects who have a damaged visual cortex, such reports are appropriately taken at face value. In theoretical contexts, however, we should not take behavioral measures just at face value. We validate and critically assess data. In particular, we probe whether introspection is accurate in these cases or provides relevant information.

A recent debate on blindsight, revisiting worries raised by John Campion et al. (1983), highlights this concern. In theoretical contexts, in taking at face value patient reports that they cannot see, one infers that these subjects are phenomenally blind. Yet an alternative is that their reports are consistent with their having preserved but very degraded vision. They report not seeing because, as suggested by Campion et al., blindsight patients have a conservative bias toward reporting the presence of seen stimuli. This claim depends on the notion of a *response criterion* formally defined in *signal detection theory*, but for present purposes, a simple example will do (see also Chapter 4.5). Consider being in a laboratory experiment tasked with finding a faint visual signal within background static. You are rewarded a small amount of cash if you score a *hit* (i.e., detect a stimulus when it is there), but you are also subject to a large penalty (a shock) if you *false alarm* (i.e., report a stimulus being there when it is not). As you dislike shocks, you report a stimulus only if it is very likely that one is present. That is, you set your criterion or threshold very high for reporting stimulus presence so as to avoid false alarms and attendant shocks. Your behavior becomes conservative, hesitating if there is notable uncertainty. Similarly, blindsight patients might have set their criterion for reporting stimuli very high so often decline to report stimuli that they see but regarding which they lack sufficient confidence (recall simple introspection, Chapter 8.2). Even in cases where they perceive a stimulus, though quite degraded in experience, they might still say that they do not see it just as you might opt to remain silent in the shock experiment even if you thought you saw a faint glimmer of the target in the static, some evidence of its presence. We cannot discuss these issues in detail (for discussion, see (Phillips 2021); for a response, see (Michel and Lau 2021). Simply note how much work introspection is doing in the empirical argument for unconscious attention.

Related worries regarding the argument for unconsciousness in the dorsal stream have been raised by Wu (2020b). The empirical argument for unconscious vision in the dorsal stream uses as a premise that subjects report not seeing stimuli they can act on. In acting selectively on the stimuli, they visually attend to them. The assumption is that the introspective report of absent consciousness gives relevant information about dorsal stream processing and attendant visual attention. Yet if we assume the standard functional account of the visual streams that treats them as functionally segregated and we link introspective report, a conceptual response to one's visual experience, to the ventral stream, then it follows that introspective reports about what one sees or doesn't see concern ventral, *not dorsal*, stream processing. For example, when DF reports not seeing, she correctly reports a deficit in ventral stream–supported vision. This report, however, carries no information about the dorsal stream since, by hypothesis, verbal report, being tied to the ventral stream, thereby has no informational connection to the dorsal stream. Introspective reports based on the ventral stream are irrelevant to inferences about the functionally segregated dorsal stream. The conclusion is not that the dorsal stream is actually conscious but that the empirical argument amounts to a non sequitur since the conclusion about the dorsal stream does not follow from premises about the ventral stream.

The received opinion remains that the examples discussed support the claim that visual attention can occur in the absence of visual consciousness, so visual attention is not sufficient for visual consciousness. Yet introspection plays a key role in those arguments, and there are reasons to query the accuracy and relevance of the proffered introspective reports.

9.3 Attentional Effects on Experience: Empirical Work

Even if we think that attention can be unconscious, it is largely uncontroversial that attention is often connected to consciousness. Does attention, when conscious, have a uniform phenomenology, a distinctive attentional character instantiated in all cases of conscious attention? Alternatively, when we m-attend to T (visually/auditorily attend to T), the link to consciousness is in attention's causal *effects* on the m-experience. For example, when we visually attend to T this alters the visual experience of T relative to when we are not visually attending to it. On this causal account, there need not be any common feature that all conscious forms of attention exemplify. There isn't a distinctive *attentional phenomenology* or *phenomenal character*. Rather, attention modulates conscious experience, possibly in different ways.

At the beginning of modern psychology, Gustav Fechner and William James disagreed on whether attention affects how things perceptually appear. Fechner claimed that "a gray paper appears no lighter, the pendulum-beat of a clock no louder, no matter how much we increase the strain of our attention upon them" (quoted in (James 1890), p. 426).[3] On the contrary, William James wrote:

> Every artist knows how he can make a scene before his eyes appear warmer or colder in color, according to the way he sets his attention. If for warm, he soon begins to *see* the red color start out of everything; if for cold, the blue.

> Similarly in listening for certain notes in a chord, or overtones in a musical sound, the one we attend to sounds probably a little more loud as well as more emphatic than it did before.
>
> (James op. cit. p. 425)

How can two noted psychologists disagree on phenomenology?

As noted in the previous chapter, introspective reports can be biased by theoretical commitments. Marisa Carrasco and colleagues reduced this bias by probing subjects' conscious awareness indirectly. Carrasco and colleagues probed conscious awareness by requiring subjects to register how things visually appear along one feature dimension in order to explicitly report on a different dimension. Subjects never explicitly reported on their conscious experience in the task but relied on that experience to inform their report on a different dimension. Consider Carrasco's first study, focusing on the perception of contrast.

Perception of contrast is a fundamental feature of visual experience. In natural scenes, think of differing luminance as in the shadowy pattern cast by a picket fence. Experimenters use Gabor patches, whose contrast and spatial frequency can be precisely adjusted. The contrast of such gratings can be calculated in different ways, but a standard is the *Michelson Contrast*, which yields a value between 0 and 1 and is often expressed as a percentage. Here is a set of stimuli of the sort used by Carrasco with their contrast values (Figure 9.2).

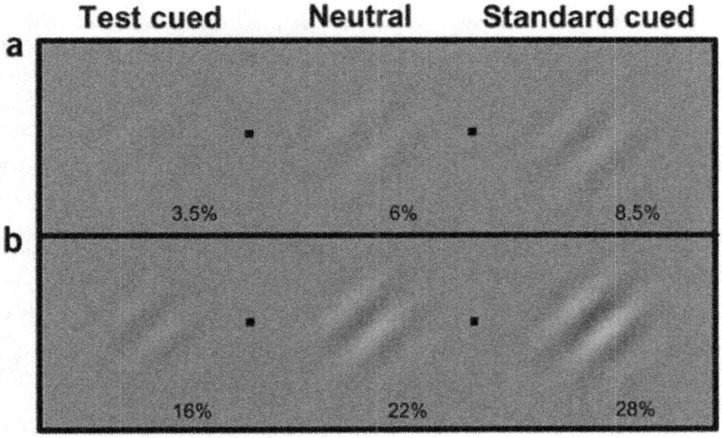

Figure 9.2 Sample stimuli from Carrasco, M., Ling, S., & Read, S. (2004). Attention alters appearance. *Nature Neuroscience*, 7(3) https://doi.org/10.1038/nn1194 reproduced with permission from Springer Nature. A set of Gabor patches at different levels of contrast (panels (A) and (B), the former including low-contrast stimuli; the latter, high-contrast).

Carrasco and colleagues had previously shown that attention improves a subject's sensitivity to contrast and argued that this was due to attention's enhancing visual representation of contrast (e.g., (Carrasco et al. 2000)). In subsequent work, Carrasco, Sam Ling, and Sarah Read investigated whether this signal enhancement was reflected in the visual *appearance* of contrast (Carrasco et al. 2004). Subjects did not directly report the contrast they experienced; rather, they reported on the orientation of a Gabor patch in light of the patch's apparent contrast. Subjects were presented with two Gabor patches of different contrasts and reported the orientation of the patch that appeared highest in contrast (the patches were tilted 45° either left or right). An experimental trial begins with subjects fixating on a central dot. This is followed by a cue either at the point of fixation (neutral, uninformative cue) or at the periphery near one of the targets (peripheral cue, so direct cueing). After an interstimulus interval between cue and stimuli of 53 milliseconds (ms), two Gabor patches appear equidistant from the fixation point on the left and right for 40 ms. One of the patches is the *standard*, kept at a specific contrast; the other, the *test* patch, varies in contrast. Subjects were given 1000 ms to report the orientation of the Gabor patch that appears highest in contrast (Figure 9.3). The experimental design uses direct cues to tap into bottom-up or endogenous attention, a form that the experimenters note peaks at about 120 ms after the cue and largely decays by 250 ms (see Figure 4.5). This explains the short presentation time of the stimuli to take full advantage of bottom-up attention.

Subjects' reports about orientation depended on how the contrast of the patches appeared to them (for a discussion of the logic of the experiment, see (Carrasco 2006)). The results suggest that attention makes the Gabor patch appear to be higher in contrast than it in fact is. This would seem to be a case where attention *affects* conscious experience. In experiments where the standard Gabor patch was of 6% contrast, attention appeared to boost apparent contrast by 2.5%. Thus, an attended 3.5% Gabor patch would appear to be the same as a 6% contrast patch. With a higher contrast standard of 22%, attention appeared to boost apparent contrast by 6%. Later work demonstrated similar effects with top-down attention (Liu et al. 2009) as well as other features (these are discussed in the first edition of this book, Chapter 4).[4] For example, Stuart Fuller and Carrasco (2006) report that attention affects the appearance of saturation but not of hue. They explain this difference in light of a difference between the two properties. Saturation, like contrast and spatial frequency, can be understood as a magnitude allowing for more or less, while hue cannot. It might be that

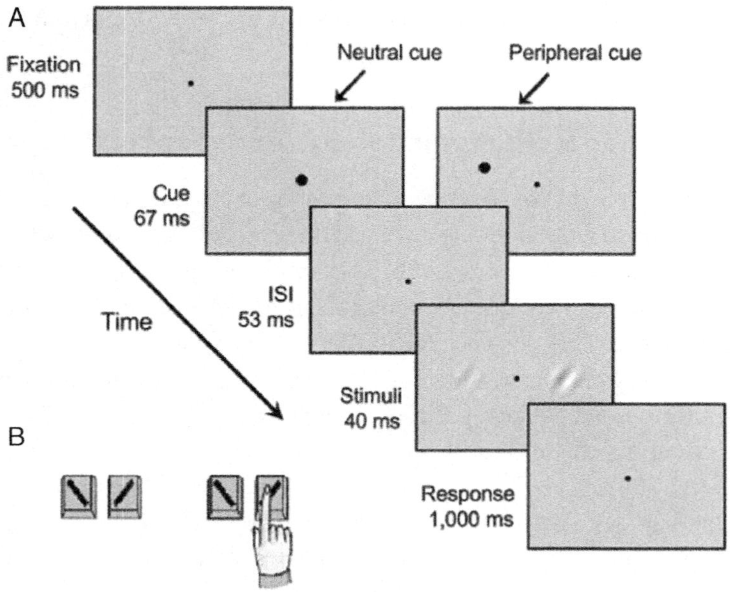

Figure 9.3 Figure reproduced from Carrasco, M., Ling, S., & Read, S. (2004). Attention alters appearance. *Nature Neuroscience*, 7(3) https://doi.org/10.1038/nn1194 reproduced with permission from Springer Nature. Subjects fixated on a central fixation point for 0.5 seconds. A cue was presented for 67 milliseconds (ms), either at the fixation point (neutral cue) or at a location near where one of the Gabor patches would appear (peripheral cue). After an inter-stimulus interval (ISI) of 53 ms, the two Gabor patches would appear for 40 ms. Subjects were required to respond within one second, reporting on the orientation of the Gabor patch that appeared to them of highest contrast.

attention affects only the representation of gradable properties such as size, speed, contrast, and saturation. There is also work showing that the contrast effects can be achieved crossmodally where attention is cued in an auditory fashion, affecting the visual experience of contrast (Störmer et al. 2009).

There have been some queries raised and alternative explanations. These discussions are somewhat technical, so I propose not engaging the issue further beyond pointing interested readers to relevant articles.[5] Rather, I note that the original study involved very short presentation times and so might not naturally capture the highlighting, focalizing, or foregrounding phenomenology that many introspectors report finding when they consider attention. How to connect the two phenomena is a task worth exploring. One thing readers might try is to maintain fixation and see if covert attention seems to make the lower contrast patch appear higher in contrast (Figure 9.2). If this seems to be the case, is this due to a cognitive bias on introspection given knowledge of the result (Chapter 8.5)? Carrasco's methodology aimed to avoid this possibility.

9.4 Attentional Phenomenology: Philosophical Accounts

The empirical results suggest that when a subject attends, this results in correlated changes in the magnitude of visible features. Attention is conscious in that it brings about (possibly distinctive) phenomenology in other mental states. To say that attention is conscious is to say that attention modulates conscious states. This does not mean that attention has its own characteristic phenomenal character. Indeed, if attention modulates the phenomenology of other mental states, then for many of these, in principle, the states might exemplify the relevant phenomenology without attention itself being conscious.

We need to separate two claims. On the one hand, attention might have its own phenomenal character that inheres in the subject's attention whatever else attention brings about. On the other, independent of attention's proprietary phenomenology (if any), attention might have specific modulations of phenomenology that are uniform for a given kind of state. We will return to proprietary attentional phenomenology in the next section. Philosophers have typically explored the distinctive phenomenal effects of attention.

James Stazicker (2011) and Bence Nanay (2010) have both emphasized that attention increases the *determinacy* of visual representations. Conscious visual attention is so called because it is always tied to increases in the determinacy of visual representations and these constitute an important aspect of visual experience. Stazicker and Nanay explain the idea of increases in determinacy in terms of the *determinable/determinate* distinction, where a determinate of a determinable can be understood as a more specific way of being that determinable. Thus, *scarlet* is a determinate of the determinable *red*, with the latter itself being a determinate of the determinable *color*. Scarlet is a (more specific) way of being red, and red is a (more specific) way of being colored. Another way to think about an increase in determinacy is in terms of a decrease in uncertainty about the feature in question. Being between 0.8 and 0.9 meters is a more determinate way of being between 0.5 and 1.0 meters, and it reduces uncertainty about the length of the line. There is more uncertainty about the exact length if you provide a larger range as opposed to a smaller range. The phenomenal conception of attention then can associate conscious attention with increases in perceptual determinacy.

Todd Ganson and Ben Bronner (2012) point out, however, that some of the effects identified in Carrasco's work do not involve increases in determinacy. For example, if attention's effect on contrast is to be understood as boosting absolute contrast level, say from 3.5% to 6% contrast, then this is not an increase in determinacy as would be the case if attention shifted contrast representations from 2%–7% contrast to 3%–6% and thus narrowed the represented range. (The same point holds for relative contrast between the two patches, say a shift from unequal to equal contrast.) Similarly, changes in experienced saturation might be due to an increase in the level of saturation as experienced. Thus, even where attention affects visual content, it need not be tied to an increase in determinacy. If so, conscious attention can be disconnected from increases in determinacy.

Elsewhere, I (Wu 2011b) and, independently, Sebastian Watzl (2011) have argued against various attempts to appeal to some aspect of perceptual content to characterize a distinctive phenomenology P that is always associated with attention. (For a critical discussion of this argument, focusing on Watzl's version, see Hemdat Lerman (2022).) To give a sense of how the argument goes, consider two illustrative proposals for distinctive attentional phenomenology in the visual domain: attentional phenomenology as tied to an apparent boost in contrast or to an apparent increase in spatial resolution. One might claim that when one attends to a Gabor patch, the relevant phenomenal upshot is that contrast appears greater than it did earlier when it was not being (focally) attended (see the notion of diachronic salience in Section 9.5). The phenomenology of attention is then the increase in the level of apparent contrast of a patch over time, between its being unattended versus its being attended. Yet, in principle, one might be able to manipulate the stimuli or even the neurons processing that portion of the visual field such that the apparent contrast of the patch decreases over time. If so, then the change in apparent contrast will be in the opposite direction of the proposal that attention boosts apparent contrast.

One might also claim that attention always increases spatial resolution. Yet the worsening of visual spatial resolution seems to be compatible with attending to an object that becomes less spatially resolved. Think of attending to letters on a screen through a lens as an optometrist adjusts various lenses in the search for one's correct eyeglass prescription. One can attend to the letters even though the object seems blurrier over time. Indeed, optometrists rely on this capacity for attention while they make adjustments that change the apparent spatial resolution of visual experience in order to generate a correct prescription (Chapter 8.5). Attention to a dimming object in the waning light or attending to an ever-more-blurry letter in an optometrist's office is not generally characterized as unconscious attention. So it seems that the two proposals for a distinctive phenomenology P always associated with attention can be decoupled from conscious attention.

The strategy is to take any proposal for P based on perceptual content and show that it is possible to have attention without P (for comments on this strategy, see (Lerman 2022, Section 4)). As I have not exhaustively considered all available options, it would be premature to draw the strong conclusion that no uniform phenomenology as tied to content will be present in each and every case of visual attention. Nevertheless, I have canvassed the initially most plausible cases in that they are grounded in Carrasco's work (for arguments against more complicated proposals for P, see my (Wu 2011b); for an argument based on the gradability of attention, see (Mitchell 2022)). If there are to be viable proposals for a uniform phenomenology tied to attention, then proposals from proponents of the phenomenal conception must be given. Until then, I suggest a tentative conclusion: for all that has been proposed thus far or are reasonable extrapolations from those proposals, namely increases in determinacy or boosting of perceptually represented magnitudes like contrast, attention does not necessitate a uniform phenomenology tied to some aspect of perceptual content. Moreover, the effects of attention on perceptual content remain a motley, non-uniform sort. This conclusion can allow that attention has a *typical* phenomenology in that, for example, when attention is directed at contrast, the effects that Carrasco suggests might generally obtain, a boost in apparent contrast or an increase in the determinacy of spatial representations. That such effects are typical can also explain why theorists gravitate toward specific metaphors to describe attention.

9.5 Salience and Structure in the Phenomenology of Attention

In considering whether there is a distinctive attentional phenomenology, we draw on metaphors of highlighting, focalization, and foregrounding. Another relevant notion is *salience*. We have already investigated salience in the technical sense tied to a saliency map (Chapter 5.5). That notion is functional-computational, not phenomenal. In this section, we begin with the idea of *phenomenal salience*. This leads to the following proposal.

Conscious attention: S *consciously*-attends to T if and only if T is phenomenally salient to S.

One might propose a different account of phenomenal salience of T, namely that T impinges on S's consciousness such that T draws on S's attention, even commands attention (Yetter-Chappell and Yetter-Chappell 2016; Watzl 2017; Archer 2022b). I do not have an argument against this proposal except to ask what happens to phenomenal salience when attention is engaged on T? If phenomenal salience is the draw on attention, is T no longer phenomenally salient when one comes to attend to it, the draw being discharged? I venture that even someone inclined to understand salience as what explains attention's engagement might still allow that when one is attending to T, indeed consciously attending to T, it is thereby phenomenally salient. Indeed, it seems to get things backwards to say that before one attends to T it is phenomenally salient, yet once T is attended, its salience is abolished. Phenomenal salience is the phenomenal aspect of conscious *attention*.

But what precisely is phenomenal salience? In the first edition of this book, I followed a strategy of studying consciousness by identifying concrete instances. In that work, I presented the following comment:

> The intuitive starting point is that in perception, attention highlights or phenomenally prioritizes a specific item. Thus, pick two perceptual objects in each modality and switch [covert] attention from one to the other: hold two objects in each hand, and [covertly] switch tactile attention between them; identify two concurrent sounds, and [covertly] switch auditory attention between them; look at two objects before you, and keeping the eyes fixed, switch attention between them. Really try it! Does the attended one in some way seem more salient than the other?...If yes, then *that* is the explanandum.
>
> (Wu 2014, 127)

Given my concerns with theory-ladened introspection, I can't help but see this instruction as a leading one, but set that aside. The challenge is to identify something uniform that corresponds to the attribution of phenomenal salience across these domains. One version of the phenomenal conception might simply assert that phenomenal salience refers to recognizable phenomenology that is available to subjects on introspecting their episodes of attention. This phenomenology, moreover, is *sui generis* or something primitive. (For the suggestion though not necessarily the endorsement, see (Speaks 2010; Chalmers 2004).) Alternatively, phenomenal salience supervenes on attention as we best understand it. If the Common Conception provides the basic conception of attention, then might phenomenal salience be explained by selection for action?

In earlier work (Wu 2011b), I noted that phenomenal salience has two temporal dimensions: diachronic and synchronic:

Diachronic phenomenal salience: The salience of an object at some time relative to that object at an earlier time.

Synchronic phenomenal salience: The salience of an object at some time relative to other objects at the same time.

When you covertly shift attention between two Gabor patches, you toggle the diachronic phenomenal salience of a single patch over time as you switch attention to and fro. When attention lands on a patch, that patch is more phenomenally salient than it was at an earlier time when attention was directed elsewhere. At the same time, when you attend to one of the patches, you render it synchronically more phenomenally salient relative to the other patch. This assumes that attention does not completely gate consciousness (Chapter 10).

The previous sections underscore that there is as yet no adequate account of a uniform attentional phenomenology. Let me now offer such an account. I proposed that phenomenal salience is a product of special cases where subjects explicitly reflect on the phenomenology of attention, namely by introspection. In reflecting on the phenomenology of attention to T, as we must to discuss conscious attention, we render the target of attention salient in thought. Specifically, the phenomenal salience of T is tied to one's demonstrative *awareness* of T. My expository emphasis on demonstrative *thought* has thrown interpreters off. Sebastian Watzl, for example, rejects the view as "overly intellectualistic", emphasizing my invocation of cognition such as in this passage: "phenomenal salience associated with conscious perception derives in part from cognition: the phenomenal salience of an attended object correlates with one's perceptual-based demonstrative thought about it, specifically a demonstrative awareness that one is attending to that object" (Wu 2011b, 95–96). But this is an initial, cagey remark in the introduction of the paper ("in part", "correlates"), not the actual explication later in the paper about what conscious attention is.

The key idea is to connect phenomenal salience to *awareness of agency*. My thought was that when we philosophers detect phenomenal salience to theorize about, we do so introspectively, focusing on what it is like for T to be a target of attention. This provides central data for our reflection on conscious attention, but in these very cases, we are also aware of attending to T since the introspection is intentionally directed. The idea of a demonstrative thought in this case is that my judgments, hypothesis, suppositions, and so on about attending to T are demonstrative representations of T in my awareness that I am attending to *that* T. But the account is broader in scope than demonstrative thought, as the later explication makes clear:

> in response to voluntarily attending to a specific object, *the subject actively thinks about it as opposed to other objects perceived, makes plans or deliberates about it as opposed to others, is aware of moving towards and acting on it rather than others and so on.* We can say that *the attended object also anchors such broadly cognitive activity*. One is in general then aware of what one is variously doing, activities that are united by a common anchor: the attended object. To the extent that these states make a subjective difference to the subject, they do so because the selected object rather than others is at the center of explanations of that subjective difference. That is, the subject is demonstratively cognitively representing that object and not others concurrently perceived.
>
> (111, emphasis added)

If we take the broad set of awareness that attends to our intentionally acting on something, as various *activities* of mind and *anchoring* as these activities being rooted in the demonstrative link to the attended target, then the proposal is this (slightly modified) for targets T, subjects S, and activities *A*:

> For *T* perceived by *S* and *S*'s (broadly) cognitive activities *A*: *T* is *phenomenally salient* to *S* if and only if *S* attends to *T* in selecting *T* such that it *anchors S*'s activities *A* (*A* involves demonstrative representations of just *T*).

The upshot is that T is phenomenally salient in that one is *consciously* attending to T. For example, T is visually phenomenally salient to you when in consciously seeing T, that experience guides some activity *A* that is (demonstratively) anchored on your attending to T. So, looking at this glowing alien mass I've dug up from my garden, I wonder, "What's that?" The mass is phenomenally salient to me. The point is that conscious attention is distinctive as a form of consciousness because of the intersection of its functional role of guiding behavior along with this guidance of one's action being anchored in an input state that is itself phenomenal.

Watzl presents his account of phenomenal salience as "a *felt* command to attend to something; or more generally: a felt instruction to restructure one's field of consciousness so that something else becomes central" (213). So, in the experience of a fire alarm, the command is (roughly): "put the experience of this fire alarm at the center of your field of consciousness" (216). Caveats with introspective reliability noted, I find that this characterization seems phenomenologically and functionally off-key (see Jonathan Mitchell who calls my critique the *tinkering objection* and his version of the objection (Mitchell 2022)). The worry is that the posited command is *inwardly* directed, to deal with one's mind in the face of danger in the external world. Instead, one would think that if something commands attention, it is to direct attention often outwards and to anchor appropriate response to its target.

Jonathan Mitchell proposes a sympathetic reading of my account:

> the view takes the relevant form of demonstrative cognition to be a kind of higher-order or reflexive awareness of attending. Perhaps in certain cases this reflexive demonstrative awareness might take the form of explicit demonstrative thoughts, but if we are being sympathetic to the view, we should note that it needn't, and can just as well take the form of a less cognitively demanding awareness of attending.
>
> (Mitchell 2022, 21)

To this, Mitchell responds: "higher-order or reflexive forms of awareness seem to go beyond the more minimal awareness of worldly objects and we might think it not entirely obvious whether all attentive episodes or experiences involve something of this kind" (ibid. 22). Perhaps not, but it's not clear to me either that all attentive episodes involve distinctively *conscious* attention rather than conscious experience that involves attention.

Mitchell's own proposal, the *Modification View*, draws on ideas of Edmund Husserl. The key idea is that there is a *preattentive perceptual field* such that when one attends to a target in the perceptual field, say the visual field, there is "a phenomenology of 'drawing out' or 'selection' of an item from the pre-affective perceptual field" (ibid., p. 24). The phenomenology of selection is present in voluntary and involuntary cases of attention and is present when one maintains attention on a target and so extends one's selection of it within a perceptual field. As Mitchell notes, this view commits one to the idea of consciousness independent of attention, but the ideas of diachronic and synchronic salience presuppose that as well. Possibly, the Modification View is a way of implementing, in Husserlian terms, the view I proposed.

My primary analysis concerns cases where one is intentionally attending to an object. This seems to leave out the cases where there is automatic conscious attention to T. Extending the analysis, if I am consciously attending to T, then my activities are anchored on T. Watzl presents a counterexample which I modify in a way that preserves his point (Watzl 2017, 190). We are listening passively to a jazz piece. In one situation, we prefer saxophones; in another, we prefer piano. Consider two cases of auditory awareness where our instrument preferences differ; Watzl asserts that in passive listening "there clearly could be a phenomenal difference" in such a case but there is no demonstrative thought. But this is just assertion in a case where, by hypothesis, you do not have agentive awareness of listening (say, you're zoning out). There might be phenomenal differences in respect of clarity of auditory representations of one instrument versus another akin to the changes in acuity demonstrated in experiments by Carrasco and colleagues for the visual case, but that's not the phenomenal difference Watzl and I agree is present, something distinctively attentional shared by both the auditory and visual case. Yet if it's not that, then one cannot just assert that there is a distinct phenomenal difference. The case must be further explicated, but then we arrive at the territory under dispute.

My claim is not that there is no phenomenal change with passive attentional capture. Indeed, although my early paper took conscious attention to be present only in intentional attending, the view can be extended to attentional capture. We then further specify the values of m in our logical frame, S m-attends to T *for* R, to distinguish between intentional conscious attending (m = *intentional conscious*) and automatic conscious attending (m = *automatic conscious*) to T. In both cases, one's attending to T anchors a variety of responses R to T. The change in our subjectivity when these activities are so anchored explains the general property of phenomenal salience, that phenomenal consciousness of T guides (anchors) various responses. These further responses can involve their own phenomenology, so the phenomenology of conscious attention is quickly differentiated. This makes extracting the core phenomenology of attention in introspection difficult, but having a theory of attention to guide investigation is crucial.

Watzl takes a different approach to explaining conscious attention: the phenomenology of attention is to be understood in terms of *structuring the conscious field*. As we saw in Chapter 7, Watzl's account of attention is that it is the mental activity of ordering one's mental state into a *priority structure*. Some states have priority over others, such as one's intention to solve a pressing problem versus one's intention to do something in the future. This ordering has a parallel in the structure of consciousness. In an early paper, Watzl expresses this succinctly as follows:

> consciously attending to something consists in the conscious mental process of structuring one's stream of consciousness so that some parts of it are more central than others.
>
> (Watzl 2011, 158)

The phenomenology of attention is tied to a structure imposed on the conscious field by attention that yields a center/periphery structure. The properties of this structure are explicated in great detail in Watzl's work, but the idea is intuitive enough. Some things are in the center of phenomenal consciousness, and some things are not. In the simplest case, take two phenomenal states, one of which has priority, such as one's seeing a person flailing in the pool versus seeing the book one is reading. In this situation, hopefully, one visually attends to the person in distress and thereby one is focally conscious of them. Parallel to the functional ordering of priority of one's visual experiences is a centering of one's conscious field on the person drowning. Watzl notes that for X to be more central to one's conscious experience than Y is for X to be prioritized over Y. (Note that the values for the variables are *mental states* not objects in the world, something I noted when considering Watzl's metaphysics of attention, Chapter 7.3.) His analysis is quite flexible, allowing for multiple centers and more fine-grained descriptions of phenomenal structure. Watzl emphasizes that this phenomenal structure is not itself an object of attention. "It is our conscious attention" (Watzl 2017, 184). This captures something distinctive about conscious attention: "that your experience is structured by relative centrality is what constitutes the phenomenal property shared by *all* conscious attention episodes" (Watzl 2017, 184). This is an attractive and intuitive account.

It seems that assessing the views in question will draw on introspection. The aim of the previous chapter was to underscore that we should not treat introspective experiences as any more sacrosanct than perceptual experiences in that both capacities are subject to noise in their deliverances which can mean that, in some contexts, the phenomenal might not be clearly presented in introspection and that corresponding judgments might be inaccurate. I raise the possibility that the discernment of a center-periphery (cf. figure-ground) structure is one of those cases.

I can only report that my introspection on conscious introspection does not clearly reveal a center-periphery structure. Indeed, I worry that we are being driven to a conceptualization of this structure that mirrors visual experience, a dominant form of consciousness many of us are intimately aware of. A common center-periphery phenomenal structure does not obviously attend cognitive consciousness (but see Mark Fortney (2018)). Consider thinking one thought rather than another. This seems to be a case where one thought is present before the mind, is being thought, while the other is not. So, in thinking that thought, it is "more salient" than the other thought, but if so, this is because I am *consciously thinking the first* and not the second. This leads to a hypothesis, the basis of my account of phenomenal salience. In each data point revealed through a philosopher's intentional introspection for theory-building, there is something common, the theorist's demonstrative anchoring of introspective judgment or, more broadly, introspective reflection on the target of attention. This functional feature, the anchoring of reactions to experience, is tied to distinctive forms of phenomenal consciousness on which one can introspectively reflect and so is present across perceptual and cognitive cases. Is my introspection right that this is the common phenomenal aspect of conscious attention? I have no idea, but it is also not obviously wrong.

What I do not find in every case of conscious attention is the center-periphery structure of the sort that Watzl describes unless it is a different way of describing the functional-phenomenal distinction I have proposed. Watzl might be right that there is something like a center-periphery structure, but I would claim that what you think of as a distinctive center-periphery structure is just a description of the functional difference where your subjectivity is differentially anchored. Your introspective judgment of center-periphery is a *complex* judgment about how you are attending while being conscious, reflecting your knowledge of what you are doing along with other beliefs you have about your subjective life. Watzl in turn will claim that I have missed a common structural feature of all perceptual experiences where attention is differentially deployed. I find it striking that this dispute mirrors that between James and Fechner, a difference in basic intuitions about the phenomenology of attention. Watzl sides with James in finding attentional phenomenology to be widely distributed across experiences; I, on the other hand, side with Fechner in finding less attentional phenomenology, though I note a constant anchor that attention provides for our responses to the world (see fn. 3).

Your introspection might lead you to side with me or to side with Watzl. But here is the point: None of that would settle the debate. The prior issue, as noted in Chapter 8, is whether introspection on its own can bear the load for specific disagreements. On each side, there are further arguments that can be given, so the present aim is not to settle the debate. Rather, it is to note that there *is* something to debate, that introspection does not provide a neutral and final tribunal to settle the phenomenal issues. What needs to be done, as we did in discussing overflow and cognitive access, is to recognize that judgments about conscious attention and phenomenal salience or phenomenal structure are *complex* judgments subject to a variety of influences that might amount to noise that obscures the phenomenal signal. So, the first step is to scrutinize introspection. That said, I will note one point. The functional-phenomenal account of phenomenal salience I bruited should be a starting point because it is undeniable that one's broadly cognitive activities can be anchored on what one is consciously attending to. My claim is that this likely exhausts the distinctively attentional phenomenology that identifies conscious attention as a distinctive form of consciousness. Watzl should agree that there is such phenomenology. His point is that there is more in the phenomenal than I have found.

9.6 Conclusion

Is attention a specific way of being conscious? I began with the Jamesian idea that perceptual attention is essentially a specific way of being conscious. Our attempt at identifying this phenomenal character has been at best equivocal (some might accuse me of being dim-witted, phenomenally speaking). Many empirically supported changes in phenomenology resulting from attention do not seem to fall under one general phenomenal category, such as increased determinacy, that can define an essential attentional phenomenology.

This leads to a central question: Have theorists misconstrued the truth in James's original description? Perhaps attention does not have a uniform phenomenology. For example, visual attention does not uniformly make things look brighter, of higher contrast, or of greater spatial determinacy. This allows that visual attention (or perceptual attention) can have a variety of effects on conscious experience, but if there is a uniform feature of attention, perhaps it is not that attention has its own distinctive phenomenal upshot but that, in light of the phenomenology of conscious experience, attention allows for a selective response to it, to functionally focalize and concentrate what is relevant to the subject as part of prioritizing attention's target to allow the subject to deal with it as she wishes. Even if there is a phenomenology of attention, what matters in respect of conscious attention is not this phenomenology but the selectivity of attention in respect of consciousness. Attention is conscious to the extent that it drives a response in myriad ways to consciousness in its myriad forms.

Suggested Readings

Robert Kentridge (2011) reviews evidence for unconscious attention. A nice overview of the empirical work discussed at the beginning of the chapter from a neuroscientific perspective can be found in Anton-Erxleben and Carrasco (2013). As far as I know, the analytical discussion of phenomenal salience was first raised in print (Wu 2011b). Sebastian Watzl (2017) has the most sustained analytic philosophical discussion of conscious attention. John Campbell's discussion of attention, reference, and consciousness is a seminal work in the analytic tradition that reinvigorated discussion of attention (Campbell 2002).

Notes

1 The changes in experience that are induced by voluntary shifts of attention are reminiscent of the changes that can be induced in the experience of ambiguous figures such as the Necker cube or the duck-rabbit figure (Tse notes this as well). That is, shifts of attention seem to allow one to flip the orientation of the Necker cube or whether one sees the figure as a duck or a rabbit.

2 Prinz (2012) presents further objections to which I respond (Wu 2013b).

3 The passage is translated by James. Fechner interestingly further notes that "everyone, on the contrary, feels the increase as that of his own conscious activity turned upon the thing" (James 1890, p. 426). I shall return to a version of this response in discussing phenomenal salience and one's awareness of one's attending to a specific target.

4 It is worth noting that Massimo Turatto et al. (2007) found that attended moving Gabor patches appeared of *lower* contrast.

5 For an alternative explanation based on a shift in decisional criteria, see (Schneider 2006; Schneider and Komlos 2011; Beck and Schneider 2017); for Carrasco's response, see (Ling and Carrasco 2007; Anton-Erxleben et al. 2010, 2011). See also (Prinzmetal et al. 2008) and a response in (Carrasco et al. 2008).

10

ATTENTION AS THE GATEKEEPER OF CONSCIOUSNESS

10.1 Introduction

William James's (1890) comments as follows on attention and conscious experience:

> Millions of items of the outward order are present to my senses which never properly enter into my experience. Why? Because they have no *interest* for me. *My experience is what I agree to attend to.* Only those items which I *notice* shape my mind—without selective interest, experience is an utter chaos. Interest alone gives accent and emphasis, light and shade, background and foreground--intelligible perspective, in a word. It varies in every creature, but without it the consciousness of every creature would be a gray chaotic indiscriminateness, impossible for us even to conceive.
>
> (402–3, James's italicization)

DOI: 10.4324/9781003223450-11

"My experience is what I agree to attend to" suggests that attention serves as a *gatekeeper* for consciousness. It determines what one is conscious of. The gatekeeper model contrasts with a common sense model where attention responds to consciousness. One is first conscious and then one selectively attends. We understand the *Complete Gatekeeping* model as endorsing the following biconditional:

> Complete Gatekeeping: One is conscious of X if and only if one attends to X.

This suggests an answer to the Metaphysical Question: attention is a selective process that is *for consciousness* (cf. attention as selection for perception, Chapter 3.7). One implementation of this idea is gatekeeping. The central questions are

> What is it for attention to be a gatekeeper for consciousness?
> What is the evidence regarding attention as gatekeeper?

Section 10.2 identifies numerous Gatekeeping conditionals. Failure to make distinctions among these has tripped up some discussions. Given putative evidence that attention is not sufficient for consciousness in Chapter 9.2, Section 10.3 focuses on the necessity claim: one is conscious of X only if one attends to X. Inattention leads to blindness in the visual domain. Section 10.4 explores what might be meant by *blindness*, and three different notions and their consequences are examined. Section 10.5 identifies three alternatives to inattentional blindness: inattentional *amnesia*, inattentional *agnosia*, and inattentional *apraxia*. Inattentional apraxia suggests that the experimental paradigms standardly used to support inattentional blindness fail to provide evidence for it. Section 10.6 returns to the early-versus-late selection debate, which is the ancestor of the question of inattentional blindness and explores attempts to demonstrate consciousness outside of attention, namely in the perception of the gist of a scene and in the visual phenomenon of crowding.

10.2 Gatekeeping Conditionals

Complete Gatekeeping takes attention to be necessary and sufficient for consciousness:

(1) Sufficiency: If S is perceptually attending to X, S is perceptually conscious of X.

(2) Necessity: If S is perceptually conscious of X, S is perceptually attending to X.

I assume that attention and consciousness are in the same modality m, so the conditionals will, for example, focus on visual consciousness and visual attention. For current purposes, "conscious of" and "attention to" are success terms implying existence of their targets. Ordinary experience seems to support Sufficiency. Whenever you attend to an object, you seem to be conscious of it. In contrast, Necessity seems false for it seems that one can be conscious of more than one attends to. Empirical work, however, suggests that Sufficiency is false while Necessity is true!

(1) and (2) provide the most natural interpretation of Gatekeeping, but once one acknowledges distinct targets of attention, there are a slew of Gatekeeping claims. The variables in (1) and (2) take the same argument, so attention and consciousness have the same target. For example, to be conscious of a bear, you have to attend to the bear, and when you attend to the bear, you are conscious of it; to be conscious of the blackness of its fur, you have to attend to the color, and where you attend to the blackness, you are conscious of it. But attention and consciousness can have different targets, and one can allow for different arguments for the variables:

(3) If S is attending to X, then S is conscious of Y where possibly $Y \neq X$.

(4) If S is conscious of X, then S is attending to Y where possibly $Y \neq X$.

Clarifying the content of gatekeeping conditionals arose in the debate about unconscious attention (Chapter 9.2). Consider these elaborations of (4):

4A. If S is conscious of object O, then S attends to O.

4B. If S is conscious of object O, then S attends to (some) feature F of O.

4C. If S is conscious of object O, then S attends to location L of O.

Does consciousness of an object imply that one is attending to it or at least to one of its properties or its spatial location? Let O be the gorilla. Likely, proponents of Gatekeeping mean (4A), but consider the possibility that when object attention, as invoked in (4A), is abolished, subjects report not seeing a gorilla. Yet (4B) might be true as well, and perhaps while not attending to objects, subjects still attend to features, such as the color of the gorilla's hair. What we might say, then, is that these subjects do not see the gorilla as a gorilla though they do see the gorilla in seeing the black hair. We might call this a type of inattentional agnosia (Section 10.5.2). To discuss Gatekeeping, we need to be explicit about which conditionals are at issue. In this chapter, consciousness and attention have the same target.

10.3 Attention as Gatekeeper for Consciousness: Initial Evidence

Restate Necessity as the *Gatekeeping Hypothesis:*

> $\text{Hypothesis}_{(GK)}$: *S* is conscious of *X* only if *S* attends to *X*.

What happens when you fail to attend to X? On this view, in vision, you will not be phenomenally visually conscious of X even if it is fully in view. Cognitive scientists speak of *inattentional blindness* and *change blindness,* terms that derive from a set of experimental paradigms. Begin with inattentional blindness. If you have never seen displays demonstrating this, stop reading and do a web search for "The Monkey Business Illusion". Watch and be sure to follow the instructions. Even if you are familiar with the paradigm, try it with this version. Don't read the next paragraph until you do!

The video demonstrates a form of inattentional blindness: by directing your attention to the ball and the number of passes, your attention is pulled away from the gorilla. Moreover, you don't report seeing it, and when shown the video again, you are surprised by the gorilla. Typically, around one half of subjects fail to notice the gorilla.

Arien Mack and Irvin Rock (1998), who coined the phrase *inattentional blindness,* used a different paradigm. A cross is flashed very briefly (200 milliseconds, ms), followed by a mask to disrupt residual visual processing of the stimulus. Subjects were required to report either (a) which arm of the cross was longer or, in some trials, (b) whether they were equal in length. After a number of trials where the cross is flashed at the same location in the visual field, an additional stimulus was presented with the cross in the *critical trial.* Subjects were never apprised of the possibility of an additional stimulus. After the critical trial, subjects were asked if they saw anything in addition to the cross, something they had not seen in previous trials. Many denied seeing anything new. Mack and Rock (1998) summarized their findings as follows:

> All the experiments described in [our] book demonstrate that when one takes the proper measures to eliminate voluntary attention or, better

> expressed, the intention to attend to what is about to be displayed, there is a drastic reduction in what is perceived, at least on a conscious level. In fact, unless certain kinds of objects are presented in our critical trial, the rule seems to be that *nothing is perceived consciously*.
>
> (163, my emphasis)

Mack and Rock endorse attention as a necessary condition for consciousness, the Gatekeeping hypothesis. While they might mean that, without attention, cognitive *access* is disrupted, I interpret them to mean something more interesting, that *phenomenal* visual consciousness is eliminated. Their focus is on top-down, intention-directed attention, but they also have bottom-up attention in mind (Chapter 10.6).

Mack and Rock found that inattentional blindness varies with the type of stimulus and with its location within the visual field. When a solid black geometrical shape was flashed in the periphery while the cross was flashed at fixation, 25% of subjects denied seeing the black shape, yet when the cross was flashed in the periphery and the black shape presented *at fixation*, so stimulating the part of the retina yielding highest spatial acuity, 60% to 80% of subjects denied seeing the shape. Finally, when the stimulus was the subject's own name, inattentional blindness dropped to 12.5% of subjects (Mack and Rock 1998, Figure 5.1, p. 117). Recall similar results by Moray in audition (the cocktail party effect, Chapter 3.3 (Moray 1959)). Consciousness aside, these experiments provide a wealth of information about what stimuli automatically grab attention. The other notable finding is that once the critical stimulus is revealed, subjects are no longer inattentionally blind (or less so) to subsequent presentation of the stimulus, such as the gorilla. They form an *expectation* that surprising stimuli are likely to appear and so are vigilant for them (cf. discussion of expectation, Chapter 4.3 and vigilance, Chapter 6.6).

Change blindness is different in that it is defined in terms of a specific target, an *event* or perhaps a *difference* across time. A typical change blindness paradigm involves flashing two nearly identical pictures in succession with an intervening mask (a gray screen), cycling from one picture to the other. (A mask is not necessary for the effect as very gradual continuous changes work as well.) As the second picture is different in some way from the first, there is a change between the two. Subjects are asked to report the change. Despite knowing that there is a change, and so expecting one, subjects often require a bit of time to spot the change, even substantial alterations involving large portions of the scene such as a whole building disappearing.

While they know a change is occurring, without specific information about where or what is changing, subjects do not easily detect the alteration. However, if you point to where the change will occur (i.e., cue attention to that location), subjects see the change immediately. In this case, if S attends to *location* L, S is aware of the *change* at L (notice that the targets of attention and awareness are different). Arguably, inattentional blindness, or unawareness, is the more general phenomenon, with change blindness as a species. Change blindness is just inattentional blindness to change. For consider this specific version of the Gatekeeping Hypothesis:

> Gatekeeping Hypothesis: if *S* does not visually attend to *X*, then *S* is not visually conscious of *X* (i.e., is blind to *X*).

This is the inattentional blindness formulation of the Gatekeeping Hypothesis. Notice that the value of X can be a material object like a gorilla or a temporal object like an event (this emphasizes that there is an implicit temporal variable). The negation of gatekeeping is *Overflow*:

> Overflow Hypothesis: There are cases where *S* does not visually attend to *X* and *S* is visually conscious of *X*.

Overflow expresses the folk conception of attention and consciousness. We can be aware of something even without attending to it. I shall argue that while the experimental evidence seems to speak decisively against Overflow and in favor of Gatekeeping, this evidence is *compatible* with both positions.

Two other phenomena are relevant: hemispatial neglect and the attentional blink. Hemispatial neglect involves a patient's unawareness of a certain side of space, typically the left side due to damage to right parietal cortex. Strikingly, neglect patients might fail to dress the left side of their body, fail to eat from the left side of their plate, or fail to report on the left side of objects. Neglect is often described as an attention deficit, an inability to attend to the left (or relevant) side of space (Losier and Klein 2001; Bartolomeo et al. 2007). The attentional blink can be demonstrated in normal subjects and is characterized by the inability to notice a second stimulus rapidly presented after an initial stimulus. After attending to the first, attention "blinks", leading to failure to select subsequent stimuli within a small temporal window (Dux and Marois 2009; Martens and Wyble 2010; Zivony and Eimer 2021). In both cases, the inability to attend to a stimulus suggests that the subject is not conscious of the stimulus.[1] We do not have the space to discuss these interesting phenomena, but the questions I shall later raise regarding inattentional blindness experiments can be applied to these cases as well.

In light of these results, cognitive scientists concluded that the absence of attention to an object is sufficient for the absence of consciousness of that object. In the visual domain, inattention suffices for blindness (i.e., inattentional blindness). That said, two questions must be answered to assess the case for Gatekeeping: What is meant by "blindness" and what conception of attention is in play?

10.4 On Blindness

What is meant by "blindness" in $\text{Hypothesis}_{(GK)}$? It can't just mean failure to notice since that is compatible with Overflow. Rather, for there to be a clash, "blindness" must be taken literally, but what does this come to? Consider these gatekeeping conditionals:

1. **Object blindness:** failure to visually attend to an O at L suffices for blindness to O

2. **Feature blindness:** failure to visually attend to an O at L suffices for blindness to O's features

3. **Location blindness:** failure to visually attend to an O at L suffices for blindness to L

The congenitally blind lack visual experience in all three senses, yet when sighted subjects are said to be inattentionally blind, which conditional is intended?

In phenomenal blindness, one lacks visual awareness of features, objects, and space, the complete absence of sight. It is not experiencing darkness, for that is a visual experience not available to the congenitally blind. To experience what it might be like to be phenomenally blind, fixate on some object before you and now hold out your thumb and slowly move it to the periphery of your field of view while you maintain fixation. At some point, you will no longer see the thumb. At the point at which the thumb disappears, it does not, I suggest, disappear into darkness. Rather, it just disappears into an area that you cannot from the current vantage point visually experience. Having a normal field of view is not like looking through a tube, an area of visibility with a penumbra of darkness. When your thumb disappears, you are literally blind to it. You have no visual experience of it. Beyond the limit where the visual field terminates, you do not have visual experiences at all. For total blindness, imagine the boundaries of the visual field collapsing but without being replaced by darkness. On this reading, the claim of blindness is stronger than the claim of failure to notice. If failure of attention is sufficient for blindness, then the Gatekeeping Hypothesis, in disputing Overflow, takes visual spatial attention to define the extent of the visual field. Anything to which one does not attend lies outside the visual field and one has no visual experience of it, whether of space, feature, or property. Inattentional phenomenal blindness entails the truth of object, feature, and location blindness.

I find it difficult to imagine what targeted inattentional blindness might be like. Let us apply phenomenal blindness to inattentional blindness of the gorilla. By hypothesis, since subjects are not attending to the gorilla, they are phenomenally blind to it. Assume that there is some configuration where the visual field covers an area including all the white- and black-clad players passing the balls and within which the gorilla appears. Given inattention, subjects are phenomenally blind to the gorilla, the object, its spatial location, and its visible properties. That part of the world lies "outside" the visual field. What then is blindness? Imagine the gorilla walking into the visual field. It acts like a magnet to the visual nothingness that characterizes the blind regions outside of the visual field, as if the boundary of the visual field now is pulled in at the spot where the gorilla first enters. As the gorilla walks, does the boundary get pulled in further, leaving a trail of blindness behind it? Or does the visual nothingness pinch off like a bubble, so that as the gorilla walks across the visual field, we have a *phenomenal hole* corresponding to its location, one that moves across the area where the players are passing the balls. Inattention leaves a hole that is not visible in any sense just as the areas outside of a normal visual field are not visible in any sense. Indeed, the location of the hole will shift as attention shifts with the ball. But is experience of the world like that? Is that what proponents of inattentional blindness intend? How would we verify this radical phenomenal consequence? By introspection? Yet introspection requires attention.

A second interpretation of "blindness" is invoked in color blindness. Consider the Ishihara color vision test that involves a set of color dots in a circle where some of the dots are differently colored and form a numeral, with the other dots forming the background. For certain colorblind individuals, given appropriate colors, the numeral cannot be discriminated from its background, and they are in that sense blind to the numeral. They cannot see it because they cannot separate the dots that constitute it from the other dots that form the background. Of course, these subjects are blind neither to the dots, which they can see quite well, nor to color, for the dots can appear colored. The problem is that they do not appear differently colored sufficient to do the task. Think also of a camouflaged animal such as a chameleon blending in with tree bark. One might see the color of the chameleon without individuating it, contrasting it against its background. In such cases, objects are not perceptually individuated, even though some of their features are perceivable.

There is then a conception of blindness exemplified by an inability to differentiate an object from the background, *individuation* blindness that leads to object blindness So one might be blind to the gorilla in the sense that one cannot distinguish it from its background or because, in some sense, only its features are revealed though the gorilla itself is not. Let the gorilla then be at location L and surrounded by background B. Blindness to the gorilla is just that the gorilla melds with its background or is not sufficiently resolved, say in the video the gorilla being unresolved relative to the black shirted distractor players; that is, they are undifferentiated from each other aside from spatial location (see inattentional agnosia, Section 10.5.2). Still some consciousness is preserved in individuation blindness: one remains aware of the location of the thing that is the gorilla and perhaps of some of the gorilla's features, say the blackness of its coat. On this conception of blindness, attention does not define the extent of the visual field. Inattentional blindness in this second sense entails object blindness but not location or feature blindness. This allows that one could be conscious of location and feature even if one is not attending to these, for one is attending to the ball. If proponents of inattentional blindness mean individuation blindness, then the Gatekeeping Hypothesis is restricted to objects: one is conscious of an object only if one attends to it.

Finally, consider *category* blindness, inattentional *associative agnosia* (see Section 10.5.2), where one is blind to the gorilla's being a gorilla. One does not see it as a gorilla. Notice, however, that while visually missing this higher-level categorization suggests a type of blindness to the gorilla, it is compatible with other ways of seeing the gorilla. For example, one might still see the gorilla as a moving black shape, one that task instructions explicitly require one to ignore (follow just the white-shirted, not black-shirted, players). Such blindness as a visual deficit in categorization of an object is compatible with consciousness of the object in another lower-level sense. There is *category* blindness but not object, feature, or location blindness. What is the difference between individuation and category blindness since both involve failing to see the gorilla as a gorilla? The difference can be subtle in that, in individuation blindness, one sees all the relevant parts but cannot separate objects. In category blindness, it might be that one also fails to see the parts. That said, if the issue is a failure at some point to yield full-level perceptual processing, then the experiential upshot of the two forms is equivalent.

These different meanings of "blindness" have different implications for the limits in visual consciousness under inattention. Many theorists seem to endorse the strongest version, inattentional phenomenal blindness of object, feature, and location, but there are more restricted forms of blindness that are compatible with the evidence. The failure to be clear about how to characterize blindness has left the basic claim of inattentional blindness unclear, namely how attention precisely gates consciousness.

10.5 What Actually Follows from Inattention?

The experimental evidence does not demonstrate total phenomenal blindness given inattention. The structure of the empirical evidence is (1) a manipulation that eliminates attention to X and (2) evidence of failure of the subject to be visually conscious of X. (1) either is achieved through experimental manipulation or is the result of brain disruption or damage. (2) involves either the failure to report X from which it is inferred that the subject did not see X or an explicit report by the subject that they did not see X. This is followed by an inference to the best explanation: the subjects are not conscious of X because they are not attending to X. This supports the Gatekeeping Hypothesis, for failure of attention to X suffices for failure of consciousness to X. The inference, however, requires that inattentional blindness be the *best* explanation among alternatives. It is not. Let us note three alternatives: inattentional amnesia, inattentional agnosia, and inattentional apraxia.

10.5.1 *Inattentional Amnesia*

The first alternative is that the observed failure to report the critical stimulus is due not to failure of consciousness but to failure of encoding a conscious content into working memory (Chapter 6). Since report of a previously seen stimulus proceeds through memory of that stimulus, failure of remembering the relevant object will suffice for failure to report even if the object was consciously experienced. In fact, this seems to be a natural explanation of change blindness, a form of inattentional blindness. If one thinks of change as a modification in the property of an object over time, such as its transition from exemplifying feature F to feature G, then to experience the change is to be aware of the difference between F and G. For example, when one notices that an object is moving, one is aware of the difference in its spatial location over time; when one notices its changing color, one is aware of the difference between the old and new color. One compares and contrasts them. Indeed, the use of "comparator" mechanisms that involve comparison between previous and new information has been postulated to explain various phenomena such as efficient motor control (Wolpert and Ghahramani 2000), why the world appears to be stable when one moves the eyes (Wurtz 2008; Wu 2013d), and why patients with schizophrenia experience auditory verbal hallucinations (Cho and Wu 2013). On this view, to see the change, one has to remember the old to contrast it with the new.

A subject can fail to detect the change by not retaining previous information. So, in conditions of inattention, one fails to select something to remember. In the experiments discussed, the required reports of unattended stimuli are generally retrospective: after the presentation of the critical stimulus, subjects are asked if they noticed anything unusual. If subjects are to accurately report the stimulus, they must remember that the stimulus was present. Since report requires memory, failure of memory can preempt the absence of conscious awareness as an explanation of the subject's failing to report the change. Note that a failure of memory can result from (1) a failure of encoding into memory or (2) success in encoding but failure of access of the encoded memory or its degradation. If so, inattentional amnesia trumps inattentional blindness.

Jeremy Wolfe (1999) proposed *inattentional amnesia* to account for the subject's failure to report the stimuli. He comments:

> If vision has no memory and if attention is the gateway to other mental representations, it follows that unattended visual stimuli may be seen, but will be instantly forgotten; hence, *inattentional amnesia*.
>
> (75)

Other researchers in this area have drawn similar conclusions (Lamme 2004; Simons and Ambinder 2005). The argument for the Gatekeeping view assumes that the best explanation of a subject's failure to report X is the subject's failure to be conscious of X. Yet inattentional amnesia provides an alternative explanation of the subject's failure to report, one that is no worse than the appeal to failure of consciousness. This alternative, if cogent, halts the inference to the best explanation to inattentional blindness.

There is, however, a problem with the appeal to inattentional amnesia as a general response to inattentional blindness. Many theorists of consciousness postulate that working memory is necessary for consciousness, specifically those who endorse the global workspace conception of consciousness (Baars 1997; Dehaene and Naccache 2001; Baars 2005; Dehaene et al. 2006; Naccache 2018). Recall our discussion in Chapter 9.6 regarding cognitive accessibility with phenomenal consciousness of X tied to X being accessible to action systems by being encoded in working memory (or the global workspace). On this view, inattentional amnesia would be sufficient for inattentional blindness, so the defense collapses if one accepts that access is a necessary condition on phenomenal consciousness. In this case, inattentional amnesia does not provide a clear alternative to the appeal to inattentional blindness since one issue is whether the former, at least given failure of encoding, entails the latter.

10.5.2 *Inattentional Agnosia*

A second alternative is *inattentional agnosia* (see Daniel Simons (2000), who attributes the idea to Jeremy Wolfe). *Agnosia* concerns an inability to see objects or to see objects as belonging to specific categories (Farah 2004). Damage to certain visual areas can lead to deficits such as the inability to see shape and hence to see objects (what is often called *apperceptive* agnosia; (Farah 2004, Chapter 2)). Imagine something like a scrambled visual world. Alternatively, some damage to the visual system leads to the inability to see objects as the type of objects they are (categorization) despite largely preserved visual shape processing (*associative* agnosia; (Farah 2004, Chapter 6)). Thus, while an apperceptive agnosic might not be able to recognize a gorilla as a gorilla because she cannot resolve its basic features, an associative agnosic might not recognize a gorilla as a gorilla even though she might be able to accurately draw it.

Given the distinction between apperceptive and associative agnosia, we can discern an echo of the early-versus-late selection debate which concerns which stimuli get further processed. Consider apperceptive inattentional agnosia of the gorilla. We can draw on early selection to characterize what it is like to see the gorilla under conditions of inattention. Since the gorilla is not selected for further processing, the gorilla, in early selection, is processed only to a limited extent. For example, it might be processed only to the level of basic visual features such as texture, contrast, color, and motion. For inattentional apperceptive agnosia, the gorilla is then only one black object among others; indeed among the set of black distractors, the subject is not likely to notice it. Notably, the inattentionally agnosic subject is not completely blind to the gorilla for the subject perceives, but does not notice, basic visual features. For associative agnosia, we might draw on a late selection model where, in fact, all items in the visual field are fully perceptually processed. Inattention leads to a failure to engage with non-perceptual systems, perhaps systems of categorization and conceptualization. Even here, though the subject sees all the gorilla's features, it is not categorized as a gorilla. If not, the subject is not likely to notice the gorilla even if she is not at all inattentionally blind to it. Failure to notice is tied to incomplete processing, but this failure of processing is consistent with seeing the gorilla.

It is not clear that inattentional blindness is a better explanation of the data than inattentional agnosia. If the two are on a par with respect to the empirical data, then might inattentional agnosia receive a slight advantage since it is compatible with folk intuitions that we do see more than we attend to?

10.5.3 *Inattentional Apraxia*

There is, however, a fatal methodological flaw in the appeal to the experiments and findings at issue as support for inattentional blindness. These findings are *neutral* between Gatekeeping and Overflow. The logic of inattentional blindness experiments and related phenomena begins with experimental conditions that abolish or hinder attention to a critical stimulus to test whether attention is necessary for consciousness. The prediction is that if attention is removed from some stimulus X, the subject will not be phenomenally conscious of X. If this empirical condition is not met, then the experiment will fail to test the necessary condition. How is attention abolished or hindered?

There are three basic ways to manipulate attention. The first is by distraction in the sense of having the subject attend to a different object distinct from the critical stimulus. So, in the gorilla experiment, subjects are tasked with counting the basketball passes of one group of players. Notice that this fixes attention by implementing an empirical sufficient condition: select a specific basketball to count passes for later report. We must grant that this suffices to ensure that attention is not directed to the gorilla when it appears. The second is by creating conditions that disrupt attention, such as in typical change blindness displays where an intervening mask between the two visual stimuli makes it difficult to integrate information to detect a change or in attentional blink studies where critical stimuli for report come too quickly one after the other, hindering the engagement of selection mechanisms. In such cases, the subject's selection of relevant stimuli for report—that is, the subject's attention to those stimuli—is disrupted. Finally, there are neuropsychological conditions that are thought to damage visual attention, such as in parietal damage that leads to neglect. For each of these, we will grant that proponents of Gatekeeping have a case where attention to X is eliminated as needed. Otherwise, the experiments are not relevant to testing Gatekeeping.

Let us consider the two moments when one might expect subjects to report on a salient stimulus, namely (a) during the experiment when the stimulus appears ("Hey, what's that gorilla doing there?") or (b) retrospectively when queried after stimulus presentation ("Oh, there was something funny…I think it was a gorilla!"). In the first case, if attention is fully siphoned away from the gorilla as is required to test Gatekeeping, then one can *predict* that the subject will not report the presence of the stimulus. Given the manipulation, there will be no selection of the gorilla for report. In the second case, one should think about what selection for retrospective report involves. If I ask you to remember the first five cards I reveal in rapidly flipping through a standard deck of cards and then to later report them, you will select those five cards for memory and then report on them by drawing on memory. Retrospective report is a memory-guided task and so selection for such reports requires selection for memory as a crucial component of selecting for action. So, in selecting an object for later report, selection for memory-guided action requires that when the stimulus is presented, it is selected for memory. If not, then the stimulus will be lost to later action. But if at the time of stimulus presentation, the capacity for attention is fully deployed elsewhere, as must be if the experiment eliminates attention as a necessary condition for consciousness, then the stimulus cannot be selected for memory so as to serve later action. That is, inattentional amnesia obtains through disrupting attention. This suggests that again where attention is completely diverted away from the critical stimulus, the possibility of report is abolished. Note that if a global workspace theorist now claims that inattentional amnesia leads to blindness, they will be begging the question against the overflow theorist.

There is a serious but unnoted challenge to those who want to conclude that consciousness requires attention from experiments that depend on failure to report. The experimental conditions in all relevant experiments or cases of neural disruption that take out attention if successful in their manipulation *guarantee* that the subject will not report the presence of the stimulus. For if attention is not available to select a stimulus, one can predict that the subject will not remember and/or report it. Thus, both Gatekeeping *and Overflow* can predict the same behavioral results in light of how attention is being manipulated. But if every position can make the same predictions, then the data cannot favor Gatekeeping against Overflow. Instead, the experiments and neuropsychological cases demonstrate inattentional apraxia, an inability to respond to the relevant stimulus precisely because attention is tied up with another task. We have the absence of *access* consciousness but not obviously of phenomenal consciousness. Accordingly, we have as yet no evidence that attention is a gatekeeper for phenomenal consciousness. This point applies to the attentional blink and hemispatial neglect. For in both, if attention is not available to be deployed to the relevant objects, then we do not expect the subject to report them.

The Gatekeeping theorist has also claimed that Overflow is not testable since the latter claims that phenomenology is present in the absence of attention. How can an Overflow theorist acquire evidence of phenomenology's presence without attention? Notice, however, that the Gatekeeping theorist is also committed to a thesis about phenomenology without attention, namely that phenomenology is absent. Turning the tables, how can the Gatekeeping theorist acquire evidence of phenomenology's absence without attention. Put another way, if attention undercuts Overflow's appeal to the presence of phenomenology, it also undercuts Gatekeeping's appeal to its absence. The two views seem to be on a par in regard to inattentional apraxia.

The data discussed do not resolve a dispute between Gatekeeping and Overflow since both make the same predictions about behavior. This is not to say that the experiments are uninformative. They are, but about attention as gate not to phenomenal consciousness but to access and action. Each tells us something important about attention across different subjects in different task contexts. For example, in the standard inattentional blindness paradigm, we learn about the balance between task-driven attention (counting the ball passes) and attentional capture (the gorilla). One can read Mack and Rock's substantial work as probing salience in a broad sense as well as attentional capture while performing a demanding task. Standard change blindness tasks examine the relation between attention and temporal aspects of perception, such as the integration of information over time that is needed to detect a change. The attentional blink tells us about the time course of attention for processing sequential stimuli at a location, the parameters of selection for encoding and response, while hemispatial neglect isolates regions of the brain that are important for supporting different aspects of attention. Each of these topics is important, logically independent of phenomenal consciousness, and does not require a connection to consciousness to be significant.

The issues discussed here recapitulate questions raised during the early-versus-late selection debate, specifically whether attentional selection resulted in blocking task-irrelevant distractors from further processing for perception. Indeed, Ulric Neisser first devised the types of videos later used in inattentional blindness as *visual analogs of dichotic listening*. Returning to dichotic listening, note that attention is also manipulated through the empirical sufficient condition, namely by tasking subjects to verbally shadow one ear rather than the other (compare visually tracking the basketball rather than other things). Notably, early selection theorists allowed that the unattended stimuli are processed to the level of low-level features, such as the pitch or intensity of sound. I suspect that the availability of certain audible features in the unattended channel disabused theorists from positing *inattentional deafness*. Instead, early selection was motivated precisely by noting the difference in apparent processing between attended and unattended channels.[2]

Overflow theorists might advert to this seminal auditory data to attest to phenomenal awareness outside of attention. After all, structurally, the manipulation is no different than in standard inattentional blindness paradigms, namely in the use of an empirical sufficient condition to eliminate attention to the critical stimulus by directing attention to something else, so long as the subject maintains attention on the task-relevant object. That said, a similar counterresponse by Gatekeeping theorists is available. After all, by the same logic, the Overflow theorist can claim that those subjects who do notice the gorilla also provide data supporting Overflow, awareness outside the target of attention. The Gatekeeping theorist can reply that all that these subjects demonstrate is that, sometimes, salient stimuli *capture* attention. So even those subjects who notice the gorilla do so because they access it involuntarily for report. I find this a coherent, indeed plausible, response since noticing allows for remembering and reporting. Applied to dichotic listening, subjects automatically attend to certain aspects of the task-irrelevant auditory channel.

For example, the global workspace theorist will hold that in accurately reporting stimuli in the unattended channel, that information is in the workspace which broadcasts it to report systems. If attention is necessary for entry into the workspace, then there is attention in the "unattended" channel. Given the possibility of automatic attention that leads to unintended entry into the workspace, Gatekeeping concerns top-down attention and so is properly expressed as follows:

> If *S* does not top-down visually attend to *X*, then *S* is not visually conscious of *X* (i.e., is blind to *X*).

It is not clear why we should think this conditional to be true, but set that aside as intuitions might differ. What is clear is that many of the experiments manipulate only top-down attention. It is problematic to reason from data that applies to only top-down attention, namely that eliminating it seems to eliminate consciousness, to the conclusion that eliminating attention *as such* eliminates consciousness. After all, bottom-up attention could engage, a possibility we are entertaining here. To sum up, the standard evidence for Gatekeeping is inadequate. Whether attention is necessary for phenomenal consciousness remains an open empirical question.

10.6 Consciousness without attention?

Let us turn the tables and now question opponents of Gatekeeping, for they claim that there is consciousness outside of attention. Can they demonstrate this? One claim is that subjects can be aware of the gist of a scene without attending to it. Arien Mack and Jason Clarke have noted that "the claim that gist perception is possible without attention is not trivial. It is the main evidence given for attention-free awareness" (Mack and Clarke 2012, 303). Perception of gist is taken to be the best counterexample to the Gatekeeping view, but what is gist? Aude Oliva (2005) has characterized it as a

> spatial representation of the outside world that is rich enough to grasp the meaning of the scene, recognizing a few objects and other salient information in the image, which includes all levels of processing, from low level features (e.g. colour, spatial frequencies) to intermediate image properties (e.g. surface, volume) and high level information (e.g. objects, activation of semantic knowledge).
>
> (251)

In her terminology, *conceptual* gist involves semantic information whereas *perceptual* gist involves visual representation. She points out that in less than 100 milliseconds (ms), observers can recognize the basic category of a scene as well as aspects of its spatial layout and its global structure. Thus, if you present a picture to me where it is flashed for only 100 ms, I might be able to grasp that it is a street scene or that there are vehicles in the picture, even if I can't report more specific details.

Can one be conscious of gist in the absence of attention to it. In models of visual search such as Guided Search 6.0 (Chapter 5.4), gist is processed in the separate nonselective pathway, so perhaps on that model, the answer is yes. Is there empirical evidence for gist being immune to inattentional blindness? In a critical trial of their inattentional blindness paradigm, Mack and Rock superimposed the cross used in their discrimination task over a photo of a breakfast scene or of a scene of two individuals petting a dog with a 200-ms presentation of the image (1998, 165–68). Performance in the cross-discrimination task was as in their previous studies, but Mack and Rock noted that no subject experienced inattentional blindness in respect of the "essence or gist of the picture" (167). Most subjects could report the gist as well as certain details.

Some claim that the Mack and Rock result provides evidence that gist is immune (Cohen et al. 2011, 1166). Mack and Rock, however, noted that

> it is the size of the scene that *attracts attention* and that once this occurs, attention may be distributed over the entire array, or perhaps those parts of the array that carry most meaning are given priority in processing and thus are more likely to be consciously perceived.
>
> (169; my emphasis)

Thus, they do not claim that a subject perceives gist without *any* attention, for bottom-up attention can be captured by gist. Accordingly, Mack and Rock's result is consistent with the claim that attention serves as a Gatekeeper, for, in this case, bottom-up attention guarantees that the gist is consciously experienced. Indeed, they conclude: "If attention is necessary for perception, then an object presented under conditions of inattention necessarily must capture attention to be perceived" (228), here emphasizing bottom-up attention. Mack has noted with bemusement that the received view seems to be that her earlier work with Rock argues that gist is immune to inattentional blindness despite their clear claim otherwise. That there is an interpretive disconnect highlights the challenge of keeping track of different gatekeeping conditionals, here the difference between top-down versus bottom-up attention. Much recent work has focused on whether gist is genuinely immune to *top-down* inattentional blindness (Li et al. 2002; Mack and Clarke 2012; Cohen et al. 2011). But given Mack and Rock's emphasis on gist triggering bottom-up attention, they can allow that top-down inattention does not lead to gist blindness. Establishing that gist is immune to top-down inattentional blindness does not provide evidence against the general Gatekeeping view even if it provides evidence against a restricted version of it, namely that consciousness of gist implies top-down attention to gist.

Let us consider attempts to empirically demonstrate or refute top-down inattentional blindness to gist. The general logic of such experiments is to identify a task that plausibly consumes *all* top-down attention and then to show that the subject is still aware of gist as revealed by report. A constant challenge is how to demonstrate that top-down attention is fully engaged and not available for the detection of gist (for questions about whether this is possible, see (Cohen et al. 2012)). In work from Christof Koch's group (Li et al. 2002; Reddy et al. 2004, 2006, 2007), top-down attention is pulled away by a demanding *central* task; namely, the subject must report whether briefly presented letters in a group at fixation are the same or whether some letters are different. At the same time, in a second *peripheral* task, subjects were presented with briefly flashed stimuli of scenes in the periphery that did or did not contain animals. Subjects were further tasked with making judgments about whether an animal was present or not (this was the gist task). In fact, both tasks were highly practiced:

> Each experiment required a significant training period. It usually took more than 10 h (approximately 12,000 trials of all different tasks combined) for a subject to coordinate their motor responses well enough to answer both a speeded peripheral task and the central task.
>
> (ibid p. 9596; cf. (Reddy et al. 2004, 108))

In a "dual task" experiment where subjects had to perform both the letter and animal judgment, Li et al. demonstrate that both tasks can be performed without decrement relative to their being performed individually. They conclude that there is awareness of the gist without top-down attention to it, the assumption being that top-down attention is fully engaged in the letter task.

Koch and colleagues often report their results as demonstrating awareness in the "near absence" of attention. Of course, some Gatekeeping theses might hold that one is conscious of X only if one is attending "more than a little" to X. This approach might buy into a resource view of attention against which we have argued (Chapter 3.4). Yet with respect to the Gatekeeping Hypothesis, if there remains even some residual attention, then one will not be testing the standard necessary condition which requires completely eliminating attention, and the results will not provide a counterexample to the standard account of Gatekeeping.[3] In fact, the Li et al. experiments enforce top-down attention in central and peripheral tasks. After all, the instructed peripheral task is precisely to report on gist vis-à-vis the peripheral display. How can that task by its very nature fail to engage top-down attention since it is a task that subjects intend to do as instructed? What the intense training schedule does is to alter the dynamics of top-down attention and hone the underlying capacities needed to perform the task so that subjects do it more efficiently. Efficiency does not entail the absence of top-down attention.

Indeed, in another version of a demanding dual-task paradigm where the peripheral stimuli were faces, subjects were required to discriminate the gender of faces, Leila Reddy, Farshad Moradi, and Christof Koch showed that the enhancement of neural response associated with attention as measured by fMRI is the *same* in the face-sensitive *Fusiform Face Area* (FFA) when subjects are performing the dual task as when they are performing the face discrimination task alone (Reddy et al. 2006, Figure 3). If we take the measured enhancement as correlated with the engagement of attention, then the engagement of attention to peripheral faces is not different between single- and dual-task conditions. Yet our point earlier was that the results do not show awareness in the absence of attention *tout court*.

Li et al. characterize their findings as showing "that rapid visual categorization of novel natural scenes requires very little or no focal attention" (9599). We should not ignore their qualifications, such as the quantification of amount of attention as well as the invocation of *focal* attention. Focal attention is often contrasted with *distributed* attention, which in this context we can individuate in terms of its targets, namely summary statistics (see Chapter 5.6–5.7; (Ariely 2001; Sang Chul Chong and Treisman 2003, 2005; Sang C. Chong and Evans 2011; Prettyman 2023)). Distributed attention then is a form of attention to features of scenes rather than to space, the latter of which one might call *diffuse* spatial attention (Goodhew 2020). If the thesis is that subjects can be aware of targets outside of focal attention, this is consistent with the Gatekeeping Hypothesis so long as gist and summary statistics are targets of distributed attention. Relatedly, when discussing the dual-task paradigm, Reddy et al. (2006) distinguish between "task-relevant" attention in the periphery and "focal" *spatial* attention at fixation where subjects had to report whether a group of letters were the same or different. Yet the fact that the targets are letters suggest that, to do the central task, subjects have to deploy feature or object attention where the targets are also task-relevant (cf. the discussion of spatial cueing in Chapter 4). These experiments are revealing of dual-task performance, but they do nothing to dislodge the Gatekeeping Hypothesis.

Finally, some experiments claim to generate inattentional blindness for detection of gist (Cohen et al. (2011); Mack and Clarke (2012)). To this, one can raise an earlier worry, namely that if these experiments succeed in tying up attention away from the gist, then one should expect subjects not to report on gist. The result does not support inattentional blindness over inattentional apraxia.

When we examine the logic of experiments taken to assess Gatekeeping versus Overflow, many complications arise, and seeing these clearly requires that we formulate the theses with conceptual rigor if the experimental results and their interpretation are to hit the right mark.

10.7 Conclusion

Striking experiments suggest an intimate relation between consciousness and attention, leading some to claim that attention gates consciousness. We have been debating these issues for some time now, and they might seem settled. Far from it! All the central questions are yet to be satisfactorily answered. For example:

- What is meant by "blindness" in inattentional blindness?
- What form of attention is in play?
- Which of the many Gatekeeping theses are proponents of inattentional blindness defending?
- How can we garner experimental evidence in favor of or against the Gatekeeping hypothesis?

In vision, we capture the Gatekeeping model by emphasizing its implication of inattentional blindness: when attention is drawn away from X, we do not visually experience X. The strongest version of Gatekeeping emphasizes literal blindness, but the extant evidence is insufficient to establish it. The challenge is to find a different experimental approach that allows us to assess Gatekeeping. This issue is far from stale, and there is much work to be done.

Suggested Readings

Mack and Rock (1998) provide an extensive overview of their work on inattentional blindness. Mole (2008a) provided some early criticisms, and Kentridge et al. (2008b) provide a reply. Among cognitive scientists, Koch and Tsuchiya (2007) argue that consciousness and attention are separate processes, though see Mole (2008b) for a reply. Simons and Ambinder (2005) specifically discuss change blindness. Dretske (2007) provides a philosophical counterpoint. Noë (2002) collects essays exploring the empirical and philosophical significance of inattentional blindness. Hutchinson (2019) provides a recent discussion. For a book length treatment of these issues, see Montemayor and Haladjian (2015).

Notes

1 For an influential model of the attentional blink (AB), see (Chun and Potter 1995). The nature of the task has a strong influence on the attentional blink. When subjects are told of the likely stimulus onset asynchrony (gap) between the two targets, the attentional blink is reduced, suggesting that the nature of the task and the subject's orientation to it such as temporal expectations (Chapter 3.2) can modulate the AB effect. How we deploy attention, namely select stimuli for action, is a critical feature in determining AB (a point also made by Awh et al. (2006)).

2 Recent imaging work by Michael Pitts and colleagues has addressed this issue in the visual domain. The upshot is that where stimuli are not attended, the visual system does process these to some extent though perhaps not completely (for a review of these and other studies, see (Hutchinson 2019)). Kathryn Schelonka et al. (2017) used electroencephalography (EEG) to record event-related potentials (ERPs) while subjects performed an attentionally demanding task, namely to detect whether any disks orbiting the fixation point changed in brightness. There were three concentric orbits each with four evenly spaced orbiting disks, so 12 targets to monitor covertly. Further, throughout the visual field were strewn a variety of "squiggles" which, centered at fixation, would sometimes resolve into words or consonant strings. In an experiment, the subject was confronted

with the moving disks overlayed on a field of squiggles for 600 to 800 ms at which point, the squiggles around fixation might resolve into a word (22.5% non-animal word, 10% animal word) or consonant string (22.5%) for 300 ms. Ten percent of the time during the 300-ms period, one of the disks would change in brightness during this interval after which another 600- to 800-ms presentation of moving disks with just squiggles would appear. This pattern of presentation would be repeated. After this first phase (Phase 1) was completed, subjects were asked a set of awareness questions with those who did not report words or letter strings identified as inattentionally blind while those who did identified as not inattentionally blind. In Phase 2, subjects executed the same task, though in this case, all subjects noticed the words or consonant strings. Finally in Phase 3, subjects ignored the disks and looked for infrequently appearing animal words. That is, in the last phase, the words or consonant strings became task-relevant. The logic was to probe neural activity during inattentional blindness with comparison to controls (non-inattentionally blind), to then examine both groups under the same condition in which all were not inattentionally blind, and then to examine intentional access to the words.

Schelonka et al. observed ERPs related to orthographic processing during inattentional blindness, here comparing ERP signatures between word forms and scrambled lines. They did not, however, observe higher-level processing: "ERP signatures of lexical processing, measured here by comparing ERPs elicited by words versus consonant strings...were absent during inattentional blindness" and suggest that "the visual system can differentiate between letters and non-letters without attention or awareness, while at least a minimal amount of attention is necessary for lexical processing" (p. 64). See also work of Juliet Shafto and Michael Pitts (2015) with a similar paradigm using faces as the critical stimulus category. They observed the absence of an early face processing ERP, the N170, during inattentional blindness conditions and observed it only when attention was plausibly engaged.

3 Again, it is worth raising questions about the conception of attention that allows for talk of *residual* attention. Further, note that in the Li et al. experiment, the question of gatekeeping was probed in a dual-task paradigm, namely that subjects performed a letter judgment task and an animal detection task. On the selection for action view, we have two forms of top-down, goal-directed attention given task instructions. It is hard to

understand why this case counts as a form of top-down attention in the central letter judgment task but not in the peripheral animal detection task. The very nature of the task instructions ensures that the selection of stimuli for report is goal-directed and top-down in both cases (given training, we expect some level of automaticity, but as I argued in Chapter 2.8, this is consistent with it being top-down). This argues against using the experimental results in support of consciousness in the absence of top-down attention.

11

ATTENTION, AUTOMATICITY, AND SKILL

11.1 Introduction

Consider top-down versus bottom-up attention. If I point to a spot on the wall and ask you to attend to it, you can do so. You intend to look where I am pointing. Your attending to *that location*, the action having that feature, is controlled because that is what you intend to do (Chapter 2.8). Contrast a bright and sudden flash at said location that captures your attention, the environment pulling your eye to it. In such bottom-up attention, attentional capture, your attending to *that location* is fully automatic because it occurs despite your having no intention to do so and indeed can work against your intentions as a powerful distractor.

As theorists have pointed out, the top-down and bottom-up dichotomy is not exhaustive. Recent work has focused on a third type of bias, a family of *historical* biases on attention (Awh et al. 2012). We can diagram this as in Figure 11.1.

In principle, attention can be assessed as good or bad, better or worse, and so on. Consider being admonished to look or listen more carefully.

DOI: 10.4324/9781003223450-12

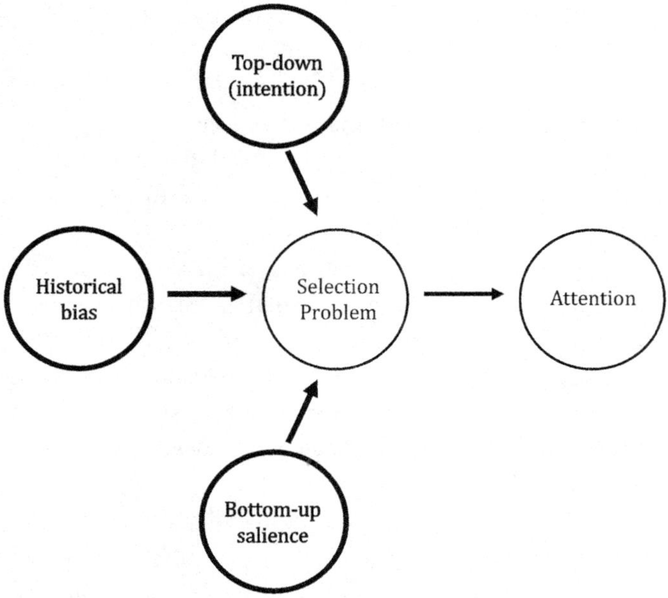

Figure 11.1 Historical influences on attention via the Selection Problem.

These evaluations are made relative to a standard within a practice or within ethical, epistemic, aesthetic, and other evaluative perspectives. As an agent's control is tied to an intention, the latter provides a controlled bias, the basis of top-down attention. Other biases yield automatic attention. Automatic attention is the topic of this chapter.

Recall that, in Yarbus's eye-tracking studies, the *pattern* of eye movements he recorded make sense given the intended task. At one level of description, his subjects' looking is controlled since subjects are *looking for task-relevant targets* to execute explicit instructions. To bring out the control in the subject's action, we use the agent's conception of what she is doing to describe specific features of her behavior. At the same time, other descriptions of her behavior, namely more specific descriptions that isolate a specific movement such as a specific saccade, its direction, speed, and target at a moment in time, are not intended yet they individuate the agent's specific looking behavior at that time. These aspects of action are automatic. Most subjects are unable to accurately report what they fixated on during visual search beyond a general description that is made available by, and perhaps inferred from, their conception of the task. For creatures with finite minds, there must be automatic features of action many of which the agent is unaware.

(For an argument for this necessity claim due to representational capacity limitations in intention, see (Wu 2023, Section 1.5).)

Control and automaticity are seamlessly integrated in intentional action. Certainly, automatic attention can disrupt action, working against control. The inattentional blindness paradigms illustrated that many subjects are distracted by unexpected salient stimuli (Chapter 10). Yet automaticity is also part of the flow of intentional behavior, and in many cases, automatic attention changes its character relative to a standard or norm, to being better or worse relative to an accepted benchmark. Because automatic attention is typically cognitively inaccessible, it can fly under the radar of first-personal assessment. Accordingly, where automatic attention in action leads to harms, mitigation and transformation can be a stark challenge. We will discuss harms in the next chapter. This chapter develops an understanding of attentional automaticity.

Section 11.2 provides a partial taxonomy of automatic biases. Section 11.3 considers habits and attention, arguing that habits draw on automatic attention. In Section 11.4, we consider value as a source of automatic attention, and Section 11.5 the influence of structure and statistics on attention. Section 11.6 looks at skill in the eye during visual search, focusing on radiology. Section 11.7 introduces the idea of attunement, a readiness to attend, part of an agent's attentional *character*.

11.2 Varieties of Automatic Bias

There are many sources of automatic biases in action. Here is a non-exhaustive list:

1. Bottom-up bias in pop-out (Chapter 5.2) and physical salience as explained by saliency and priority maps (Chapter 5.5).

2. Knowledge of statistical features of the environment that is *implicitly* learned so not acquired by intentional learning. This includes learning summary statistics (Chapter 5.8) and gist (Chapter 10.6). Some expectations belong in this category.

3. Associations where X comes to be associated with Y through learning and experience where, as in statistical learning (2), the agent need not intend to pick up the association.

4. Various long-term memories, such as episodic or semantic, that influence the agent's behavior without the agent intentionally recalling them.

5. Emotions and moods which the agent can be aware of but which have some independence from the agent's intention, such as anxiety, fear, anger, envy, lust, and love.

6. Priming, the pre-activation of representations and capacities needed for action with those capacities being influenced in the immediate or recent past. For example, my continued performance of an action on the same target changes how I respond to it when it appears again in the near future.

7. The learning of a value, positive or negative, associated with an outcome of an action or with a stimulus in the environment of one's actions. Some values are acquired without an intention to do so.

8. Desires and other conative states that are disconnected from intention, a pro-attitude (Scanlon 1998, Chapter 1).

9. Arousal and other internal states, a general alertness that shifts the causal influence of other internal states.

This is a disparate lot with interesting interrelations (Figure 11.2): one might be a species of another; some might overlap. Refining the initial

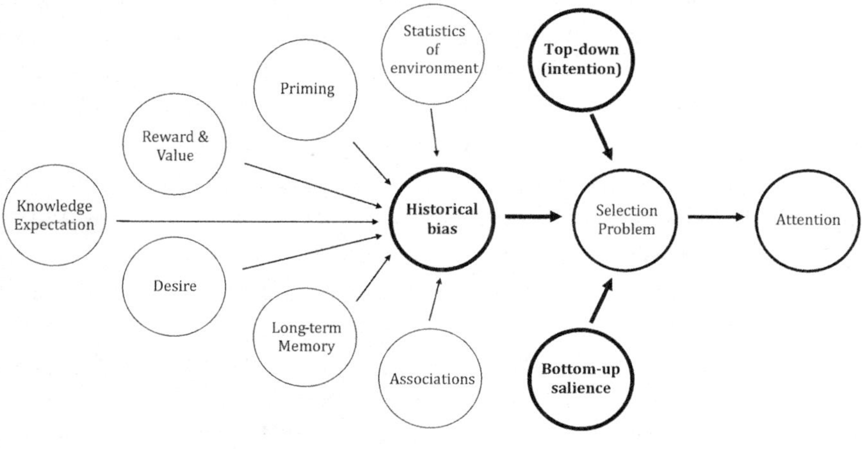

Figure 11.2 Some of the biases on attention through the Selection Problem.

taxonomy is a research task we will not undertake here. The present list yields key words to aid researchers to investigate further topics of interest. As noted, many of the biases are sources of automatic attention. If a person is salient to me because I love them, then my attending to them, an emotion-biased attention, is automatic.

For ease, I follow the standard tripartite division of biases: top-down, bottom-up and historical. I will emphasize historical biases which have substantial philosophical import explored in the next two chapters of the book (Chapters 12 and 13). We begin with the automaticity of attention in habitual action.

11.3 Habits and Attention

Habits are characterized as automatic, such as turning right at an often-traversed intersection, flicking on a light switch as you enter a familiar room, or hitting the Instagram icon on your phone right after you intentionally close the application. They include mannerisms such as tapping fingers, playing with one's hair, or using specific turns of phrase in speech. Addiction can lead to habitual behaviors such as having a smoke after a departmental seminar. Philosophers have also spoken of virtuous habits (Pollard 2003; Snow 2006), and Aristotle placed habituation at the center of his conception of practical wisdom (Aristotle 2014).

In cognitive science, Ann Graybiel describes characteristic features of habitual action: "fully acquired habits are performed almost automatically, virtually nonconscious, allowing attention to be focused elsewhere" (Graybiel 2008, 361). Graybiel inserts appropriate qualifiers, but consider an extreme reading of her description: Habits are fully automatic, done unconsciously and *without any attention*. Is the performance of a habit independent of *all* attention? Given our logical frame, S m-attends to T for R, should we read Graybiel's observation as maintaining that *no* modes of attention are in play? That is, where S acts in a habitual way, S is not in any way attending to T for performance of the habitual response? That would be a strong reading. What empirical evidence would support it?

Consider a common history of habit formation. Let us begin with three instances of attention arguably present while learning an action such as the proper way to draw a bow across a violin string: (1) one *visually* attends to the *instrument* and environmental *cues*; (2) one *perceptually* attends to one's bodily response, the *overt behavior* (e.g., proprioceptively); and (3) one *cognitively* attends (remembers) one's teacher's verbal *instructions* on how to do the action one is trying to learn. One form of attention likely disappears with learning, namely having to remember specific instructions in (3). As one automatizes behavior, cognitive attention to what one is doing, minutely described, diminishes and ultimately disappears. If one has learned, one does not explicitly think about how to act. One just does. So, later, on picking up the violin to play a piece, one habitually (automatically) draws the bow correctly to play a note. (See (Cooper et al. 2014) on the reduced need for "attentional control" (246) meaning "attention to action" as in (3), fn. 1.)

What of the other two forms of attention: perceptual attention to the behavior (movement) and perceptual attention to one's environment? When one is learning to play an instrument, one's focus is initially on the environment and on the body. Attention is initially *controlled* in that one directs cognitive attention to task instructions which then biases perceptual attention to highlight parts of the body (form your grip in a certain way) and parts of external objects (make sure the bow contacts the string *here*). The resulting task conception (*task set*) establishes an *attention set*, resulting in perceptual focus on relevant elements of the behavior and the environment. Perceptual attention changes character as one learns, transitioning from controlled through explicit instructions (focus on holding the grip *thus*, hitting bow *here*) to automatic attention to the same targets. Attention does not disappear. It is transformed from being controlled (top-down) to automatic. There is then an ambiguity in the bald claim that perceptual attention is not required in habits. This might be true only in that top-down perceptual attention, attention intentionally deployed, is not required after one habituates. To argue for the stronger claim that, in habits, *neither* controlled *nor* automatic perceptual attention is present requires a powerful argument. The observed automatization of behavior does not entail that attention is fully absent.

Attention, like bodily movements, can become habitual or automatic. Recent work argues for habits of attention (Anderson 2016a; Seger 2018). Rebecca Todd et al. (2012) speak of an "affective control setting as a habitual 'mental set,' based on our history of experience with what is motivationally relevant in a given context, which biases attention prior to an event" (365). On their account, we have affective states setting vigilance which leads to a type of automatic attention when attention is engaged. Drawing on affective biasing and other historical biases, Laura Bickel (2024) has argued that habits require attention and that we must expand control to include not only executive modulation but also affective influence. Note that our conceptualization contrasts affective influence as distinct from control (intention/explicit expectation), but we can agree that affective influences bias attention. Yuhong Jiang and Caitlin Sisk (2019), in summarizing certain properties of habits, suggest that some forms of attention have the following characteristics: "automatic, fixed action sequences gradually acquired within-specific contexts. Although the behavior is initially reinforced, once established, it may persist without reinforcement, even when it is detrimental" (65). Present theories of attention make room for the automaticity and habituation of attention.

While automaticity can disrupt intentional action, it is often coordinated with control. Every intentional action involves automaticity, so were automaticity to always disrupt control, nothing would get done. Yarbus's work shows how control and automaticity are integrated (Chapter 2.3). In intentionally carrying out Yarbus's tasks, his subjects act intentionally, and their automatic saccades are *goal-sensitive* even if not explicitly intended. Habits in attention are not purely environmentally driven but are in some way integrated with intentional control in action.

Consider the familiar case of taking a habitual right turn at an oft-traveled intersection to go home. This habit is sometimes unfortunate as when one has promised one's partner to pick up medicine for one's sick child, this requiring an atypical *left* turn to go to the pharmacy. Unfortunately, when the time comes, one unthinkingly, habitually turns right. In this instance, the habit has a negative consequence (in (Wu 2023, Chapter 3), I discuss this as a failure of *steadfastness*). One comes home without the medicine. Still, the habitual turn is done in the context of an intention to go home, indeed an intention to go home by way of the pharmacy. This failure of cognitive control is due to the disruptive influence of one's habits despite the specific content of the intention. On other days, the habit coheres with one's intention to drive home. We are not at the mercy of our habits as if our actions are purely driven by the environment, fixed by our prior experiences. Rather, habits support intentions and in many cases seamlessly merge with them.

11.4 Reward and Value as Automatic Bias

Biases on attention are often learned. This learning can be intentional as when we explicitly acquire information in improving performance through practice. Yet learning can also skirt awareness. It can proceed despite any intention. One powerful influence on attention is reward-based learning and the automatic acquisition of a valuation where a specific feature dimension is associated with a reward. This valuation can bias attention.

An early study by Chiara della Libera and Leonardo Chelazzi (2006) suggested that reward can modulate attention in *intertrial priming*, specifically *negative* priming. In negative priming, an ignored stimulus in a previous experimental trial that is reused as a target in the present trial leads to slower reaction time compared with cases where the target did not previously function as a distractor. This is as if previous withdrawal from the stimulus, since it was irrelevant, carries over and affects subsequent attention to it, even when it becomes task-relevant. della Libera and Chelazzi observed that when the previous trial involved a high reward, subjects were even slower to respond to a previously irrelevant stimulus now serving as a target. Reward enhanced the negative priming effect in a way that affected selective response. As Brian Anderson recounts, "Using a priming task, [della Libera and Chelazzi] showed that the ability to select a target was impaired if participants were highly rewarded for ignoring that stimulus on the previous trial" (Anderson 2016a, 24).

A foundational experiment on reward and attention was conducted by Anderson, Patryk Laurent, and Steven Yantis (2011), who had their subjects visually search for targets among distractors. The targets were red and green circles among distractors of other colors. In this task, red and green are task-relevant. On identifying the relevant colored circle, subjects reported the orientation of a line within it. Subjects were differentially rewarded for correct performance, with a higher reward more frequently paired with one target color. For example, the reward frequency for correct performance might be as follows: when the target is green, subjects receive a high reward on 80% of trials, low reward on 20% with the reverse payout frequency for when the target is red, so 20% high, 80% low. The subjects were not explicitly told of this statistical structure but learned it during the task. Subjects on the same day and several days later performed a different task where color was now task-*irrelevant*. They were asked to identify the orientation of a line within a target defined by its unique *shape*. Distractor shapes were presented in different colors. In some trials, a distractor was colored green, say where this was the high-valued target color from the previous task. Anderson and colleagues observed that the green object functioned as a powerful distractor as evidenced by significant increases in reaction time, as if the green of the object captured attention even though color was no longer task-relevant. The prior association between color and reward bled over to automatically bias attention in the second task, leading to reward-based distraction.

Anderson and Yantis (2012) demonstrated that the distraction was observable in eye movements as the first saccade was often made to the high-valued distractor (see also (Hickey and Van Zoest 2012; Theeuwes and Belopolsky 2012; Hickey and van Zoest 2013)). Strikingly, the effect was still present six months after the initial learning (Anderson and Yantis 2013). Similar results were shown for spatial attention using a modified version of Posner spatial cueing (Failing and Theeuwes 2014) where rewarded cues grabbed spatial attention. Anderson, Laurent, and Yantis provided evidence that the reward–color associations established using the 2011 paradigm could carry over to another task (Anderson et al. 2012). These effects are also observed in the auditory domain where a rewarded letter sound learned during training captured attention during the line-discrimination task noted earlier (Anderson 2016b).[1]

Reward-based bias on attention is acquired automatically in that subjects were never tasked with learning the reward structure. Further, even if they had relevant knowledge so as to counter the automatic reward bias by forming a strategic intention, the automatic influence can remain. Clayton Hickey, Leonardo Chelazzi, and Jan Theeuwes (2010) asked subjects to report the orientation of a line in a target defined by being an oddball shape, such as a target diamond among circle distractors. Each stimulus, six total around a fixation point, was colored, though color was *never* task-relevant. In every array, one distractor circle was colored differently from the other objects. For example, the array could consist of red circles and a red target diamond along with one green colored distractor circle. Subjects received either a low or high reward for correct performance on that trial (n). On the next trial (n+1), the colors might be *swapped* so that the color associated with the previous target diamond (say red) would now be the color of the unique distractor (that is, a distractor red circle among green circles and the new n+1 target, a green diamond). Even though color is never task-relevant, if the color of the highly rewarded unique shape target in the previous trial was swapped so that it became the color of a distractor circle, this led to an increase in reaction time, suggesting that the subject was distracted by a task-irrelevant color that was previously *associated* with a highly rewarded *shaped* target (see Figure 1b, p. 11097). The task-irrelevant color of the target was automatically associated with a high reward even though color was not task-relevant. That is, the association was learned despite task irrelevance of one of the associates.

In another experiment in the study, half of the subjects were told that if they received a large reward, there was a high probability (80%) that the colors would swap in the next trial. So, a highly rewarded red target shape in the nth trial would indicate that the target in the n+1 trial would likely be a different color, namely green. Hickey et al. reasoned that strategic subjects would plan to ignore items of the previous target color, so they would ignore the red shape and get ready for green shapes (see vigilance, Chapter 6.6). Yet informed subjects did not show statistically significant differences in response from uninformed subjects (Figure 2, p. 11098; see also (Munneke et al. 2016), exp. 3). Put another way, strategic subjects who formed intentions to use the statistical knowledge to their advantage failed to counter the reward-based bias that they automatically learned (cf. Stroop, Chapter 2.6). The intention did not suppress the automatic reward association, and the highly rewarded, task-irrelevant color continued to distract.

The studies just canvassed are foundational studies in a large and rapidly expanding literature on the relation between reward, value, and attention. These results prompt a suggestive if very speculative line of thought: a simple visual feature such as color, when associated with a reward, can be a powerful pull on attention. This association can be acquired quickly and is long-lasting even without further reinforcement. Intentional strategies designed to counter the automatic bias can be ineffective. Automaticity can dominate. If we now consider how we put others into boxes using categories like race where color can be a visual feature that guides our response, hence where we visually attend to said feature, then we can formulate hypotheses about how and why we automatically tune to certain features and how we respond to them in normatively significant contexts. What the present analysis adds is a concrete empirical construct to potentially illuminate such automatic biases. This suggests a line of research to explain socially significant bias of perceptual attention. We can deploy the full power of empirical understanding of attention to dive more deeply into the mechanics of bias and, in doing so, perhaps improve interventions that might make a difference in a biased world.

11.5 Structural and Statistical Bias

Another bias on attention comes from the agent's context. We shall focus on external visual contexts, specifically general properties of visual scenes. An initial coarse division is between biases that are *image-computable* and those that are not. A saliency map is a paradigm of an image-computable bias in that the map depends on computations over basic feature maps (Chapter 5.5). In contrast, the priority map is not image-computable in that, by definition, it takes in factors that are not entailed or derivable from the image, such as a feature's being task-relevant. Task relevance is derived from the agent's intention, not the image. It is prima facie plausible that scene meaning or semantics are *not* image-computable properties just as the meaning of a word cannot be computed just from its shape. Much will depend on what is theoretically meant by scene semantics or meaning. For example, if meaning is tied to value, then such meaning, tied to reward history, is not image-computable.

Caitlin Sisk, Roger Remington, and Yuhong Jian distinguish between *array-based* and *scene-based* biases (Sisk et al. 2019, 284). Let's begin with a well-studied array-based bias. Marvin Chun and Yuhong Jiang (1998) noted that "visual context guides the deployment of visual attention, critical for processing complex visual inputs. Global properties of an image can prioritize objects and regions in complex scenes for selection, recognition, and control of action" (30), an effect they dubbed *contextual cueing*. They argued that such cueing arose from implicit learning. Here, this means that their subjects did not intend nor were explicitly aware of such learning. Their experimental paradigm demonstrating the effect involved visual search for a rotated "T" among distractor "L"s. The "T" could be rotated so its base was oriented left ("–|") or right "|–", and subjects were tasked with reporting one orientation or the other (a target was always present). Arrays divided between *old* and *new* were presented across 30 blocks of 24 trials each (Experiment 1). Old arrays (12 total) were repeated throughout the experiment, each individual old array presented once each block. New arrays were not repeated.

> Subjects were not informed that the spatial configurations of the stimuli in some trials would be repeated, nor were they told to attend to or encode the global array. They were simply given instructions on the visual search task procedure and shown sample displays of what the targets and nontargets looked like.
>
> (35)

Strikingly, reaction time was reduced for old versus new arrays (Chun and Jiang 1998, Figure 2). Chun and Jiang introduced *context maps*, "memory representations of visual context," that encoded "the rich informational structure present in the visual environment" (op. cit. 62). The context map, once acquired through experience, biases the deployment of attention.[2]

There has been a lot of work done over the past two decades regarding other features of scenes. We have already discussed gist (Chapter 10.6).

Here, we consider recent work on scene semantics. One approach has been undertaken by John Henderson and colleagues in developing *meaning maps* (Henderson and Hayes 2017). Meaning maps contribute to explaining visual search: "A meaning map can be taken as a conceptual analogue of a saliency map, capturing the distribution of semantic properties rather than image properties across a scene" (op. cit. 743). They are constructed by asking subjects to rate patches of images for meaningfulness (see op. cit. Figures 1b–d for examples of patches):

> Subjects were instructed to assess the meaningfulness of each patch based on how informative or recognizable they thought it was. Subjects were first given examples of two low-meaning and two high-meaning scene patches to make sure they understood the rating task. Subjects then rated the meaningfulness of test patches on a six-point Likert scale ('very low', 'low', 'somewhat low', 'somewhat high', 'high', 'very high').
>
> (Henderson and Hayes 2017, 746)

Meaning maps of images seemed to explain fixations better than standard saliency maps, leading Henderson and Hayes to conclude that "meaning is the driving force guiding attention through real world scenes" (op. cit. p. 743; for a review, see (Henderson et al. 2019); for a related approach, see Melissa Võ (2021)).

Recently, the explanatory power of meaning maps has been disputed. Marek A. Pedziwiatr et al. (2021a) have argued that meaning is not the driver of attention (for an exchange, see (Henderson et al. 2021; Pedziwiatr et al. 2021b)). Rather, they argue that attention is driven by high-level visual features that are associated with "image-computable" properties of objects. Perhaps this would include gestalt properties. Semantics are not image-computable for a given image-computable property is compatible with many semantic properties. High-level visual features are not themselves semantic properties. Plausibly, Pedziwiatr et al. observe that the original instructions to judge a patch as meaningful might amount to subjects marking meaning by identifying structures strongly correlated with meaning (see (Henderson et al. 2018, Figure 1d)). One important issue to make clear in this debate is what semantics and meaning come to with respect to scenes. In any event, there is structure in the environment that we can automatically learn through repetition (habituation), and in so learning, we acquire biases that shape attention to improve performance.

11.6 Skill in the Eye

Learning is visible in an agent's eye movements. In many domains, an agent's eye movements change as the agent becomes skilled such as in sports (for a philosopher's overview of some of the literature, see (Wu 2020a)). In this section, we shall highlight radiological skill in visual search for anomalies in medical images, focusing on assessing two-dimensional static chest X-ray images and mammograms.

Consider this striking sequence of eye movements in a study by Tim Donovan and Damien Litchfield that illustrates the transition in terms of the development of an attentional skill (for similar results, see also (Kelly et al. 2016, Figure 4) and data from Kundel and La Follette (1972) redrawn in Figure 12.2 in (Wolfe et al. 2018)). Here, we draw on two sets of concepts in our initial description of the movements: (a) salience and priority and (b) control and automaticity. Donovan and Litchfield tracked the fixations of subjects

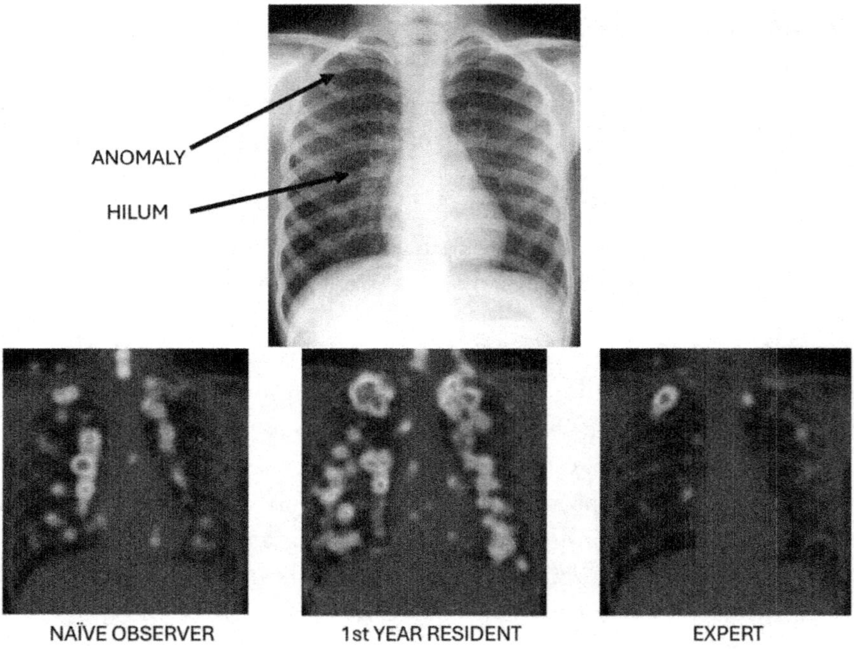

Figure 11.3 Heat map of fixations across three groups with different levels of training from naïve, untrained subjects; first-year trainees; and expert radiologists. Hot (darker) regions indicate longer time spent at fixation. An anomaly is present in the upper right lung. Note also the hilum, a normal structure. I'm grateful to Tim Donovan for providing the raw images from (Donovan and Litchfield 2013).

at different levels of radiological training, from (1) subjects who had no training, (2) first- and third-year trainees, and (3) established radiologists. The image provides a heat map of where subjects tended to fixate, this correlating with overt visual attention (saccades).

We treat all subjects as intentionally undertaking the task of looking for anomalies. They begin with the same task conception, fixed by instructions. Thus, by definition, each group illustrates a level of control in that their search behavior of looking for an anomaly is intentional. Since a given image might or might not contain an anomaly, their locating a specific target in the sense of *fixating* it is *automatic*. This is as per our definition of automaticity: locating the target *at its actual location* L was not intended. After all, if you already know where an anomaly is located, then that would be part of your conception of your task, say as a teacher to point to the anomaly at location L once the students have had a chance to search for it. What the sequence of changes in pattern of overt visual search suggests is the acquisition of automatic biases on overt attention. What are these biases?

Begin with some notion of low-level salience in the novice group. Novices seem driven to focus on an interesting spidery structure that is a normal, if typically unfamiliar, structure (the *hila*). Whether the structure is strictly salient in the sense of a saliency map is unclear, but given that the novice doesn't know that the hila are normal structures, attention is drawn toward that part of the image. Experienced radiologists know to not dwell on it. Some type of common bias leads novices to automatically look at irrelevant regions (Donovan and Litchfield 2013). In contrast, trainees often aim to be systematic in their search, something inculcated in their training often through an explicit rule. We can see a broader distribution of fixations across the image relative to novices. An interesting finding is that systematicity of search does not always correlate with better detection (Kok et al. 2016), and well-trained radiologists exhibit a more efficient search (Kundel and La Follette 1972, Figures 1, 3, 4). Speculatively, the broader distribution of eye movements in trainees might be due to applying a rule to ensure systematic search, such as looking according to an instructed pattern. In this way, trainees might have a more detailed intention than novices or experts: trainees intend to look for the anomaly by applying a rule. Trainees might differ in that, early in training, they must *remember the rule* and so incorporate it into their conception of their task. More experienced trainees automatically apply the rule and so need not explicitly represent it in their task representation. They just intend to look for an anomaly.

The striking panel is the experienced radiologist. Again, their locating the anomaly must be automatic since in a new image, they will not antecedently know whether there is an anomaly and where it is. In this example, it is as if the eye is pulled to the anomaly like an alarm. The radiologist stays there to examine it in more detail. Arguably, the anomaly is not physically salient (saliency map). Instead, the region has a medical *priority*. That it draws the expert's attention reflects a host of automatic biases acquired during proper training. Once the eye lands on it, the radiologist can examine it further. Importantly, the radiologist's finding it is intentional but automatic. In beginning the assessment, the radiologist does not know if and where there is an anomaly.

If we treat the sequence as coarse snapshots of the process of developing radiological skill, we begin with (a) a type of naïve intentional search where the novice's eye movements gravitate around salient but clinically unimportant structures, to (b) search where the trainee explicitly implements a search rule to encompass the entire region of interest though this rule can be automatized and so no longer explicitly intended in later years of training (recall habit formation), to (c) expert search where training leads to an automatic recognition of a feature that should be clinically prioritized. The images suggest a developmental trajectory of radiological skill in visual search, hence in visual attention. The sequence highlights a normative dimension to attention in that, for radiological practice, there are *better and worse* ways to attend within that domain, and the goal of good training is to ensure that one's ability to attend improves toward an ideal, such as efficient, reliable, and accurate detection of radiological anomalies.

We are using eye movements as a proxy for attentional selection, but we should not forget that these are proxies. The underlying action structure of saccades during visual search is the visual selection of a location L to program an eye movement. Where this movement occurs successfully, the eye will land on L and we can say that the subject both covertly and overtly attends to L. Consequently, in visual search, where the eye does not land on L, we might infer that the subject failed to visually attend to L. If the target in question, say a radiological anomaly, is at L, then the subject will have not noticed it, and the language of inattentional blindness gets a grip (Chapter 10). Failing to attend, we fail to be aware of the anomaly. Even if the eye lands on L, this need not secure success. As we saw in Chapter 10.3, even if the eye is directed at L where a target is, the subject might still fail to notice it in the sense that the subject might not select L or the item therein for further processing beyond programming the eye movement. Specifically, the subject might fail to select the anomaly for decision making, deciding whether it is an anomaly or not. This is what Kundel and Nodine called a *recognition error*. One way we can put this is that the recognitional response, namely "This is an anomaly", might not be engaged. Finally, the subject might focus on the anomaly and deliberate about whether it genuinely is anomalous yet *wrongly conclude that it is normal*. This is what Kundel and Nodine called a *decision error* (Chia-Chien Wu and Jeremy Wolfe depict the three types of error (Wu and Wolfe 2019, Figure 5)). As we think about normative assessment of attention, we must bear in mind that attention is tied up with action and that a proper assessment of attention must bring in the various links to the agent's response or failure thereof. After all, a subject *m*-attends *T* for response *R*.

Since the anomaly is not physically salient, the pattern of eye movement in the expert is the result of other biases set by good radiological training. Here, we consider the hypothesis that visual search in eye movement is guided by extracting gist and higher-order structure. To frame the issues, we begin with a general hypothesis of how such structures affect radiological search and set this in the context of Jeremy Wolfe's model of Guided Search (Chapter 5.4). The general hypothesis exemplifies a *holistic* approach, a label that identifies a family of theories of radiological visual search (Sheridan and Reingold 2017). These approaches posit that global processing guides local processing. One version of this is that the "gist" of a radiological image can help guide detection of anomalies. We can set this within the Guided Search model: the non-selective pathway that processes high-level scene properties biases processing in the selective pathway needed to locate visual objects like the radiological anomaly. We posit that radiologists during training improve their skills such that they become attuned to global features that facilitate detection of clinically relevant local features. Here, we use "gist" to refer to those specific properties.

Behavioral evidence is consistent with the hypothesis that quickly processed global properties guide visual search. For example, in a study of radiologists searching mammograms, 67% of anomalies were fixated *within the first second*, though, as a sobering statistic, only 63% of these fixations led to correct decision, indicating a substantial decision error (Kundel et al. 2008). Donovan and Litchfield (2013) observed that 33% of cancers were fixated in a chest X-ray within 1 second of search, and 56% by 2 seconds. Further, a number of studies have demonstrated that brief glimpses of radiological images allow substantially better than chance categorization of these as either normal or abnormal. Kundel and Nodine observed that radiologists could detect 70% of abnormal X-ray images even at a 200-millisecond (ms) presentation (Kundel and Nodine 1975). Karla Evans et al. (2013) demonstrated high sensitivity in expert radiologists identifying abnormal mammograms at 250-ms presentations while naïve subjects' performance was at chance (Evans et al. op. cit. Figure 2b). Interestingly, radiologists were nevertheless *at chance in localizing* the anomaly in X-rays that they correctly identified as abnormal (Evans et al. op. cit. Figure 2c).

Relevant information can be encoded at different spatial frequencies (Schyns and Oliva 1994; Oliva and Schyns 1997). In a study following up on their observation that radiologists can identify abnormalities in as short as a 250-ms presentation of a mammogram, Evans et al. (2016) posited that there seems to be a gist of "abnormality" such that when looking at the mammogram of the "normal" breast, namely the pair of the abnormal one detected in the brief presentation, *radiologists were still above chance* (right panel, Figure 3, p. 10294). Further, converting the abnormal mammogram into low- and high-frequency components and retesting categorization suggested that the relevant information used to detect abnormal mammograms is encoded in high spatial frequency bands (Figure 4, p. 10294). The proposal is that there is a "gist of healthy/unhealthy" tissue that is encoded at high spatial frequencies and that is present in both breasts, the one with the anomaly and the one without.

Monica Castelhano and John Henderson (2007) provided evidence that brief presentations of scenes, a *preview*, aided subsequent search for objects in that scene when it was re-presented. If structural information, gist, can aid search and be extracted quickly, then previews should facilitate search. Subjects were presented with a natural scene for 250 ms followed by a mask to eliminate visual traces after scene offset. They were then given a two-second presentation of a word that specified a target before searching a target image. Visual search was restricted to a window that revealed only a two–visual degree portion of the image around fixation, literally like a spotlight strictly gating what was visible. Consequently, subjects could not see the entire image while they searched. If visual search was biased, it would be on the basis of information extracted from the scene previewed earlier. Castelhano and Henderson observed more efficient search when the actual search scene was previewed versus preview of a different or neutral scene (Table 2, p. 756; cf. Experiment 3, Table 4). This seems to support the role of gist, a quickly extracted structure, in guiding target search.

Radiological search might be different. We noted that Evans et al. (2013) showed that while radiologists correctly identified an abnormal mammogram at a 250-ms presentation, they were at chance in localizing the abnormality. Using the method reported by Castelhano and Henderson, Litchfield and Donovan (2016) tested whether there is also a preview benefit in visual search for anomalies in chest X-rays. They replicated Castelhano and Henderson's observation of a preview benefit for natural images in their pool of radiologists and novices (Experiment 1). They then used chest X-rays as the target image to test whether previews facilitated radiological search. While radiologists performed better than novices (as expected), radiologists did not show a preview effect in respect of diagnostic accuracy or sensitivity (Table 2 and discussion, p. 987). Interestingly, naïve observers performed *worse* when they were presented with a preview, and the authors speculate that since naïve observers tend to be distracted by irrelevant but noticeable elements in a chest X-ray, the preview might have biased them toward such features. This result raises initial questions about the holistic model for radiological search. One possibility to be explored is that difficult search such as in radiological images relies more on a continuous interaction between global properties processed in the nonselective channel and local search in the selective channel (Sheridan and Reingold 2017). This continuous interaction is disrupted in brief previews.

Radiological search is salient for us as a case of learned expertise in attention. How subjects attend to an image shifts during training, and the ability to automatically locate anomalies putatively depends on acquiring the right type of biases which shapes radiological skill. What these biases are and how they influence attention remain unclear, and given that the biases are implicitly acquired, radiologists are unable to identify these factors for us. We have explored a possible bias based on holistic models where radiologists extract high-level information ("gist") to bias search. While there is evidence that gist can be extracted in previews to bias search of subsequent natural images, the evidence for a similar effect in radiological search is less clear. Nevertheless, the question is not whether there is a bias that is correlated with expertise but what precisely this bias is, how it is acquired, and how it shifts selection to guide expert judgment.

The broader significance is that in learning and experience, we acquire biases that shape how we attend to the world. In concerted training, these biases can lead to the wonders of human skill and expertise, and in speaking of such agents as doing better or worse in a practice, we introduce a normative element to the discussion of attention. In radiology as well in other domains, the *correct* shifts in automatic attention depend on the *right* biases, and this on *good* training. We will discuss these issues in more depth in the next chapter by exploring ethical norms and attention.

11.7 Attunement

Let me introduce the idea of *attunement* as a character trait, the agent's attentional potential or attentional character. In many ways, this potential is shaped by learning. Vigilance is one form of attunement that is established by what the subject intends to do. If you intend to search for a radiological anomaly, you are vigilant for it, and this involves in part readying the appropriate input capacities so as to better visually attend to what you intend to find if it is there. Similarly, saliency maps provide the basis of a subject's attunement to space because they explain the agent's subsequent shift of spatial attention. Given the agent's spatial orientation as set by a saliency map, the agent is inclined to visually attend to the salient location. As a representation of the agent's visual state prior to the shift of attention, saliency maps implement spatial attunement. In general, different varieties of attunement support all manner of automatic attention in our responding to the world by preparing the way. In habitual behavior, attunement keys in on regular features of the environment tied to specific responses, rigidified by past repetition. In skillful action, regularities also sharpen our sensitivities but in ways that support the emergence of excellence.

The studies with radiologists highlight a common attunement when we are confronted with the new and unknown: attention is driven by some sort of "salience". We impose control on attention by an intention to highlight appropriate features of the new unknown, perhaps drawing on instruction, perhaps by thinking things through, developing a plan. In the background remain various forces that can work in harmony or disharmony with the bias provided by intention. As these factors work themselves out over time, an interplay between control and automaticity, they leave an impression on the agent's different capacities for attention. In concerted training such as medical practice, the net result can be a skillful capacity such as the ability to quickly and accurately diagnose anomalies in radiological images. This is built on properly molding the agent's attunement, developing appropriate sensitivities and propensities to notice so that good attention can emerge. In the next chapter, we shall focus on the ethical dimension to attunement and attention.

11.8 Conclusion

The dynamics of attention over time involve a tug-of-war between automaticity and control that reflects the subject's experience with the world and what she learns. Learning of various forms instills a bias that shapes the subject's attention through molding their readiness to attend in specific ways, how they are attuned to things. In concerted cases where subjects intentionally train, these biases lead to attention that is judged good, proper, and skilled. Here, normative frameworks engage. Yet where there is good, there is bad. On the flip side, negative biases can also develop due to poor training and learning. Some of these biases are the result of problematic intentions to go against what is right and appropriate, but more often, the distortions in attention result from learning that is automatic, an acquisition of structures that pull us away from where we ought to, and want to, be. The result is a set of automatic attentional capacities of which we are often unaware. To see this clearly, we need to understand the automaticity of attention and its role in behavior.

Suggested Readings

Caitlin Sisk, Roger Remington, and Yuhong Jiang give a tutorial overview of contextual cueing (Sisk et al. 2019). Brian Anderson provides a recent overview of value-based attention in (Anderson et al. 2021). John Henderson gives a concise and accessible overview of his work on meaning maps in (Henderson 2020). Melissa Võ discusses her work on scene grammar in (Võ 2021). Monica Castelhano and Karolina Krzyś discuss the role of spatial layout and relations in scene processing, an area not explored in this chapter (Castelhano and Krzyś 2020). For a recent review of radiological search, see (Brunyé et al. 2019). I provide an initial discussion of vigilance and attunement in (Wu 2023, Chapter 3).

Notes

1 The reaction time differences are often quite small though statistically significant, on the order of tens of milliseconds between relevant conditions. Li Sha and Yuhong Jiang (2016) emphasized the importance of ruling out an effect of target repetition as explaining changes in reaction time independent of the reward schedule. For example, one can demonstrate a difference in reaction time with different levels of reward. The original results from (Anderson et al. 2011) were reproduced with a larger sample size (n = 40) by Brian Anderson and Madeline Halpern (2017). Reaction time for the (distractor with) high reward, low reward, and distractor absent conditions were 698, 689, and 688 milliseconds, respectively, but the

differences between the high reward condition and the other conditions were statistically significant: vs no distractor $t(39) = 2.73$, $p = 0.009$, $d = 0.43$, and vs low-value distractor conditions, $t(39) = 2.30$, $p = 0.027$, $d = 0.36$ (Experiment 1). See also their reanalysis of the data from Anderson et al. 2011. also showing differences between the high reward condition versus low reward and no distractor conditions (p. 1006–7).

2 Caitlin Sisk, Roger Remington, and Yuhong Jiang (2019) note that there are two competing but compatible models of contextual cueing effects. On one model, the effect is on attentional selection; on the other model, the effect is on response. Evidence that supports an effect on attention includes alterations in eye movement where there is a reported increase in the number of first saccades that land on the target in the old versus new array (Peterson and Kramer 2001, Figure 3) along with fewer fixations needed to find the old target versus the new (Peterson and Kramer 2001, Figure 4), though as Sisk et al. note, these are small effects (see Peterson and Kramer 2001, pp. 1231–3). With electrophysiological measures, there is an increase in an event-related potential component that is correlated with attentional selection within a hemifield, again in the old versus new array ((Johnson et al. 2007, Figure 3b); cf. (Olson et al. 2001)). There remain a variety of issues to sort out, but the key point is that subjects are sensitive to structure in their environment, and where there are useful associations such that the structure carries information relevant to improving performance, subjects can learn this structure such that it can bias their attention and behavior.

12

ATTENTION AND THE ETHICAL

12.1 Introduction

Are there norms of attention? Sebastian Watzl (2022) has argued that if a mental phenomenon is descriptively central to understanding the mind, then it should be normatively central. Drawing on the ethics of belief, Watzl's strategy is to point out that if we take seriously an ethics of belief, we should also take seriously an ethics of attention, both aspects of mind being descriptively central (see his argument, op. cit., p. 92). Is the posited link between the descriptive and the normative too permissive? For example, it might be that states of arousal as general alertness will be central to descriptions of the mind, but are these states normatively assessable?

A different approach links the ethics of attention to that of agency. The Common Conception emphasizes attention as a central component of action, the subject's selectivity that guides their behavior. Attention emerges from the agent's attunement that identifies her propensities to attend in different contexts. Attunement is part of the agent's character, something that is acquired in learning, and so attunement and the attention it engenders

DOI: 10.4324/9781003223450-13

can be assessed as part of the agent's character. The issue is not whether attention is normatively evaluable ("You ought to pay more attention!"). Rather, it is whether attention raises *distinctive* normative issues.

Section 12.2 canvasses recent discussions about attention norms tied to *salience*. Section 12.3 notes a distinctive picture of ethical attention due to Iris Murdoch and Simone Weil. That picture, I suggest, resonates with *attunement* (Chapter 11.7), the agent's attentional potential discussed in Section 12.4, emphasizing how proper attunement is acquired as part of an agent's character. Section 12.5 considers recent work on attention and the virtues, focusing on modesty. Finally, Section 12.6 considers issues about attention in democracy and the role of media not as a marketplace for attention, the attention economy, but as a locus for learning and acquisition of relevant biases, attentional virtues for democratic citizens.

12.2 Salience

In ordinary speech, anything we can psychologically register can be salient. Recent work has deployed salience to illuminate the ethics of attention (Archer 2022a). Salience in ethical discussions is broader than the technical notion of salience tied to saliency maps (Chapter 5.5). In previous work, I have provided a taxonomy of salience in philosophical discussions.

The first division is between *objective* and *subjective* salience. Objective salience in normative contexts concerns states of affairs. Consider a person before me in severe distress. That fact is morally significant. It imposes a demand on me to aid them. I might not, however, *notice* said person, so an objectively salient item might not be subjectively salient to me. If I do

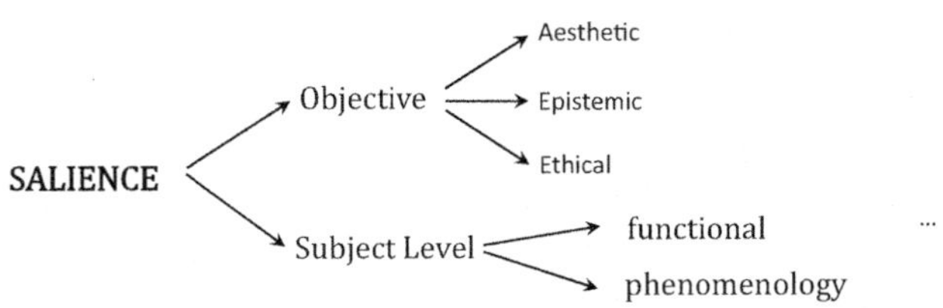

Figure 12.1 Map of different saliencies and their relations, adapted from Wu 2023.

not notice, I do not act (inattentional apraxia, Chapter 10.5.3). Here, the reason to act constituted by the person's being in distress fails to motivate me because I do not notice. I set objective salience aside and focus on the psychological conditions for normatively sensitive action. If there are normative reasons to respond to, they must be subjectively salient to motivate the agent to act.

Salience is tied to attention. There are two approaches to explaining salience: a target T's being salient either (1) entails that the agent is attending to T or (2) only entails that the agent is able, disposed, or inclined to attend to T. A number of theorists have disconnected salience from actual attention, holding instead that T's salience is exhibited as a *pull* on attention. Richard Yetter Chappell and Helen Yetter-Chappell (2016) speak of salience "in terms of an agent's disposition to attend, by which [they] mean specifically this kind of active draw on involuntary attention" (450). They argue that

> all else being equal, negligent inaction is less blameworthy (and less indicative of a problematic callousness in one's character) when the neglected moral considerations are less salient to the agent—in contrast to cases where the agent fails to act because they simply do not care.
>
> (450)

Denis Buehler (2022b) deploys the priority map to explain how attention is pulled. Sophie Archer has argued that we can be held responsible for what we find or do not find salient. In certain cases, normative evaluation focuses on salience, not attention. Where something that ought to be salient is not, Archer notes that "you are not being held responsible for what you attend to exactly, but for what is and is not salient to you in the first place" (Archer 2022b, 113–14).

Consider an alternative account of "something's pulling on attention" in the sense of the subject being attuned to such things. This allows us to speak of vigilance or preparatory attention, phenomena already discussed in cognitive science. On this view, while attunement does not entail actual attention, salience does. We make T salient by attending to it and drawing others' attention to it. In general, something is salient because you are attending to it. Salience tracks attention and disappears when attention does. The pull on attention is then explained via forms of attunement such as vigilance or other sensitivities.

Ella Whiteley has noted *cognitive salience perspectives* (2022), emphasizing harms due to "relative attentional surplus on the wrong property" (Whiteley 2023, 506). In certain cases, attention renders the property salient in a harmful way. Consider one of her primary examples, quoting Rebecca Buxton and Lisa Whiting, who, noting an association between maleness and philosophy, comment that "a result of this is that women are often remembered as women first: they are seen more as women than they're seen as philosophers....we forget that they are principally philosophers" (Buxton and Whiting 2021). Whiteley diagnoses the consequent harm as attention to the wrong property, here to the person's being a woman rather than to her being a philosopher, and argues that this introduces a problematic quantity of attention, namely too much attention to the property of being a woman and that this is a relative surplus, too much attention to being a woman relative to being a philosopher.

What needs to be clarified is an attentional *surplus*, a quantitative notion. Is attention such that there can be too much of it? In what sense too much? If attention is literally a resource, then it is subject to quantification. I have argued that we should not identify attention with a resource but instead take it to be constrained by resources (Chapter 3.4). This is not to deny that attention is associated with quantitative *features* since attention is tied to action, and these properties can be graded in various ways (e.g., correct performance, reaction time) even if attention itself is not a resource. Yet if we think attention itself is gradable, how might we make sense of this? Consider Whiteley's noting that "the absolute end of surplus attention is fixation. Only paying attention to an individual's body, for instance—so that one lavishes their attention on it to an extreme amount—looks to be a particularly clear case of morally problematic attention" (509–10). Consider visual fixation which can be characterized temporally, one's holding the eye on T over time. Contrast two cases: your interlocutor's eye briefly landing on your chest as one of their many saccades versus the interlocutor visually fixating on your chest. Yet is visual fixation over time on its own harmful?

"Fixation" as Whiteley means it is not foveation but an attentional focusing. Consider then a literal inner spotlight of attention whose intensity and breadth are gradable. What would it be to differentially attend to a person's being a woman versus her being a philosopher? Perhaps my attentional spotlight is centered on her being a woman with her being a philosopher at the edge of the spotlight where the intensity is lower. In this sense, I am attending more to her being a woman than her being a philosopher. This means that the person's being a woman is more salient than her being a philosopher, a surplus of attention. But why should that in itself be more harmful? There are, after all, times where it is appropriate to pay more attention to her being a woman than to her being a philosopher (Whitely emphasizes the importance of context in op. cit. p. 516).

As an alternative, on the Common Conception, what matters is the *response* which can define a context. One might focus on a person's being a woman as part of a joint enterprise with her in writing a paper about the harms of inordinate or skewed attention of the sort Whitely investigates. The amount of attention in this case might be equal to that in the harmful case by any measure of attention. What differs is the response for which selection of the individual's being a woman serves. To shift to a related example relevant in the context of affirmative action, in many contexts, I would be unhappy to find out that I was invited to a conference not because I am a philosopher working on X but because I am an *Asian* philosopher. The light shined on my being Asian is one thing, but what the light is for is what matters. In shifting to a response-centered account of attentional harms, we can still agree with Whiteley's insights on attentional harms (for more discussion, see Wu n.d.). There can be inappropriate salience.

12.3 Ethical Attention: Murdoch and Weil

Iris Murdoch argued for the importance of attention as the basis of ethical engagement with the world, an account that also owes much to work of Simone Weil. A focal point of Murdoch's exposition is a case of ethical engagement with a person through a "just and loving gaze" (Murdoch 2013, 16ff):

> A mother, whom I shall call M, feels hostility to her daughter in-law, whom I shall call D. M finds D quite a good-hearted girl, but while not exactly common yet certainly unpolished and lacking in dignity and refinement. D is inclined to be pert and familiar, insufficiently ceremonious, brusque, sometimes positively rude, always tiresomely juvenile. M does not like D's accent or the way D dresses. M feels that her son has married beneath him. Let us assume for purposes of the example that the mother, who is a very 'correct' person, behaves beautifully to the girl throughout, not allowing her real opinion to appear in any way. We might underline this aspect of the example by supposing that the young couple have emigrated or that D is now dead: the point being to ensure that whatever is in question as happening happens entirely in M's mind.

> Thus much for M's first thoughts about D. Time passes, and it could be that M settles down with a hardened sense of grievance and a fixed picture of D, imprisoned (if I may use a question begging word) by the cliché: my poor son has married a silly vulgar girl. However, the M of the example is an intelligent and well-intentioned person, capable of self-criticism, capable of giving careful and just attention to an object which confronts her. M tells herself: 'I am old-fashioned and conventional. I may be prejudiced and narrow-minded. I may be snobbish. I am certainly jealous. Let me look again.' Here I assume that M observes D or at least reflects deliberately about D, until gradually her vision of D alters. If we take D to be now absent or dead this can make it clear that the change is not in D's behaviour but in M's mind. D is discovered to be not vulgar but refreshingly simple, not undignified but spontaneous, not noisy but gay, not tiresomely juvenile but delightfully youthful, and so on. And as I say, ex hypothesi, M's outward behaviour, beautiful from the start, in no way alters.
>
> (Murdoch op. cit. pp. 16–17)

Murdoch emphasized that M's outward behavior "in no way alters." The moral significance of M's actions is in being "morally active" in her "inner life". What M is "attempting to do is not just to see D accurately but to see her justly or lovingly" (22): "M looks at D, she attends to D, she focuses her attention. M is engaged in an internal struggle. She may for instance be tempted to enjoy caricatures of D in her imagination" (22). The struggle to block harmful distraction is part of "a progressive attempt to see a particular object clearly" (23), a never-ending mental activity. The beauty of this investigation is the emphasis on the ethics of an inner life, centrally tied to a distinctive way of attending to a person.

Despite Murdoch's claims of not "suggesting anything in the least esoteric" (29), her account of ethical attention can seem elusive. My own view is that Murdoch and Weil, at least in salient instances, are talking about a very specific way of attending in the sense we have been discussing in this book, not a different kind of attention. That said, let us first try to make sense of distinctively ethical (Murdochian/Weilian) attention without the conceptual apparatus of contemporary theories of attention.

Weil writes in "Reflections on the Right Use of School Studies with a View to the Love of God" (Weil 2021):

> Attention consists of suspending our thought, leaving it detached, empty and ready to be penetrated by the object, it means holding in our minds,

> within reach of this thought, but on a lower level and not in contact with it, the diverse knowledge we have acquired which we are forced to make use of. Our thought should be in relation to all particular and already formulated thoughts, as a man on a mountain who, as he looks forward, sees also below him, without actually looking at them, a great many forests and plains. Above all our thought should be empty, waiting, not seeking anything, but ready to receive in its naked truth the object which is to penetrate it.
>
> (35)

For Weil, attention's canonical exemplification is in prayer. This connection might not help illuminate ethical attention for those who do not pray, but Weil's essay strikingly adduces study (homework!) as a way to cultivate the ethical capacity in question:

> paradoxical as it may seem, a Latin prose or a geometry problem, even though they are done wrong, may be of great service one day, provided we devote the right kind of effort to them [waiting, not seeking]. Should the occasion arise, they can one day make us better able to give someone in affliction exactly the help required to save him, at the supreme moment of his need.
>
> (36)

In a passing remark, Murdoch says that she borrows "the word 'attention'" from Weil, though she does not provide a citation. The quote from Weil does seem to illuminate Murdoch's ideas.

Recall attention in the non-moral sense as exemplified in visual search. In the cognitive domain under consideration, attentional search might be understood as "seeking" and "searching" for the answer by "looking" for more facts, as when surveying propositions believed, remembered, or entertained. Weil explicitly contrasts this familiar conception of attention with the idea of "waiting". Waiting is not passive, for Weil emphasizes that it is often a form of *intentional concentration* (34). This brings us back to M and D. It seems to me too strong to hold that moral attention never involves searching and scrutinizing in the sense of seeking and uncovering more facts. Julia Driver notes that Murdoch provides us with a case of moral reflection: "Attention to detail gets us further at the truth. But we have to approach such cases with mental descriptions that are general, and then search for more detail" (Driver 2011, 302). That said, as Christopher Cordner (2016) brings out, scrutiny in the search for more detail would not be a loving gaze. Such search is compatible with a cold, analytic scrutiny that is anything but loving.

I think the distinctiveness of ethical attention in Murdoch and Weil's sense is brought out by stipulating that all that can be discovered in search, all the relevant materials, are in view. Even then, there is work for a just and loving gaze. Weil's discussion of attention is part of her advocacy of a way of studying subjects like geometry, consequently of a way of distinctively giving attention to the "data" (35). In being given problems to work out in problem sets, all that is needed to solve the problem is present if one's teacher can write good assignments. Attention as selection can be a means of gathering data, but that is not when attention is distinctively ethical. Rather, it is in the way we deal with the data that distinctively moral activity emerges. The aim then is not attentional search but intentional waiting. One might say *vigilance*. The idea is that if all the facts are present, then the inputs to a Selection Problem are set. What matters is the response, a way of conceptualizing, cognizing, *seeing* the target of attention.

M's achievement in seeing D more clearly is embodied in a shift to a different set of evaluative concepts, applied by hypothesis to the same "perceptible" features that led to M's initial negative characterization. As a result, "D is discovered to be not vulgar but refreshingly simple, not undignified but spontaneous, not noisy but gay, not tiresomely juvenile but delightfully youthful" (Murdoch 2013, 17). Murdoch speaks of these concepts as *normative epithets*. The case is fashioned so that the shift in normative evaluation arrives at a correct view of D, for as Murdoch notes, M's initial view led to "convincingly coherent but false pictures of the world, complete with systematic vocabulary. (M seeing D as pert-common-juvenile, etc.) Attention is the effort to counteract such states of illusion" (31). M achieves a correct view of D because "love involves *knowledge* of the individual" (Murdoch 2013, 27; my emphasis). Note, this leaves open a different scenario involving M and D where D is really vulgar and tiresomely juvenile, but one suspects that even there, M's view of D will not remain unchanged, for even in the vulgar, there can be beauty.

How does the operation of ethical attention involve openness and waiting? We need a conceptualization of waiting that is active not because one must search for more detail, for as stipulated, all the facts are on the table. Rather, the activity comes in the automatic engagement of a way of thinking along with the constant development of ethical concepts. Here, the concept of a bias provides a different perspective on M's activity. M's reflection of her past attention to D leads to an important self-recognition that she is old-fashioned and conventional, prejudiced and narrow-minded, snobbish and jealous. One way we might understand these factors is that they are negative biases shaping M's attending, one that moves her from the data to an illusory picture involving the incorrect application of a set of evaluative concepts. While we have spoken of bias in previous chapters as operating at the level of input, given all the relevant facts being in view, there need not be a need for a bias to aid sifting between inputs. Rather, M's biases also affect the *outputs*, the concepts that she wrongly deploys. She is, in a jealous, narrow-minded, and snobbish frame of mind, inclined to see D's traits uncharitably. In turn, justice and love in attention involve counteracting these negative biases to eliminate a distortion of reality. When M draws on the right set of concepts (i.e., when her attention to D guides application of the appropriate conceptual responses), she enriches her picture of the world and achieves a better view of the reality constituted by other individuals. In linking D's attributes to a different set of normative epithets, M achieves a just view of D, one that constitutes a further development of M's understanding of those concepts, namely that they do, in fact, apply to D. The extension of specific moral epithets is thereby altered as is the agent's attention in the coupling of perceived facts to proper epithets. This is a moral, conceptual, development.

The waiting for a solution to appear is for reality to insert itself into thought, namely for D's traits to engage the right concepts in M's cognitive, interpretive, and evaluative response. This is a way of developing a just attention, a loving sensitivity for reality to engage the correct concepts of simplicity, spontaneity, gaiety, and youthfulness, all the time doing battle with the illusion that is imposed by the wrong concepts advanced by M's early biases. Consequently, M *learns* something, not just about D but about how to think by proper conceptualization in light of attentional selection of D's features.

In the end, I am not sure that I have the correct interpretation of ethical attention as Murdoch and Weil conceived of it. The exegetical issues would require a deeper investigation of their texts, as Silvia Panizza has done (Panizza 2022; Panizza and Hopwood 2022). Murdoch and Weil's emphases on waiting for reality to engage thought correctly and on the corresponding *struggle* against illusory conceptions that are driven by biases in how we respond when we are unjust connect to ideas we have discussed. In this waiting, I am *vigilant* for the solution. In being ready to attend so as to yield the appropriate response, be it to the geometry problem or to my daughter-in-law, my being properly attuned (appropriate waiting) enables an accurate conceptualization of the reality of these targets. When a correct view of a person is achieved, one thinks of a problem or of an individual "aright".

12.4 Attunement and Attentional Structure

A lesson inspired by Murdoch and Weil is what I am calling *attunement*, something that can be seen in waiting to grasp a correct picture of the world, to link data with the correct conception of normative reality. Attunement is the agent's readiness to attend to various targets, accordingly a readiness to selectively respond to them in specific ways. Attunement in many cases is an active orientation of mind, a pressure to attend. For that reason, the concept of a disposition might not do all the explanatory work needed in a psychological account of attunement even if being attuned to X, namely being inclined to attend to X, implies a disposition.

To introduce attunement in an ethical context, let me outline a familiar story (for more discussion, see (Wu 2023, Chapter 5)). In various academic contexts, a question-and-answer period (Q&A) follows a colloquium presentation. Q&As typically involve the audience members raising their hands while a moderator calls sequentially on questioners, inviting them to interrogate the speaker. Question slots are a limited resource, an epistemic good, and how such goods are apportioned is a question of epistemic distributive justice. Many departments have noticed that the queue, and hence the moderator, is often biased, overweighting certain stakeholders over others. In particular, students were often ignored, deprioritized relative to faculty. As Leonie Smith and Alfred Archer note, such situations constitute an "unjust scenario in which someone is paid less epistemic attention than they ought to be paid" (Smith and Archer 2020, 779).

Given our criticisms of the resource conception of attention, we can make sense of the idea of less attention paid given how queues are constructed (cf. Whiteley's invocation of fixation, Chapter 12.2). The moderator must search for hands and, on the basis of locating a hand, enter the person's name in the queue. If, given the number of students and faculty hands raised, students gain fewer slots than they ought while faculty members gain more than they ought, one possibility is that the moderator failed to select the student or did so less frequently than they ought. The moderator's eye landed less often on students than on faculty over time (fewer fixations on students, cf. a search error in the radiology context, Chapter 11.6). We can treat this as an *implicit* bias in visual search on the assumption that moderators do not intend to exclude students.

Many departments have adopted rules that counterbias the inadvertent tendency to exclude students. A common rule is this: the initial *n* questions or first *n* minutes in the Q&A go to students. The moderator, armed with an explicit rule, conducts visual search in a rule-based way (cf. radiological trainees who are given a scanning rule, Chapter 11.6). Yet the intention to apply the rule also sets *vigilance*, establishing a readiness to attend to students that was not in place in past Q&As before the rule was made policy. Deploying a rule, moderators are ready to attend to known students, and this propensity, set by intention, is exercised when a student with hand raised is (more likely) noticed. This has largely worked in that explicit rules have corrected imbalances in Q&A queues. Note that the moderator who applies a selection rule is similar to the trainee radiologist who applies a scanning rule. Yet in every practical domain, our goal should be increasing skill to attain expertise. By analogy, if the aim of radiological training is to achieve a level of attunement to medical anomalies that does not require explicitly applying a rule in order to get the job done, the aim of good moderation is to acquire attunement to underrepresented stakeholders that does not require explicit rules to achieve an equitable queue. Vigilance is the first step. We want automatic attunement to what matters, an appropriate readiness to attend.

Vigilance is attunement often tied to intention. Other attunements are based on automatic biases, biases that yield automatic attention. That attunement, and correspondingly attention, can be intimately connected to automaticity emphasizes that consequential responses can be driven in ways that fly beneath the radar of our self-awareness because they happen without intention. Austin Baker (Baker, n.d.) has discussed various forms of what they call *nonverbal marginalization*. Many of these are driven by biased attention and, in generating marginalization, can cause harm. Consider a familiar case that fits Baker's analysis. Many of us in social situations find ourselves talking to another person whose eyes frequently enough look past us, say over our shoulder. In what sense might this amount to nonverbal marginalization? Consider two individuals, *A* and B, where while *A* speaks, B's eyes dart about occasionally in the way noted. Let *A* and B be (respectively)

- New member to the social group versus an old hand
- Student versus faculty
- Junior *X* (e.g., faculty) versus senior *X*
- Person of a marginalized group versus person of non-marginalized group.

The values of *A* and B define elements of a context where the eye movements might be socially and ethically consequential. If during the conversation, the flicking of the eyes constantly happens, this might start to be at least rude. (It seems like you're not listening. Is there someone you'd rather be talking to? Am I boring you?) Baker argues that, in certain cases, such behavior can amount to harmful marginalization.

Sometimes, there are good reasons for one's fleeting visual search. "I'm sorry, I'm a little distracted. I'm concerned about my partner who just went outside to take a phone call about their seriously ill parent. I might need to run off. . . ." Other times, fleeting glances are just that. It would be uncomfortable for both parties to just stare at each other without any break in eye contact. That said, there are also contexts where nonverbal marginalization can occur. In Chapter 11, we noted some factors that automatically bias attention, such as visible structures, value/reward, and statistics associated with gist. These influences often reflect learned features of our environment that themselves are results of marginalizing factors. Consider the following hypothesis: *A* is a graduate student, B a junior faculty member, both at a conference. Each might, relative to their standing in the profession, be marginalized. Students have been marginalized in Q&As, unjustly deprioritized relative to faculty. The same might be true of junior faculty relative to senior faculty.

In the conference context, B's eyes flick about during the conversation at the social hour. Consequently, *A* feels that they are not being attended to. They feel devalued, perhaps their self-esteem lowered. B does not intend to devalue *A*, to marginalize them, and would deny it if the issue was raised. Yet value can be automatically learned and influence attention (Chapter 11.5). So B need not intend to marginalize *A* yet nevertheless can be biased in a way that reflects a value structure that favors other faculty over *A*. For example, senior faculty from other institutions who might be important writers of tenure letters are targets of B's attunement. The point is not that this is the only explanation of B's behavior, just that it could be. Value/reward provides a way in which attunement, and hence overt attention in gaze, can be biased. Should B be confident that their propensity to attend did not reflect structures that they would disavow? Given the automaticity of bias, certainty in one's uprightness is not warranted. The challenge for theorists of moral psychology and ethics is how to develop a framework for discussing the ethical significance of attunement, attention, and the different factors that shape it.

Jessie Munton (2023) has argued that prejudice can be constituted by a problematic *salience structure*. A salience structure is an ordering of information characterized by accessibility to a subject. This structure is tied to the informational structure of the agent's psychology as well as that of her social and physical environment. Consider beliefs as an illustration. Just knowing that an agent believes that *p* and believes that *q* says little about how the agent might behave. Let the two beliefs concern an outgroup O and let one be positive, the other prejudicial: say, *p* is that O's have played an important recent role in progress in some technical field, and *q* is that O's generally have poor hygiene. The first belief is true, the second false. While the belief that *q* is prejudicial, it might never influence behavior. Alternatively, the subject might be explicitly prejudicial, always thinking about the apparent poor hygiene of O's, going out of their way to avoid O's in social contexts. The different accessibility of beliefs, evinced by differential access in guiding the subject's behavior, identifies a difference in the subject's salience structure (cf. Henry Taylor on beliefs vis-à-vis attention (Taylor 2015)).

The relevant information is not just in the mind but also in the environment. One of Munton's examples is a red mailbox one has yet to look at. The red item is salient, ready to grab attention relative to a grey metallic trash bin, even if both were side-by-side and equidistant from the observer's standpoint. Salience structures are determined by the mind and the world, relative to where the agent is. They are *centered* structures (Munton, forthcoming). For a given moment in time and a given perspective and layout of the world, there will be a set of accessibility relations for a subject that fixes their salience structure at that time and place. On the flip side, there will also be a propensity to pay attention to various targets correlated with accessibility. Information that is more accessible given a subject's salience structure is consequently more likely to be attended. The construct of a salience structure provides a systematic explanation of attentional accessibility.

A subject can have a prejudicial outlook in that the outlook is constituted by a salience structure. Presumably, two subjects who have the same prejudice can differ in terms of the accessibility of the prejudicial belief. The more likely the subject is to access that belief, the more prejudicial their outlook. Strikingly, because Munton's salience structures include accessible information in the environment that is not actually *accessed*, this leaves open the possibility of increasing the subject's prejudiced outlook by changing the informational access relations. Munton notes that

> if there are fewer books written about Black film directors, or if those books are only available in specialist bookshops, then that information is less accessible to the subject than information about white film directors.

> We therefore need to consider not just the cognitive effort that a subject has to put in to accessing that information, but also the run of the mill physical effort of conducting an enquiry in a given environment. (12)

Assume that the bookstore has been taken over by a right-wing proprietor who believes that having some books with racist content is part of the freedom of ideas. He removes many books he deems "woke" and adds a small section on white supremacy and racist ideology. Has someone who lives nearby the bookstore become (ever-so-slightly) more prejudiced given the imbalance of books regarding film directors even if she is never aware of the change in informational accessibility? This raises a question regarding the relation between prejudicial structures of a subject and prejudicial structures of the subject's environment. That said, whether we wish to say that subjects in the neighborhood become ever-so-slightly more prejudiced given the change in informational accessibility, alterations in salience structures in our environment shape our potential and actual engagement with the world, including possibilities for attention.

12.5 Attention and Virtue

Attunement as part of the agent's character is connected to virtues and vices. Virtues and vices are manifest in patterns of thought and action and so in patterns of attention. For example, the exercise of many virtues will be prompted by targets that "call" for one to act virtuously. These targets will be targets of attention that guide virtuous response. So the danger that calls for courage, the benefits that call for gratitude, the achievements that call for humility or modesty, cases of need that call for empathy, injustice that calls for righteous anger, and so on are what the virtuous agent is sensitive to and will typically attend to in response. Attention will be an important part of understanding specific virtues and, perhaps, virtue as such.

Nicholas Bommarito's (2013) original account of modesty as a virtue makes central patterns of attention and, correlatively, inattention (see also Bommarito 2018). The appropriate patterns are captured by highlighting what the modest person does and does not attend to. Let us speak of the *object* of modesty, what one is modest about, such as an achievement, trait, a loved one, or one's country. The objects of modesty are seemingly broad. Regarding what the modest agent attends to, Bommarito distinguishes between *quality inattention*, attention away from the object's quality, and *value inattention*, attention away from its value. Second, even when the modest person does attend to the quality and value of the object of their modesty, such as a skill, their attention shifts to the conditions that make one's skill possible, "the outside causes and conditions that played a role in developing it" (103). Modest patterns of attention also involve appropriate deflection of attention.

Consider one of Bommarito's cases of modesty as quality inattention, Sean, an outstanding driver.

> Consider Sean, who has several good qualities as a driver. He not only drives safely and has a good sense of direction but also has a knack for knowing where there will be traffic and where the police will be. Sean doesn't think about these things though; he does not pay conscious attention to his driving at all. He just does his best to get from one place to another without any reflection. He would never boast about his driving skills or even think of bringing up the issue of his driving skills, mostly because such things are just not on his mind.
>
> (Bommarito 2013, 101)

Let us distinguish between (a) the person being modest and (b) instances of their exemplifying modesty. On the one hand, Sean is modest in that his attentional character tends not to engage immodestly with the relevant object. In Sean's case, he is not attuned to his driving skill so that it becomes a focus of his attention. Yet is inattention sufficient for modesty? Doesn't the pervasiveness of inattention (cf. inattentional blindness) make modesty too easily achievable? Recognizing that there have to be constraints on appropriate inattention, Bommarito writes:

> [people's] inattention to their own good qualities is not an instance of modesty if it is the result of a clinical attention disorder or a pessimistic temperament. However, they are modest if their inattention is the result of a lack of certain bad desires or concerns, such as a desire to ogle their own self-image. Just as one's inattention to the TV in a bar can display one's lack of concern for sports, [a subject's] inattention is modest when it reveals that certain bad desires or values are absent.
>
> (op. cit. 104)

The worry is that the relevant inattention is still too easy. Inattention is a natural byproduct of attention, for a given X and Y, there are many contexts where if I attend to X, I am thereby inattentive to Y. The reasons for one's inattention to Y, such as one's skill, can be mundane even if it is also true that it is not due to bad desires or pathologies. For any quality Y that we could be immodest about, in the normal course of being an agent, we must attend to some X where X ≠ Y. For any agent, there will be many times that she is not attending to Y just because she is attending to something else. Does it suffice for *exemplifications* of modesty that one is just too busy with other things? There seems to be a general challenge to an appeal to inattention as a way to characterize any virtue: inattention is pervasive, the automatic byproduct of attention to other things.

Should an attention theory of a virtue focus first on the deployment of attention? For me, a core case of a subject exemplifying modesty is exactly when their skill is brought to their attention. Here, Bommarito's modest agent deflects attention away from the skill so that one comes to be inattentive to it. Bommarito considers a case of an engineer who focuses on his quality as an engineer and its value to society yet remains modest. Bommarito comments: "Though he attends to his skills and their importance, he more often considers how fortunate he has been to have the opportunities that led him to where he is" (102). This is a sort of inattention, yet it is not clear that such inattention is necessary for modesty even if the engineer in thinking about the conditions of his success is modest.

Consider another case where one is trying to improve a skill, the quality one could be immodest about. Practice, training, and retraining require focused attention on the skill and its quality and consequences (including value). One has to make it salient in order to improve it. One's focusing on the skill on its own does not make such attention immodest. Further, in attending in this directed way, modesty does not require thinking about the external conditions that made such skill possible to deflect immodesty. Indeed, there is no doing better without such focused attention. Attention being fully locked onto the skill and its benefits to others might be part of appropriate training. At the very least, this seems consistent with *being* modest. It seems that modest agents can practice their skills without becoming immodest. Intuitively, for certain exemplifications of modesty, inattention to quality and value is not needed, nor is attention to the external conditions that made it possible. (Here, as with many cases in ethics and epistemology, I am unsure about the status of my intuitions.)

I agree with Bommarito that attention is central to explaining virtues whose exemplification is tied to virtuous action. But the putative counterexample about the person in focused training suggests that we have to say more about attention deployed beyond generic talk of attentional patterns. The modest and immodest agent can both attend to their skill for the purpose of improving it. Here, I think that focusing just on the object of attention is not going to be sufficient. The Common Conception suggests that the resulting *response* informed by attention is relevant to separating the modest from immodest person in the training example.

Prideful responses guided by attention will be problematic to modesty. Let's call those responses *immodest*. Similarly, modest responses guided by attention will be at the core of an agent's exercise of modesty for some quality Q. Then the characterization of modesty in terms of attention will entail that given a quality Q to which one exhibits modesty, to exercise modesty with respect to Q involves a pattern of attention such that one's selecting Q, say in thought, guides *modest* responses and does not guide *immodest* responses. The set of modest and immodest responses need not be complements as there might be responses that are neutral. In general, for a given virtue, *V*, and paired vice, *C*, *virtuous* attention will guide *V-responses* and not *C-responses*. This gloss on attention in modesty is circular as a schema for *defining* virtue, so what is offered cannot be a satisfactory analysis. Rather, in gathering data for an account of modesty, most of us will agree on an initial partitioning of responses as *V-responses* and others as *C-responses*. In clarifying such responses, one can attempt to develop the virtues. Highlighting the role of attention goes hand-in-hand with highlighting the responses guided by it. Just as in the cases of skill noted in Chapter 11, we cannot develop the virtues without learning to express them, and to do that, we must selectively respond in the right way.

Laura Frances Callahan (Callahan 2022, 2024) presents a different account of modesty (or *humility* as she prefers). She aims to satisfy two constraints: *inclusivity* in that anyone can partake in the virtue of modesty, even those who are oppressed or disadvantaged, and *uniqueness* in identifying what is distinctive about modesty as a virtue. Taking on the idea that virtues are often paired with vices, Callahan defines modesty in contrast to not just pride as such but *vicious pride*: a person who is modest is one who is not disposed to be viciously proud. What then is vicious pride? Not just an immoderate concern with one's qualities, for "in the viciously proud person, the self occupies too large a place in one's thought and desires, specifically by *crowding out* other things one ought more properly to be focused on. Vicious pride always makes us liable to distraction" (Callahan 2022, 632).

There is a challenge to the claim that modesty is (a disposition to) freedom from vicious pride in the sense of freedom from "the self [occupying] too large a place in one's thought and desires." Consider the *efficiently* immodest person. Every time one of his qualities comes up in conversation or otherwise is a target of his attention, he thinks: "Wow, I'm f*#!!! awesome at this!" The person then goes back to what he was doing, shifting attention back to the task at hand. His pride is intense, focused, and fleeting. It does not distract him in any notable way. Indeed, it might facilitate action by increasing motivation, but that is not essential to the point. While I am hesitant to trade on intuitions here, I would not judge such a person as modest. Being disposed to briefly think of oneself, even correctly, to be awesome every time the quality arises seems the opposite of modesty. Imagine the subject always voicing the immodest thought! And yet such pride need not be distracting.

Callahan has a reply to such cases when she joins "something of a chorus of philosophers who reject the sufficiency of a belief about your own goodness or superiority, for either humility or pride" (Callahan, 2024, 5–6). A person might have the relevant thoughts but not be distracted. How then might such a proud person become viciously proud? That they think of their awesomeness very often? But that seems not immodesty but obsession. The case of the efficiently proud person suggests that attending to certain self-reflective contents can be sufficient for immodesty, the lack of humility, even if it does not crowd out other thoughts. I suspect we have different intuitions on such cases.

Callahan also suggests that the background pride can cognitively load the agent's behavior, with emphasis on making her less able to do well on the tasks she intends. This suggests that pride can be understood as a *bias* on how one attends, deflecting attention, a causal influence that strikes me as very plausible. Let's say that we're both philosophers where you are coming to issues of attention for the first time whereas I've done a bit of work on it. My pride in my standing as an attention theorist might lead me to overweight (bias) my opinions on attention over yours. Our joint reasoning might be perfectly perspicuous, and at the end, we end up disagreeing. As it turns out, I'm right about the matter even though the answer isn't obvious. In the background of our discussion is not just my correct reasons supporting my conclusion. There is also my overconfidence based on my pride which is potentially distortive. This bias did not lead me astray in the imagined case, but in other contexts, it could lead me to the wrong results, overruling others when they are right. Pride as a bias can lead to all sorts of distractions such as those Callahan has in mind. The efficiently proud person is momentarily distracted but in a way that seems to me to reflect immodesty. Callahan is inclined to locate the relevant immodesty with increased distraction. Can modesty, and pride, be graded? Perhaps, but an advantage of Callahan's approach is that, plausibly, distractibility is graded. We can be more or less distracted. She speaks of pride crowding out other thoughts, and we can make this concrete by looking at patterns of attention over time and the influence of pride as a bias on what and how we attend.

The Common Conception provides a framework for thinking substantively about attention in modesty and in the virtues proper. The emphasis on biases on attention, targets of attention, and the responses that attention guides are elements that we can use to characterize any virtue, beginning with these fruitful discussions of modesty. One goal of the philosophical theory of attention will be to use extant discussions as roadmaps to characterize other virtues and vices.

12.6 Media and Responsible Attention

Recent popular discussions have focused on the notion of an *attention economy*. We are said to have sold our attention. Sometimes attention is stolen. I find this emphasis on attention as a commodity a distortion. This is not to say that there are no insights in those discussions, but since they often operate without a concrete conception of attention, I am going to set aside that framing and apply the Common Conception to illuminate related issues regarding the political information economy.

A central concern in the attention economy literature is our interaction with various forms of media, including the growing toxic effects of engagement with it. There has been increased discussion of the ethics, epistemology, and politics of attention within a world of diverse and hyper-engaging media outlets (Kärki and Kurki 2023; Kärki 2024). Here, I go old school and consider print media, and Susanna Siegel's discussion of it, bringing out the issue of *responsible attention in (context)* C. While engaging with print media is different from engaging with smart phones and computers, the Common Conception brings out overlapping issues.

Siegel (2022) points out that at the beginnings of print journalism in the 1920s, newspapers "institutionalized a *salience principle of importance*: make salient information that is important for the public to know about" (237). Something is salient, on Siegel's account, if it is put forward "as both demanding attention and deserving it" (239). This raises a *problem of democratic attention* for journalism in democracies: "democracy imposes an attentional demand that can't easily be met" (237). A role for newspapers in a democracy is to engage readers as part of the democratic process, including being informed about matters of relevance to their political existence. The problem of *democratic attention* then suggests a specific democratic function for journalism. It is not just to make salient items of political interest but to engage readers thereon. A thriving democracy depends on citizens who take an active role in learning about news. The problem is that "for much important information, many readers have no antecedent interest in it, and feel no prior motivation for taking it in" (238). In this way, "the public is *not* disposed to pay attention to news that *does* fill the importance principle" (245). Constraints that lead to a failure of attention include the cognitive demands that a barrage of news, and noise, can impose on readers and the fact that, well, news can be boring. One bad solution is to simplify news, sprinkled with low-calorie garnish (cf. any current primetime U.S. network news).

Siegel's solution is the *public-as-protagonist principle* which suggests "framing and selecting information to invite readers to view themselves and one another as potential political participants" (250) and, in doing so, engage and cultivate their attitudes and, potentially, their agency as democratic citizens. I want to connect this goal to attunement. As Siegel notes, citizens might be insufficiently motivated to attend to matters of political interest. Newspapers can certainly contribute to lowering the activation barrier to engagement, but engagement is a two-way street. There is also the challenge of *democratic attunement*. What would it be to be appropriately attuned to the world in a way that exhibits a type of democratic virtue or excellence? How does one achieve such attunement? Siegel's protagonist principle emphasizes attempts to engage attention, an engagement that is constrained by readers' attunement, such as attunement shaped by prior interests. The media–citizen interaction can shift the interests, attitudes, of readers, but one of the lessons of automatic attention is that configurations of attunement are shaped by factors of which we need not be, and often are not, aware.

So consider that Donald Trump is, as of this writing, the former President of the United States and the nominee of the Republican Party for the 2024 U.S. election. Given Trump's own publicly stated intentions of his actions were he to be re-elected, there is a plausible danger of the U.S. shifting from its form of democracy to a more authoritarian form of government. Here, news media have a choice in how to describe him, one that connects to the importance principle and what to make salient. For example, to simply report ("sane-wash") unhinged statements that he makes "objectively" might be taken to normalize what is pathological political behavior. Concretely, here are two among many possible descriptors, each accurate: refer to Trump first as the Republican 2024 nominee for president or refer to him as a convicted felon. Both descriptions are true. How these descriptions are used in media shapes what is salient to those reading the news and in turn how their attention is engaged.

Rendering Trump's status of being convicted salient in a systematic way is not just to engage with readers. The reader-as-protagonist principle conceptualizes the reader as an agent who is subject to various performance and capacity limitations. A newspaper's selection of some information rather than others, or its prioritization of some information over others, shapes an agent's action space, and this can encourage readers toward democratic responses. In then making salient specific descriptions, newspapers invite readers to engage in specific ways. We should not forget, however, that newspapers are sources of information and readers learn about the world through them. Some of this learning is intentional. I'm interested in recent fires in Canada, given frequent air-quality warnings due to the fires remaining uncontrolled (as of this writing). With this interest, I intend to read the newspaper or other sources to find out more. Yet, as I have noted, much learning is *automatic*. So I can learn about Trump's legal challenges by reading the newspaper, and those facts do not change if he is referred to as the former president or as an indicted citizen. At the same time, the uses of those descriptions establish biases on how I attend in the future. This raises the question about newspapers as sources of learning. Should not how we frame information be sensitive to how we automatically influence readers?

At the same time, a newspaper's choice to initiate a biasing association through the descriptions deployed in describing an individual or event, indeed the choice to inculcate an *implicit* bias to think of an individual in specific ways, smacks of a type of unwholesome or problematic *manipulation*, one which in other contexts we are likely to judge as a bad thing, such as social media feeds that have an untoward influence on the autonomy of young minds. Yet the brain is an information sponge. Unless we shut ourselves up in a room, in engaging with the world, the brain automatically learns structures, including associations and statistics of the local and global environment. We cannot shut off this channel just like that, and the power of explicit intentions to control it is limited. An important political, epistemic, and ethical question will be not just to combat misinformation but to recognize that the route into the mind and heart of subjects is also the automatic learning of information, learning that shapes the automatic ways that we respond to the world. This is an important and indeed substantial part of behavior. To put it in stark terms, perhaps one of the most powerful instruments for new media in a democracy is not *just* engagement of explicit attitudes but inculcation of implicit biases through automaticity.

The media has a role to play in shaping *collective* action. Christopher Mole has recently written of *emancipatory attention*, by which he intends to highlight attention's distinctive role in confronting large-scale social and moral problems. Drawing on a selection for action framework, Mole emphasizes that combatting something like racial injustice is not just grounded in acquiring new knowledge, recognizing epistemic gaps, or raising consciousness. Rather, it also is tied to a type of attentive engagement with one's environment. Critically, an important part of emancipatory attention is a call not just to look more carefully (cf. our discussion of Murdoch and Weil, Chapter 12.4; Mole draws on Marilyn Frye (Frye 1983)) but to engage attention with action. This depends on the "circulation of information that would enable a socially distributed set of capabilities to be selectively coordinated around a coherent goal" (41). Addressing injustices will require attention within a group's establishing a space of possible actions that reflect the relevant targets and the possibilities of responding to them. Here, media can play a facilitatory role via the public-as-protagonist principle where the public can also be thought of as a group agent. Media can play a constructive role in the shaping of social attention in ways that can support democracy and justice. The unfortunate flip side is that media can also play a destructive role.

12.7 Conclusion

If attention plays a central role in action, then it is within the purview of normative assessment. We have discussed the interrelated notions of *salience* as that which is prioritized because one attends to it, of *attunement* as the propensity of a subject to attend in specific ways given a background set of biases typically learned, intentionally or not, and the resulting shaping of ethical and political *virtues* and their manifestation. These are all grounded in the agent as an attentive being. We are only beginning to explore the normative significance of this aspect of human agents, an area ready for further development and insight. What I want to emphasize again is that the Common Conception from folk and empirical psychology can provide a shared starting point for engaging these critical issues with theoretical precision and systematicity.

Suggested Readings

Sophie Archer's edited volume, *Salience*, collects essays touching on many dimensions of salience both within and outside of ethics (Archer 2022a). Jessie Munton's forthcoming book discusses salience in relation to ethics and epistemology (Munton forthcoming). I review some recent work on norms of attention (Wu 2024a). A wide-ranging perspective is provided by Georgi Gardiner (2022). Murdoch and Weil have received renewed attention, and Silvia Panizza (2022) provides a recent book-length discussion of their views as it relates to ethics. For work connecting attention to core issues in epistemology, see Abrol Fairweather and Carlos Montemayor (Fairweather and Montemayor 2017). A recent review of attention and epistemology is given by Catherine Saint-Croix (Saint-Croix 2024).

13

THINKING, REASONING, AND COGNITIVE MEANDERING

13.1 Introduction

William James noted that attention is exemplified in grasping a train of thought. Thinking in its various forms exemplifies attention, what we call *cognitive* attention, attention that is based in various cognitive states broadly understood. On the Common Conception, the agent's selecting a target for response suffices for their attending to it. Cognitive selection can be the subject's recalling a specific memory to inform their report, the memory state being the grounds of their attention. It can also be the subject's focusing on a proposition as material for reasoning, their belief or other cognitive attitude being the grounds of their attention. In intentional thinking, one sets oneself to a task through selective cognition. At the same time, there is also spontaneous thinking that is not task-driven, such as mind wandering, rumination, or fixation. Further, the intentional and the spontaneous intermingle in bouts of thinking.

To get started, consider the following trace over a two-dimensional field as a very coarse representation of the mind's cognitive movements over time. This wouldn't be an effective way to represent thoughts, for what are the relevant (two) dimensions? (cf. Christoff et al. (Christoff et al. 2016,

DOI: 10.4324/9781003223450-14

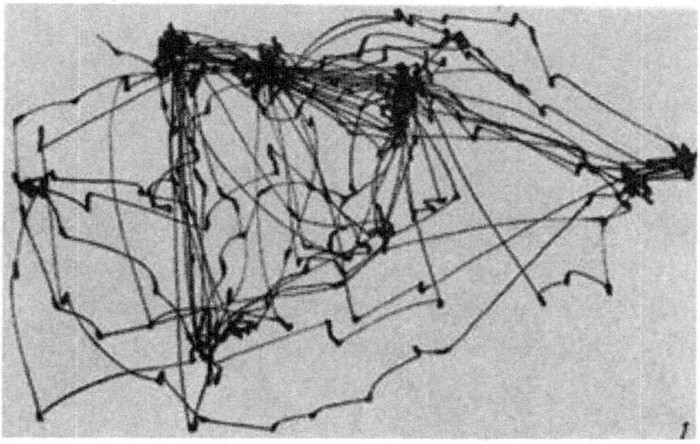

Figure 13.1 Trace of movements of attention.

Figure 1); Figure 13.3). The present point is just that the mind moves across a cognitive space that we here project onto these two dimensions. Crudely, the depicted movements could be across the subject's memories where each discontinuity in the trajectory is a moment of recollection, perhaps intentional, perhaps not.

This is, as you might have guessed, actually a trace of eye movements from Yarbus's experiments, in this case free viewing of Ilya Repin's *They Did Not Expect Him*. The subject is asked to have a look, with no further goal. Thus, the viewing is not completely spontaneous, but there is a freedom of exploratory movement.

A bias to faces is readily apparent. Yet the eye also moves to other locations, and why the eye lands at those places is less clear. As has been a constant

Figure 13.2 Free view and painting.

refrain in this book, there are many forces on visual attention such as in visual search. The same applies to cognitive attention, in cognitive search and mental meandering as Figure 13.1 was meant to evoke. This chapter provides a selective review of the large terrain of cognitive attention in thinking.

Section 13.2 considers the role of attention in epistemic justification where we draw conclusions based on reasons for belief, and Section 13.3 summarizes work on the role of attention in securing perceptual demonstrative thought. Section 13.4 discusses epistemic bias, and Section 13.5 considers the automaticity of thought, with emphasis on mind wandering.

13.2 Attention and Justification

Here is a basic case of good, justified, reasoning: normally, when I have a visual experience of a blue car passing before me, this leads to a belief that there is a blue car passing by. Given that the circumstances are normal, the resulting belief is *based* in an epistemically appropriate way on my experience. In part, this is because the experience provides evidence or reasons for my belief. Perception plays a rational role in belief formation by justifying my belief.

Attention is necessary. Whether I form the belief about the car depends on whether I notice or attend to the car. For assume that I fail to notice it because attention is diverted elsewhere. The lesson of inattentional blindness is that I will not form the relevant belief about its color—or indeed any belief about it—based on my perceptual experience of it. If so, my experience provides evidence regarding the color of the car, but given that my attention is directed elsewhere, I do not notice the evidence and do not take advantage of it. The same points can be made using "reason" instead of "evidence": my experience gives me reason for a belief which I do not respond to given my inattention. (I will be somewhat lax about usage of "reason" and "evidence", using them interchangeably.) To reason to belief, I must attend to relevant evidence. It is a further question whether attention is needed for the experience to provide evidence. After all, one might say that the evidence is there whether I notice it or not. Having evidence or providing reasons is one thing; being attuned to and noticing it another.

Consider two notions of justification: propositional versus doxastic justification. Propositional justification can be characterized as follows:

> Propositional Justification: if experience *E* provides reasons, evidence or support for *p*, then *E* propositionally justifies *p*.
>
> (Silins and Siegel 2014)

It is a small step to then speak of E as propositionally justifying a belief with the content p. As noted earlier, a subject might have an experience E that justifies the belief that p yet not form that belief. So the subject can have an experience that provides propositional justification without ever taking advantage of it. This might happen because the subject does not notice the relevance of the experience or because the subject does not appropriately respond to it. *Doxastic* justification occurs when the subject forms that belief appropriately on the basis of E: the belief that p is doxastically justified by E.[1] Doxastic justification of the belief that p by E implies propositional justification of that belief by E. With this distinction concerning justification in place, one can then ask about the epistemic role of attention by considering its possible connection to propositional and doxastic justification. We shall focus on doxastic justification since what is at issue is a belief formed as a response to E.

Is attention necessary for doxastic justification? Isn't the answer obviously *yes*, given the earlier example of noticing: to form a belief on the basis of experience, one must notice the relevant aspects of experience. This suggests a more general way to argue for the necessity of attention for doxastic justification, one that draws on our discussion of attention and agency in Chapter 2.[2] Let us begin with an observation by John Turri:

> In evaluating beliefs we are evaluating a kind of performance, the performance of a cognitive agent in representing the world as being a certain way, and when performing with materials (which, in cognitive affairs, will include reasons or evidence), the success, or lack thereof, of one's performance will depend crucially on the way in which one makes use of those materials.
>
> (Turri 2010, 315)

In many cases, this seems exactly right. If belief aims at truth, then fixing belief involves figuring out the truth, a cognitive activity, something often done intentionally. For example, one might pose the question "Is p true?" to oneself, and this initiates epistemic actions of evidence gathering and reasoning. How effectively this activity is carried out depends on the manner of execution and on the materials at hand. To focus on perception-based beliefs, good epistemic standing depends on whether experiences provide propositional justification and whether beliefs are formed in a way such that they are doxastically justified. In aiming for the truth, one often has to do things: searching for relevant evidence or reasons, such as by looking or otherwise experiencing the world, and considering and weighing the evidential options. Will it rain in the afternoon? One could, of course, hazard a guess, but to know the truth, one will look for and assemble relevant evidence and, on that basis, form a belief about the weather. For example, one can ask a knowledgeable friend, check a reliable weather service, or just look.

For mundane cases of figuring out the truth, there is cognitive action, and where there is action, the Selection Problem applies. This application involves delineating the relevant action space, in this case an *epistemic* action space. Specifically, the space is structured by inputs as sources of evidence for belief and various beliefs as outputs. Generally, there are many sources of evidence or reasons: experience, beliefs, memories, and such. I will focus on a subpart of a typical epistemic behavior space, namely where the inputs are perceptual experiences and the outputs beliefs, or judgements, that could be based on those experiences.

There are at least three experience-belief mappings to consider. First, the simplest mappings are experiences and beliefs that have content with the same accuracy conditions and thus the belief that *p* and the experience that *p*. Second, more complicated mappings are beliefs whose contents are propositionally justified by the available experiences, a category that will include more beliefs than in the first case. Finally, there will be beliefs that are only apparently propositionally justified by the set of available experiences. That is, a subject might falsely think that certain beliefs are propositionally justified by a certain experience and form those beliefs on that mistaken basis. Adding this third type of belief into the mix yields a complicated behavior space where experiences are connected to (a) beliefs with which they share the same content, (b) beliefs for which the experiences provide actual propositional justification (which include (a)), and (c) beliefs for which they provide apparent propositional justification, from the subject's perspective. Of course, the space is more complicated than this, but the current layout suffices for our discussion. The epistemic Selection Problem then defines a space of possible perception-based beliefs. That there are so many possible paths is driven by the idea that which path one takes depends on what one notices (i.e., on what one attends to).

"Base" here is used in a broader sense than in epistemology where much focus has been directed at the *basing relation*. Ram Neta writes:

> [The basing relation] is that relation *the obtaining of which* makes it the case that the reasons that stand on one side of the relation are *the reasons for which* the creature holds the belief that stands on the other side of the

> relation. In other words, the basing relation is that relation which is such that, when it obtains between a belief B and a reason R for which the belief is held, its obtaining is what makes it the case that R is the reason (or at least *a* reason) for which B is held.
>
> (Neta 2010, 109)

If one thinks that visually experiencing that the car is blue provides evidence for one's belief that the car is blue, then where believing that it is blue is based in the relevant way on that experience, this amounts to a case where the perceptual reason is why the belief is formed. The resulting belief is well founded. Here, the evidence propositionally justifies belief and the relevant basing relation holds, so the belief is also doxastically justified. The more general notion of basing as used to define the epistemic action space includes the epistemic basing relation as one among several mappings linking perception to belief. Epistemic basing is one among many ways to form one's beliefs. In the epistemic action space, there are three salient cases for experience E and belief B where B is based (in the general sense tied to the Selection Problem) on E:

1. E propositionally and doxastically justifies B (i.e., B is properly based on E).

2. E propositionally but does not doxastically justify B.

3. E does not propositionally justify B yet B is based on E

Recall that the behavior space characterizes the goal-directed activity of figuring out what to believe. If beliefs aim at the truth, in figuring out what to believe, one figures out what is true. It is natural in this context to "look" for specific evidence or good reason and, in this way, interrogate one's evidential sources selectively. When one finds relevant evidence, one focuses on it, considers it, and evaluates it in respect of other evidence. Attention is part of this activity of focusing, interrogating, and considering. Call the epistemic behavior space at issue the space of experience-based belief. The argument for the necessity of attention for doxastic justification is just the argument for the necessity of attention for beliefs based on experience in the cognitive activity of figuring out what is true, that is in solving a Selection Problem. As doxastic justification is one of the three forms noted previously, the necessity of attention for doxastic justification follows from the necessity of attention for cognitive action. To figure out what is true is an activity that culminates in traversing a specific path in behavior space, and the selectivity at issue, namely the specific belief formed in light of a specific perceptual experience, implicates attention. Think of attention here as selection of perceptual content to inform the fixation of belief. So, in the cases of cognitive activity for the sake of determining what to believe, attention is necessary for basing belief on experience in the general sense of basing, and, *a fortiori*, attention is necessary for doxastic justification where a specific epistemic basing relation is required, whatever that relation turns out to be. It follows that the epistemic basing relation will involve attention.

Nico Silins and Susanna Siegel have raised doubts about whether attention is necessary for doxastic justification even if it often serves this role. Here is one of their cases:

> Consider a distracted subject navigating the environment, such as a distracted driver, or a walker lost in thought. Such a subject can still adjust their behavior in response to the environment in a way that is not merely instinctive, operating the brake, the clutch, the defrosting system, the steering wheel, and so on. Further, they arguably can do so while remaining distracted from the environment, without their attention being captured by the obstacles that they are successfully avoiding, or by the equipment that they are manipulating. Despite being superficially automatic, such behavior is far from being a mere reflex, and has a strong claim to being rational. In addition, the subject would satisfy the central diagnostics for having various beliefs about her immediate situation, such as the belief that the car is running and operating as it should be. They are disposed to endorse this proposition if asked, and they are acting in a way that would be advisable, given their desire to continue driving, if the proposition is true. In such a case, their inattentive experience is feeding into well-founded perceptual beliefs.
>
> (Silins and Siegel 2014, 159)

The emphasis on inattentive experience feeding into beliefs suggests that attention is not present. We can agree that selective feeding into beliefs is not based on an intention to infer in that way, so such inferences are not intentional. This leaves open the possibility of automatic attention and inference, and, if so, the example is not a counterexample to the claim that attention is necessary for doxastic justification. One still has to notice relevant reasons, intentionally or not.

Of course, much rides on what unvarnished talk of inattention ultimately comes to. In characterizing core cases of attention via the Common Conception as selection for guiding action, attention has a necessary connection to guided action as when we form beliefs on the basis of evidence. The present proposal is that one can capture the intuitive idea of inattention in Siegel and Silins's example without denying that attention is engaged. To do this, we need only draw on the contrast between control and automaticity, with Siegel and Silins's conception of attention in their example as correlated with control, inattention with automaticity. For the case to pose a counterexample requires that the selection they acknowledge in behavioral adjustment not amount to attention. This claim is theoretically controversial. That said, to the extent that we focus on selection that influences behavior, we might find processes for which the epistemic-justificatory notion of being doxastically well founded will be off kilter. There are going to be cases at the edges where intuitions will differ, and, then, a well-substantiated theory can add its weight. It is enough, however, to acknowledge, as I think many will, that in core cases of belief arrived at on the basis of good reason, attention is involved in one's noticing the relevant reasons and responding to them appropriately. We need only remember that automatic attention is a type of attention. In acknowledging this, we make room for automatic inferences that need be no less well grounded than their intentional relatives.

13.3 Demonstrative Thought

Consider perception-based (or perceptual) demonstrative thoughts about objects, thoughts typically expressed by the use of demonstratives such as "this" or "that" ("demonstrative thought" henceforth means perception-based demonstrative thought).[3] For example, imagine Jane pointing at a building in a skyline and saying, "*That* is the tallest of the lot." She uses the sentence to express what she is thinking, and a companion can understand her immediately by looking at what she points to. In contrast, imagine that in a different time and place, a stranger reads a written report of Jane's exact words. By merely reading the sentence "That is the tallest of the lot", the stranger would not understand the specific thought Jane expressed. Why? A natural answer is that the stranger would in some sense not know which object Jane referred to with the demonstrative "that", something that Jane's companion knows by looking at what Jane refers to. This suggests two conditions for grasping Jane's perception-based demonstrative thought:

(a) *The know-which condition*: one understands Jane's thought only if one knows to which building she referred.
(b) *The perception condition*: seeing the building Jane was pointing to is necessary to understand the perception-based thought she expresses.

John Campbell (2002) compellingly argued that attention must also play a role by considering a *sea of faces*. Imagine facing a crowd where your companion singles out a woman with the expression "that woman". Campbell writes:

> It is only when I have finally managed to single out the woman in my experience of the room, when it ceases to be a sea of faces and in my experience I focus on that person, that I would ordinarily be said to know who was being referred to. So it does seem to be compelling to common sense that conscious attention to the object is needed for understanding of the demonstrative.
>
> (9)

Campbell speaks of "conscious" attention, but the core claim is that we must attend to what the speaker refers to in order to understand demonstrative reference. Accounts of the role of attention in demonstrative reference were also developed in related but distinct ways by Declan Smithies (2011b) and Imogen Dickie (2011, 2015). All three not only emphasize attention's causal and informational role but also connect attention to justification and normativity. Thus, Campbell emphasizes attention as setting standards for assessing the appropriateness of information processing, Smithies underscores attention's making available propositional justification in a form of rational access, and Dickie highlights the appropriateness of attention as a luck-eliminating referential skill that satisfies the agent's referential intentions and indeed needs.

The role of attention in demonstrative reference is, arguably, well established in the philosophical literature. I want to return to Campbell's emphasis on *conscious* attention. He writes:

> If I am to understand a demonstrative referring to an object, it is not enough merely that the object be there somewhere in my visual field; I have

> to attend to it. But the attention that is needed here is, as it were, a matter of experiential highlighting of the object; it is not enough that there be some shifts in the architecture of my information-processing machinery, remote from consciousness.
>
> (Campbell 2002, 2)

I take talk of "highlighting" to add a phenomenal character to attention, for what is needed is not just selective information processing "remote from consciousness" but a change in consciousness itself. Smithies writes of "a phenomenal distinction to be drawn between the attended foreground and the unattended background of one's experience" (229) (cf. Watzl's phenomenal account of attention discussed in Chapter 7.3). This loads an additional element onto attention in its role in securing demonstrative thought. Here, I simply want to highlight two different views and leave it to the reader to assess which is more plausible. We might agree that to be capable of entertaining a perceptual-based demonstrative thought, one must consciously perceive the referent. This leads to distinct proposals:

(I) Conscious attention is necessary for understanding demonstrative reference in the sense that one must attend to the consciously perceived referent.

(II) Conscious attention is necessary for understanding demonstrative reference in the sense that one must phenomenally attend to the (consciously) perceived referent.

In (I), attention might have no further phenomenal upshot than selecting consciously perceived targets to fix reference in a way that allows the perceiver to understand a demonstrative thought.

Smithies gives an explicit argument for something in the area of (II):

(1) Attention is what makes information fully accessible for use in the rational control of thought and action.

(2) But what makes information fully accessible for use in the rational control of thought and action is a distinctive mode of consciousness.

(3) Therefore, attention is a distinctive mode of consciousness. (Smithies 2011a, 248)

This argument leads him to posit a distinctive conception of attention as *rational access consciousness*.

Yet if we draw on the Common Conception as a broadly accepted starting place, the role of attention is not to establish the *accessibility* of perception. Arguably, that perception is phenomenally conscious might secure its accessibility. Rather, the role of attention is to access perception in the control of thought and action. It thus plays a role in rational control. If we then change the first premise to, (IA) attention is what makes information fully *accessed* for the rational control of thought and action, the argument fails to go through. Attention is plausibly needed to secure perceptual demonstrative reference, but it is a stronger demand to require that attention itself must be conscious.

13.4 Bias and Epistemic Injustice

We have discussed epistemic injustice when considering the recent history of queue construction during Q&As, how underrepresented groups had been perhaps systematically, even if inadvertently, ignored and how a counterbias was introduced to address the inequitable distribution of epistemic resources (Chapter 12.4). The result was to shift the deployment of visual attention to accord people their due attention (Smith and Archer 2020). There are, unfortunately, other cases of epistemic injustice.

Siegel poses the following plausible case:

> Outgroup hiring: A group of evaluators harbor implicit, ill-founded views about a group of people who constitute an "outgroup" relative to them. Due to those views, evaluators disproportionately focus (without knowing it) on the weakest parts of an outgroup candidate *X*'s application. The negative features of *X*'s application are not fabricated, but a fuller picture of *X*'s candidacy would contain positive features that the evaluators did not consciously register, or did not take in at all. In response to the evidence they have about *X*, the evaluators conclude that *X* is unqualified.
>
> ((Siegel 2017, 158); one might consider this case from a Murdochian conception of attention, Chapter 12.3)

Let's say that the evaluators have an implicit prejudice against members of the outgroup. There is then something wrong with the inference, and on Siegel's telling of this case, the problem is "unwitting" so is difficult to pin down. This means that the prejudice is not among the explicitly entertained premises in the inference (it does not appear in her list of premises, Table 9.1, p. 166). Rather, it functions to select and anti-select putative evidence. Perhaps it functions as a *bias* in the sense we have discussed. Siegel refers to it as a *mechanism* and characterizes what she calls the *anti-selection* of relevant evidence as follows: "When a mechanism causes you not to notice an object or a feature, we can say that the object or feature was anti-selected" (157). One response is that not noticing something is the statistical norm, so most things that are available to one are not selected (inattentional blindness). Since this failure to select does not require a mechanism, many things missed will not be anti-selected. So, even if there is a mechanism of anti-selection, there remains the question of why we were not attuned to the many things merely missed even when they are relevant. Let's set this issue aside and focus on the central point, "prejudice...influences the selection of evidence" (162), namely in preventing the intake of "uncongenial" evidence counter to one's prejudicial attitudes (164). The epistemic problem in Outgroup Hiring resides therein.

In reconstructing the evaluator's reasoning regarding a job candidate's file, Siegel notes two inferences. First, the evaluator undertakes a subinference from *some* mediocre features of the file to the first subconclusion that the file contains *mainly* mediocre features. One might object that this is already a poor inference, but the issue is whether it is poor, in addition, because of the agent's prejudice? That is, is the inference prejudicial, not just "quantificationally impetuous" in moving too quickly from *some* to *many*? The second subinference Siegel notes seems reasonable on its own, an inference from the premise that the file has mainly mediocre features to the conclusion that the candidate should be rejected. So why is the inference prejudicial? How does prejudice figure in an explanation of the assessor's reasoning? Siegel's diagnosis is that the prejudice blocks the evaluator from entertaining evidence that speaks in favor of the candidate, namely features of excellence and qualification.

There is much to agree with in Siegel's characterization, and we are in a position to elaborate the issues she raises by incorporating the case within the framework for attention we have been developing in this book. (Siegel doesn't delve into the attention literature in her discussion nor give more details about the mechanism.) Perhaps the most basic phenomenon is that a given bias opens up attention to some things and closes it to others. The prejudicial bias, whatever it ultimately comes down to, can play a familiar functional role that we have seen exemplified by a variety of biases of which intention is a paradigm case as seen in inattentional blindness paradigms.

Bias explains certain cases of partiality in the assessment of evidence, and the discussion of previous chapters highlights how bias, elaborated in terms of disparate factors on solving the Selection Problem, changes both attunement and selection for response.

We can analogize Siegel's case to that of the Q&A queue. There, the problem we noted was a failure of attunement that we mitigated by intention-driven vigilance for student questioners. It might be too strong to say that the moderator is prejudiced against students in the Q&A case as the evaluator is prejudiced against outgroup members in the CV case, but the net result can be the same, attention to a narrow subset of reasons for action and the resulting unjust partiality in the agent's response. So a bias explains the shape of the agent's attunement, their propensity for attention, which then explains their subsequent failure to notice relevant reasons.

13.5 The Automaticity of Thought

As we have seen, biases shape the character of attention. When an agent intends to act, the intention biases attention in task-relevant ways. The framework of automaticity and control we have been working with identifies the agent's control relative to features of her action that are intended. Yet most features of action are unintended, hence automatic. The interplay of automaticity and control shows up in attention. Sometimes, the agent intends to attend in a specific way, and where she does so, attention as she intends is controlled. For example, the agent intends to think about what to have for lunch today, and her having that train of thought, described as centered on *lunch*, is controlled. Yet most of the features of attention are automatic. That she thinks about *hamburgers* rather than *salad*, or vice versa, reflects the automaticity of thought in respect of her thinking about *those* specific items. The automaticity of her thought is reflected in the unintended even if task-relevant specific targets of cognitive attention, in this case, burgers versus salad. These specific food items "pop" into mind.

The automaticity of thought is seen most clearly in the *meandering* of attention. A notable focus in recent philosophy, and indeed in psychology, has been on *mind wandering*. Given our invocation of automaticity and control, consider a related proposal of Kalina Christoff et al. (2016) that presents a dynamic framework for thought, one encapsulated in the following figure (Figure 1 in their paper):

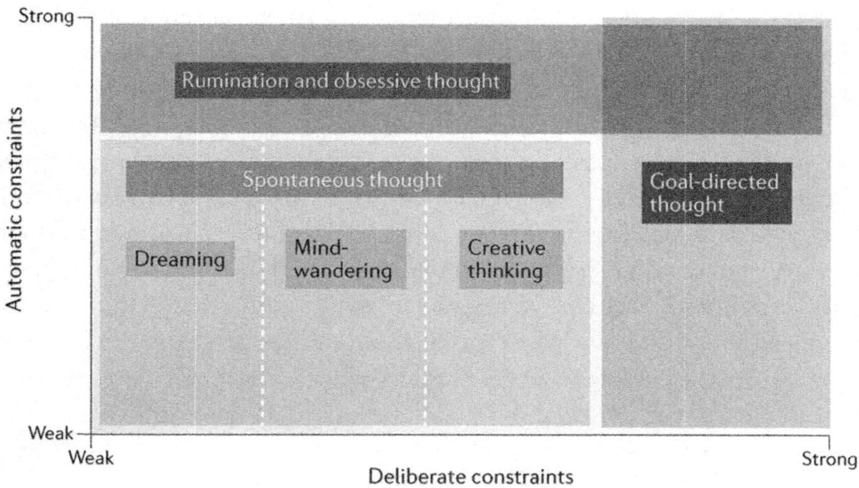

Figure 13.3 Map of different types of thought. The automatic and deliberate constraints indicate the dynamics of thought content. Figure is from Christoff, K., Irving, Z. C., Fox, K. C. R., Spreng, R. N., & Andrews-Hanna, J. R. (2016). Mind-wandering as spontaneous thought: A dynamic framework. *Nature Reviews Neuroscience*, 17(11), Article 11. https://doi.org/10.1038/nrn.2016.113 with permission of Springer Nature.

I think mapping different forms of thought with respect to automaticity and control ("deliberative constraints") is the right approach, but let's consider a few points with his mapping. One concerns the idea of automatic and deliberative constraints as *graded*. In our discussion, a property of a process counts as controlled if it figures in the content of the intention. Otherwise, it is automatic. That perspective does not treat the automaticity or control of a feature as graded, though perhaps such a conception can be developed. What Christoff et al. likely have in mind is appeal to a control *process* where control can be literally dialed up or down and so assigned an increasing or decreasing scalar value. Similar points apply to automatic constraints. It would be good to be given concrete details about the processes that inform a two-dimensional representation of thought kinds along the noted gradable dimensions and whether the categorizations of different kinds of thought are in some way derivable from the dimensions. For example, why are the boundaries between thought kinds drawn where they are? Second, with respect to automatic constraints, the perspective of this book is that automatic biases are myriad. This suggests the need for a multidimensional representation of different forms of thought (cf. the "family resemblances view" of mind wandering, (Seli et al. 2018b)). These issues aside, we converge on the central idea that automaticity is a crucial factor.

Theorists assert that we know what mind wandering is. Well, there are salient cases that are likely to garner wide agreement as exemplars of mind wandering, but I want to begin with two cases that puzzle me. Here is the first. Writing a paper on a difficult topic, a conundrum arises, and I don't know how to solve it. Yet I must, so I intend to reflect in order to figure things out. To do this, I begin to consider a variety of options, quickly surveying them, recalling different past solutions. My mind shifts rapidly as if running on an obstacle course where drastic, spontaneous shifts of direction are required, all as part of searching for an unclear goal under time constraints. I need to dramatically meander to discover a way out of my cognitive conundrum. Is this mind wandering? Second, I'm sitting in a lecture that is mind-numbingly dull. Indeed, the lecturer is so ill equipped that, as a student, I feel insulted that I am required to sit through the session while the teacher has hardly spent the time to be properly prepared. So, in silent protest, I intend to *not* do what I am supposed to. I tune out the droning lecture and return to my conundrum, mentally running my obstacle course in search of the elusive goal. Is this mind wandering? Does it matter if in my protest, I *intend* to deal with my conundrum or just *find myself* so dealing with it?

I don't know. Really. The first is an intentional action, though it involves quite a bit of automaticity and desultory movement, indeed meandering, in the search of an end. Each move, though automatic, is shaped by my goal, and if I am focused, the cognitive leaps are exactly what is needed to solve my problem (recall Figure 13.1). I'm not inclined to call this mind wandering, but my choice lacks high confidence in my grasp of the phenomenon. The second, if done intentionally, is often classified by theorists as a type of *intentional* mind wandering, but if the first case isn't a case of mind wandering despite meandering, why should the second case be? How would we decide who is right? If there's a challenge, I don't think it is because these are "edge cases". I raise them to ask how clear our conception of mind wandering is.

Mind wandering is said to be introspectively apparent. Jonathan Smallwood and Jonathan Schooler note:

> Introspective evidence is often suspect; yet, certain mental phenomena are so self-evident their existence can hardly be questioned. Our propensity for mind wandering is such a phenomenon.
>
> (Smallwood and Schooler 2006, 946)

Yet again, I am uncertain (cf. (Seli et al. 2015b)). Recalling our discussion of introspection in Chapter 8, we should investigate how subjects introspect that they are currently mind wandering. Christoff, Zachary Irving, and colleagues have emphasized the dynamic, desultory character of mind wandering. To wander here and there takes time. If cognitive meandering is a central diagnostic feature of mind wandering, a reasonable hypothesis is that to recognize that a thought is an instance of mind wandering requires a temporal perspective on thinking that allows this dynamic to unfold. It seems that introspective sampling cannot be focused on just a temporal instant. Restricting one's view to an instant, or short stretch of time, cannot reveal wandering as a temporally extended phenomenon. Rather, some extended period of thought must be tracked, so portions of past thought must be remembered to determine whether wandering occurs. For example, to mind-wander entails that where one *is* cognitively is at some distance from where one *was* cognitively. How much distance would count as properly wandering and how would we measure such distance? (Note, the property of "cognitive distance" is not derivable from our notion of automaticity and control nor from the two-dimensional representation by Christoff et al. Figure 13.3; cf. similar worries by Seli et al. (2018b), Box 1.) Given that some cross-temporal comparison of episodes of mind wandering is needed, introspection will likely be memory based to monitor mental movements across time. Even if introspection can, at a moment, access a punctate memory, that memory must capture a stretch of time.

Here is a second way that we might go about introspecting mind wandering, drawing on a conception of mind wandering common to scientists who study the phenomenon: mind wandering as *task-unrelated thought*. On this conception, a subject can introspect an episode of cognition as mind wandering by assessing whether it is on task or not. How does the subject introspect this property of thought? If we hypothesize that subjects know at a moment what they are intentionally doing (Anscombe 1957) and, given this, that they can come to know whether what they are currently doing conforms to what they intended to do, then the subject can accurately assess whether a given instance of thinking is, at that moment, a case of mind wandering in the sense of being task-unrelated.

Philosophers might contend that this form of introspection relies on the agent's distinctive and accurate access to her intention (Anscombe 1957) and an ability to arbitrate whether her present action accords with what she intends. How such access is implemented is not an obvious matter, and we lack a theory of such access. One possibility, inspired by the motor control literature, is that intentions lead to forward models of predicted consequences which can be compared to actual movements in a self-monitoring process to assess whether the movement is intended or not (Wolpert 2009). How to apply this idea to thought is an open question (Campbell 1999), but the present point is that introspection of the property of task-unrelatedness might not require a broad temporal perspective as in the introspection of the property of wandering. Accordingly, there are at least two possible ways that judgments of mind wandering might be engendered. If this sketch of two ways of introspecting mind wandering is at least in outline possible, then two features associated with common conceptions of mind-wandering can lead to introspection of differing temporal scope and so potentially to introspective processes with different mechanistic and evidential bases. How the subject introspects their own mind wandering will then say something about what they take mind wandering to be.

In our discussion of introspective accuracy, we have focused on the deployment of attention. How attention is deployed can be biased by how the subject conceives of the intended target. One of the assumed advantages of the task-unrelated thought description of mind wandering in experimental contexts is that it seems easy to grasp by experimental subjects. Accordingly, one might hope that this would lead to more accurate introspection because a clear conception can better direct attention in the right direction. Matters are, however, complicated. As Samuel Murray et al. discuss (Murray et al. 2020), the concept of task-unrelated thought is in many ways insufficiently determinate. For example, many probes for mind wandering ask subjects to rate in some way whether they are thinking about something *other than what they are doing*. There are, however, many trains of thought that fit that description yet are not clear cases of mind wandering. After all, I might be able to both do the task while intentionally thinking about something else. Mind wandering might often be task-unrelated thought, but many instances of the latter are not the former. In the case just noted, the task-unrelated thinking is clearly an intentional action. I agree with Murray et al. that the description "task-unrelated thought" is in many experimental contexts too open-ended to narrow the scope of introspection to paradigm cases of mind wandering. This means that while subjects might be accurate in introspecting their task-unrelated thought under that description, they might nevertheless be inaccurate in identifying instances of mind wandering.

As a theorist, task-unrelatedness is one of the properties of thought that I gravitate to as characteristic of mind wandering. Is it *necessary* for mind wandering? On an *expansive* conception, task-unrelatedness is a diagnostic sign of mind wandering but not necessary. On a *narrow* conception, task-unrelatedness is an essential feature. This brings us back to the idea of intention and mind wandering raised in my two puzzling cases. The expansive conception leaves it open that one can intend to wander and do so. The narrower conception denies that this is possible, so intentional mind wandering is *paradoxical*. Paul Seli and colleagues have argued that we must allow for intentional mind wandering. Various studies suggest that experimental subjects recognize the category. In one study, 113 student subjects were instructed to categorize mind wandering during task performance as follows:

> Mind-wandering can occur either because you INTENTIONALLY decided to think about things that are unrelated to the task OR because your thoughts UNINTENTIONALLY drifted away to task-unrelated thoughts, despite your best intentions to focus on the task.
>
> ((Selie et al. 2016a), supplementary materials, DS1)

The primary task was the sustained attention to response task (SART), which involved pressing one key in response to all numerals sequentially presented on the screen from "1" to "9" save one, the numeral "3", which required a different key as response. Because the task is boring, adequate performance requires sustained attention. The researchers presented an easy and difficult SART, the former with numerals presented in order, hence predictable, the latter with numerals presented in random sequence. Seli et al. observed that intentional mind wandering occurred more frequently in the easy versus difficult task (cf. (Forster and Lavie 2009, 351), Figure 3).

In an earlier study, Seli et al. (2015) reported that in 166 students, 41% of all mind-wandering episodes uncovered by thought probes during a SART were of the intentional sort ("intentionally thinking about task unrelated thoughts", p. 1419). Similarly, Wammes et al. (Wammes et al. 2016) reported that half of the mind-wandering episodes in 154 students probed during a lecture across a semester were of the intentional form defined as "willfully thinking about things unrelated to the current lecture" (p. 18). These cases fit my "insulted student" case earlier: "This is so stupid, I have better things to do like figure out my conundrum." Here, it seems that intentionally thinking about something else can just be a *change in task*. There is a task one ought to be doing and a task that one intends to do. This does not seem to me to be a standard case of mind wandering versus that of intentionally changing tasks. The descriptions offered in the instructions capture both genuine mind-wandering episodes and those where students opt to do something else even though they are supposed to be attending to lecture. For this reason, the studies seem to me inconclusive in supporting the existence of intentional thinking that is a form of mind wandering. Put another way, introspective probes require concepts that are as sharply defined as possible. A thought that occurs because one "intentionally decided to think about things that are unrelated to the task" can just be a change in plan. If so, then the conceptualization is too broad. It does not capture only mind wandering and, in certain cases, might not capture mind wandering at all.

To what extent can an intention be involved in mind wandering? One suggestion is that its role in mind wandering should be different than its role in active intentional thinking. Consider a different form of task-unrelated mind wandering: *acquiescence* to meandering. Sophie Foster and Nillie Lavie instructed their subjects as follows: "Sometimes people may, for one reason or another, *deliberately allow their mind to wander* from a task that they are performing. This is a deliberate [Task unrelated thought]" ((2009, 350), my emphasis). Similarly, Seli and colleagues have used a *Mind-Wandering: Deliberate* (MW-D) scale to measure intentional mind wandering. This scale consists of four items: "I allow my thoughts to wander on purpose", "I find mind wandering is a good way to cope with boredom", "I enjoy mind wandering", and "I allow myself to get absorbed in pleasant fantasy" (Carriere et al. 2013, 22). Yet *allowing* one's mind to wander is different from intentionally thinking in a task-unrelated way as in the defiant student case. After all, the former can occur via meta-cognitive awareness of mind wandering in the absence of intervention whereas the latter involves an intention to think about something task-unrelated (see also (Seli et al. 2015a)). Given the different ways of probing introspection of mind wandering, the notion of intentional mind wandering in the empirical literature might pick out different phenomena ((Seli et al. 2016b) note this (p. 613)).

These points on the introspection of mind wandering raise important questions about whether there is a uniform phenomenon of mind wandering. At the very least, we can ask whether there is a uniform folk conception of mind wandering and whether these conceptions help us draw theoretically adequate boundaries. Why think that the folk can reliably and accurately identify instances of mind wandering. If they can, how do they do so? What conception of mind wandering do they use? Do these ways of identifying mind wandering identify the same phenomenon? To raise these questions is not to deny that various automaticities in thought provide interesting cognitive phenomena that have philosophical significance. It is instead to emphasize that reliance on introspection should not assume that subjects have unvarnished access to a phenomenon they report on. The generation of those reports is a complicated matter as we have previously discussed (Chapter 8) and which is visible in the present case.

Let us now turn to philosophical discussions of mind wandering that have pinned it explicitly to attention. Zachary Irving has argued that mind wandering is *unguided* attention. Irving is right to characterize this cognitive wandering as attention. The Common Conception allows for cognitive attention in thinking, the mind's taking possession of a train of thought. James's description of attention emphasizes active thinking where the train of thought is part of the mind's taking possession of thought contents and so best exemplified in intentional cogitation. Mind wandering, however, might be better described as the taking possession *of* the mind *by* a train of thought. Mind wandering is, in a sense, passive.

The differentiating feature of mind wandering on Irving's account is that it is unguided attention. What does he mean by "unguided". In this book's apparatus, mind wandering is *automatic* and so does not exemplify the control found in ordinary intentional cogitation. Irving writes:

> An agent *A* is guided to focus her attention on some information *i* if and only if she has two dispositions:
>
> 1. A is reliably disposed to focus her attention on i, and
> 2. If *A*'s attention isn't focused on *i*, she notices, feels discomfited by, and is thereby disposed to correct this fact.
>
> (Irving 2016, 565)

The main point of the account is to explain guidance in terms of the disposition in (2), an approach that implements a Frankfurtian framework for agentive guidance (Frankfurt 1978). Here, I will make explicit what is implicit in Irving's condition, namely that guidance involves keeping one's thinking on task, such as in the service of a goal. This might involve thinking about i at the present moment, but in some cases, one might come to think of j where j ≠ i. This will induce a correction during guidance only if thinking j at this moment in time does not serve the agent's goals. Mind wandering as unguided attention lacks this capacity (disposition) for correction.

I will assume, as seems Irving's intention, that in *thinking* i (i.e., in cognitively attending to i), such attention is guided. This suggest that we should understand the left side as claiming that *A*'s current attend*ing* to i is guided.

The subject is, in fact, attending such that it can be guided. If so, the biconditional as written cannot then be correct since the right side identifies dispositions and not their exercise. At a given moment in time, the agent might not be thinking i and yet satisfy (1) and (2). An agent can be reliably disposed to attend to i and have the tendency in (2) without yet exercising those dispositions, say in thinking i. Since the analysis is a version of the Frankfurtian approach to action, one which explicates guidance via dispositions and counterfactual conditions, it reveals a lacuna. What is needed to explain actively guided thinking is the *expression* of relevant dispositions. This presents a challenge to Frankfurtian theories of guidance as theories of an agent's *controlling* her action in *acting* ((Wu 2023, 50–51) (cf. (Hendrickx 2023)). Appeal just to dispositions will not explain the activity of control.

This is a technical problem, and an initial response is to stipulate explicitly that the biconditional covers cases of active thinking about i. But now consider *unguided* attention (i.e., attention that is *not* guided). This involves the negation of the right side of the biconditional, so not (1) or not (2). But this means that *A* not being reliably disposed to focus attention on i is sufficient for attention to I to be unguided. An agent, however, might not be reliably disposed to focus her attention on i and yet, aim to think about i and manage to do so given her intention. In this case, the agent's thought about i does not seem to be a case of mind wandering but of goal directed thought even if she faces the challenge of lacking a reliable disposition to focus. That is, she is able, with effort, to exercise an unreliable disposition in concerted thinking. I suspect there is a fix here since it's clear what Irving intends, and the general idea seems correct. Still, the analysis needs further workup.[4]

In light of the noted difficulties, we might try a different way of capturing unguided attention given the framework of automaticity and control that we have been deploying. On this account, the central explanatory conception is not a disposition but a bias. Thought is unguided in that it is automatic, not controlled. So a thought about i is automatic with respect to being the subject's thinking about i if the subject, in thinking about i, did not intend to. In effect, this is to make the automaticity of a thought about i tied to the fact that it is not the agent's intended task at that time to think about i. This fits most of the standard cases of "spontaneous" thought though automaticity does not, alone, divide different kinds of automatic thought. After all, there are different types of automatic bias. Perhaps Christoff, Irving, and others are correct that what distinguishes mind wandering is the meandering. So mind wandering is automatic *meandering* thought. Whether wandering cognition amounts to an interesting category is worth further discussion, but as many researchers on mind wandering have begun to emphasize, so long as we are clear on what we intend to study under the rubric "mind wandering", this might suffice for the theory of the relevant thought type.

13.6 Conclusion

Attention in thought is a pervasive feature of our lives, for as Descartes noted, we are thinking things. Cognitive attention is exemplified in many varieties, and the limited discussion of this chapter touches on only some of them: deductive reasoning, reasoning leading to the formation of beliefs in the project of discerning the truth, biases on thinking that can lead to negative effects, and automatic thought as reflected in recent discussions of mind wandering. Clearly, gaps remain in a full accounting of thought as a way of attending.

The central outputs of this book provide a foundation for thinking about other forms of cognition through the lens of attention. This provides a productive and unifying framework that theorists of cognition should take up. As James noted, the mind in attending can do so by grasping a train of thought among possible trains of thought. The automatic form of attention in thought is the mind's being grabbed by a train of thought. The interplay between control and automaticity provides a framework to view the richness of thought, particularly in the different forms of bias that influence how we think. Some of these biases have substantial epistemic significance, including negative effects on how we engage with others. At the same time, just as biases can be altered to provide the basis of skill in the case of perception, they can also be modulated to yield skillful cognition. This brings us to large issues regarding how we might become better reasoners, inquirers, and creators. It would be wonderful to have a sustained discussion of these issues. Here, we simply conclude with the hope that in the next decade of philosophical (and empirical) work on attention, we might bring more of these central forms of human activity into a theoretical frame for attention.

Suggested Readings

Galen Strawson (Strawson 2003) has engagingly examined the automaticity of thought as a way to argue against mental action, and a reply drawing on the automaticity–control distinction is given in (Wu 2013). I discuss cognitive attention in thinking in deduction in Chapter 6 of (Wu 2023). Leonie Smith and Alfred Archer discuss epistemic injustice with emphasis on the attention economy in (Smith and Archer 2020). Abrol Fairweather and Carlos Montemayor discuss attention in epistemology systematically in (Fairweather and Montemayor 2017), Georgi Gardiner reviews cognitive virtues and epistemic attention in (Gardiner 2022), and Cat Saint-Croix gives an overview of the epistemology of attention, including social epistemology, in (Saint-Croix 2024). Susanna Siegel discusses attention and print media in (Siegel 2022). Aaron Glasser and Zachary Irving give an accessible philosophical introduction to mind wandering in their (Irving and Glasser 2019).

Notes

1 "Appropriately" here is due to cases of "bad basing" to be discussed below.

2 I'm grateful to Nico Silins for suggesting this line of argument.

3 There are other demonstrative thoughts that are based on memory or testimony that we will not discuss. Note that we should distinguish between demonstrative thoughts and demonstrative expressions. On a classic and influential discussion of linguistic demonstratives, see (Kaplan 1985). For a pioneering discussion of demonstratives in thought that discusses this distinction as well as non-perception-based demonstrative thoughts, see (Evans 1982).

4 In a later paper (Irving 2021, 622), Irving talks about a specific form of guidance by goal, giving a similar analysis except that although he refers to the first disjunct as a disposition, he describes it as when the agent "reliably focuses her attention". To be nitpicky, this would be the *expression* of a disposition. In any event, this is a move in the right direction from the earlier paper. It still faces a problem raised for the negated biconditional. After all, it might seem that the agent's not reliable focusing of attention can nevertheless be attention guided by a goal. As a friendly amendment, I suggest that Irving remove the first disjunct entirely.

CONCLUSION

Whatever most theorists want to say about attention, I suggest that all will agree that it plays, to varying degrees, a central role in the production of behavior. Often, what we care about when we focus on attention is precisely this behavioral role. One can see the discussion in this book as providing an account of attention that allows theorists of any stripe to approach interesting cases of behavioral guidance, with support by an extensive science of attention and a developing philosophical theory of attention. Clearly, there is much work to be done, but it should be clear that so much has already been achieved.

Although the book does not pursue these topics in sufficient detail, or at all, what we might call the *humanity* of attention should receive more scrutiny by philosophers. There is, as we noted, new work in this direction, but a few strands of attention's influence are worth noting. The first consists of alterations in and disorders of attention that can have substantial impact on people's lives, such as in those with obsessive-compulsive disorder, addiction, schizophrenia, depression, and attention-deficit/hyperactivity disorder. In many of these, deformations and disruptions of attention are a key strand in understanding the challenges faced by subjects who confront them. The second consists of the biases on attention that have substantial

DOI: 10.4324/9781003223450-15

social significance. There has been much work on implicit biases, but I hope it is clear that there are diverse biases on attention that affect how we interact with each other and whose basis we are in a position to clarify and, in doing so, potentially mitigate and change. Finally, there is pervasive talk of an attention economy where attention is said to be "harvested" or "stolen" by social media companies and other maleficent actors. These metaphorical glosses no doubt capture some truth, but the perspective of this book is that for core problems of attention, we should not stop short of understanding in deep and substantive ways what attention is, what it is for, what its relevant features are, and its biological basis. In this way, we can understand not just its philosophical significance but its clinical and social significance as well. I am pleased to see how much we have accomplished and how we are in the right place to accomplish much more.

GLOSSARY

Access Consciousness — A state or content is access-conscious if it is poised for use to inform or control thought and action.

Architectural Level — A level of analysis not in the original Marrian explanatory scheme. In this book, it captures processing architectures that link different algorithmic processing modules.

Attentional Capture — Often described as when a stimulus automatically draws attention in a bottom-up or stimulus-driven way.

Automaticity — Automaticity is contrasted with control. In this book, automaticity is defined relative to some feature *F* exemplified by a process (e.g., the duration of the process), where the process is automatic relative to *F* if and only if it is not controlled relative to *F*. Attention is automatic when some of its features are.

Bias — In this book, "bias" refers to an internal factor that sets attention, such as by influencing as an input the construction of a priority map. Some biases are negative, leading to negatively biased behavior and, in some cases, to implicit bias.

Biased Competition — Proposed neural mechanism for attention where multiple stimuli compete for limited neural processing resources such that biasing one of the stimuli, say by top-down control, allows it to win the competition and be further processed.

Blindsight — A visual condition due to damage in primary visual cortex. Blindsight subjects claim to be blind to regions of the visual field, but when prompted to "guess" about stimuli in their blind field, give better than chance reports regarding them. This ability is mediated by subcortical pathways that provide input to later cortical visual areas.

Bottom-up Attention — Often spoken of as *endogenous* or *stimulus*-driven attention, bottom-up attention can be roughly understood as attention which is engaged due purely to sensory input.

Capacity Limitations — A fundamental constraint on processing thought to necessitate attention such as a limit on how much information can be processed at a time (the informational capacity of a channel). A challenge is to provide a precise quantification of capacity limitations.

Capture of Attention — A generic way to describe common situations where attention is pulled to a stimulus such as a sudden noise. Such attention is typically bottom-up attention but can also result contingently from internal states (e.g., value-based attention).

Change Blindness — An inability to detect changes. Experimentally demonstrated using displays, typically two visual images separated by a mask. There is often a substantial difference between the two images. Subjects typically do not locate changes immediately.

Conjunction Search — A form of visual search involving identification of a target based on two features (e.g., shape and color). These features are separately exemplified by distractor objects making visual search difficult.

Control — Opposite of automatic. Defined here in terms of features of a process, roughly a process is controlled in respect of one of its features *F* if the process's having *F* is due to the agent's intention (or, if one wishes, other higher-order cognitive states).

Crowding — A phenomenon where closely grouped figures result in a disruption of object perception. For example, a sequence of letters, "XAX", is such that the flanking "Xs" crowd the "A" making it difficult to discern.

Demonstrative Concepts — Typically linguistically expressed with demonstratives such as "this" and "that". Perception-based demonstrative concepts are concepts of some X where these concepts are made available by perceptual attention to X.

Dichotic Listening Paradigm — A paradigm where experimental subjects are required to track, attend to, one of two verbal streams presented to the ears (each ear constituting a channel). Subjects are typically required to verbally shadow one of the two streams, namely to verbally repeat what is said. A standard result is that few of the properties of the unattended channel are accurately reported.

Direct Cue — A cue that occurs at or near the target location. Contrasted with an indirect cue.

Divisive Normalization — A proposed computation performed by neurons where a neuron's response to a stimulus is divided by the response of a population of neurons that constitute its normalization pool. This computation is used to explain effects of attention on neural response.

Doxastic Justification — A belief is said to be doxastically justified when it is appropriately based on propositional justification.

Early Selection — The operation of selective mechanisms early in perceptual processing of basic stimulus features and prior to higher-level processing such as semantics.

Early Versus Late Selection — An early debate in modern attention research concerning whether filtering of information occurs early or late in perceptual processing.

Empirical Sufficient Condition — If a subject S perceptually selects X for some task T, then S perceptually attends to X for T. Instantiated in experimental paradigms for attention in order to set attention.

Feature Attention — Attention that is directed at perceptible properties of an object such as color or shape in vision or pitch or semantics in audition.

Feature Integration Theory — A theory proposed by Anne Treisman that postulates a role for attention in binding features from different visual feature maps to form a visual representation of an object.

Feature Search — A form of visual search where a target is defined by a single feature.

Filter, Attentional — An early conception of attention proposed by Donald Broadbent that emphasized attention as a filter that sifts through information allowing only a subset for further processing.

Firing Rate — The number of spikes generated by a neuron per unit time.

Fixation Point — A location where one fixes the eyes, allowing the location to stimulate the fovea.

Fovea — A small region in the retina that provides for highest spatial acuity.

Gabor Patch — A visual stimulus generated by multiplying a sinusoidal wave (function) with a Gaussian function, resulting in a contrast gradient, where the contrast in the wave decreases as it moves away from the center.

Gatekeeping View — A view that characterizes attention as a gatekeeper for phenomenal consciousness. Typically, the view holds that a subject is conscious of X only if the subject attends to X.

Inattentional Agnosia — The failure of forming higher-level perceptual representations, say of category, due to inattention.

Inattentional Amnesia — Failure to encode information in working memory because of inattention.

Inattentional Apraxia — Failure to act on information because of not attending to that information.

Inattentional Blindness — Failure to be visually (phenomenally) aware of a stimulus because of inattention.

Indirect Cue — Sometimes called a symbolic cue, such as an arrow, an indirect cue is used to indicate the location of a target.

Inhibition of Return — A measured delay in response to stimuli at a location to which attention was previously directed. The idea is that attention is inhibited from returning to recently attended locations.

Introspection — To introspect is to perform an action of accessing one's inner life and is often taken to involve attention of an internally directed sort. As discussed in this book, this natural idea can be disputed.

Invalid Cue — A cue that does not correctly indicate target location (e.g., in spatial cueing tasks).

Late Selection — Theories of attentional selection that hold that perceptual processing is not limited in capacity, so selection of perceptual information is post-perceptual and hence late.

Load Theory — Theory that explains early and late selection effects as a function of the perceptual load in a task, namely the demands a task makes on processing.

Mind Wandering — An automatic form of cognitive attention or thinking, though its characterization has been debated, such as whether it is task-irrelevant thought or whether there can be forms of intentional mind wandering.

Multiple Object Tracking — Experimental paradigm developed by Zenon Pylyshyn. Subjects track a subset of visual objects that move on a screen, typically four or five objects.

Necessary Condition — Expressed as a conditional, "if p then q", q is a necessary condition for p. If q fails to obtain, then p does not obtain.

Object Attention — Attention that is directed at objects, such as a sound (conversation) in audition or a material object in vision.

Partial Report Paradigm — As used by George Sperling, subjects are prompted to report only a portion of a stimulus array to which they attend. Contrasted with *total report* where subjects attempt to report the entirety of the stimulus array.

Perceptual Load — The amount of available perceptual processing resources used by current processing.

Phenomenal Consciousness — A state is phenomenally consciousness if there is something that it is like to be in that state.

Pop-out — Experimentally, tied to visual search paradigms where search is not affected by distractor set-size. This should be distinguished from colloquial talk of pop-out as attentional capture.

Preferred Stimulus — The stimulus that drives the strongest response from a neuron when that stimulus is placed in the neuron's receptive field.

Premotor Theory — A theory of spatial visual attention that posits spatial attention as a result of motor programming of eye movements to a location.

Priority Map — A postulated map constructed in visual processing that assigns a priority value to each represented location. Priority maps are computed over a variety of internal factors such as stimulus information (see "Saliency map") and the agent's goals. Priority maps are typically taken to be spatial and so do not represent features or objects.

Reaction Time — A standard measure in behavioral tasks, namely how long it takes for a subject to perform a task, say locating a target.

Receptive Field, Spatial — In vision, the spatial receptive field of a neuron is that region of the retina, stimulation of which drives a neuron to generate spikes. Alternatively, the receptive field is that area of external space where the presence of a stimulus causes the neuron to spike.

Response Accuracy — A standard measure in behavioral tasks (such as reaction time), measuring the accuracy of response for a given task such as correct reports of the features of a stimulus.

Retro-cue Paradigm — Typically, subjects are presented with items to hold in working memory. After stimuli disappear, subjects are given a cue, retroactively, and subsequently tested on the original array in some respect (e.g., a change detection task). As in spatial cueing, subjects tend to show similar cost-benefits with invalid versus valid cues.

Salience — Definitionally, that which attracts attention.

Saliency Map — A postulated map constructed in visual processing that assigns a salience value to each represented location and where, on many models, overt or covert visual attention shifts to the location of highest salience. Note that saliency maps do not represent the objects or features at a location. Unlike the priority map, saliency maps compute only stimulus information.

Selection for Action — A theory of attention that treats attention to X as the selection of X for action. It is also expressed in William James's famous description of attention.

Selection Problem — Given that typically, agents are faced with multiple inputs and multiple possible responses, the Problem concerns how to couple selectively a specific set of inputs to a specific set of responses.

Spatial Attention — Attention directed to a spatial location.

Spatial Cueing — An experimental paradigm that directs spatial attention using different types of cues (direct or indirect) that indicate the location of a target. Where attention is cued in this way with a valid cue (direct or indirect), detection of the target is improved as measured by decrease in reaction time and increase in report accuracy relative to a neutral cue.

Spatial Frequency — For simple visual patterns that can be represented as a sinusoidal function, the spatial frequency of the pattern is given in cycles per visual degree.

Spike — The electrical discharge of a neuron.

Spotlight — A pervasive metaphor for spatial attention, implying changes in perception in light of attention akin to spotlighting attended areas (and items) in space.

Sufficient Condition — A sufficient condition is typically expressed as a conditional. "If p, then q" expresses the claim that p is sufficient for q. Thus, if p obtains, then q obtains.

Top-down Attention — Often called endogenous or goal-directed attention, it generally refers to attention influenced by higher-order cognitive states like intention or knowledge.

Valid Cue — A cue that correctly indicates target location. Invalid cues do not correctly indicate target location.

Vigilance — Often thought to be a non-selective form of attention, colloquially, a sense of readiness or openness. Technically, explication of vigilance often points to selection.

Visual Acuity — A measure of spatial resolution in vision, typically tested in optometry offices using Snellen diagrams (sequences of letters of decreasing size) or Landolt figures.

Visual Degree — A unit of measurement of the visual field. The width of your thumb held at arm's length subtends an angle roughly of two visual degrees.

Visual Search — A paradigm used where a target is to be located among a set of distractors.

Working Memory — A type of active short-term memory that can be understood as memory for work, namely memory that immediately serves ongoing behavior.

REFERENCES

Allport, Alan. 1987. "Selection for Action: Some Behavioral and Neurophysiological Considerations of Attention and Action." In *Perspectives on Perception and Action*, edited by Herbert Heuer and Andries F. Sanders, 395–419. Hillsdale, NJ: Lawrence Erlbaum Associates, Publishers.

Allport, Alan. 1993. "Attention and Control: Have We Been Asking the Wrong Questions? A Critical Review of Twenty-Five Years." In *Attention and Performance XIV (Silver Jubilee Volume): Synergies in Experimental Psychology, Artificial Intelligence, and Cognitive Neuroscience*, edited by David E. Meyer and Sylvan Kornblum, 183–218. Cambridge, MA: MIT Press.

Anderson, Brian A. 2016a. "The Attention Habit: How Reward Learning Shapes Attentional Selection." *Annals of the New York Academy of Sciences* 1369 (1): 24–39. https://doi.org/10.1111/nyas.12957

Anderson, Brian A. 2016b. "Value-Driven Attentional Capture in the Auditory Domain." *Attention, Perception and Psychophysics* 78 (1): 242–250.

Anderson, Brian A., and Madeline Halpern. 2017. "On the Value-Dependence of Value-Driven Attentional Capture." *Attention, Perception, & Psychophysics* 79 (4): 1001–1011. https://doi.org/10.3758/s13414-017-1289-6

Anderson, Brian A., Haena Kim, Andy J. Kim, Ming-Ray Liao, Lana Mrkonja, Andrew Clement, and Laurent Grégoire. 2021. "The Past, Present, and Future of Selection History." *Neuroscience & Biobehavioral Reviews* 130 (November): 326–50. https://doi.org/10.1016/j.neubiorev.2021.09.004

Anderson, Brian A., Patryk A. Laurent, and Steven Yantis. 2011. "Value-Driven Attentional Capture." *Proceedings of the National Academy of Sciences* 108 (25): 10367–71. https://doi.org/10.1073/pnas.1104047108

Anderson, Brian A., Patryk A. Laurent, and Steven Yantis. 2012. "Generalization of Value-Based Attentional Priority." *Visual Cognition* 20 (6): 647–58. https://doi.org/10.1080/13506285.2012.679711

Anderson, Brian A., and Steven Yantis. 2012. "Value-Driven Attentional and Oculomotor Capture during Goal-Directed, Unconstrained Viewing." *Attention, Perception and Psychophysics; Austin* 74 (8): 1644–53.

Anderson, Brian A., and Steven Yantis. 2013. "Persistence of Value-Driven Attentional Capture." *Journal of Experimental Psychology: Human Perception and Performance* 39 (1): 6–9. https://doi.org/10.1037/a0030860

Anderson, Britt. 2011. "There Is No Such Thing as Attention." *Frontiers in Theoretical and Philosophical Psychology* 2: 246. https://doi.org/10.3389/fpsyg.2011.00246

Anderson, Britt. 2023. "Stop Paying Attention to 'Attention'." *WIREs Cognitive Science* 14 (1): e1574. https://doi.org/10.1002/wcs.1574

Anscombe, G.E.M. 1957. *Intention*. Oxford: Blackwell Publishers.

Anton-Erxleben, Katharina, Jared Abrams, and Marisa Carrasco. 2010. "Evaluating Comparative and Equality Judgments in Contrast Perception: Attention Alters Appearance." *Journal of Vision* 10 (11): 6. https://doi.org/10.1167/10.11.6

Anton-Erxleben, Katharina, Jared Abrams, and Marisa Carrasco. 2011. "Equality Judgments Cannot Distinguish between Attention Effects on Appearance and Criterion: A Reply to Schneider (2011)." *Journal of Vision* 11 (13): 1–8. https://doi.org/10.1167/11.13.8

Anton-Erxleben, Katharina, and Marisa Carrasco. 2013. "Attentional Enhancement of Spatial Resolution: Linking Behavioural and Neurophysiological Evidence." *Nature Reviews. Neuroscience* 14 (3): 188–200. https://doi.org/10.1038/nrn3443

Archer, Sophie, ed. 2022a. *Salience: A Philosophical Inquiry*. Abingdon, UK: Routledge.

Archer, Sophie, ed. 2022b. "Salience and What Matters." In *Salience: A Philosophical Inquiry*, edited by Sophie Archer, 113–29. Abingdon, UK: Routledge.

Ariely, Dan. 2001. "Seeing Sets: Representation by Statistical Properties." *Psychological Science* 12 (2): 157–62. https://doi.org/10.1111/1467-9280.00327

Aristotle. 2014. *Aristotle: Nicomachean Ethics*. Translated by Roger Crisp. Cambridge, UK: Cambridge University Press.

Awh, E., E. K. Vogel, and S. H. Oh. 2006. "Interactions between Attention and Working Memory." *Neuroscience* 139 (1): 201–8.

Awh, Edward, Artem V. Belopolsky, and Jan Theeuwes. 2012. "Top-down versus Bottom-Up Attentional Control: A Failed Theoretical Dichotomy." *Trends in Cognitive Sciences* 16 (8): 437–43. https://doi.org/10.1016/j.tics.2012.06.010

Baars, Bernard J. 1997. *In the Theater of Consciousness: The Workspace of the Mind*. Oxford: Oxford University Press.

Baars, Bernard J. 2005. "Global Workspace Theory of Consciousness: Toward a Cognitive Neuroscience of Human Experience." In *Progress in Brain Research*, edited by Steven Laureys, 150: 45–53. Elsevier. https://doi.org/10.1016/S0079-6123(05)50004-9

Baddeley, Alan D. 1992. "Working Memory." *Science* 255 (5044): 556–59.

Baddeley, Alan D. 1996. "Exploring the Central Executive." *Quarterly Journal of Experimental Physiology Section A*, 49: 1–25.

Baddeley, Alan D. 2002. "Fractionating the Central Executive." In *Principles of Frontal Lobe Function*, edited by Donald T. Stuss and Robert T. Knight, 246–60. Oxford: Oxford University Press.

Baddeley, Alan D., and Graham J. Hitch. 1974. "Working Memory." In *The Psychology of Learning and Motivation*, edited by Gordon H. Bower, 8: 47–89. New York: Academic Press.

Baddeley, Alan D., Graham J. Hitch, and Richard J. Allen. 2019. "From Short-Term Store to Multicomponent Working Memory: The Role of the Modal Model." *Memory & Cognition* 47 (4): 575–88. https://doi.org/10.3758/s13421-018-0878-5

Baddeley, Alan D., and Robert H. Logie. 2012. "Working Memory: The Multiple-Component Model BT - Models of Working Memory." In *Models of Working Memory*, 28–61. Cambridge, UK: Cambridge University Press.

Bahmani, Zahra, Kelsey Clark, Yaser Merrikhi, Adrienne Mueller, Warren Pettine, M. Isabel Vanegas, Tirin Moore, and Behrad Noudoost. 2019. "Prefrontal Contributions to Attention and Working Memory." In *Processes of Visuospatial Attention and Working Memory*, edited by Timothy Hodgson, 129–53. Current Topics in Behavioral Neurosciences. Cham: Springer International Publishing. https://doi.org/10.1007/7854_2018_74

Baker, Austin. n.d. "Nonverbal Marginalization."

Balan, Puiu F., and Jacqueline Gottlieb. 2006. "Integration of Exogenous Input into a Dynamic Salience Map Revealed by Perturbing Attention." *The Journal of Neuroscience: The Official Journal of the Society for Neuroscience* 26 (36): 9239–49. https://doi.org/10.1523/JNEUROSCI.1898-06.2006

Bartolomeo, Paolo, Michel Thiebaut de Schotten, and Fabrizio Doricchi. 2007. "Left Unilateral Neglect as a Disconnection Syndrome." *Cerebral Cortex* 17 (11): 2479–90. https://doi.org/10.1093/cercor/bhl181

Battistoni, Elisa, Timo Stein, and Marius V. Peelen. 2017. "Preparatory Attention in Visual Cortex." *Annals of the New York Academy of Sciences* 1396 (1): 92–107. https://doi.org/10.1111/nyas.13320

Bear, Mark, Barry Connors, and Michael A. Paradiso. 2020. *Neuroscience: Exploring the Brain, Enhanced Edition: Exploring the Brain, Enhanced Edition*. Burlington, MA: Jones & Bartlett Learning.

Beck, Jacob, and Keith A. Schneider. 2017. "Attention and Mental Primer." *Mind & Language* 32 (4): 463–94. https://doi.org/10.1111/mila.12148

Benoni, Hanna, and Yehoshua Tsal. 2013. "Conceptual and Methodological Concerns in the Theory of Perceptual Load." *Frontiers in Psychology* 4. https://doi.org/10.3389/fpsyg.2013.00522

Bichot, Narcisse P., Andrew F. Rossi, and Robert Desimone. 2005. "Parallel and Serial Neural Mechanisms for Visual Search in Macaque Area V4." *Science (New York, NY)* 308 (5721): 529–34.

Bickel, Laura. 2024. "Why the Performance of Habit Requires Attention." *Mind & Language* 39 (2): 260–70. https://doi.org/10.1111/mila.12467

Bisley, James W., and Koorosh Mirpour. 2019. "The Neural Instantiation of a Priority Map." *Current Opinion in Psychology*, Attention & Perception, 29 (October):108–12. https://doi.org/10.1016/j.copsyc.2019.01.002

Block, Ned. 1995. "On a Confusion about the Function of Consciousness." *Behavioral and Brain Sciences* 18:227–47.

Block, Ned. 2007. *Consciousness, Function, and Representation*. Cambridge, MA: MIT Press.

Block, Ned. 2011. "Perceptual Consciousness Overflows Cognitive Access." *Trends in Cognitive Sciences* 15 (12): 567–75.

Bommarito, Nicolas. 2013. "Modesty as a Virtue of Attention." *Philosophical Review* 122 (1): 93–117. https://doi.org/10.1215/00318108-1728723

Bommarito, Nicolas. 2018. *Inner Virtue*. Oxford: Oxford University Press.

Borji, Ali, and Laurent Itti. 2013. "State-of-the-Art in Visual Attention Modeling." *IEEE Transactions on Pattern Analysis and Machine Intelligence* 35 (1): 185–207. https://doi.org/10.1109/TPAMI.2012.89

Boynton, Geoffrey M. 2009. "A Framework for Describing the Effects of Attention on Visual Responses." *Vision Research* 49 (10): 1129–43. https://doi.org/10.1016/j.visres.2008.11.001

Brass, Marcel, Baptist Liefooghe, Senne Braem, and Jan De Houwer. 2017. "Following New Task Instructions: Evidence for a Dissociation between Knowing and Doing." *Neuroscience & Biobehavioral Reviews*, 81 (October): 16–28. https://doi.org/10.1016/j.neubiorev.2017.02.012

Broadbent, Donald Eric. 1958. *Perception and Communication*. London: Pergamon Press.

Bruce, N. D. B., and J. K. Tsotsos. 2009. "Saliency, Attention, and Visual Search: An Information Theoretic Approach." *Journal of Vision* 9 (3): 5.

Brunyé, Tad T., Trafton Drew, Donald L. Weaver, and Joann G. Elmore. 2019. "A Review of Eye Tracking for Understanding and Improving Diagnostic Interpretation." *Cognitive Research: Principles and Implications* 4 (1): 7. https://doi.org/10.1186/s41235-019-0159-2

Buehler, Denis. 2018a. "A Dilemma for 'Selection-for-Action'." *Thought: A Journal of Philosophy* 7 (2): 139–49. https://doi.org/10.1002/tht3.378

Buehler, Denis. 2018b. "The Central Executive System." *Synthese* 195 (5): 1969–91. https://doi.org/10.1007/s11229-017-1589-3

Buehler, Denis. 2019. "Flexible Occurrent Control." *Philosophical Studies* 176 (8): 2119–37. https://doi.org/10.1007/s11098-018-1118-3

Buehler, Denis. 2022a. "Agential Capacities: A Capacity to Guide." *Philosophical Studies* 179 (1): 21–47. https://doi.org/10.1007/s11098-021-01649-6

Buehler, Denis. 2022b. "Explicating Agency: The Case of Visual Attention." *The Philosophical Quarterly*, July, pqac034. https://doi.org/10.1093/pq/pqac034

Bundesen, Claus, Søren Kyllingsbaek, Kristján Jul Houmann, and Rune Møller Jensen. 1997. "Is Visual Attention Automatically Attracted by One's Own Name?" *Perception & Psychophysics* 59 (5): 714–20. https://doi.org/10.3758/BF03206017

Burge, T. 2007. "Psychology Supports Independence of Phenomenal Consciousness." *Behavioral and Brain Sciences* 30 (5–6): 500–501.

Buxton, Rebecca, and Lisa Whiting. 2021. "Women or Philosophers? - The Philosophers' Magazine." February 4. https://www.philosophersmag.com/essays/230-women-or-philosophers

Callahan, Laura Frances. 2022. "Humility for Everyone: A No-Distraction Account." *Philosophy and Phenomenological Research* 104 (3): 623–38. https://doi.org/10.1111/phpr.12803

Callahan, Laura Frances. 2024. "Intellectual Humility: A No-Distraction Account." *Philosophy and Phenomenological Research* 104 (2): 320–37. Accessed July 17, 2023. https://doi.org/10.1111/phpr.12965

Campbell, John. 1999. "Schizophrenia, the Space of Reasons, and Thinking as a Motor Process." *Monist* 82 (4): 609–25.

Campbell, John. 2002. *Reference and Consciousness*. Oxford: Oxford University Press.

Campion, John, Richard Latto, and Y. M. Smith. 1983. "Is Blind-Sight an Effect of Scattered Light, Spared Cortex, and Near-Threshold Vision." *Behavioral and Brain Sciences* 6 (3): 423–48. https://doi.org/10.1017/S0140525X00016861

Carandini, Matteo, and David J. Heeger. 2012. "Normalization as a Canonical Neural Computation." *Nature Reviews Neuroscience* 13 (1): 51–62. https://doi.org/10.1038/nrn3136

Carrasco, Marisa. 2006. "Covert Attention Increases Contrast Sensitivity: Psychophysical, Neurophysiological and Neuroimaging Studies." *Progress in Brain Research* 154:33–70.

Carrasco, Marisa. 2011. "Visual Attention: The Past 25 Years." *Vision Research* 51 (13): 1484–1525. https://doi.org/10.1016/j.visres.2011.04.012

Carrasco, Marisa, Stuart Fuller, and Sam Ling. 2008. "Transient Attention Does Increase Perceived Contrast of Suprathreshold Stimuli: A Reply to Prinzmetal, Long, and Leonhardt (2008)." *Perception & Psychophysics* 70 (7): 1151–64.

Carrasco, Marisa, S. Ling, and S. Read. 2004. "Attention Alters Appearance." *Nature Neuroscience* 7 (3): 308–13.

Carrasco, Marisa, C. Penpeci-Talgar, and M. Eckstein. 2000. "Spatial Covert Attention Increases Contrast Sensitivity across the CSF: Support for Signal Enhancement." *Vision Research* 40 (10–12): 1203–15.

Carriere, Jonathan S. A., Paul Seli, and Daniel Smilek. 2013. "Wandering in Both Mind and Body: Individual Differences in Mind Wandering and Inattention Predict Fidgeting." *Canadian Journal of Experimental Psychology* 67 (1): 19–31. https://doi.org/10.1037/a0031438

Carruthers, Peter. 2015. *The Centered Mind.* Oxford: Oxford University Press.

Castelhano, Monica S., and John M. Henderson. 2007. "Initial Scene Representations Facilitate Eye Movement Guidance in Visual Search." *Journal of Experimental Psychology: Human Perception and Performance* 33 (4): 753–63. https://doi.org/10.1037/0096-1523.33.4.753

Castelhano, Monica S., and Karolina Krzyś. 2020. "Rethinking Space: A Review of Perception, Attention, and Memory in Scene Processing." *Annual Review of Vision Science* 6 (1): 563–86. https://doi.org/10.1146/annurev-vision-121219-081745

Chalmers, David J. 2004. "The Representational Character of Experience." In *The Future for Philosophy*, edited by Brian Leiter, 153–81. Oxford: Oxford University Press.

Chalmers, David J. 2009. *The Character of Consciousness.* New York: Oxford University Press.

Chelazzi, L., J. Duncan, E. K. Miller, and R. Desimone. 1998. "Responses of Neurons in Inferior Temporal Cortex during Memory-Guided Visual Search." *Journal of Neurophysiology* 80 (6): 2918–40.

Cherry, E. Colin. 1953. "Some Experiments on the Recognition of Speech, with One and with Two Ears." *Journal of the Acoustical Society of America* 25 (5): 975–79.

Cho, Raymond, and Wayne Wu. 2013. "Mechanisms of Auditory Verbal Hallucination in Schizophrenia." *Schizophrenia* 4: 155. https://doi.org/10.3389/fpsyt.2013.00155

Chong, Sang C., and Karla K. Evans. 2011. "Distributed versus Focused Attention (Count vs Estimate)." *WIREs Cognitive Science* 2 (6): 634–38. https://doi.org/10.1002/wcs.136

Chong, Sang Chul, and Anne Treisman. 2003. "Representation of Statistical Properties." *Vision Research* 43 (4): 393–404. https://doi.org/10.1016/S0042-6989(02)00596-5

Chong, Sang Chul, and Anne Treisman. 2005. "Attentional Spread in the Statistical Processing of Visual Displays." *Perception & Psychophysics* 67 (1): 1–13. https://doi.org/10.3758/BF03195009

Christoff, Kalina, Zachary C. Irving, Kieran C. R. Fox, R. Nathan Spreng, and Jessica R. Andrews-Hanna. 2016. "Mind-Wandering as Spontaneous Thought: A Dynamic Framework." *Nature Reviews Neuroscience* 17 (11): 718–31. https://doi.org/10.1038/nrn.2016.113

Christophel, Thomas B., P. Christiaan Klink, Bernhard Spitzer, Pieter R. Roelfsema, and John-Dylan Haynes. 2017. "The Distributed Nature of Working Memory." *Trends in Cognitive Sciences* 21 (2): 111–24. https://doi.org/10.1016/j.tics.2016.12.007

Chun, Marvin. M., J. D. Golomb, and N. B. Turk-Browne. 2011. "A Taxonomy of External and Internal Attention." *Annual Review of Psychology* 62: 73–101.

Chun, Marvin M., and Mary C. Potter. 1995. "A Two-Stage Model for Multiple Target Detection in Rapid Serial Visual Presentation." *Journal of Experimental Psychology: Human Perception and Performance* 21 (1): 109.

Chun, Marvin M., and Yuhong Jiang. 1998. "Contextual Cueing: Implicit Learning and Memory of Visual Context Guides Spatial Attention." *Cognitive Psychology* 36 (1): 28–71. https://doi.org/10.1006/cogp.1998.0681

Clark, Andy. 2001. "Visual Experience and Motor Action: Are the Bonds Too Tight?" *Philosophical Review* 110 (4): 495–520.

Cohen, Jonathan D., Kevin Dunbar, and James L. McClelland. 1990. "On the Control of Automatic Processes: A Parallel Distributed Processing Account of the Stroop Effect." *Psychological Review* 97 (3): 332–61. https://doi.org/10.1037/0033-295X.97.3.332

Cohen, Marlene R., and John H. R. Maunsell. 2011. "Using Neuronal Populations to Study the Mechanisms Underlying Spatial and Feature Attention." *Neuron* 70 (6): 1192–1204.

Cohen, Jonathan D. 2017. "Cognitive Control." In *The Wiley Handbook of Cognitive Control*, edited by Tobias Egner, 1–28. Chichester: John Wiley & Sons, Ltd. https://doi.org/10.1002/9781118920497.ch1

Cohen, Michael A., George A. Alvarez, and Ken Nakayama. 2011. "Natural-Scene Perception Requires Attention." *Psychological Science* 22 (9): 1165–72. https://doi.org/10.1177/0956797611419168

Cohen, Michael A., Patrick Cavanagh, Marvin M. Chun, and Ken Nakayama. 2012. "The Attentional Requirements of Consciousness." *Trends in Cognitive Sciences* 16 (8): 411–17. https://doi.org/10.1016/j.tics.2012.06.013

Colflesh, Gregory J. H., and Andrew R. A. Conway. 2007. "Individual Differences in Working Memory Capacity and Divided Attention in Dichotic Listening." *Psychonomic Bulletin & Review* 14 (4): 699–703. https://doi.org/10.3758/BF03196824

Conway, Andrew R. A., Nelson Cowan, and Michael F. Bunting. 2001. "The Cocktail Party Phenomenon Revisited: The Importance of Working Memory Capacity." *Psychonomic Bulletin & Review* 8 (2): 331–35. https://doi.org/10.3758/BF03196169

Conway, Andrew R. A., Michael J. Kane, Michael F. Bunting, D. Zach Hambrick, Oliver Wilhelm, and Randall W. Engle. 2005. "Working Memory Span Tasks: A Methodological Review and User's Guide." *Psychonomic Bulletin & Review* 12 (5): 769–86. https://doi.org/10.3758/BF03196772

Cooper, Richard P., Nicolas Ruh, and Denis Mareschal. 2014. "The Goal Circuit Model: A Hierarchical Multi-Route Model of the Acquisition and Control of Routine Sequential Action in Humans." *Cognitive Science* 38 (2): 244–74. https://doi.org/10.1111/cogs.12067

Corbetta, Maurizio, Gaurav Patel, and Gordon L. Shulman. 2008. "The Reorienting System of the Human Brain: From Environment to Theory of Mind." *Neuron* 58 (3): 306–24.

Corbetta, Maurizio, and Gordon L. Shulman. 2002. "Control of Goal-Directed and Stimulus-Driven Attention in the Brain." *Nature Reviews Neuroscience* 3 (3): 201–15. https://doi.org/10.1038/nrn755

Cordner, Christopher. 2016. "Lessons of Murdochian Attention." *Sophia* 55 (2): 197–213. https://doi.org/10.1007/s11841-016-0540-2

Coull, Jennifer T., and Anna C. Nobre. 1998. "Where and When to Pay Attention: The Neural Systems for Directing Attention to Spatial Locations and to Time Intervals as Revealed by Both PET and fMRI." *Journal of Neuroscience* 18 (18): 7426–35. https://doi.org/10.1523/JNEUROSCI.18-18-07426.1998

Cova, Florian, Maxence Gaillard, and François Kammerer. 2021. "Is the Phenomenological Overflow Argument Really Supported by Subjective Reports?" *Mind & Language* 36 (3): 422–50. https://doi.org/10.1111/mila.12291

Cowan, Nelson. 2012. *Working Memory Capacity*. Psychology Press.

Cowan, Nelson. 2017. "The Many Faces of Working Memory and Short-Term Storage." *Psychonomic Bulletin & Review; New York* 24 (4): 1158–70.

Dang, Jasmine S., Ivonne J. Figueroa, and William S. Helton. 2018. "You Are Measuring the Decision to Be Fast, Not Inattention: The Sustained Attention to Response Task Does Not Measure Sustained Attention." *Experimental Brain Research* 236 (8): 2255–62. https://doi.org/10.1007/s00221-018-5291-6

Dehaene, Stanislas, Jean-Pierre Changeux, Lionel Naccache, Jérôme Sackur, and Claire Sergent. 2006. "Conscious, Preconscious, and Subliminal Processing: A Testable Taxonomy." *Trends in Cognitive Sciences* 10 (5): 204–11. https://doi.org/10.1016/j.tics.2006.03.007

Dehaene, Stanislas, and Lionel Naccache. 2001. "Towards a Cognitive Neuroscience of Consciousness: Basic Evidence and a Workspace Framework." *Cognition* 79 (1): 1–37.

Della Libera, Chiara, and Leonardo Chelazzi. 2006. "Visual Selective Attention and the Effects of Monetary Rewards." *Psychological Science* 17 (3): 222–27. https://doi.org/10.1111/j.1467-9280.2006.01689.x

Denison, Rachel N. 2024. "Visual Temporal Attention from Perception to Computation." *Nature Reviews Psychology*, March, 1–14. https://doi.org/10.1038/s44159-024-00294-0

Desimone, Robert, and John Duncan. 1995. "Neural Mechanisms of Selective Visual Attention." *Annual Review of Neuroscience* 18 (1): 193–222. https://doi.org/10.1146/annurev.ne.18.030195.001205

D'Esposito, Mark, and Bradley R. Postle. 2015. "The Cognitive Neuroscience of Working Memory." *Annual Review of Psychology* 66 (1): 115–42.

Deutsch, J. Anthony, and Diana Deutsch. 1963. "Attention: Some Theoretical Considerations." *Psychological Review* 70 (1): 80–90.

Diamond, Adele. 2013. "Executive Functions." *Annual Review of Psychology* 64 (1): 135–68. https://doi.org/10.1146/annurev-psych-113011-143750

Dickie, Imogen. 2011. "Visual Attention Fixes Demonstrative Reference by Eliminating Referential Luck." In *Attention: Philosophical and Psychological Essays*, edited by Christopher Mole, Declan Smithies, and Wayne Wu, 292–322. New York: Oxford University Press.

Dickie, Imogen. 2015. *Fixing Reference*. Oxford University Press.

Donovan, Tim, and Damien Litchfield. 2013. "Looking for Cancer: Expertise Related Differences in Searching and Decision Making." *Applied Cognitive Psychology* 27 (1): 43–49. https://doi.org/10.1002/acp.2869

Dow, B. M., A. Z. Snyder, R. G. Vautin, and R. Bauer. 1981. "Magnification Factor and Receptive Field Size in Foveal Striate Cortex of the Monkey." *Experimental Brain Research* 44 (2): 213–28. https://doi.org/10.1007/BF00237343

Dretske, Fred. 1995. *Naturalizing the Mind*. Cambridge, MA: MIT Press.

Dretske, Fred. 2007. "What Change Blindness Teaches about Consciousness." *Philosophical Perspectives* 21 (1): 215–20.

Driver, Jon. 2001. "A Selective Review of Selective Attention Research from the Past Century." *British Journal of Psychology* 92 (Part 1): 53–78.

Driver, Julia. 2011. "'For Every Foot Its Own Shoe': Method and Moral Theory in the Philosophy of Iris Murdoch." In *Iris Murdoch, Philosopher*, edited by Justin Broackes, 292–305. Oxford: Oxford University Press. https://doi.org/10.1093/acprof:oso/9780199289905.003.0012

Dux, P. E., and R. Marois. 2009. "The Attentional Blink: A Review of Data and Theory." *Attention, Perception, & Psychophysics* 71 (8): 1683–1700.

van Ede, Freek, and Anna C. Nobre. 2023. "Turning Attention Inside Out: How Working Memory Serves Behavior." *Annual Review of Psychology* 74 (1): 137–65. https://doi.org/10.1146/annurev-psych-021422-041757

Egeth, Howard E., Robert A. Virzi, and Hadley Garbart. 1984. "Searching for Conjunctively Defined Targets." *Journal of Experimental Psychology: Human Perception and Performance* 10 (1): 32–39. https://doi.org/10.1037/0096-1523.10.1.32

Elazary, Lior, and Laurent Itti. 2008. "Interesting Objects Are Visually Salient." *Journal of Vision* 8 (3): 3–3. https://doi.org/10.1167/8.3.3

Engle, Randall W. 2002. "Working Memory Capacity as Executive Attention." *Current Directions in Psychological Science* 11 (1): 19–23. https://doi.org/10.1111/1467-8721.00160

Engle, Randall W. 2018. "Working Memory and Executive Attention: A Revisit." *Perspectives on Psychological Science* 13 (2): 190–93. https://doi.org/10.1177/1745691617720478

Engle, Randall W., Stephen W. Tuholski, James E. Laughlin, and Andrew R. A. Conway. 1999. "Working Memory, Short-Term Memory, and General Fluid Intelligence: A Latent-Variable Approach." *Journal of Experimental Psychology: General* 128 (3): 309–31. https://doi.org/10.1037/0096-3445.128.3.309

Evans, Gareth. 1982. *The Varieties of Reference*. Oxford: Oxford University Press.

Evans, Karla K., Diane Georgian-Smith, Rosemary Tambouret, Robyn L. Birdwell, and Jeremy M. Wolfe. 2013. "The Gist of the Abnormal: Above-Chance Medical Decision Making in the Blink of an Eye." *Psychonomic Bulletin & Review* 20 (6): 1170–75. https://doi.org/10.3758/s13423-013-0459-3

Evans, Karla K., Tamara Miner Haygood, Julie Cooper, Anne-Marie Culpan, and Jeremy M. Wolfe. 2016. "A Half-Second Glimpse Often Lets Radiologists Identify Breast Cancer Cases Even When Viewing the Mammogram of the Opposite Breast." *Proceedings of the National Academy of Sciences* 113 (37): 10292–97. https://doi.org/10.1073/pnas.1606187113

Failing, Michel F., and Jan Theeuwes. 2014. "Exogenous Visual Orienting by Reward." *Journal of Vision* 14 (5): 6–6. https://doi.org/10.1167/14.5.6

Fairweather, Abrol, and Carlos Montemayor. 2017. *Knowledge, Dexterity, and Attention: A Theory of Epistemic Agency*. Cambridge, UK: Cambridge University Press.

Farah, Martha J. 2004. *Visual Agnosia*. Second. Cambridge, MA: MIT Press.

Fish, William. 2009. *Perception, Hallucination, and Illusion*. Oxford: Oxford University Press.

Folk, Charles L., Roger W. Remington, and James C. Johnston. 1992. "Involuntary Covert Orienting Is Contingent on Attentional Control Settings." *Journal of Experimental Psychology Human Perception and Performance* 18: 1030–1030.

Forster, Sophie, and Nilli Lavie. 2009. "Harnessing the Wandering Mind: The Role of Perceptual Load." *Cognition* 111 (3): 345–55. https://doi.org/10.1016/j.cognition.2009.02.006

Fortney, Mark. 2018. "The Centre and Periphery of Conscious Thought." *Journal of Consciousness Studies* 25: 112–36.

Franco, Kateryna Samoilova. 2024. "Pluralism about Introspection." *Mind & Language* 39(2): 293–309. https://doi.org/10.1111/mila.12483.

Frankfurt, Harry G. 1978. "The Problem of Action." *American Philosophical Quarterly* 15 (2): 157–62.

Fridland, Ellen. 2014. "They've Lost Control: Reflections on Skill." *Synthese* 191 (12): 2729–50. https://doi.org/10.1007/s11229-014-0411-8

Fridland, Ellen. 2017. "Automatically Minded." *Synthese* 194 (11): 4337–63.

Frye, Marilyn. 1983. "On Being White: Thinking toward a Feminist Understanding of Race and Race Supremacy." In *The Politics of Reality: Essays in Feminist Theory*, 110–27. Berkeley: Crossing Press.

Fukuda, Keisuke, Edward Vogel, Ulrich Mayr, and Edward Awh. 2010. "Quantity, Not Quality: The Relationship between Fluid Intelligence and Working Memory Capacity." *Psychonomic Bulletin & Review* 17 (5): 673–79. https://doi.org/10.3758/17.5.673

Fuller, Stuart, and Marisa Carrasco. 2006. "Exogenous Attention and Color Perception: Performance and Appearance of Saturation and Hue." *Vision Research* 46 (23): 4032–47. https://doi.org/10.1016/j.visres.2006.07.014

Ganeri, Jonardon. 2017. *Attention, Not Self.* Oxford University Press.

Ganson, Todd, and Ben Bronner. 2012. "Visual Prominence and Representationalism." *Philosophical Studies* 164 (2): 405–18. https://doi.org/10.1007/s11098-012-9853-3

Gardiner, Georgi. 2022. "Attunement: On the Cognitive Virtues of Attention." In *Social Virtue Epistemology*, edited by Mark Alfano, Jeroen de Ridder, and Colin Klein, 48–72. New York: Routledge.

Gayet, Surya, Anastasia Kiyonaga, and Mark D'Esposito. 2018. "Reaffirming the Sensory Recruitment Account of Working Memory." *Trends in Cognitive Sciences* 22 (3): 190–92.

de Gelder, Beatrice, Marco Tamietto, Geert van Boxtel, Rainer Goebel, Arash Sahraie, Jan van den Stock, Bernard M. C. Stienen, Lawrence Weiskrantz, and Alan Pegna. 2008. "Intact Navigation Skills after Bilateral Loss of Striate Cortex." *Current Biology* 18 (24): R1128–29. https://doi.org/10.1016/j.cub.2008.11.002

Gertler, Brie. 2001. "Introspecting Phenomenal States." *Philosophy and Phenomenological Research* 63 (2): 305–28.

Gertler, Brie. 2011. *Self-Knowledge.* Abingdon, UK: Routledge.

Gertler, Brie. 2012. "Renewed Acquaintance." In *Introspection and Consciousness*, edited by Declan Smithies and Daniel Stoljar, 93–128. New York: Oxford University Press.

Giesbrecht, Barry, Daniel H. Weissman, Marty G. Woldorff, and George R. Mangun. 2006. "Pre-Target Activity in Visual Cortex Predicts Behavioral Performance on Spatial and Feature Attention Tasks." *Brain Research* 1080 (1): 63–72. https://doi.org/10.1016/j.brainres.2005.09.068

Giustina, Anna. 2021. "Introspection without Judgment." *Erkenntnis* 86 (2): 407–27. https://doi.org/10.1007/s10670-019-00111-8

Giustina, Anna. 2022. "Introspective Knowledge by Acquaintance." *Synthese* 200 (2): 128. https://doi.org/10.1007/s11229-022-03578-1

Giustina, Anna. 2023. "Introspective Acquaintance: An Integration Account." *European Journal of Philosophy* 31 (2): 380–97. https://doi.org/10.1111/ejop.12690

Goldhill, Olivia. 2018. "Psychology Will Fail If It Keeps Using Ancient Words like 'Attention' and 'Memory'." *Quartz*. April 7, 2018. https://qz.com/1246898/psychology-will-fail-if-it-keeps-using-ancient-words-like-attention-and-memory

Gomez-Lavin, Javier. 2020. "Working Memory Is Not a Natural Kind and Cannot Explain Central Cognition." *Review of Philosophy and Psychology* 49 (A): 1–27. https://doi.org/10.1007/s13164-020-00507-4

Goodhew, Stephanie C. 2020. *The Breadth of Visual Attention*. Cambridge, UK: Cambridge University Press.

Graybiel, Ann M. 2008. "Habits, Rituals, and the Evaluative Brain." *Annual Review of Neuroscience* 31: 359–87.

Green, David Marvin, and John A. Swets. 1966. *Signal Detection Theory and Psychophysis*. New York: Wiley.

Greene, Michelle R., and Aude Oliva. 2009. "The Briefest of Glances: The Time Course of Natural Scene Understanding." *Psychological Science* 20 (4): 464–72. https://doi.org/10.1111/j.1467-9280.2009.02316.x

Griffin, Ivan C., and Anna C. Nobre. 2003. "Orienting Attention to Locations in Internal Representations." *Journal of Cognitive Neuroscience* 15 (8): 1176–94. https://doi.org/10.1162/089892903322598139

Groos, Karl. 1896. *Die Spiele der Tiere*. Jena: G. Fischer.

Hafed, Ziad M., Klaus-Peter Hoffmann, Chih-Yang Chen, and Amarender R. Bogadhi. 2023. "Visual Functions of the Primate Superior Colliculus." *Annual Review of Vision Science* 9 (1). https://doi.org/10.1146/annurev-vision-111022-123817

Harman, Gilbert. 1990. "The Intrinsic Quality of Experience." In *Philosophical Perspectives, 4 Action Theory and Philosophy of Mind*, 31–52. Atascadero, CA: Ridgeview Publishing.

Harrison, Stephenie A., and Frank Tong. 2009. "Decoding Reveals the Contents of Visual Working Memory in Early Visual Areas." *Nature* 458 (7238): 632–35. https://doi.org/10.1038/nature07832

Hatfield, Gary. 1998. "Attention in Early Scientific Psychology." In *Visual Attention*, edited by Richard D. Wright, 3–25. Oxford: Oxford University Press.

Henderson, John M., G.L. Malcolm, and C. Schandl. 2009. "Searching in the Dark: Cognitive Relevance Drives Attention in Real-World Scenes." *Psychonomic Bulletin and Review* 16 (5): 850–56. https://doi.org/10.3758/PBR.16.5.850

Henderson, John M. 2020. "Meaning and Attention in Scenes." In *Psychology of Learning and Motivation*, edited by Kara D. Federmeier and Elizabeth R. Schotter, 73: 95–117. Gazing Toward the Future: Advances in Eye Movement Theory and Applications. Academic Press. https://doi.org/10.1016/bs.plm.2020.08.002

Henderson, John M., and Taylor R. Hayes. 2017. "Meaning-Based Guidance of Attention in Scenes as Revealed by Meaning Maps." *Nature Human Behaviour* 1 (10): 743–47. https://doi.org/10.1038/s41562-017-0208-0

Henderson, John M., Taylor R. Hayes, Candace E. Peacock, and Gwendolyn Rehrig. 2019. "Meaning and Attentional Guidance in Scenes: A Review of the Meaning Map Approach." *Vision* 3 (2): 19. https://doi.org/10.3390/vision3020019

Henderson, John M., Taylor R. Hayes, Candace E. Peacock, and Gwendolyn Rehrig. 2021. "Meaning Maps Capture the Density of Local Semantic Features in Scenes: A Reply to Pedziwiatr, Kümmerer, Wallis, Bethge & Teufel (2021)." *Cognition* 214 (September):104742. https://doi.org/10.1016/j.cognition.2021.104742

Henderson, John M., Taylor R. Hayes, Gwendolyn Rehrig, and Fernanda Ferreira. 2018. "Meaning Guides Attention during Real-World Scene Description." *Scientific Reports* 8 (1): 13504. https://doi.org/10.1038/s41598-018-31894-5

Hendrickx, Malte. 2023. "Agentially Controlled Action: Causal, Not Counterfactual." *Philosophical Studies*, September. https://doi.org/10.1007/s11098-023-02033-2

Hickey, Clayton, Leonardo Chelazzi, and Jan Theeuwes. 2010. "Reward Changes Salience in Human Vision via the Anterior Cingulate." *Journal of Neuroscience* 30 (33): 11096–103. https://doi.org/10.1523/JNEUROSCI.1026-10.2010

Hickey, Clayton, and Wieske Van Zoest. 2012. "Reward Creates Oculomotor Salience." *Current Biology* 22 (7): R219–20. https://doi.org/10.1016/j.cub.2012.02.007

Hickey, Clayton, and Wieske van Zoest. 2013. "Reward-Associated Stimuli Capture the Eyes in Spite of Strategic Attentional Set." *Vision Research* 92 (November): 67–74. https://doi.org/10.1016/j.visres.2013.09.008

Holt, Nigel, Andy Bremner, Ed Sutherland, Michael Vliek, Michael Passer, and Ronald Smith. 2019. *Psychology: The Science of Mind and Behaviour.* 4th ed. McGraw Hill.

Hommel, Bernhard. 2000. "The Prepared Reflex: Automaticity and Control in Stimulus-Response Translation." In *Control of Congitive Processes: Attention and Performance XVIII*, edited by S. Monsell and J. Driver, 247–73. Cambridge, MA: MIT Press.

Hommel, Bernhard, Craig S. Chapman, Paul Cisek, Heather F. Neyedli, Joo-Hyun Song, and Timothy N. Welsh. 2019. "No One Knows What Attention Is." *Attention, Perception & Psychophysics* 81 (7): 2288–2303.

Hutchinson, Brendan T. 2019. "Toward a Theory of Consciousness: A Review of the Neural Correlates of Inattentional Blindness." *Neuroscience & Biobehavioral Reviews* 104 (September): 87–99. https://doi.org/10.1016/j.neubiorev.2019.06.003

Iamshchinina, Polina, Thomas B. Christophel, Surya Gayet, and Rosanne L. Rademaker. 2021. "Essential Considerations for Exploring Visual Working Memory Storage in the Human Brain." *Visual Cognition*. 1–12. https://doi.org/10.1080/13506285.2021.1915902

Irvine, Elizabeth. 2012a. *Consciousness as a Scientific Concept: A Philosophy of Science Perspective*. Springer Science & Business Media.

Irvine, Elizabeth. 2012b. "Old Problems with New Measures in the Science of Consciousness." *British Journal for the Philosophy of Science* 63 (3): 627–48.

Irving, Zachary C. 2016. "Mind-Wandering Is Unguided Attention: Accounting for the 'Purposeful' Wanderer." *Philosophical Studies* 173 (2): 547–71. https://doi.org/10.1007/s11098-015-0506-1

Irving, Zachary C. 2021. "Drifting and Directed Minds: The Significance of Mind-Wandering for Mental Agency." *The Journal of Philosophy* 118 (11): 614–44. https://doi.org/10.5840/jphil20211181141

Irving, Zachary C., and Aaron Glasser. 2019. "Mind-Wandering: A Philosophical Guide." *Philosophy Compass* 6 (5): 548–15. https://doi.org/10.1111/phc3.12644

Itti, Laurent, Christof Koch, and Ernst Niebur. 1998. "A Model of Saliency-Based Visual Attention for Rapid Scene Analysis." *IEEE Transactions on Pattern Analysis and Machine Intelligence* 20 (11): 1254–59. https://doi.org/10.1109/34.730558

Itti, Laurent. 2007. "Visual Salience." *Scholarpedia* 2 (9): 3327. https://doi.org/10.4249/scholarpedia.3327

Itti, Laurent, and Christof Koch. 2000. "A Saliency-Based Search Mechanism for Overt and Covert Shifts of Visual Attention." *Vision Research* 40 (10): 1489–1506. https://doi.org/10.1016/S0042-6989(99)00163-7

Itti, Laurent, and Christof Koch. 2001a. "Computational Modelling of Visual Attention." *Nature Reviews. Neuroscience* 2 (3): 194–203. https://doi.org/10.1038/35058500

Itti, Laurent, and Christof Koch. 2001b. "Feature Combination Strategies for Saliency-Based Visual Attention Systems." *Journal of Electronic Imaging* 10 (1): 161–69. https://doi.org/10.1117/1.1333677

James, William. 1890. *The Principles of Psychology*, Vol. 1. Boston, MA: Henry Holt and Co.

Jennings, Carolyn Dicey. 2015. "Consciousness without Attention." *Journal of the American Philosophical Association* 1 (2): 276–95.

Jennings, Carolyn Dicey. 2020. *The Attending Mind*. Cambridge, UK: Cambridge University Press.

Jennings, Carolyn Dicey. 2022. *Attention and Mental Control*. Cambridge, UK: Cambridge University Press.

Jiang, Yi, Patricia Costello, Fang Fang, Miner Huang, and Sheng He. 2006. "A Gender- and Sexual Orientation-Dependent Spatial Attentional Effect of Invisible Images." *Proceedings of the National Academy of Sciences* 103 (45): 17048–52. https://doi.org/10.1073/pnas.0605678103

Jiang, Yuhong V., and Caitlin A. Sisk. 2019. "Habit-like Attention." *Current Opinion in Psychology*, Attention & Perception, 29 (October): 65–70. https://doi.org/10.1016/j.copsyc.2018.11.014

Johnson, Jeffrey S., Geoffrey F. Woodman, Elsie Braun, and Steven J. Luck. 2007. "Implicit Memory Influences the Allocation of Attention in Visual Cortex." *Psychonomic Bulletin & Review* 14 (5): 834–39. https://doi.org/10.3758/BF03194108

Jonides, John. 1981. "Voluntary versus Automatic Control over the Mind's Eye's Movements." In *Attention and Performance*, edited by J. B. Long and A D Baddeley, 9: 187–203. Hillsdale, NJ: Lawrence Erlbaum Association Inc.

Jonides, John, Stephen C. Lacey, and Derek Evan Nee. 2005. "Processes of Working Memory in Mind and Brain." *Current Directions in Psychological Science* 14 (1): 2–6.

Jonides, John, and Steven Yantis. 1988. "Uniqueness of Abrupt Visual Onset in Capturing Attention." *Perception & Psychophysics* 43 (4): 346–54. https://doi.org/10.3758/BF03208805

Kahneman, Daniel, and Anne Treisman. 1984. "Changing Views of Attention and Automaticity." In *Varieties of Attention*, edited by R. Parasuraman and D. R. Davies, 29–61. New York: Academic Press.

Kahneman, Daniel. 1973. *Attention and Effort*. Englewood Cliffs, NJ: Prentice-Hall.

Kammerer, François, and Keith Frankish. 2023. "What Forms Could Introspective Systems Take? A Research Programme." *Journal of Consciousness Studies* 30 (9–10): 13–48. https://doi.org/10.53765/20512201.30.9.013

Kaplan, D. 1985. "Demonstratives." In *Themes from Kaplan*, 481. Oxford: Oxford University Press.

Kärki, Kaisa, and Visa Kurki. 2023. "Does a Person Have a Right to Attention? Depends on What She Is Doing." *Philosophy & Technology* 36 (4): 86. https://doi.org/10.1007/s13347-023-00673-0

Kärki, Kaisa. 2024. "Digital Distraction, Attention Regulation, and Inequality." *Philosophy & Technology* 37 (1): 8. https://doi.org/10.1007/s13347-024-00698-z

Kayser, Christoph, Christopher I. Petkov, Michael Lippert, and Nikos K. Logothetis. 2005. "Mechanisms for Allocating Auditory Attention: An Auditory Saliency Map." *Current Biology* 15 (21): 1943–47. https://doi.org/10.1016/j.cub.2005.09.040

Kelly, Brendan S., Louise A. Rainford, Sarah P. Darcy, Eoin C. Kavanagh, and Rachel J. Toomey. 2016. "The Development of Expertise in Radiology: In Chest Radiograph Interpretation, 'Expert' Search Pattern May Predate 'Expert' Levels of Diagnostic Accuracy for Pneumothorax Identification." *Radiology* 280 (1): 252–60. https://doi.org/10.1148/radiol.2016150409

Kentridge, R. W. 2011. "Attention Without Awareness: A Brief Review." In *Attention: Philosophical and Psychological Essays*, edited by Christopher Mole, Declan Smithies, and Wayne Wu, 228–46. New York: Oxford University Press.

Kentridge, R. W., C.A. Heywood, and L. Weiskrantz. 1999. "Attention without Awareness in Blindsight." *Proceedings of the Royal Society London B* 266: 1805–11.

Kentridge, R. W., T.C.W. Nijboer, and C.A. Heywood. 2008a. "Attended but Unseen: Visual Attention Is Not Sufficient for Visual Awareness." *Neuropsychologia* 46: 864–69.

Kentridge, R. W., L. H. de-Wit, and C. A. Heywood. 2008b. "What Is Attended in Spatial Attention?" *Journal of Consciousness Studies* 15 (4): 105–11.

Kind, Amy. 2003. "What's So Transparent about Transparency." *Philosophical Studies* 115: 225–44.

Klein, Raymond. 1980. "Does Oculomotor Readiness Mediate Cognitive Control of Visual Attention." In *Attention and Performance VIII*, edited by R. S. Nickerson, 8: 259–76. Hillsdale, NJ: Lawrence Erlbaum Associates, Publishers.

Klein, Raymond M., and Michael A. Lawrence. 2012. "On the Modes and Domains of Attention." In *Cognitive Neuroscience of Attention*, 2nd ed., edited by Michael I. Posner and Liqiang Huang, 11–28. New York: Guilford Press.

Koch, Christof, and Naotsugu Tsuchiya. 2007. "Attention and Consciousness: Two Distinct Brain Processes." *Trends in Cognitive Sciences* 11 (1): 16–22. https://doi.org/10.1016/j.tics.2006.10.012

Koch, Christof, and Shimon Ullman. 1985. "Shifts in Selective Visual Attention: Towards the Underlying Neural Circuitry." *Human Neurobiology* 4 (4): 219–27.

Koehler, Kathryn, and Miguel P. Eckstein. 2017. "Beyond Scene Gist: Objects Guide Search More than Scene Background." *Journal of Experimental Psychology: Human Perception and Performance* 43 (6): 1177–93. https://doi.org/10.1037/xhp0000363

Koester, John D., Sarah H. Mack, and Steven A. Siegelbaum, eds. 2021. "Visual Processing for Attention and Action." In *Principles of Neural Science*, 6th ed. New York: McGraw Hill. www.neurology.mhmedical.com/content.aspx?aid=1180642180

Kok, Ellen M., Halszka Jarodzka, Anique B. H. de Bruin, Hussain A. N. BinAmir, Simon G. F. Robben, and Jeroen J. G. van Merriënboer. 2016. "Systematic Viewing in Radiology: Seeing More, Missing Less?" *Advances in Health Sciences Education* 21 (1): 189–205. https://doi.org/10.1007/s10459-015-9624-y

Koralus, Philipp. 2014. "The Erotetic Theory of Attention: Questions, Focus, and Distraction." *Mind and Language* 29 (1): 26–50.

Krauzlis, Richard J., Anil Bollimunta, Fabrice Arcizet, and Lupeng Wang. 2014. "Attention as an Effect Not a Cause." *Trends in Cognitive Sciences* 18 (9): 457–64. https://doi.org/10.1016/j.tics.2014.05.008

Krauzlis, Richard J., Lupeng Wang, Gongchen Yu, and Leor N. Katz. 2023. "What Is Attention?" *WIREs Cognitive Science* 14 (1): e1570. https://doi.org/10.1002/wcs.1570

Kundel, Harold L., and Paul S. La Follette. 1972. "Visual Search Patterns and Experience with Radiological Images." *Radiology* 103 (3): 523–28. https://doi.org/10.1148/103.3.523

Kundel, Harold L., and Calvin F. Nodine. 1975. "Interpreting Chest Radiographs without Visual Search." *Radiology* 116 (3): 527–32. https://doi.org/10.1148/116.3.527

Kundel, Harold L., Calvin F. Nodine, Elizabeth A. Krupinski, and Claudia Mello-Thoms. 2008. "Using Gaze-Tracking Data and Mixture Distribution Analysis to Support a Holistic Model for the Detection of Cancers on Mammograms." *Academic Radiology* 15 (7): 881–86. https://doi.org/10.1016/j.acra.2008.01.023

Lambert, Anthony, Edward Spencer, and Naresh Mohindra. 1987. "Automaticity and the Capture of Attention by a Peripheral Display Change." *Current Psychology* 6 (2): 136–47. https://doi.org/10.1007/BF02686618

Lamme, Victor A. F. 2004. "Separate Neural Definitions of Visual Consciousness and Visual Attention; a Case for Phenomenal Awareness." *Neural Networks: The Official Journal of the International Neural Network Society* 17 (5–6): 861–72. https://doi.org/10.1016/j.neunet.2004.02.005

Landman, Rogier, Henk Spekreijse, and Victor A. F. Lamme. 2003. "Large Capacity Storage of Integrated Objects before Change Blindness." *Vision Research* 43 (2): 149–64. https://doi.org/10.1016/S0042-6989(02)00402-9

Lavie, Nilli. 2005. "Distracted and Confused?: Selective Attention under Load." *Trends in Cognitive Sciences* 9 (2): 75–82. https://doi.org/10.1016/j.tics.2004.12.004

Lavie, Nilli, and Yehoshua Tsal. 1994. "Perceptual Load as a Major Determinant of the Locus of Selection in Visual Attention." *Perception & Psychophysics* 56 (2): 183–97. https://doi.org/10.3758/BF03213897

Lee, Joonyeol, and John H. R. Maunsell. 2009. "A Normalization Model of Attentional Modulation of Single Unit Responses." *PLoS ONE* 4 (2): e4651. https://doi.org/10.1371/journal.pone.0004651

Lerman, Hemdat. 2022. "Attention, Salience, and the Phenomenology of Visual Experience." In *Salience: A Philosophical Inquiry*, edited by Sophie Archer, 24–49. Abingdon, UK: Routledge.

Levi, Dennis M. 2008. "Crowding—An Essential Bottleneck for Object Recognition: A Mini-Review." *Vision Research* 48 (5): 635–54.

Li, Fei Fei, Rufin VanRullen, Christof Koch, and Pietro Perona. 2002. "Rapid Natural Scene Categorization in the near Absence of Attention." *Proceedings of the National Academy of Sciences of the United States of America* 99 (14): 9596–9601. https://doi.org/10.1073/pnas.092277599

Ling, Sam, and Marisa Carrasco. 2007. "Transient Covert Attention Does Alter Appearance: A Reply to Schneider (2006)." *Perception & Psychophysics* 69 (6): 1051–58.

Litchfield, Damien, and Tim Donovan. 2016. "Worth a Quick Look? Initial Scene Previews Can Guide Eye Movements as a Function of Domain-Specific Expertise but Can Also Have Unforeseen Costs." *Journal of Experimental Psychology. Human Perception and Performance* 42 (7): 982–94. https://doi.org/10.1037/xhp0000202

Liu, Taosheng, Jared Abrams, and Marisa Carrasco. 2009. "Voluntary Attention Enhances Contrast Appearance." *Psychological Science* 20 (3): 354–62.

Losier, Bruno J.W., and Raymond M. Klein. 2001. "A Review of the Evidence for a Disengage Deficit Following Parietal Lobe Damage." *Neuroscience & Biobehavioral Reviews* 25 (1): 1–13. https://doi.org/10.1016/S0149-7634(00)00046-4

Lovejoy, Lee P., and Richard J. Krauzlis. 2010. "Inactivation of Primate Superior Colliculus Impairs Covert Selection of Signals for Perceptual Judgments." *Nature Neuroscience* 13 (2): 261–66. https://doi.org/10.1038/nn.2470

Lovejoy, Lee P., and Richard J. Krauzlis. 2017. "Changes in Perceptual Sensitivity Related to Spatial Cues Depends on Subcortical Activity." *Proceedings of the National Academy of Sciences* 114 (23): 6122–26. https://doi.org/10.1073/pnas.1609711114

Lu, Zhong-Lin, and Barbara Anne Dosher. 2009. "Mechanisms of Perceptual Learning." *Learning & Perception* 1 (1): 19–36.

Luck, Steven J., Nicholas Gaspelin, Charles L. Folk, Roger W. Remington, and Jan Theeuwes. 2021. "Progress toward Resolving the Attentional Capture Debate." *Visual Cognition* 29 (1): 1–21. https://doi.org/10.1080/13506285.2020.1848949

Luo, Thomas Zhihao, and John H. R. Maunsell. 2015. "Neuronal Modulations in Visual Cortex Are Associated with Only One of Multiple Components of Attention." *Neuron* 86 (5): 1182–88. https://doi.org/10.1016/j.neuron.2015.05.007

Luo, Thomas Zhihao, and John H. R. Maunsell. 2018. "Attentional Changes in Either Criterion or Sensitivity Are Associated with Robust Modulations in Lateral Prefrontal Cortex." *Neuron* 97 (6): 1382–1393.e7. https://doi.org/10.1016/j.neuron.2018.02.007

Luo, Thomas Zhihao, and John H. R. Maunsell. 2019. "Attention Can Be Subdivided into Neurobiological Components Corresponding to Distinct Behavioral Effects." *Proceedings of the National Academy of Sciences* 116 (52): 26187–94. https://doi.org/10.1073/pnas.1902286116

Mack, Arien, and Jason Clarke. 2012. "Gist Perception Requires Attention." *Visual Cognition* 20 (3): 300–327. https://doi.org/10.1080/13506285.2012.666578

Mack, Arien, and Irvin Rock. 1998. *Inattentional Blindness*. Cambridge, MA: MIT Press.

Mackworth, Norman H. 1948. "The Breakdown of Vigilance during Prolonged Visual Search." *Quarterly Journal of Experimental Psychology* 1 (1): 6–21. https://doi.org/10.1080/17470214808416738

Macmillan, Neil A., and C. Douglas Creelman. 2004. *Detection Theory: A User's Guide*. Psychology Press.

Marr, David. 1982. *Vision*. San Francisco: W. H. Freeman and Company.

Marshall, J. C., and P. W. Halligan. 1988. "Blindsight and Insight in Visuo-Spatial Neglect." *Nature* 336 (6201): 766–67. https://doi.org/10.1038/336766a0

Martens, S., and B. Wyble. 2010. "The Attentional Blink: Past, Present, and Future of a Blind Spot in Perceptual Awareness." *Neuroscience & Biobehavioral Reviews* 34 (6): 947–57.

Martin, Michael G.F. 2002. "The Transparency of Experience." *Mind and Language* 17 (4): 376–425.

Meiran, Nachshon, Michael Cole, and Todd Braver. 2012. "When Planning Results in Loss of Control: Intention-Based Reflexivity and Working-Memory." *Frontiers in Human Neuroscience* 6. https://www.frontiersin.org/articles/10.3389/fnhum.2012.00104

Michel, Mathias, and Hakwan Lau. 2021. "Is Blindsight Possible under Signal Detection Theory? Comment on Phillips (2021)." *Psychological Review* 128 (3): 585–91. http://dx.doi.org.pitt.idm.oclc.org/10.1037/rev0000266

Miller, George A., Eugene Galanter, and Karl H. Pribram. 1960. *Plans and the Structure of Behavior*. New York: Holt, Rinehart and Winston.

Milner, A. David, and Melvyn A. Goodale. 1995. *The Visual Brain in Action*. Oxford: Oxford University Press.

Mitchell, Jonathan. 2022. "The Phenomenal Contribution of Attention." *Inquiry*: 1–32. https://doi.org/10.1080/0020174X.2022.2107061

Miyake, Akira, and Priti Shah. 1999. "Toward Unified Theories of Working Memory: Emerging General Consensus, Unresolved Theoretical Issues, and

Future Research Directions." In *Models of Working Memory: Mechanisms of Active Maintenance and Executive Control*, edited by Akira Miyake and Priti Shah, 442–82. Cambridge, UK: Cambridge University Press. https://doi.org/10.1017/CBO9781139174909.016

Mole, Christopher. 2008a. "Attention and Consciousness." *Journal of Consciousness Studies* 15 (4): 86–104.

Mole, Christopher. 2008b. "Attention in the Absence of Consciousness?" *Trends in Cognitive Sciences* 12 (2): 44.

Mole, Christopher. 2009. "Illusions, Demonstratives and the Zombie Action Hypothesis." *Mind* 118 (472): 995–1011.

Mole, Christopher. 2011. *Attention Is Cognitive Unison: An Essay in Philosophical Psychology*. New York: Oxford University Press.

Mole, Christopher. 2013. "Embodied Demonstratives: A Reply to Wu." *Mind* 122 (485): 231–39. https://doi.org/10.1093/mind/fzt031

Mole, Christopher. 2023. "Attention And Attentiveness: A Defence of The Argument for Adverbialism." *Australasian Journal of Philosophy*: 1–16. https://doi.org/10.1080/00048402.2023.2289109

Mole, Christopher, and Aaron Henry. 2023. "What Is Attention? Adverbialist Theories." *WIREs Cognitive Science* 14 (1): e1588. https://doi.org/10.1002/wcs.1588

Molyneux, Bernard. 2009. "Why Experience Told Me Nothing about Transparency." *Noûs* 43 (1): 116–36.

Montemayor, Carlos, and Harry Haroutioun Haladjian. 2015. *Consciousness, Attention, and Conscious Attention*. Cambridge, MA: MIT Press.

Moore, Cathleen M., and Jeremy M. Wolfe. 2001. "Getting beyond the Serial/Parallel Debate in Visual Research: A Hybrid Approach." In *The Limits of Attention: Temporal Constraints in Human Information Processing*, 178–98. New York: Oxford University Press. https://doi.org/10.1093/acprof:oso/9780198505150.003.0009

Moore, Tirin, and M. Fallah. 2001. "Control of Eye Movements and Spatial Attention." *Proceedings of the National Academy of Sciences of the United States of America* 98 (3): 1273–76. https://doi.org/10.1073/pnas.021549498

Moore, Tirin, and Katherine M. Armstrong. 2003. "Selective Gating of Visual Signals by Microstimulation of Frontal Cortex." *Nature* 421 (6921): 370–73. https://doi.org/10.1038/nature01341

Moors, Agnes. 2016. "Automaticity: Componential, Causal, and Mechanistic Explanations." *Annual Review of Psychology* 67: 263–87. https://doi.org/10.1146/annurev-psych-122414-033550

Morales, Jorge. 2023. "Mental Strength: A Theory of Experience Intensity." *Philosophical Perspectives* 37 (1): 1–21. https://doi.org/10.1111/phpe.12189

Morales, Jorge. 2024. "Introspection Is Signal Detection." *British Journal for the Philosophy of Science* 75 (1): 99–126.

Moray, Neville. 1959. "Attention in Dichotic Listening: Affective Cues and the Influence of Instructions." *Quarterly Journal of Experimental Psychology* 11 (1): 56–60. https://doi.org/10.1080/17470215908416289

Muhle-Karbe, Paul S., John Duncan, Wouter De Baene, Daniel J. Mitchell, and Marcel Brass. 2017. "Neural Coding for Instruction-Based Task Sets in Human Frontoparietal and Visual Cortex." *Cerebral Cortex* 27 (3): 1891–1905. https://doi.org/10.1093/cercor/bhw032

Muhle-Karbe, Paul S., Nicholas E. Myers, and Mark G. Stokes. 2021. "A Hierarchy of Functional States in Working Memory." *Journal of Neuroscience* 41 (20): 4461–75. https://doi.org/10.1523/JNEUROSCI.3104-20.2021

Munneke, Jaap, Artem V. Belopolsky, and Jan Theeuwes. 2016. "Distractors Associated with Reward Break through the Focus of Attention." *Attention, Perception and Psychophysics* 78 (7): 2213–25. https://doi.org/10.3758/s13414-016-1075-x

Munoz, Douglas P. 2002. "Commentary: Saccadic Eye Movements: Overview of Neural Circuitry." *Progress in Brain Research* 140: 89–96. https://doi.org/10.1016/S0079-6123(02)40044-1

Munton, Jessie. 2023. "Prejudice as the Misattribution of Salience." *Analytic Philosophy* 64 (1): 1–19. https://doi.org/10.1111/phib.12250

Munton, Jessie. Forthcoming. *Priority and Prejudice: The Epistemic Evaluation of Attention and Salience*. Oxford: Oxford University Press.

Murdoch, Iris. 2013. *The Sovereignty of Good*. Routledge.

Murphy, Gillian, John A. Groeger, and Ciara M. Greene. 2016. "Twenty Years of Load Theory—Where Are We Now, and Where Should We Go Next?" *Psychonomic Bulletin & Review* 23 (5): 1316–40. https://doi.org/10.3758/s13423-015-0982-5

Murray, Samuel, Kristina Krasich, Jonathan W. Schooler, and Paul Seli. 2020. "What's in a Task? Complications in the Study of the Task-Unrelated-Thought Variety of Mind Wandering." *Perspectives on Psychological Science* 15 (3): 572–88.

Myers, Nicholas E., Mark G. Stokes, and Anna C. Nobre. 2017. "Prioritizing Information during Working Memory: Beyond Sustained Internal Attention." *Trends in Cognitive Sciences* 21 (6): 449–61. https://doi.org/10.1016/j.tics.2017.03.010

Naccache, Lionel. 2018. "Why and How Access Consciousness Can Account for Phenomenal Consciousness." *Philosophical Transactions of the Royal Society B: Biological Sciences* 373 (1755): 20170357. https://doi.org/10.1098/rstb.2017.0357

Nakayama, Ken, and Gerald H. Silverman. 1986. "Serial and Parallel Processing of Visual Feature Conjunctions." *Nature* 320 (6059): 264–65. https://doi.org/10.1038/320264a0

Nanay, Bence. 2010. "Attention and Perceptual Content." *Analysis* 70 (2): 263–70.

Navon, David, and Daniel Gopher. 1979. "On the Economy of the Human-Processing System." *Psychological Review* 86 (3): 214–55. https://doi.org/10.1037/0033-295X.86.3.214

Neider, Mark B., and Gregory J. Zelinsky. 2006. "Scene Context Guides Eye Movements during Visual Search." *Vision Research* 46 (5): 614–21. https://doi.org/10.1016/j.visres.2005.08.025

Neisser, Ulric. 1967. *Cognitive Psychology*. London: Prentice-Hall International, Inc.

Neta, Ram. 2010. "The Basing Relation." In *The Routledge Companion to Epistemology*, edited by Sven Bernecker and Duncan Pritchard, 109–18. Abingdon, UK: Routledge.

Neumann, Odmar. 1987. "Beyond Capacity: A Functional View of Attention." In *Perspectives on Perception and Action*, edited by H. Heuer and A.F. Sanders, 361–94. Hillsdale: Lawrence Erlbaum Associates, Publishers.

Ni, Amy M., Supratim Ray, and John H. R. Maunsell. 2012. "Tuned Normalization Explains the Size of Attention Modulations." *Neuron* 73 (4): 803–13. https://doi.org/10.1016/j.neuron.2012.01.006

Nobre, Anna C., and Freek van Ede. 2018. "Anticipated Moments: Temporal Structure in Attention." *Nature Reviews Neuroscience* 19 (1): 34–48. https://doi.org/10.1038/nrn.2017.141

Nobre, Anna C. (Kia), and M.-Marsel Mesulam. 2014. "Large-Scale Networks for Attentional Biases." In *The Oxford Handbook of Attention*, edited by Anna C. Nobre and Sabine Kastner, 106–51. New York: Oxford University Press. https://doi.org/10.1093/oxfordhb/9780199675111.013.035

Nobre, Kia, and Sabine Kastner, eds. 2018. *The Oxford Handbook of Attention*. Oxford: Oxford University Press.

Noë, Alva. 2002. *Is the Visual World a Grand Illusion?* Imprint Academic.

Norman, Donald A. 1968. "Toward a Theory of Memory and Attention." *Psychological Review* 75 (6): 522–36. https://doi.org/10.1037/h0026699

Norman, Liam J., Charles A. Heywood, and Robert W. Kentridge. 2013. "Object-Based Attention without Awareness." *Psychological Science* 24 (6): 836–43. https://doi.org/10.1177/0956797612461449

Oberauer, Klaus. 2002. "Access to Information in Working Memory: Exploring the Focus of Attention." *Journal of Experimental Psychology: Learning, Memory, and Cognition* 28 (3): 411–21. https://doi.org/10.1037/0278-7393.28.3.411

Oberauer, Klaus. 2009. "Design for a Working Memory." In *Psychology of Learning and Motivation*, 51: 45–100. The Psychology of Learning and Motivation. Academic Press. https://doi.org/10.1016/S0079-7421(09)51002-X

Oberauer, Klaus. 2019. "Working Memory and Attention – A Conceptual Analysis and Review." *Journal of Cognition* 2 (1): 223–98.

Oberauer, Klaus, Stephan Lewandowsky, Edward Awh, Gordon D. A. Brown, Andrew Conway, Nelson Cowan, Christopher Donkin, et al. 2018. "Benchmarks for Models of Short-Term and Working Memory." *Psychological Bulletin* 144 (9): 885–958.

Oken, B. S., M. C. Salinsky, and S. M. Elsas. 2006. "Vigilance, Alertness, or Sustained Attention: Physiological Basis and Measurement." *Clinical Neurophysiology: Official Journal of the International Federation of Clinical Neurophysiology* 117 (9): 1885–1901. https://doi.org/10.1016/j.clinph.2006.01.017

Oliva, Aude. 2005. "Gist of the Scene." In *Neurobiology of Attention*, edited by Laurent Itti, Geraint Rees, and John Tsotsos, 251–56. Burlington, MA: Elsevier Academic Press.

Oliva, Aude, and Philippe G. Schyns. 1997. "Coarse Blobs or Fine Edges? Evidence That Information Diagnosticity Changes the Perception of Complex Visual Stimuli." *Cognitive Psychology* 34 (1): 72–107. https://doi.org/10.1006/cogp.1997.0667

Olivers, Christian N. L., Frank Meijer, and Jan Theeuwes. 2006. "Feature-Based Memory-Driven Attentional Capture: Visual Working Memory Content Affects Visual Attention." *Journal of Experimental Psychology: Human Perception and Performance* 32 (5): 1243–65. https://doi.org/10.1037/0096-1523.32.5.1243

Olivers, Christian N. L., Judith Peters, Roos Houtkamp, and Pieter R. Roelfsema. 2011. "Different States in Visual Working Memory: When It Guides Attention and When It Does Not." *Trends in Cognitive Sciences* 15 (7): 327–34.

Olson, Ingrid R., Marvin M. Chun, and Truett Allison. 2001. "Contextual Guidance of Attention: Human Intracranial Event-Related Potential Evidence for Feedback Modulation in Anatomically Early Temporally Late Stages of Visual Processing." *Brain* 124 (7): 1417–25. https://doi.org/10.1093/brain/124.7.1417

Orabona, Francesco, Giorgio Metta, and Giulio Sandini. 2007. "A Proto-Object Based Visual Attention Model." In *Attention in Cognitive Systems. Theories and Systems from an Interdisciplinary Viewpoint*, edited by Lucas Paletta and Erich Rome, 198–215. Lecture Notes in Computer Science. Berlin, Heidelberg: Springer. https://doi.org/10.1007/978-3-540-77343-6_13

Palmeri, Thomas. 2006. "Automaticity." In *Encyclopedia of Cognitive Science*, edited by Lynn Nadel, 290–301. John Wiley & Sons.

Panizza, Silvia Caprioglio. 2022. *The Ethics of Attention: Engaging the Real with Iris Murdoch and Simone Weil*. New York: Routledge. https://doi.org/10.4324/9781003164852

Panizza, Silvia Caprioglio, and Mark Hopwood, eds. 2022. *The Murdochian Mind*. London: Routledge. https://doi.org/10.4324/9781003031222

Pashler, Harold. 1998. *The Psychology of Attention*. Cambridge, MA: MIT Press.

Patel, Gaurav H., Danica Yang, Emery C. Jamerson, Lawrence H. Snyder, Maurizio Corbetta, and Vincent P. Ferrera. 2015. "Functional Evolution of New and Expanded Attention Networks in Humans." *Proceedings of the National Academy of Sciences* 112 (30): 9454–59. https://doi.org/10.1073/pnas.1420395112

Peacocke, Christopher. 1998. "Conscious Attitudes, Attention, and Self-Knowledge." In *Knowing Our Own Minds*, 63–98. Oxford: Oxford University Press.

Pedziwiatr, Marek A., Matthias Kümmerer, Thomas S. A. Wallis, Matthias Bethge, and Christoph Teufel. 2021a. "Meaning Maps and Saliency Models Based on Deep Convolutional Neural Networks Are Insensitive to Image Meaning When Predicting Human Fixations." *Cognition* 206 (January): 104465. https://doi.org/10.1016/j.cognition.2020.104465

Pedziwiatr, Marek A., Matthias Kümmerer, Thomas S. A. Wallis, Matthias Bethge, and Christoph Teufel. 2021b. "There Is No Evidence That Meaning Maps Capture Semantic Information Relevant to Gaze Guidance: Reply to Henderson, Hayes, Peacock, and Rehrig (2021)." *Cognition* 214 (September): 104741. https://doi.org/10.1016/j.cognition.2021.104741

Peelen, Marius V., and Sabine Kastner. 2011. "A Neural Basis for Real-World Visual Search in Human Occipitotemporal Cortex." *Proceedings of the National Academy of Sciences* 108 (29): 12125–30. https://doi.org/10.1073/pnas.1101042108

Pelli, Denis G. 2008. "Crowding: A Cortical Constraint on Object Recognition." *Current Opinion in Neurobiology* 18 (4): 445–51.

Petersen, Steven E., and Michael I. Posner. 2012. "The Attention System of the Human Brain: 20 Years After." *Annual Review of Neuroscience* 35 (1): 73–89. https://doi.org/10.1146/annurev-neuro-062111-150525

Peterson, Matthew S., and Arthur F. Kramer. 2001. "Attentional Guidance of the Eyes by Contextual Information and Abrupt Onsets." *Perception & Psychophysics* 63 (7): 1239–49. https://doi.org/10.3758/BF03194537

Phillips, Ian. 2011. "Perception and Iconic Memory: What Sperling Doesn't Show." *Mind and Language* 26 (4): 381–411.

Phillips, Ian. 2021. "Blindsight Is Qualitatively Degraded Conscious Vision." *Psychological Review* 128 (3): 558–84. https://doi.org/10.1037/rev0000254

Pollard, Bill. 2003. "Can Virtuous Actions Be Both Habitual and Rational?" *Ethical Theory and Moral Practice* 6 (4): 411–25. https://doi.org/10.1023/B:ETTA.0000004561.34480.d4

Posner, Michael I., Mary Jo Nissen, and William C. Ogden. 1978. "Attended and Unattended Processing Modes: The Role of Set for Spatial Location." In *Modes of Perceiving and Processing Information*, edited by H. L. Pick Jr. and E. Saltzman, 137–57. New York: Psychology Press.

Posner, Michael I., and Steven E. Petersen. 1990. "The Attention System of the Human Brain." *Annual Review of Neuroscience* 13 (1): 25–42. https://doi.org/10.1146/annurev.ne.13.030190.000325

Posner, Michael I., C.R. Snyder, and B.J. Davidson. 1980. "Attention and the Detection of Signals." *Journal of Experimental Psychology: General* 109 (2): 160–74.

Potter, Mary C. 1976. "Short-Term Conceptual Memory for Pictures." *Journal of Experimental Psychology: Human Learning and Memory* 2 (5): 509–22. https://doi.org/10.1037/0278-7393.2.5.509

Potter, Mary C., and Ellen I. Levy. 1969. "Recognition Memory for a Rapid Sequence of Pictures." *Journal of Experimental Psychology* 81 (1): 10–15. https://doi.org/10.1037/h0027470

Pouget, Pierre, Iwona Stepniewska, Erin A. Crowder, Melanie W. Leslie, Erik E. Emeric, Matthew J. Nelson, and Jeffrey D. Schall. 2009. "Visual and Motor Connectivity and the Distribution of Calcium-Binding Proteins in Macaque Frontal Eye Field: Implications for Saccade Target Selection." *Frontiers in Neuroanatomy* 3: 2. https://doi.org/10.3389/neuro.05.002.2009

Prettyman, Adrienne. 2023. "What Is Diffuse Attention?" *Mind & Language* 38 (2): 374–93. https://doi.org/10.1111/mila.12365

Prinz, Jesse. 2012. *The Conscious Brain*. Oxford: Oxford University Press.

Prinz, Jesse. 2022. "The Attending Mind." *The Philosophical Review* 131 (3): 390–93. https://doi.org/10.1215/00318108-9743939

Prinzmetal, William, Virginia Long, and James Leonhardt. 2008. "Involuntary Attention and Brightness Contrast." *Perception & Psychophysics* 70 (7): 1139–50. https://doi.org/10.3758/PP.70.7.1139

Quinlan, Philip T. 2003. "Visual Feature Integration Theory: Past, Present, and Future." *Psychological Bulletin* 129 (5): 643–73. https://doi.org/10.1037/0033-2909.129.5.643

Reddy, Leila, Farshad Moradi, and Christof Koch. 2007. "Top–down Biases Win against Focal Attention in the Fusiform Face Area." *NeuroImage* 38 (4): 730–39. https://doi.org/10.1016/j.neuroimage.2007.08.006

Reddy, Leila, Lavanya Reddy, and Christof Koch. 2006. "Face Identification in the Near-Absence of Focal Attention." *Vision Research* 46 (15): 2336–43. https://doi.org/10.1016/j.visres.2006.01.020

Reddy, Leila, Patrick C. Wilken, and Christof Koch. 2004. "Face-Gender Discrimination Is Possible in the near-Absence of Attention." *Journal of Vision* 3 (9): 106–17. https://doi.org/10.1167/3.9.576

Reeder, Reshanne R., Francesca Perini, and Marius V. Peelen. 2015. "Preparatory Activity in Posterior Temporal Cortex Causally Contributes to Object Detection in Scenes." *Journal of Cognitive Neuroscience* 27 (11): 2117–25. https://doi.org/10.1162/jocn_a_00845

Renero, Adriana. 2019. "Modes of Introspective Access: A Pluralist Approach." *Philosophia* 47 (3): 823–44. https://doi.org/10.1007/s11406-018-9989-2

Rensink, Ronald A. 2000. "The Dynamic Representation of Scenes." *Visual Cognition* 7 (1–3): 17–42. https://doi.org/10.1080/135062800394667

Reynolds, John H., and David J. Heeger. 2009. "The Normalization Model of Attention." *Neuron* 61 (2): 168–85. https://doi.org/10.1016/j.neuron.2009.01.002

Rizzolatti, Giacomo, Lucia Riggio, and Bori M. Sheliga. 1994. "Space and Selective Attention." In *Attention and Performance XV: Conscious and Nonconscious Information Processing*, edited by Carlo Umiltà and Morris Moscovitch, 231–65. Cambridge, MA: MIT Press.

Robbins, Trevor W. 1998. "Arousal and Attention: Psychopharmacological and Neuropsychological Studies in Experimental Animals." In *The Attentive Brain*, 189–220. Cambridge, MA: The MIT Press.

Rosenholtz, Ruth. 2016. "Capabilities and Limitations of Peripheral Vision." *Annual Review of Vision Science* 2 (1): 437–57. https://doi.org/10.1146/annurev-vision-082114-035733

Rosenholtz, Ruth. 2020. "Demystifying Visual Awareness: Peripheral Encoding plus Limited Decision Complexity Resolve the Paradox of Rich Visual Experience and Curious Perceptual Failures." *Attention, Perception, & Psychophysics* 82 (3): 901–25. https://doi.org/10.3758/s13414-019-01968-1

Rosenholtz, Ruth. 2024. "Visual Attention in Crisis." *The Behavioral and Brain Sciences*, May, 1–32. https://doi.org/10.1017/S0140525X24000323

Rosenholtz, Ruth, Jie Huang, and Krista Ehinger. 2012a. "Rethinking the Role of Top-Down Attention in Vision: Effects Attributable to a Lossy

Representation in Peripheral Vision." *Frontiers in Psychology* 3: 13. https://doi.org/10.3389/fpsyg.2012.00013

Rosenholtz, Ruth, Jie Huang, Alvin Raj, Benjamin J. Balas, and Livia Ilie. 2012b. "A Summary Statistic Representation in Peripheral Vision Explains Visual Search." *Journal of Vision* 12 (4): 14. https://doi.org/10.1167/12.4.14

Ruff, Christian C., Felix Blankenburg, Otto Bjoertomt, Sven Bestmann, Elliot Freeman, John-Dylan Haynes, Geraint Rees, Oliver Josephs, Ralf Deichmann, and Jon Driver. 2006. "Concurrent TMS-fMRI and Psychophysics Reveal Frontal Influences on Human Retinotopic Visual Cortex." *Current Biology* 16 (15): 1479–88. https://doi.org/10.1016/j.cub.2006.06.057

Rungratsameetaweemana, Nuttida, and John T Serences. 2019. "Dissociating the Impact of Attention and Expectation on Early Sensory Processing." *Current Opinion in Psychology*, Attention & Perception, 29 (October):181–86. https://doi.org/10.1016/j.copsyc.2019.03.014

Russell, Alexander F., Stefan Mihalaş, Rudiger von der Heydt, Ernst Niebur, and Ralph Etienne-Cummings. 2014. "A Model of Proto-Object Based Saliency." *Vision Research* 94 (January):1–15. https://doi.org/10.1016/j.visres.2013.10.005

Russell, Bertrand. 1910. "Knowledge by Acquaintance and Knowledge by Description." *Proceedings of the Aristotelian Society* 11: 108–28.

Saint-Croix, Catharine. 2024. "The Epistemology of Attention." In *The Blackwell Companion to Epistemology*, 3rd ed., edited by Kurt Sylvan, Ernest Sosa, Jonathan Dancy, and Matthias Steup. Wiley Blackwell.

Scanlon, T.M. 1998. *What We Owe to Each Other.* Cambridge, MA: Harvard University Press.

Schelonka, Kathryn, Christian Graulty, Enriqueta Canseco-Gonzalez, and Michael A. Pitts. 2017. "ERP Signatures of Conscious and Unconscious Word and Letter Perception in an Inattentional Blindness Paradigm." *Consciousness and Cognition*, 54 (September): 56–71. https://doi.org/10.1016/j.concog.2017.04.009

Schneider, Keith A. 2006. "Does Attention Alter Appearance?" *Perception & Psychophysics* 68 (5): 800–814.

Schneider, Keith A, and Marcell Komlos. 2011. "Attention Alters Decision Criteria but Not Appearance: A Reanalysis of Anton-Erxleben, Abrams, and Carrasco (2010)." *Journal of Vision* 11 (13): 1–10. https://doi.org/10.1167/11.13.7

Schneider, Walter, and Richard M. Shiffrin. 1977. "Controlled and Automatic Human Information Processing: I Detection, Search, and Attention." *Psychological Review* 84 (1): 1–66. https://doi.org/10.1037/0033-295X.84.1.1

Schwitzgebel, Eric. 2011. *Perplexities of Consciousness.* Cambridge, MA: MIT Press.

Schwitzgebel, Eric. 2012. "Introspection, What?" In *Introspection and Consciousness*, edited by Declan Smithies and Daniel Stoljar, 29–48. Oxford: Oxford University Press.

Schyns, Philippe G., and Aude Oliva. 1994. "From Blobs to Boundary Edges: Evidence for Time-and Spatial-Scale-Dependent Scene Recognition." *Psychological Science* 5 (4): 195–200. https://doi.org/10.1111/j.1467-9280.1994.tb00500.x

Scimeca, Jason M., Anastasia Kiyonaga, and Mark D'Esposito. 2018. "Reaffirming the Sensory Recruitment Account of Working Memory." *Trends in Cognitive Sciences* 22 (3): 190–92. https://doi.org/10.1016/j.tics.2017.12.007

Seger, Carol A. 2018. "Corticostriatal Foundations of Habits." *Current Opinion in Behavioral Sciences*, Habits and Skills, 20 (April):153–60. https://doi.org/10.1016/j.cobeha.2018.01.006

Seli, Paul, Jonathan S. A. Carriere, and Daniel Smilek. 2015a. "Not All Mind Wandering Is Created Equal: Dissociating Deliberate from Spontaneous Mind Wandering." *Psychological Research* 79 (5): 750–58. https://doi.org/10.1007/s00426-014-0617-x

Seli, Paul, Tanya R. Jonker, James Allan Cheyne, Kassandra Cortes, and Daniel Smilek. 2015b. "Can Research Participants Comment Authoritatively on the Validity of Their Self-Reports of Mind Wandering and Task Engagement?" *Journal of Experimental Psychology: Human Perception and Performance* 41 (3): 703–9. https://doi.org/10.1037/xhp0000029

Seli, Paul, Michael J. Kane, Thomas Metzinger, Jonathan Smallwood, Daniel L. Schacter, David Maillet, Jonathan W. Schooler, and Daniel Smilek. 2018a. "The Family-Resemblances Framework for Mind-Wandering Remains Well Clad." *Trends in Cognitive Sciences* 22 (11): 959–61. https://doi.org/10.1016/j.tics.2018.07.007

Seli, Paul, Michael J. Kane, Jonathan Smallwood, Daniel L. Schacter, David Maillet, Jonathan W. Schooler, and Daniel Smilek. 2018b. "Mind-Wandering as a Natural Kind: A Family-Resemblances View." *Trends in Cognitive Sciences* 22 (6): 479–90. https://doi.org/10.1016/j.tics.2018.03.010

Seli, Paul, Evan F. Risko, and Daniel Smilek. 2016a. "On the Necessity of Distinguishing Between Unintentional and Intentional Mind Wandering." *Psychological Science* 27 (5): 685–91. https://doi.org/10.1177/0956797616634068

Seli, Paul, Evan F. Risko, Daniel Smilek, and Daniel L. Schacter. 2016b. "Mind-Wandering with and without Intention." *Trends in Cognitive Sciences* 20 (8): 605–17. https://doi.org/10.1016/j.tics.2016.05.010

Serences, John T., and Geoffrey M. Boynton. 2007. "Feature-Based Attentional Modulations in the Absence of Direct Visual Stimulation." *Neuron* 55 (2): 301–12. https://doi.org/10.1016/j.neuron.2007.06.015

Serences, John T., Edward F. Ester, Edward K. Vogel, and Edward Awh. 2009. "Stimulus-Specific Delay Activity in Human Primary Visual Cortex." *Psychological Science* 20 (2): 207–14. https://doi.org/10.1111/j.1467-9280.2009.02276.x

Serences, John T., Sarah Shomstein, Andrew B. Leber, Xavier Golay, Howard E. Egeth, and Steven Yantis. 2005. "Coordination of Voluntary and Stimulus-Driven Attentional Control in Human Cortex." *Psychological Science* 16 (2): 114–22. https://doi.org/10.1111/j.0956-7976.2005.00791.x

Sha, Li Z., and Yuhong V. Jiang. 2016. "Components of Reward-Driven Attentional Capture." *Attention, Perception and Psychophysics* 78 (2): 403–14. http://dx.doi.org.cmu.idm.oclc.org/10.3758/s13414-015-1038-7

Shafto, Juliet P., and Michael A. Pitts. 2015. "Neural Signatures of Conscious Face Perception in an Inattentional Blindness Paradigm." *Journal of Neuroscience* 35 (31): 10940–48. https://doi.org/10.1523/JNEUROSCI.0145-15.2015

Shannon, Claude Elwood. 1949. *The Mathematical Theory of Communication.* University of Illinois Press.

Sheridan, Heather, and Eyal M. Reingold. 2017. "The Holistic Processing Account of Visual Expertise in Medical Image Perception: A Review." *Frontiers in Psychology* 8. https://doi.org/10.3389/fpsyg.2017.01620

Shomstein, Sarah, Xiaoli Zhang, and Dick Dubbelde. 2023. "Attention and Platypuses." *WIREs Cognitive Science* 14 (1): e1600. https://doi.org/10.1002/wcs.1600

Shulman, Gordon L., and Maurizio Corbetta. 2012. "Two Attentional Networks: Identification and Function within a Larger Cognitive Architecture." In *Cognitive Neuroscience of Attention*, 2nd ed., edited by Michael I. Posner and Liqiang Huang, 113–28. New York: Guilford Press.

Siegel, Susanna. 2017. *The Rationality of Perception.* Oxford University Press.

Siegel, Susanna. 2022. "Salience Principles for Democracy." In *Salience*, edited by Sophie Archer, 235–66. Abingdon, UK: Taylor and Francis.

Siewert, Charles. 2004. "Is Experience Transparent?" *Philosophical Studies* 117: 15–41.

Silins, Nicholas, and Susanna Siegel. 2014. "Consciousness, Attention, and Justification." In *Scepticism and Perceptual Justification*, edited by Elia Zardini and Dylan Dodd, 149–72. Oxford: Oxford University Press.

Simons, Daniel J., and C. F. Chabris. 1999. "Gorillas in Our Midst: Sustained Inattentional Blindness for Dynamic Events." *Perception* 28 (9): 1059–74.

Simons, Daniel J. 2000. "Attentional Capture and Inattentional Blindness." *Trends in Cognitive Sciences* 4 (4): 147–55. https://doi.org/10.1016/S1364-6613(00)01455-8

Simons, Daniel J., and M. S. Ambinder. 2005. "Change Blindness Theory and Consequences." *Current Directions in Psychological Science* 14 (1): 44–48.

Sisk, Caitlin A., Roger W. Remington, and Yuhong V. Jiang. 2019. "Mechanisms of Contextual Cueing: A Tutorial Review." *Attention, Perception, & Psychophysics* 81 (8): 2571–89. https://doi.org/10.3758/s13414-019-01832-2

Smallwood, Jonathan, and Jonathan W. Schooler. 2006. "The Restless Mind." *Psychological Bulletin* 132 (6): 946–58. https://doi.org/10.1037/0033-2909.132.6.946

Smith, Daniel T, and Thomas Schenk. 2012. "The Premotor Theory of Attention: Time to Move On?" *Neuropsychologia* 50 (6): 1104–14. https://doi.org/10.1016/j.neuropsychologia.2012.01.025

Smith, Leonie, and Alfred Archer. 2020. "Epistemic Injustice and the Attention Economy." *Ethical Theory and Moral Practice* 23 (5): 777–95. https://doi.org/10.1007/s10677-020-10123-x

Smithies, Declan. 2011a. "Attention Is Rational-Access Consciousness." In *Attention: Philosophical and Psychological Essays*, edited by Christopher Mole, Declan Smithies, and Wayne Wu. New York: Oxford University Press.

Smithies, Declan. 2011b. "What Is the Role of Consciousness in Demonstrative Thought?" *Journal of Philosophy* 108 (1): 5–34.

Smithies, Declan, and Daniel Stoljar. 2012. *Introspection and Consciousness.* Oxford University Press.

Snow, Nancy E. 2006. "Habitual Virtuous Actions and Automaticity." *Ethical Theory and Moral Practice* 9 (5): 545–61. https://doi.org/10.1007/s10677-006-9035-5

Soto, David, John Hodsoll, Pia Rotshtein, and Glyn W. Humphreys. 2008. "Automatic Guidance of Attention from Working Memory." *Trends in Cognitive Sciences* 12 (9): 342–48. https://doi.org/10.1016/j.tics.2008.05.007

Soto, David, Glyn W. Humphreys, and Pia Rotshtein. 2007. "Dissociating the Neural Mechanisms of Memory-Based Guidance of Visual Selection." *Proceedings of the National Academy of Sciences* 104 (43): 17186–91. https://doi.org/10.1073/pnas.0703706104

Souza, Alessandra S., and Klaus Oberauer. 2016. "In Search of the Focus of Attention in Working Memory: 13 Years of the Retro-Cue Effect." *Attention, Perception, & Psychophysics* 78 (7): 1839–60. https://doi.org/10.3758/s13414-016-1108-5

Speaks, Jeff. 2010. "Attention and Intentionalism." *Philosophical Quarterly* 60 (239): 325–42.

Spener, Maja. 2024. *Introspection: First-Person Access in Science and Agency*. Oxford, New York: Oxford University Press.

Sperling, George. 1960. "The Information Available in Brief Visual Presentations." *Psychological Monographs: General and Applied* 74 (11): 1–29.

Stazicker, James. 2011. "Attention, Visual Consciousness and Indeterminacy." *Mind & Language* 26 (2): 156–84.

Stemmann, Heiko, and Winrich A Freiwald. 2019. "Evidence for an Attentional Priority Map in Inferotemporal Cortex." *Proceedings of the National Academy of Sciences of the United States of America* 116 (47): 23797–805.

Stokes, Mark G. 2011. "Top-down Visual Activity Underlying VSTM and Preparatory Attention." *Neuropsychologia* 49 (6): 1425–27. https://doi.org/10.1016/j.neuropsychologia.2011.02.004

Stokes, Mark, Russell Thompson, Anna C. Nobre, and John Duncan. 2009. "Shape-Specific Preparatory Activity Mediates Attention to Targets in Human Visual Cortex." *Proceedings of the National Academy of Sciences* 106 (46): 19569–74. https://doi.org/10.1073/pnas.0905306106

Stoljar, Daniel. 2004. "The Argument from Diaphanousness." In *Language, Mind and World: Special Issue of the Canadian Journal of Philosophy*, 341–90. Calgary: University of Calgary Press.

Störmer, Viola S. 2019. "Orienting Spatial Attention to Sounds Enhances Visual Processing." *Current Opinion in Psychology* 29 (October):193–98. https://doi.org/10.1016/j.copsyc.2019.03.010

Störmer, Viola S., John J. McDonald, and Steven A. Hillyard. 2009. "Cross-Modal Cueing of Attention Alters Appearance and Early Cortical Processing of Visual Stimuli." *Proceedings of the National Academy of Sciences* 106 (52): 22456–61. https://doi.org/10.1073/pnas.0907573106

Strawson, Galen. 2003. "Mental Ballistics or the Involuntariness of Spontaniety." *Proceedings of the Aristotelian Society* 103 (3): 227–57.

Summerfield, Christopher, and Tobias Egner. 2009. "Expectation (and Attention) in Visual Cognition." *Trends in Cognitive Sciences* 13 (9): 403–9.

Summerfield, Christopher, and Floris P. de Lange. 2014. "Expectation in Perceptual Decision Making: Neural and Computational Mechanisms." *Nature Reviews Neuroscience* 15 (11): 745–56. https://doi.org/10.1038/nrn3838

Taylor, Henry. 2023. "Attention as a Patchwork Concept." *European Journal for Philosophy of Science* 13 (3): 36. https://doi.org/10.1007/s13194-023-00538-5

Taylor, J. Henry. 2015. "Against Unifying Accounts of Attention." *Erkenntnis* 80 (1): 39–56. https://doi.org/10.1007/s10670-014-9611-3

Theeuwes, Jan. 1992. "Perceptual Selectivity for Color and Form." *Perception & Psychophysics* 51 (6): 599–606. https://doi.org/10.3758/BF03211656

Theeuwes, Jan, and Artem V. Belopolsky. 2012. "Reward Grabs the Eye: Oculomotor Capture by Rewarding Stimuli." *Vision Research* 74 (December): 80–85. https://doi.org/10.1016/j.visres.2012.07.024

Theeuwes, Jan, Christian N. L. Olivers, and Artem Belopolsky. 2010. "Stimulus-Driven Capture and Contingent Capture." *WIREs Cognitive Science* 1 (6): 872–81. https://doi.org/10.1002/wcs.83

Todd, Rebecca M., William A. Cunningham, Adam K. Anderson, and Evan Thompson. 2012. "Affect-Biased Attention as Emotion Regulation." *Trends in Cognitive Sciences* 16 (7): 365–72. https://doi.org/10.1016/j.tics.2012.06.003

Todd, Rebecca M., and Maria G. M. Manaligod. 2018. "Implicit Guidance of Attention: The Priority State Space Framework." *Cortex*, 102 (May):121–38. https://doi.org/10.1016/j.cortex.2017.08.001

Torralba, Antonio, Aude Oliva, Monica S. Castelhano, and John M. Henderson. 2006. "Contextual Guidance of Eye Movements and Attention in Real-World Scenes: The Role of Global Features in Object Search." *Psychological Review* 113 (4): 766–86. https://doi.org/10.1037/0033-295X.113.4.766

Treisman, Anne. 1960. "Contextual Cues in Selective Listening." *Quarterly Journal of Experimental Psychology* 12 (4): 242–48.

Treisman, Anne. 1969. "Strategies and Models of Selective Attention." *Psychological Review* 76 (3): 282–99. https://doi.org/10.1037/h0027242

Treisman, Anne. 1985. "Preattentive Processing in Vision." *Computer Vision, Graphics, and Image Processing* 31 (2): 156–77.

Treisman, Anne. 1988. "Features and Objects: The Fourteenth Bartlett Memorial Lecture." *The Quarterly Journal of Experimental Psychology Section A* 40 (2): 201–37. https://doi.org/10.1080/02724988843000104

Treisman, Anne. 1998. "Feature Binding, Attention and Object Perception." *Philosophical Transactions of the Royal Society of London. Series B: Biological Sciences* 353 (1373): 1295–1306.

Treisman, Anne. 2006. "How the Deployment of Attention Determines What We See." *Visual Cognition* 14 (4–8): 411–43.

Treisman, Anne, and Garry Gelade. 1980. "A Feature-Integration Theory of Attention." *Cognitive Psychology* 12: 97–136.

Treisman, Anne, and Hilary Schmidt. 1982. "Illusory Conjunctions in the Perception of Objects." *Cognitive Psychology* 14 (1): 107–41. https://doi.org/10.1016/0010-0285(82)90006-8

Tse, Peter U. 2005. "Voluntary Attention Modulates the Brightness of Overlapping Transparent Surfaces." *Vision Research* 45 (9): 1095–98. https://doi.org/10.1016/j.visres.2004.11.001

Tsotsos, John K. 2011. *A Computational Perspective on Visual Attention*. Cambridge, MA: MIT Press.

Turatto, Massimo, Massimo Vescovi, and Matteo Valsecchi. 2007. "Attention Makes Moving Objects Be Perceived to Move Faster." *Vision Research* 47 (2): 166–78.

Turner, Marilyn L., and Randall W. Engle. 1989. "Is Working Memory Capacity Task Dependent?" *Journal of Memory and Language* 28 (2): 127–54. https://doi.org/10.1016/0749-596X(89)90040-5

Turri, John. 2010. "On the Relationship between Propositional and Doxastic Justification." *Philosophy and Phenomenological Research* 80 (2): 312–26.

Tye, Michael. 1995. *Ten Problems of Consciousness: A Representational Theory of the Phenomenal Mind*. Cambridge, MA: MIT Press.

Tye, Michael. 2000. *Consciousness, Color and Content*. Cambridge, MA: MIT Press.

Uejima, Takeshi, Ernst Niebur, and Ralph Etienne-Cummings. 2020. "Proto-Object Based Saliency Model with Texture Detection Channel." *Frontiers in Computational Neuroscience* 14. https://www.frontiersin.org/articles/10.3389/fncom.2020.541581

Ungerleider, L.G., and M. Mishkin. 1982. "Two Cortical Systems." In *Analysis of Visual Behavior*, 549–86. Cambridge, MA: MIT Press.

Unsworth, Nash. 2016. "The Many Facets of Individual Differences in Working Memory Capacity." In *Psychology of Learning and Motivation*, edited by Brian H. Ross, 65: 1–46. Academic Press. https://doi.org/10.1016/bs.plm.2016.03.001

Veale, Richard, Ziad M. Hafed, and Masatoshi Yoshida. 2017. "How Is Visual Salience Computed in the Brain? Insights from Behaviour, Neurobiology and Modelling." *Philosophical Transactions of the Royal Society B: Biological Sciences* 372 (February):1–14. https://doi.org/10.1098/rstb.2016.0113

Vecera, Shaun P., and Matthew Rizzo. 2003. "Spatial Attention: Normal Processes and Their Breakdown." *Neurologic Clinics* 21 (3): 575–607. https://doi.org/10.1016/s0733-8619(02)00103-2

Võ, Melissa Le-Hoa. 2021. "The Meaning and Structure of Scenes." *Vision Research* 181 (April):10–20. https://doi.org/10.1016/j.visres.2020.11.003

Wallhagen, Morgan. 2007. "Consciousness and Action: Does Cognitive Science Support (Mild) Epiphenomenalism?" *The British Journal for the Philosophy of Science* 58 (3): 539.

Walther, Dirk, and Christof Koch. 2006. "Modeling Attention to Salient Proto-Objects." *Neural Networks* 19 (9): 1395–1407. https://doi.org/10.1016/j.neunet.2006.10.001

Wammes, Jeffrey D., Pierre O. Boucher, Paul Seli, J. Allan Cheyne, and Daniel Smilek. 2016. "Mind Wandering during Lectures I: Changes in Rates across an Entire Semester." *Scholarship of Teaching and Learning in Psychology* 2 (1): 13–32. https://doi.org/10.1037/stl0000053

Watzl, Sebastian. 2011. "Attention as Structuring of the Stream of Consciousness." In *Attention: Philosophical and Psychological Essays*, edited by Christopher Mole, Declan Smithies, and Wayne Wu, 145–73. New York: Oxford University Press.

Watzl, Sebastian. 2017. *Structuring Mind: The Nature of Attention and How It Shapes Consciousness*. Oxford: Oxford University Press.

Watzl, Sebastian. 2022. "The Ethics of Attention: An Argument and a Framework." In *Salience: A Philosophical Inquiry*, edited by Sophie Archer, 89–112. Abingdon, UK: Routledge.

Weil, Simone. 2021. *Waiting for God*. Abingdon, UK: Routledge.

Weiskrantz, Lawrence. 1999. *Consciousness Lost and Found: A Neuropsychological Exploration*. Oxford: Oxford University Press.

White, Brian J., David J. Berg, Janis Y. Kan, Robert A. Marino, Laurent Itti, and Douglas P. Munoz. 2017. "Superior Colliculus Neurons Encode a Visual Saliency Map during Free Viewing of Natural Dynamic Video." *Nature Communications* 8 (1): 14263. https://doi.org/10.1038/ncomms14263

Whiteley, Ella. 2022. "Harmful Salience Perspectives." In *Salience: A Philosophical Inquiry*, edited by Sophie Archer, 193–212. London: Routledge.

Whiteley, Ella Kate. 2023. "'A Woman First and a Philosopher Second': Relative Attentional Surplus on the Wrong Property." *Ethics* 133 (4): 497–528. https://doi.org/10.1086/724538

Whitney, David, and Dennis M Levi. 2011. "Visual Crowding: A Fundamental Limit on Conscious Perception and Object Recognition." *Trends in Cognitive Sciences* 15 (4): 160–68.

Wolfe, Jeremy. 2012. "Establishing the Field: Treisman and Gelade." In *From Perception to Consciousness: Searching with Anne Treisman*, edited by Jeremy M. Wolfe and Lynn C. Robertson, 97. Oxford University Press.

Wolfe, Jeremy M. 1994. "Guided Search 2.0 A Revised Model of Visual Search." *Psychonomic Bulletin and Review* 1 (2): 202–38.

Wolfe, Jeremy M. 1998. "What Can 1 Million Trials Tell Us About Visual Search?" *Psychological Science* 9 (1): 33–39. https://doi.org/10.1111/1467-9280.00006

Wolfe, Jeremy M. 1999. "Inattentional Amnesia." In *Fleeting Memories: Cognition of Brief Visual Stimuli*, edited by Coltheart, Max, 71–94. Cambridge, MA: MIT Press.

Wolfe, Jeremy M., ed. 2020a. "A Special Issue in Honor of the Contributions of Anne Treisman, Part 1." *Attention, Perception, & Psychophysics* 82 (1), 1–6.

Wolfe, Jeremy M., ed. 2020b. "A Special Issue in Honor of the Contributions of Anne Treisman, Part 2." *Attention, Perception, & Psychophysics* 82 (2), 1–6.

Wolfe, Jeremy M. 2020c. "Visual Search: How Do We Find What We Are Looking For?" *Annual Review of Vision Science* 6 (1). 539–62. https://doi.org/10.1146/annurev-vision-091718-015048

Wolfe, Jeremy M. 2021. "Guided Search 6.0: An Updated Model of Visual Search." *Psychonomic Bulletin & Review*, February. https://doi.org/10.3758/s13423-020-01859-9

Wolfe, Jeremy M., Kyle R. Cave, and Susan L. Franzel. 1989. "Guided Search: An Alternative to the Feature Integration Model for Visual Search." *Journal of Experimental Psychology: Human Perception and Performance* 15 (3): 419–33. https://doi.org/10.1037/0096-1523.15.3.419

Wolfe, Jeremy M., Karla K. Evans, and Trafton Drew. 2018. "The First Moments of Medical Image Perception." In *The Handbook of Medical Image Perception and Techniques*, edited by Ehsan Samei and Elizabeth A. Krupinski, 2nd ed., 188–96. Cambridge, UK: Cambridge University Press. https://doi.org/10.1017/9781108163781.012

Wolfe, Jeremy M., Melissa L. -H. Võ, Karla K. Evans, and Michelle R. Greene. 2011. "Visual Search in Scenes Involves Selective and Nonselective Pathways." *Trends in Cognitive Sciences* 15 (2): 77–84. https://doi.org/10.1016/j.tics.2010.12.001

Wolfe, Jeremy, and Lynn Robertson, eds. 2012. *From Perception to Consciousness: Searching with Anne Treisman.* New York: Oxford University Press US.

Wolpert, Daniel M. 2009. "Forward Models." *Oxford Companion to Consciousness*, February, 295–96.

Wolpert, D.M., and Z. Ghahramani. 2000. "Computational Principles of Movement Neuroscience." *Nature Neuroscience* 3 (Suppl): 1212–17.

Workman, Lance, and Sandie Taylor. 2021. "Attention and Perception." In *Cognitive Psychology: The Basics*, 50–83. London: Routledge.

Wright, Richard D., and Lawrence M. Ward. 2008. *Orienting of Attention.* Oxford: Oxford University Press.

Wu, Chia-Chien, and Jeremy M. Wolfe. 2019. "Eye Movements in Medical Image Perception: A Selective Review of Past, Present and Future." *Vision* 3 (2): 32. https://doi.org/10.3390/vision3020032

Wu, Wayne. 2008. "Visual Attention, Conceptual Content, and Doing It Right." *Mind* 117 (468): 1003–33. https://doi.org/10.1093/mind/fzn082

Wu, Wayne. 2011a. "Confronting Many-Many Problems: Attention and Agentive Control." *Noûs* 45 (1): 50–76. https://doi.org/10.1111/j.1468-0068.2010.00804.x

Wu, Wayne. 2011b. "What Is Conscious Attention?" *Philosophy and Phenomenological Research* 82 (1): 93–120.

Wu, Wayne. 2013a. "Mental Action and the Threat of Automaticity." In *Decomposing the Will*, edited by Andy Clark, Julian Kiverstein, and Tillman Vierkant, 244–61. Oxford: Oxford University Press.

Wu, Wayne. 2013b. "The Case for Zombie Agency." *Mind* 122 (485): 217–30. https://doi.org/10.1093/mind/fzt030

Wu, Wayne. 2013c. "The Conscious Brain: How Attention Engenders Experience, by Jesse Prinz." *Mind* 122 (488): 1174–80.

Wu, Wayne. 2013d. "Visual Spatial Constancy and Modularity: Does Intention Penetrate Vision?" *Philosophical Studies* 165 (2): 647–69. https://doi.org/10.1007/s11098-012-9971-y

Wu, Wayne. 2014. *Attention*. London: Routledge. https://doi.org/10.4324/9781315777603

Wu, Wayne. 2018. "Action Always Involves Attention." *Analysis* 36: 311–95.

Wu, Wayne. 2019. "Structuring Mind: The Nature of Attention and How It Shapes Consciousness, by Sebastian Watzl." *Mind* 128 (511): 945–53.

Wu, Wayne. 2020a. "Automaticity, Control and Attention in Skill." In *The Routledge Handbook of Philosophy of Skill and Expertise*, edited by Ellen Fridland and Carlotta Pavese, 207–18. London: Routledge.

Wu, Wayne. 2020b. "Is Vision for Action Unconscious?" *Journal of Philosophy* 117 (8): 413–33.

Wu, Wayne. 2023. *Movements of the Mind*. Oxford: Oxford University Press.

Wu, Wayne. 2024a. "On Attention and Norms: An Opinionated Review of Recent Work." *Analysis* 84 (1): 173–201. https://doi.org/10.1093/analys/anad056

Wu, Wayne. 2024b. "We Know What Attention Is!" *Trends in Cognitive Sciences* 28 (4): 304–18. https://doi.org/10.1016/j.tics.2023.11.007

Wu, Wayne. n.d. "Attention as Selection for Action Defended." *Philosophy and Phenomenological Research* (n/a). Accessed September 17, 2024. https://doi.org/10.1111/phpr.13101

Wurtz, Robert H. 2008. "Neuronal Mechanisms of Visual Stability." *Vision Research* 48 (20): 2070–89.

Wyart, Valentin, Anna Christina Nobre, and Christopher Summerfield. 2012. "Dissociable Prior Influences of Signal Probability and Relevance on Visual Contrast Sensitivity." *Proceedings of the National Academy of Sciences* 109 (9): 3593–98. https://doi.org/10.1073/pnas.1120118109

Xu, Yaoda. 2017. "Reevaluating the Sensory Account of Visual Working Memory Storage." *Trends in Cognitive Sciences* 21 (10): 794–815. https://doi.org/10.1016/j.tics.2017.06.013

Xu, Yaoda. 2020. "Revisit Once More the Sensory Storage Account of Visual Working Memory." *Visual Cognition* 28 (5–8): 433–46. https://doi.org/10.1080/13506285.2020.1818659

Yantis, Steven, and John Jonides. 1984. "Abrupt Visual Onsets and Selective Attention: Evidence from Visual Search." *Journal of Experimental Psychology: Human Perception and Performance* 10 (5): 601–21.

Yantis, Steven S., and John J. Jonides. 1990. "Abrupt Visual Onsets and Selective Attention: Voluntary versus Automatic Allocation." *Journal of Experimental Psychology Human Perception and Performance* 16 (1): 121–34.

Yarbus, Alfred L. 1967. *Eye Movements and Vision*. New York: Plenum Press.

Yeshurun, Yaffa, and Marisa Carrasco. 1998. "Attention Improves or Impairs Visual Performance by Enhancing Spatial Resolution." *Nature* 396 (6706): 72–75. https://doi.org/10.1038/23936

Yetter-Chappell, Richard, and Helen Yetter-Chappell. 2016. "Virtue and Salience." *Australasian Journal of Philosophy* 94 (3): 449–63. https://doi.org/10.1080/00048402.2015.1115530

Zénon, Alexandre, and Richard J. Krauzlis. 2012. "Attention Deficits without Cortical Neuronal Deficits." *Nature* 489 (7416): 434–37. https://doi.org/10.1038/nature11497

Zivony, Alon, and Martin Eimer. 2021. "The Diachronic Account of Attentional Selectivity." *Psychonomic Bulletin & Review*, December. https://doi.org/10.3758/s13423-021-02023-7

INDEX

Pages in *italics* refer to figures and pages followed by "n" refer to notes.

Printed in Dunstable, United Kingdom

76658794R00212